JIMMY'S BOY
Devils, Angels and Miracles

True Story of a Blessed Child

By Bob Walsh

June 28, 2014

Dear Nick & Jean,
  May God continue to bless
you and your loved ones always!

        God bless,
        Bob Walsh

JIMMY'S BOY
Devils, Angels and Miracles
True Story of a Blessed Child

ISBN 978-0-9911717-0-5

Printed and bound in the United States of America

Books are available in quantity for promotional use.

Visit us at www.jimmysboy.com

PRAYER TO ST. MICHAEL THE ARCHANGEL
Prayer for Protection from Evil Spirits

"St. Michael the Archangel, defend us in battle; be our protection against the wickedness and snares of the devil. May God rebuke him, we humbly pray: and do thou, O Prince of the heavenly host, by the power of God, thrust into hell Satan and all the evil spirits who prowl about the world seeking the ruin of souls. Amen."

AUTHOR'S NOTES

The Catholic Congregation for the Propagation of the Faith

The decree issued by the Catholic Congregation for the Propagation of the Faith (AAS 58, 1186, approved by Pope Paul VI on October 14, 1966) rules that Nihil Obstat and Imprimatur are no longer required for publications that deal with private revelations, apparitions, prophesies, and miracles provided that nothing is stated that is in contradiction of faith and morals.

The author, a faithful Catholic in good standing with the church, hereby affirms that the contents of this book are true events, and that they do not in any way contradict Roman Catholic faith and morals.

Respecting the Privacy of Others

While the events described in this book are based upon actual events, the author has changed many of the names of people and places in order to respect the privacy of those involved.

DEDICATION

This book is dedicated to God and to all those who helped me see and follow the light of Christ in my life. I thank God for the gift of life, the family and friends He sent my way, and the spiritual gifts He entrusted to me. I thank Him also for opening the gates of paradise, and for blessing me with a guardian angel who has guided and protected me on my journey through life.

To my beloved parents, Ellen Marie Sheridan Walsh and Patrick Victor Walsh, I extend my heartfelt appreciation for their love, sacrifice, encouragement, and guidance. My life is a reflection of them since they were the first to teach me about God, our Christian faith, how to love and be loved. Heaven is now all the more beautiful with their presence.

Much love and gratitude go to my seven sisters and four brothers, my first and lasting friends. They have shared all the joys, adventures, challenges and tribulations growing up together in our large, Irish American Catholic family. Like many who grew up in New York City during the 1940s and 1950s, we were poor in terms of worldly possessions but we felt rich in terms of what matters most in life: we had each other, and we were taught to love and respect God, family and country.

Special thanks go to my brother, Larry, my best friend growing up. Ever by my side, he witnessed many of the extraordinary events shared in this story, and accordingly, was able to provide additional facts and details surrounding the events depicted in this book.

To my beloved bride, Margie Holly Walsh, my soul mate, I extend my heartfelt love and appreciation. She has shared life with me, hand-in-hand, from our teenage years through the best and worst of times. Ever loving, hard-working, and self-sacrificing, she has been a beacon of light and love for me, for our family, and others. A lady of many talents, Margie also helped edit this manuscript.

My appreciation goes as well to my wonderful children and grandchildren who grace my life in so very many ways.

Thanks go to my good friend, Tom Aguirri, who provided the technical skills without which this book could not have been produced.

Finally, I extend my heartfelt gratitude to all the nuns, priests, and holy men and women who showed me the way on my spiritual journey.

Thank you all. May God continue to bless, protect, and reward you until the day we stand together in Paradise.

Bob Walsh

CONTENTS

FOREWORD

Many wonderful people who know my life story offered to share their thoughts on the extraordinary events they witnessed. For this, I am grateful, but this is reserved for the one who knows me best… God. His words as recorded in the bible provide insight into understanding the remarkable experiences I have been privileged to enjoy. I offer His words from scripture as a reflection on my life as a "blessed child of God."

"You did not choose me; I chose you, and I appointed you to go and bear fruit, fruit that will last, so that the Father will give you whatever you ask Him in My Name."   John 15:16

"As you go, proclaim the good news, 'The Kingdom of God has come near. Cure the sick, raise the dead, cleanse the lepers, cast out demons. You received without payment; give without payment."   Matthew 10:7

"Take care that you do not despise one of these little ones; for, I tell you, in heaven their angels continually see the Face of My Father in heaven."   Matthew 18:10

"He will command His angels concerning you to guard you in all your ways. On their hands they will bear you up, so that you will not dash your foot against a stone."   Psalm 91:11

"Discipline yourselves, keep alert. Like a roaring lion your adversary the devil prowls around, looking for someone to devour."   1 Peter 5:8

"That evening they brought to Him (Jesus) many who were possessed with demons; and He cast out the spirits with a word, and cured all who were sick."   Matthew 8:16

"Very truly I tell you, the one who believes in Me will also do the works that I do, and, in fact, will do greater works than these because I am going to the Father."   John 14:12

"John said to Him, 'Teacher, we saw someone casting out demons in Your Name, and we tried to stop him, because he was not following us.' But Jesus said, 'Do not stop him; for no one who does a deed of power in My Name will be able soon afterward to speak evil of Me. Whoever is not against us is for us."   Mark 9:38

"I can do all things through Him Who strengthens me."
Philippians 4:13

"Even though I walk through the darkest valley, I fear no evil, for You are with me."   Psalm 23:4

"Let your light shine before others, so they may see your good works and give glory to your Father in heaven."   Matthew 5:16

"As God's chosen ones, holy and beloved, clothe yourselves with compassion, kindness, humility, meekness, and patience. Bear with one another and, if anyone has a complaint against another, forgive each other; just as the Lord has forgiven you. Above all, clothe yourselves with love."
Colossians 3:12

"From everyone to whom much is given, much will be required."
Luke 12:48

"The Son of Man is to come with His angels in the glory of His Father, **and then He will repay everyone for what has been done.**"
Matthew 16:27

PREFACE

In "Jimmy's Boy," the author, Bob Walsh, shares the remarkable, true story of his personal experiences as a "blessed child" endowed by God with spiritual gifts centered around healing. His extraordinary, early life story provides a first-hand account, a "peek behind the curtains," into the very real existence of devils, angels... and miracles.

Recognizing that he is a blessed child of God, demons turn his life experience into a living nightmare beginning in childhood and continuing to present time. By all outward appearances, Bob was like most other children his age but those who spent time around him soon perceived there was something special about him in a spiritual sense.

Bob sensed it himself, as did his family and friends, and in time, Catholic clergy. Not surprisingly, those who knew him were convinced he was destined to become a priest one day... but God had other plans... very different plans. Ultimately, Bob was called to live as a layperson in situations where priests had little or no access.

As a devout Catholic, Bob is well founded and educated in the Catholic faith, and is in good standing with the church. One of twelve children, he grew up in a four room apartment in the Yorkville section of New York City's Eastside. He married at twenty and with his wife of over 48 years, Margie Holly Walsh, raised their three children while he worked as a bank executive on Wall Street. When his parents died at an early age, Bob and his wife also cared for Bob's younger sisters.

He has ministered to people wherever God led him in his personal and professional life. Along the way, he has witnessed countless healing miracles and serves as a lay assistant for Catholic exorcists. For those without access to an exorcist, Bob conducts lay deliverance prayer in cases of demonic obsession or oppression.

Following his career on Wall Street, Bob served as a U.S. Goodwill Ambassador to Russia and Ukraine where he ministered to the poor in cancer hospitals and orphanages. As the Right to Life Party candidate for Governor of New York in 1994 and for U.S. Congress in 2000, he spoke in defense of life and the less-fortunate wherever he campaigned.

In his parish of Ss. Cyril and Methodius in Deer Park, Long Island, Bob has been an Eucharistic Minister since 1978, served as Director of the Respect Life Ministry, a Catechist, member of the Holy Name Society, and member of the Knights of Columbus.

In defense of the most vulnerable, God's children in the womb, Bob has worked as Board Member of the Life Center of Long Island, Board Member of the Legal Center for the Defense of Life, and a member of the Long Island Coalition for Life.

He also formerly served as Board Member of Morality in Media

xii

(fighting pornography), Founder and Editor of the Catholic Chronicle Newspaper, Director of the Rockville Centre Diocesan Pastoral Assistance Program, and served as an Eucharistic Minister and Lector at St. Patrick's Cathedral in New York City.

Bob conducts presentations on "Miracles and Healings," and he leads healing prayer for those suffering with afflictions of the mind, body, and spirit. While doing so, he has witnessed countless miracles when God healed those who cried out to Him.

In fact, Bob presents himself as living proof that miracles still happen when people turn to God in faith. In 2009, he was diagnosed with three different types of malignant cancer, and Hemochromatosis, ("iron-overload") requiring a pint of blood be withdrawn every few weeks. Bob survived extensive surgeries to remove two of the different cancers, then God miraculously removed the third form of cancer!

Bob's early years as shared in "Jimmy's Boy" is evidence of the very real presence of devils, angels, and miracles in our lives. His hope in sharing his true-life experiences is that others will come to recognize this reality, and accept Christ's invitation to "follow Him" in all they do.

INTRODUCTION

"Jimmy's Boy" is the remarkable true story of a child blessed by God from birth with the extraordinary spiritual gifts of healing, visions, and the ability to recognize the presence and work of demons.

Much of what is shared in "Jimmy's Boy" is possible because God also blessed the child with a photographic memory from his earliest days of life. His remarkable journey began in infancy… and continues to this day.

In the nursery of Bellevue Hospital on First Avenue in New York City where he was born, nurses who handled him detected something very special about this child. Reports circulated throughout the hospital about the extraordinary feelings of inner peace and well-being experienced by those who came near this baby. As word spread, more and more hospital staff came to see "the special child" in the nursery.

Evidence this child was blessed came when a nurse suffering from painful arthritis held the child as others looked on. As she prayed that God would send His healing graces to her through the baby in her arms, the baby opened his eyes. Although it is generally understood that infants are not able to see this early, the nurse swears that the child was looking deeply into her eyes as an exhilarating sensation swept over her.

Her pain was gone.

It wasn't long before similar events were added to a growing list of amazing stories. Soon, a nurse called a Catholic priest and told him about the child, and strongly encouraged him to come and see for himself. When the priest came, he stood by the baby for quite a while simply looking down at the child who was sleeping peacefully.

Then as the priest was making the sign of the cross over the baby, he suddenly paused in the middle of the blessing and simply stared down at the baby. He appeared to be seeing or hearing something quite extraordinary. After completing the blessing, the nurse asked if anything special happened.

The priest, still in deep thought, did not answer so the nurse repeated her question a little louder.

"Excuse me, Father." she practically shouted. "Did you sense anything 'special' about the child?"

"Oh, I am sorry," the priest apologized. "Yes, there is something very special about that child, something extraordinary… something good and holy. In all my years as a priest, I've never experienced anything like it."

"What do you mean, Father?" the nurse asked.

"While I was standing over the child, I felt an unmistakable glow of love and goodness radiating from him."

"Yes, Father, that is what I was trying to tell you. Everyone feels something like that around him," the nurse shares.

"As I was blessing him," the priest adds, "he opened his eyes and looked right at me! This may sound crazy but I felt like he understood what I was doing.

"Then… I felt like I was being blessed!"

Another nurse interrupts, "So you, too, Father, think the baby is 'blessed?'"

"Blessed? Oh, yes, I do believe that child is blessed. Thank you for telling me about him. I'd like you to call and let me know everything that happens while he's here in the hospital. Before I go, I must speak with his mother. Which room is she in?"

As the priest made his way to speak with the child's mother, the nurses quickly set about spreading this latest exciting news about their "blessed child."

When the priest shared his thoughts with the baby's mother, she told him that the nurses had been telling her similar stories about her "special gift from God."

"He is my third child, Father," the mother explained, "but carrying him for nine months I could tell there was something very different from my first two children. I could feel this child was special... in a religious sense. I could tell this child was holy."

Unfortunately, for this child, Satan was also aware that God had greatly blessed this child. In its efforts to impede him from using God's gifts, the devil wasted no time in launching its pursuit and torment of the child... beginning in the crib. This book chronicles the miraculous events and demonic torments experienced by this child exactly as they happened.

I know… because I am that boy.

The third oldest of twelve children in a poor but highly traditional Irish Catholic family, I and my siblings were guided and nurtured by our loving parents, Patrick Victor Walsh and Ellen Marie Sheridan Walsh. For the first seventeen years of my life, I lived in an old, brownstone, tenement apartment building nestled in the Yorkville section of Manhattan in the heart of New York City. Large families like mine were common on New York's East Side at the time where "God, family and country" truly guided the lives of those who lived and worked in Yorkville.

From my earliest moments, I felt the presence of these spiritual gifts centered around healing. These led over the years to miraculous experiences of every form and nature. But they also drew the attention of Satan and its demons resulting in countless attacks and harassments from the evil horde.

While I have found that most people believe in the existence of God, angels, and miracles, many find it difficult to accept the reality that demons exist and actively impede our lives... even in childhood.

For these, I refer to what Jesus says in the New Testament of the bible in Mark 9:20-21, "And they brought the boy to Him. When the spirit saw Him, immediately it convulsed the boy, and he fell on the ground, and rolled about foaming at the mouth. Jesus asked the father, 'How long has this been happening to him?' And he said... **'from childhood.**"

Jesus words clearly tell us that the devil is able to pursue, torment and possess anyone... even children as early as infancy. While Jesus warns us about this terrible reality of what Satan can do, He also tells us how a father's love and faith led to the child's liberation from the grip of the devil. God's grace and goodness is greater than the devil's hatred and evil deeds.

Christ's central message here is clear. Anyone with enough love and concern for a loved one who is suffering under the wiles and wickedness of the devil, can help free that loved one by turning to Christ in faith and asking Him to drive the demon away.

Mark does not provide information about the life of the boy, who was possessed from infancy, or what torments the devil inflicted upon this poor child and his family before Jesus cast the demon out. We can only imagine how nightmarish this must have been. However, hearing my first-hand experiences can provide a glimpse into this terrible reality.

There is a very real, fierce battle being waged everyday between good and evil throughout society. The devil is a living, hate-filled, highly intelligent creature... the greatest enemy of every man, woman, and child. Despite this, the devil enjoys a formidable advantage since many people today do not believe it exists. I have been told by many people, including some of God's ordained men and women, that talk of the devil is "medieval nonsense!" Nothing could be farther from the truth, or more dangerous to believe.

St. Padre Pio once said if we could see all the demons that lurk about seeking the ruin of our souls, they are so numerous, they would block out the sun! The saying, "Knowing the enemy is half the battle," has never been more appropriate and important. Our immortal souls are at stake, and where we get to spend all eternity hangs in the balance. How we live, and the choices we make during our journey through physical life, forms a path leading us to God in heaven or... to the devil in hell.

My hope is that sharing this part of my life's story will help others recognize this reality and encourage all to allow the light of God to guide their way through the darkness of physical life.

Chapter 1

THE SPECTER

January 1946

It was coming!

I remember being startled out of a sound sleep in my crib in the middle of that cold, dark night of January 25, 1946, my first birthday. A fearsome creature filled with pure hatred and consummate evil was slowly approaching. It radiated a nature that was hell bent on ravaging, tormenting and destroying anything of God.

And it was coming after me.

It had just materialized off in the distance behind the apartment building where I lived since birth. Instinctively, I knew that it was aware that I was conscious of its presence, its essence, and... the fact that it was coming to inflict unspeakable harm upon me.

The apartment where I grew up during the 1940's and 1950's was a railroad-style apartment comprised of four rooms (five if you count the bathroom) located on the second floor of a brownstone tenement located in the heart of the Yorkville section of Manhattan in New York City. The rooms followed one another in a straight line, like the cars in a train; hence its name, railroad rooms. Such apartments were quite common at that time throughout the east side of Manhattan. The kitchen, the first room in our apartment, looked out on the darkened back alley behind the building.

Our family was poor but greatly blessed with deeply devout, loving parents, Patrick Victor Walsh and Ellen Marie Sheridan Walsh. They ensured that we were well educated in the Catholic faith and our rich Irish heritage and traditions. As the third oldest of twelve children in a four room flat, I never felt alone... except that night.

Allow me to take you back to those first terrifying moments... and to the extraordinary years that followed in my early childhood.

As the evil mass slowly approaches, I sit perfectly still in my crib in this cold dark room shivering and worrying about why this terrible creature is coming after me. I can sense its essence; it is consummate evil. It enters our home passing silently and effortlessly through the large double-hung window in the far right diagonal corner of the kitchen. A feeling of helplessness overwhelms me. I feel defenseless with no place to hide from it. I am so frightened I cannot move, and dare not cry out for fear the evil thing will rush at me... and consume me.

The sounds of laughter and celebration from my first birthday party

1

earlier today now seem so long ago. A pleasant vision from earlier events flashes before my mind's eye. As everyone sang "Happy Birthday," one candle on the cake burned brightly while another candle in the middle was unlit. Mommy explained it is a family tradition to leave one candle in the center unlit for good luck. The flickering of the lighted candle cast its light on the smiling faces of Daddy, Mommy, and my older siblings, Paddy, and Kitty.

The luxury of such a joyful reflection quickly fades as I sit with my back to the end section of the crib that rests against the wall. Crème-colored wooden slats border all sides of my crib. Grabbing onto one of the cold wooden slats to my right, I peer into the darkened room where I see Mommy and Daddy sleeping soundly in the bed to the immediate right of my crib.

Against the opposite wall and to the right of my crib is a four-foot wide closet with two large wooden doors on top and two drawers side by side on the bottom. To the left of the closet is a silver heat pipe that rises straight up through the floor and extends all the way up into a hole in the ceiling where it continues to the apartment above. Up by the ceiling is where all the roaches can always be seen scurrying around. Mommy told me that these pipes, and radiators, carry scalding hot water throughout the building from a furnace located down in the basement of the building.

To the left of the hot water pipe is a large double-hung window set in the wall at a forty-five degree angle to the rest of the room. This window overlooks an airway that is enclosed by the surrounding tenement buildings.

Off to the extreme right of my room is a pair of French-style glass-paneled doors each of which is two feet wide. There are thin curtains I can see through as they hang decoratively down the full length of each French door. These doors are to the left of Mommy and Daddy's bed, and they lead into the last room of our home, the living room, located at the front of our building. Beyond our living room is the outside world of our neighborhood.

My three-year-old brother, Paddy, is asleep in a bed by himself in the next room to my left located between my room and the kitchen. As is the tradition of Irish families, the first-born, Paddy, is named after Daddy, Patrick Victor Walsh. My two-year-old sister, Kitty, is sleeping at the other end of this crib that we share. She is named after Daddy's Mother, Catherine Marie Clarke Walsh.

Although surrounded by my family, I feel so alone in the utter darkness of our apartment home because I am the only one who is awake while the dark figure slowly approaches. All sound in our home is gone now as if something sucked it all out leaving an eerie, unnatural silence, a lifelessness permeating everything. Nothingness fills the air.

Why is this thing coming after me? Where can I hide? What can I do? What is going to happen to me? I feel defenseless against this monstrous entity. Since my crib is located against the wall next to the open doorway in the front of my room, it is not physically possible for me to look out through the rooms toward the kitchen in the direction of the approaching thing.

I sit perfectly still and breathe as quietly as possible as I listen intently and worry about what may happen. What is this bad thing and why is it coming to harm me? It continues to approach as it moves very, very slowly. Soon it will be upon me. In my mind's eye, I can envision it entering the next room, the second room off the kitchen where Paddy is still sleeping peacefully. Slowly, it glides past him without pausing. It is obviously only after me.

I look over to Mommy and Daddy for help but they are still sleeping in the bed a few feet from my crib... completely unaware that some terrible presence has entered our home. Kitty also continues to sleep at the other end of my crib as the entity approaches the open doorway to my room. I pull the covers closer for protection as I lie down... watch... and listen.

I realize once again that it knows I am aware of its presence and that I am terribly afraid of it. A sense of isolation, helplessness, and impending doom overwhelms me. I am too afraid to cry out and draw more attention to myself.

Why doesn't someone wake up and help me? Kitty stirs a little but does not wake. Mommy and Daddy continue sleeping, unaware that an evil entity has entered our home. Where I am in the crib, my feet and toes are protruding slightly beyond my blanket and through the end slats of my crib. Too frightened to pull my feet back, I leave them exposed and lie as still as possible hoping the dark, threatening figure will think I am asleep and leave.

Slowly gliding into my room, the "thing" pauses at the foot of my crib and turns menacingly in my direction. It is a loathsome creature clothed within a charcoal black shroud composed of consummate evil with no love or goodness in it. It is very, very bad... the essence of pure hatred. It is so black it stands out starkly in the darkness of the room. Its head slopes directly down onto its shoulders as if it has no neck. There are no features, no hair, no ears, no eyes, no nose, no chin... and no goodness. It is composed of pure evil.

Its head is only a foot higher than the end of my crib. I sense that it is peering down and into me casting a feeling of isolation and emptiness over me. I am so frightened.

It remains suspended there, perfectly still, glaring down on me. I close my eyes but can feel it is examining me, measuring me, reading me. Unable to move, I am at the mercy of this unholy presence. The warmth of my urine spills out from under my cloth diaper and flows out onto my legs and the mattress sheet below. I am so frightened I can hardly breathe.

Suddenly, sharp razor-like claws scratch my toes sending shock waves of pain and terror ripping throughout my mind and body! It has attacked me! I burst upright and scream as I pull my feet back away from the point of attack. Quickly withdrawing away, I pull myself up and look toward the end of the crib. The black thing is still there. It has not moved. So what scratched me? Looking down toward the floor, I see two eerie-looking eyes glaring in the dark right back up at me!

It is Blackie, our large jet black colored family cat! It is hissing menacingly, and is crouched as if it is going to pounce up on me in the crib. I cry out loudly for Mommy and Daddy to come protect me from our wicked cat and the evil thing but they continue to sleep!

Worrying about Blackie distracted me from the evil presence. It is no longer stationed at the foot of the crib but I can sense it is lurking somewhere nearby in the darkness of my room.

Gradually, I begin to sense another presence, a presence of pure love and goodness, a loving, caring presence. I turn in the direction of this good presence and cry out to it using my innermost feelings. It understands. Instantly, the room is filled with a glorious white light that surrounds and blankets me with a feeling of utter love and safety. The montrous evil spirit and Blackie have fled, chased away by this glorious presence.

Immersed in this presence of love and goodness, I ease myself down knowing that I am safe for the moment from the evil thing... and our crazy family cat.

I would later come to learn that this evil entity is the worst of all creatures... a demon dispatched from hell to hinder any good I might do in life... and to consume my life force, my soul, in the process.

Chapter 2

THE GOLD OF THE DAY

March 1946

Since my frightening encounter with the evil spirit and Blackie, our cat, I live in constant fear that either one may return at any time and attack me once again. This fear remains despite the fact a holy presence chased them away.

I am so afraid to be alone; I stay close to Mommy everywhere she goes becoming virtually inseparable from her. Despite her attempts to shake free from me at times, I cling tenaciously to her forcing her to take me with her... even when she has to go to the bathroom. At night when all the lights are turned off, I call out to her as loudly and persistently as I can until she comes and takes me to bed with her where I can snuggle close to her for protection with my eyes closed tightly.

Mommy is a loving, strong, strikingly beautiful woman. Her sparkling hazel eyes serve as a centerpiece for her pretty face free of wrinkles or blemishes. Her hair, dark brown with a twinge of auburn, flows softly with a silky, shiny appearance. She is slender, five foot eight inches tall, and extraordinarily graceful in her movements. Her voice is clear and pleasant to hear especially when she sings as she so often does. Her physical beauty reflects her personality and the wonderful person she is: loving, joyful, humorous, caring, confident, intelligent... and religious.

I love Mommy so much and greatly appreciate the comfort, security, and joy of her presence. She often teases Daddy saying that we children got our good looks and intelligence from her side of the family, the Sheridans and the Dupres.

Mommy's family is mostly Irish with a little German ancestry on her mother's side. Her mom, Mary Agnes Dupre, our maternal grandmother, Mommy tells us, was a refined, elegant lady. She is with God now in heaven. Mommy's father, James Aloysius Sheridan, is our maternal grandfather. Mommy says he is a deeply religious Irishman. She has one brother, Uncle Sonny (James), and six sisters, Aunt Anna, Aunt Flo, Aunt Margie, Aunt Rita, Aunt Tessie, and Aunt Vera.

Sadly, Aunt Margie died many years ago when she was only nineteen years old. She had appendicitis and when they operated on her, she bled to death. The autopsy that followed showed that, unknown to everyone, Aunt Margie was diabetic. The doctors said that she died of related complications.

One morning finds Paddy, Kitty, and me playing with wooden building blocks in the last room, the living room. The colorful letters on each block fascinate me; they also taste strange. I enjoy stacking them on top of each other as high as I can until they topple over, or are knocked over by Paddy who laughs mischievously after doing so. Rather than simply stacking the blocks in a column, I decide to arrange them in a square like that of a house. Watching me do this, Paddy and Kitty begin building similar structures.

Looking around, I realize that Mommy is no longer in the room watching us play. A quick look through our railroad-style rooms straight ahead locates her standing four rooms away in the middle of our sun-drenched kitchen at the other end of our apartment.

Beautiful-sounding music is coming from a little brown radio resting on a small shelf just over Mommy's right shoulder. From where I am sitting on the living room floor, Mommy seems so far away.

She is ironing clothes on the old ironing board that extends straight out from a narrow storage compartment in the middle of the back wall of the kitchen. Every once in a while, she places the little black iron on the fire on the stove behind her to her left. A small cloth wrapped around the handle of the iron protects her hand from being burned.

Since the terrifying encounter with the evil figure and Blackie, our family cat, I feel insecure whenever I am not in Mommy's immediate presence. Therefore, I decide to leave Paddy and Kitty playing with the building blocks and go out to where Mommy is working in the kitchen.

Although I started walking at ten months, I still prefer crawling because I can move much faster that way. Crawling out of the last room, I am fascinated by the colorful pictures of flowers imprinted on the shiny linoleum floor covering in the next room. Every room has similar linoleum on the floor but each has a different, distinct pattern.

As usual, I pause to try to pick the flowers off the linoleum. I am convinced that if I try hard enough, I can get them off the linoleum so I can eat them. No matter how hard I rub at the printed flowers, however, I cannot dislodge them. After a while, I become frustrated and resolve to try again... some other time.

Resuming my journey, I look ahead to see Mommy standing with her back to the bright sunlight still streaming in through the large window behind her in the far right corner of the kitchen. The sunlight illuminates the first two rooms of our apartment. This beautiful sunlight reminds me of the light that appeared in my room that chased away the evil spirit and Blackie.

Halfway there, I pause by the tall, dark brown wooden dresser positioned to my immediate left just past the open doorway between the second and third rooms. I have a sense of danger coming from something lurking to my left in the next room.

Looking past this dresser, I study the massive looking wooden bathroom door to my left. The door is closed as if by design for some sinister purpose... or to conceal something that is behind it. Since I cannot sense who or what is behind the door, I am reluctant to go any further into the room. Unless I do, however, I realize that I will not be able to get to Mommy.

This is so scary, I feel sick inside.

Eventually, I proceed slowly and keep my eyes fixed on the closed bathroom door to my left. As soon as I am safely past the door, I pick up the pace and quickly crawl ahead. In the middle of the room, I sense something off to my left so I pause and look around the room.

To my left, there is a tall bed with nothing underneath but a few shoes shrouded in darkness along with the eerie-looking eyes of Blackie. Fear sweeps over me as I realize that our dreaded cat is sitting in the dark shadows in the far corner underneath the bed... staring at me.

It is not moving, content to stay where it is as long as I do not approach it. Before proceeding, I look to my right to study another large, dark brown wooden bureau towering high above me as it rests on four sturdy-looking legs. This is where Mommy puts our clothes in the drawers. She puts them there after she has washed the clothes in the kitchen washbasin and then dried them by pinning them on the clothesline outside our kitchen window.

My attention is drawn to lilting music coming from that little brown radio resting on the small shelf in the center of the far wall in the kitchen. I recognize the sound of Mommy's favorite singer, Bing Crosby, as he sings a soft, pleasant tune. Mommy is singing along as she zips the little black iron on top of the clothes she is ironing.

I can barely see out into the kitchen from where I am sitting because of the blinding sunlight pouring down upon me from the corner window of the kitchen behind Mommy's left side. Content to just sit here and enjoy the moment, I bask in the sunlight with my eyes closed as I listen to Mommy sing along with Bing Crosby to the song on the radio, "Where the Blue of the Night Meets the Gold of the Day."[1]

When the song ends, I open my eyes and struggle to focus my sight as I adjust to the bright sunlight flooding the kitchen. Curious to see how Paddy and Kitty are doing with their building blocks, I turn around and gaze in toward the opposite end of our apartment. There I see Kitty totally engrossed in watching Paddy build a high stack of wooden blocks.

---

[1] "Where the Blue of the Night Meets the Gold of the Day" was recorded in1931 by the singer, Bing Crosby, who contributed lyrics so the writers, Roy Turk and Fred E. Ahlert, included him in the songwriting credit.

Suddenly, the bright warm sunlight on my back fades leaving me in a cold dark shadow. A strong sense of danger envelops me as I focus on the area between Paddy and Kitty and me. There I see a dark black mass lying on the floor facing me! I turn away and crawl as fast as I can to where Mommy is standing. Pulling myself up on her leg, I cry hoping she will pick me up.

Mommy complains that she cannot pick me up because she is ironing! I cry out even louder, more desperately, for her to save me. She obviously does not understand what is wrong. Finally, she puts the iron aside, leans down, and places her strong hands under my armpits and hoists me straight up in the air onto the safety of her right hip. I clasp firmly onto her and bury my face against her neck so I can hide from the evil thing.

"Oh, Bobby, what I am going to do with you?" Mommy complains. "I have so much work to do; I can't be holding you all the time. Besides, you are getting too heavy for me to be picking up like this."

She asks what is troubling me, but I do not know how to tell her what I saw. Looking around the kitchen, I do not see the evil black mass here but I continue to cling onto Mommy anyway.

Soon, the bright sunlight returns filling the room once again with its beautiful, comforting appearance. Apparently recognizing that I am no longer upset, Mommy lowers me down to the floor and tells me to go inside to play with Paddy and Kitty. There is no way I am going to leave. I am just going to sit right here in the middle of the kitchen floor with the warm sunlight pouring down on me.

Why would I want to crawl back through the rooms where the evil thing and Blackie are lurking somewhere in the darkness… waiting to pounce out on me.

Chapter 3

CARL SCHURZ PARK

June 1946

The familiar sounds of the noisy sanitation truck wake me up at the crack of dawn. The "garbage men," as Daddy calls them, always drag the heavy metal trashcans across the sidewalk out to the waiting garbage truck in the street. This makes very loud, annoying noises. Daddy explained the garbage cans are often filled with burned coal ashes from our apartment building and others in Yorkville. This alone makes the cans too heavy to lift so they drag the cans across the sidewalk. Even without the ashes, the cans can be very heavy from all the garbage from tenants in the apartment buildings.

The garbage men dump the ashes into the back of the garbage truck, and then one of the garbage men pulls on a lever on the side causing a panel to come down and pull all the ashes and garbage into the inside of the truck. When the truck is full, they take it to a "garbage dump" where all the ashes and garbage are dumped on top of other garbage there.

The early morning sunlight streams in through our kitchen window warming and illuminating our entire apartment. A flurry of activity and excitement fills our home as everyone eagerly prepares for what Mommy promises will be a wonderful day at Carl Schurz Park. It is located only a few blocks from our home, nestled between 84th and 90th Streets on East End Avenue overlooking the East River in Manhattan.

Mommy looks so pretty as she stands in the sunlight ironing Daddy's white short-sleeve shirt. His shirt is so big it looks more like a tent than a shirt. I can understand why it is so large. Daddy is a large, powerfully built man, five feet ten inches tall, and weighing two hundred forty-five pounds of solid muscle. His watery-blue eyes are set in a strikingly handsome face, and his wavy light brown hair is always neatly combed.

Most of the time, Daddy is a happy, kind, and loving person who likes to sing and whistle his favorite tunes. I love to hear him singing and whistling, and telling us jokes that he laughs at harder than we do. He attributes our good looks, intelligence, and spirituality to our rich Irish heritage passed down to us from his side of the family and from Mommy's.

In addition, he often says, "God, family, and country, is what life is all about, kids. Remember that always."

We are now waiting for Daddy so we can leave for the park. Paddy, Kitty, and I are standing anxiously by the entrance door to our apartment. Daddy comes into the kitchen smiling, then suddenly runs toward us and begins to tickle us. Rolling around on the floor laughing and squirming, we try to avoid his strong fingers because they dig into our stomachs and sides as he tickles us. I know he does not intend to hurt us, but his tickling really hurts.

Just when I think I cannot take anymore, Mommy calls out to Daddy and tells him to stop and put on his shirt so we can leave for the park. Amused, I watch Daddy's fingers struggle with the little buttons on his shirt. It is amazing how such a large shirt fits so snugly on him.

Mommy scoops me up and holds me securely as she watches Daddy push the brown wicker baby carriage out our front door. As he disappears into the dark hallway on the other side of our kitchen door, I worry that he may leave without us.

Moments later, Daddy comes back and picks Kitty up, grabs Paddy's hand, then briskly walks out the door so quickly he practically drags them with him. Mommy follows right behind them into the cool, dark hallway as she balances me with one arm while she fumbles with the key to lock the front door of our second floor apartment.

We descend the winding flight of stairs, three sections divided by two landings. At the bottom, we turn right into a long, shadow-filled, very dark narrow hallway that leads to the street. As we march in single file, the outside world with its brilliant sunlight and exciting sounds grows brighter and louder with every step.

The end of the hallway leads to a small four-by-four foyer area where all the mailboxes are located on the sidewalls facing each other. Under each mailbox is a nameplate and doorbell for the family that lives in the apartments of our building. The only thing that separates us now from the outside world is the set of two glass-paneled doors that swing out onto the concrete stoop in front of our building.

In a flash, we are outside where the whole world explodes with noise, color, motion, and activity everywhere. Mommy pauses on top of the stoop and surveys the street. She first looks to her left, then to her right in the direction of East End Avenue. The stoop we are standing on is about six feet wide and three feet deep. The metal handrails on either side of the stoop lead down four steps to the sidewalk below.

I am curious about what Mommy is looking for so I join her in canvassing the street. There are so many things to see. Mommy looks down at the four steps as she carefully maneuvers her way down and holds me tightly to herself. At the bottom, Mommy puts me down into the carriage and puts a cloth harness around my left and right arms, pulls the two sides of the zipper together in front of me and then zips them up effectively locking me in. Our wicker carriage squeaks every time it is moved the slightest bit.

Mommy then lifts Kitty into the bottom of the carriage and puts her down next to my feet.

Kitty's golden blond hair is blowing in the wind as she faces me. She hardly ever walks because walking causes pain in her hip. The handle bar extends from the carriage directly behind Kitty. That is where Mommy is located as she now pushes the carriage. Paddy meanwhile is stationed alongside the carriage to the left clutching onto the handlebar with his left hand. His eyes and face look so much like Daddy's appearance. They both have water-blue eyes. Aunt Marion, Daddy's older sister, always says that Paddy looks just like Daddy did when he was a little boy.

As Mommy pushes the carriage, I am intrigued by the sensation of going backward and by the accompanying squeaking sounds cascading all around me from the wicker carriage and its hood. Looking up, I scan the endless number of windows lining the brownstone tenements as we whisk past them on our way down the street heading toward the East River.

Here and there are open windows where old people are stationed looking out at the street below. I am surprised to see so many wrinkled faces framed in white hair returning my stare. Some of them return my smile; some of them just stare like Blackie the cat does.

As we near the end of our street, I look back up the block at our building. Just then, Mommy turns our carriage to cross the street to the other side. Before I am able to focus on our building again, Mommy tips the front of our carriage up causing me to slide down on top of Kitty's legs. Kitty looks startled by the sudden turn and tipping of our carriage. Afraid that I might keep sliding until Kitty and I fall out of the carriage, I desperately grab onto the sides of the carriage for support.

One loud, hard bounce later and we have survived Mommy's maneuvering from the sidewalk curb to the street only eight inches lower, and then back up again on the other side. Kitty is giggling, obviously pleased now with this "ride" compliments of Mommy.

Kitty can see that I am a little rattled by the jarring tips and bounces of the carriage. Reaching out to me, she reassures me that everything is all right, and adds that Mommy is just giving us a ride! This is not a very nice ride, I think; it is too rough and uncomfortable for me.

Kitty likes to "mother" me since I am the baby in the family. She is in her protective mode now as she smiles affectionately at me. Her light blond hair blows in the wind and glistens brilliantly in the sunlight framing her soft blue eyes and sweet smiling face. Leaning forward, she pets my face while she chatters incessantly, certain that she is soothing me.

Paddy looks so happy and excited about our trip to the park. Smiling, his hand is still clamped onto the handlebar as if glued to it. Looking up, I see Daddy gesturing as he speaks non-stop to Mommy who occasionally nods her head. She does not seem to be listening. I can tell when Mommy is not really listening... she gets a faraway look in her eyes. Daddy does most of the talking, and Mommy does most of the listening.

With my family about me, I feel safe as we reach Carl Schurz Park on the northeast corner of 84th Street and East End Avenue. A quick turn to the right and we enter the park.

The first thing I detect is a wonderful fragrance filling the air from the many trees and flowers. Then I notice a flock of birds happily chirping away as they frolic in the trees high overhead. They are playing among thousands of tree leaves dancing merrily in the gentle breeze whipping about us. There is also a strange rhythmic sound mingled in with the cheerful voices of children playing nearby.

Mommy immediately turns left, then a quick right as we enter the playground. Once inside, she takes another left turn and settles on one of the many wood-slatted benches facing the children's wading pool in the center of the playground. I again notice that strange rhythmic sound now coming from an area directly behind us. Curious to see what it is, I lean forward so I can see past the hood of the carriage. To my surprise, I discover the sounds are coming from a row of metal swings where children are soaring high up and down on the swings. Some of them look like they are going to fly off into the trees behind them or off into the air in front of their swings!

Paddy and Kitty hurriedly take off their shorts exposing their bathing suits underneath. In a flash, Paddy goes dashing off into the wading pool while Kitty slowly limps after him. They soon disappear into the sea of colors and wildly gyrating little figures under the sprinkler.

I am fascinated by the water gushing upward toward the powder blue sky and puffy white clouds. Droplets of water cascade down on the tiny writhing bodies and blend with the bright sunshine to form a dazzling display of colors. It is so interesting to watch so many boys and girls running around having lots of fun in the pool.

Looking to my left, I see a flagpole that rises higher than all the trees in the area. At its base, there are children circling the pole and singing a song. Farther back, I see mothers sitting close together. They are all talking together while rocking their baby carriages.

To my right, there are several children gathered by the water fountain in the far right corner of the playground. They are waiting in line to get a drink. Just to their left is the boys' bathroom where a constant flow of boys goes in and out. At the girls' bathroom to the far left on the other side of the playground, there are only a few girls going in and out.

Between the two bathrooms is a long, open area with a roof that spans the entire opening. Looking closely at this open area, I see two boys playing a game of table tennis called "Ping-Pong." Each time one of them hits the little white ball, it makes a strange, distinctive sound. The ball moves so fast, I am amazed that the boys can hit it back and forth, as they are doing.

I suddenly have the feeling I am being watched. A quick look around the area surrounding my carriage does not disclose anything that appears threatening. Strangely, however, all the birds in the trees overhead and nearby have left. Mommy notices that I am trying to look around at the park so she lowers the hood of my carriage enabling me to see the area around us more easily. Now she places my milk bottle in my hands and forces me to lie down as she urges me to drink my bottle and take a nap.

I squint my eyes and turn away from the blinding sunlight in the sky above as Mommy rocks my carriage and sings her familiar lullaby,

"Rockabye, Bobby, in the tree top,
When the wind blows, the cradle will rock,
When the bow breaks, the cradle will fall,
And down will come Bobby, cradle and all."

Since I am not tired, Mommy soon realizes her lullaby is not working so she decides to change my cloth diaper. This provides a welcome feeling of comfort, but it also leaves me feeling vulnerable as I lay there with the cool breeze blowing over my bare legs and bottom. After Mommy finishes attaching the pins on my fresh cloth diaper, she tucks me under my light blue blanket so tightly that I can hardly move. She shoves the edges of my blanket under the sides of my mattress completing my imprisonment.

It is so tight, I feel trapped because I cannot turn or sit up as Mommy begins to rock my carriage back and forth once again as she sings another of her favorite lullabies, "An Irish Lullaby."[2]

"Over in Kilarney, many years ago,
Me mother sang a song to me
In tones so sweet and low.
Just a simple little ditty
In her good old Irish way.
And I'd give the world
If she could sing that song
To me this day.
Too ra loo ra loo ra,

---

[2] "An Irish Lullaby" is a classic Irish song originally written in 1914 by the composer, James Royce Shannon (1881-1946), and popularized by the singer, Bing Crosby, in the 1944 movie, "Going My Way."

Too ra loo ra li,
Too ra loo ra loo ra,
Hush now don' you cry!
Too ra loo ra loo ra,
Too ra loo ra li,
Too ra loo ra loo ra,
That's an Irish lullaby.
Oft in dreams I wander
To that cot again
I feel her arms a-hugging me
As when she held me then
And I hear her voice ahumming
To me as in days of yore
When she used to rock me fast asleep
Outside the cabin door.
Too ra loo ra loo ra,
Too ra loo ra li,
Too ra loo ra loo ra,
Hush now don' you cry!
Too ra loo ra loo ra,
Too ra loo ra li,
Too ra loo ra loo ra,
That's an Irish lullaby!"

I close my eyes with a sense of great peace and tranquility and let my senses gradually fade from the outside world while Mommy sings.

Soon, I awaken to Daddy's booming voice, "Come on, kids, we're going to go down by the East River where we can watch the boats sail by."

The birds have since returned to the trees overhead as they happily chirp and fly about the tree branches gently swaying in the warm breeze. I wonder if the swaying branches are scaring them, or if the birds are causing the branches to move when they take off and land. Either way, I love to listen to them singing and watch them flying about. Way above them, are beautiful, puffy, white clouds in the powdery-blue colored sky.

Paddy is so excited by Daddy's invitation to go watch the boats he grabs Daddy's hand and starts pulling him to go right now. Mommy gathers up the towels and our other belongings, puts Kitty back in the carriage, and before I know it, we are all heading toward the river located less than one hundred yards away. As we move past the wading pool on our left on our way out toward the playground exit on the left side, the riverside, I listen to rustling sounds coming from the bushes ahead of us, and wonder what is in there.

As we exit the playground down via a winding path, I see the source of the rustling sounds in the bushes… squirrels chasing one another! They quickly scurry up the side of the small trees and disappear amid the branches.

At the bottom of the winding path, Mommy turns left and heads toward the river. This pathway is only about one hundred feet long with a canopy of trees overhead and thick bushes on either side of the walkway. This leads to a wide walkway that towers above the East River. My carriage thumps over the ridges of hexagon-shaped concrete blocks on the ground as Mommy pushes on.

Soon we are past the trees and bushes, and out into an open area where Mommy turns left. Off to our right is a three-foot black wrought iron fence that is curved up and inward toward us. Its purpose, Daddy explains, is to prevent people from accidentally falling over the side into the East River located about forty feet below. The fence rests securely on top of a two-foot high concrete wall that looks like it is filled with hundreds of round pebbles.

Just in front of the fence are benches made of wooden slats. The benches, lining the walkway as far as I can see, have people sitting on them looking out over the river. On my left, there is a play area that is lower than this promenade. Down there, children are roller-skating while older boys are playing basketball at the far left end. The metal wheels of the skates make loud, annoying noises on the pavement as the children happily whisk about.

We stop for a while to watch a little red tugboat heading slowly up-river from my right to my left against the current. A soft, sweet summer breeze blows gently against my face. It mingles with the distinctive smell of the East River.

Peering out through the bars of the fence, I see two men walking around on the narrow wooden deck of the tugboat. There is a single solitary light shining brightly inside the center room on the top section of the tugboat. Out in front, little white puffs of foam continuously spill up and over as the tugboat steadily plows through the river. I hear the distinctive sounds of the tugboat as it parts the waters.

Paddy and Kitty wave and call out to the men on the tugboat. To my great surprise, one of the men waves back! The tugboat blasts its horn for us making a loud, shrill noise. After it passes, waves caused by the little tugboat roll in slanted lines in our direction until they splash loudly against the rocks below.

Daddy tells us that although the tugboat is very small, it can pull much larger, heavier boats through the water. Paddy obviously does not believe this as he shakes his head. He probably thinks Daddy is kidding us as he so often does. But Daddy explains that little tug boats can pull much larger boats because the tugboats have very strong engines inside. Mommy adds that pulling something in water is much easier than on land because when things float in water they are much lighter. This makes sense to me.

Kitty asks Daddy if he was ever on a tugboat. Looking at Kitty, Daddy smiles as he apparently thinks about how to respond. Finally, he shakes his head no but says that he has been on another kind of boat, a ferryboat.

\   "I don't like to go out on boats, kids," he explains, "I don't feel safe being way out there over deep water with land so far away... even though I am a pretty good swimmer."

"You know, your uncle, Eddie Walsh, is a **great** swimmer," he proudly announces.

"As a matter of fact, he used to swim in the East River all the time with his friends from 78th Street. Those were the good old days, heh, Ellie? You never see anyone swimming in the river anymore."

Looking mischievous, Mommy shakes her head and quips, "Yeah, that's because people have more brains in their heads these days than they did years ago! Who wants to be run over and drowned by one of the boats? Cheeez!"

Daddy chuckles in response, "I guess you're right; it can be very dangerous. Everybody goes swimming in the pool at John Jay Park these days because it's much safer and cleaner there."

"Patsy, do you remember the time Eddie tried to swim across the East River to Welfare Island, and almost drowned?"

Mommy's question sounds like a challenge to Daddy's assessment of Uncle Eddie's swimming abilities.

Daddy's smile vanishes as he snaps, "Yes, I do. He thought he could make it across to Welfare Island because it looks a lot closer than it actually is. Anyone could make that mistake; it's very deceiving. Eddie badly misjudged the distance... and... he didn't realize how strong the river's current was that day. He's lucky the Coast Guard happened to come by and rescue him when they did. I don't think Eddie would have been able to make it to the other side. He told me he was completely exhausted."

Off in the distance, I see a larger, different shaped boat with many lights and windows. It is leaving Welfare Island on the other side of the East River.

Daddy says, "That's the 'Welfare Island Ferry,' a boat that takes people back and forth from the 78th Street dock in Manhattan to Welfare Island where there's a large hospital filled with many sick people."

I watch as the orange-colored ferry makes its way slowly across the water. Farther down the river, there are long bridges that span all the way across the river. The evening's summer sky blends with soft breezes to

16

provide an unforgettable setting of beauty, peace, and tranquility.

With twilight quickly setting in, Mommy suggests that we go see the fire boats docked on the East River near 90th Street, so off we start in that direction. I am fascinated by the fence bars to my right because they appear to wiggle as we move past them. We have gone only a short way when I notice that the road ahead of us curves downward in the direction of the river. It looks like Mommy is pushing my carriage straight down into the dark turbulent waters of the East River below!

Something moves about in the midst of the darkened trees and shrubbery off to my left as an evil, threatening voice screams, "You're going right into the river! Look at the pounding waves! You're going to drown and be eaten by the fierce creatures in the water!"

I cry out in terror as the road ahead winds down looking like it is leading directly into the dark pounding waves of the raging river now only a few feet below us! Peering out over the wildly gyrating river, I watch as wave after wave smashes thunderously below us. We are going right down into the raging river!

I scream out again, and struggle mightily against the cloth straps that have me imprisoned in the carriage. I have to get out of the carriage before it rolls down into the river!

Daddy says, "Ellie, what's wrong with Bobby?"

"I don't know, Patsy; something has scared him."

"No kidding, Sherlock!" he jokes.

While Mommy checks to see if there is an open pin in my cloth diaper, Daddy repeatedly asks me to point to what is scaring me. I point out at the river, desperately wanting him to understand that I am afraid we are heading right into the river and must turn away now before the river comes up and sweeps us all away.

Daddy just doesn't understand. As I continue to scream and struggle against my restraining straps, I worry that they may decide to keep going forward and downward toward the river.

Exasperated, Daddy says, "I give up, Ellie, I don't know what the hell is wrong with him. Let's start back home; it's getting dark anyway."

Paddy and Kitty look very concerned by my frantic actions. I can tell that they don't understand the problem with the river. To my great relief, Mommy agrees with Daddy and says she thinks I am probably afraid of being too close to the river.

Mommy usually understands me. She reassures me that I am safe, and that she wouldn't let anything bad happen to me. Slowly, she maneuvers the carriage away from the river whose raging waters now look like they are only a foot from flowing over the edge and engulfing us!

As we slowly make our way through the now fully darkened park, I sense there is a sinister, evil entity lurking nearby, watching us. Looking to my right, then my left, I see only two people strolling along in the distance. The pathway through the park leading from the East River and the park is deadly silent.

As we pass underneath the canopy of trees adjacent to the playground, I sense great danger nearby. I think Mommy also senses it. She appears unusually watchful and nervous as she looks left and right while pushing the carriage at an ever-increasing speed.

Passing the playground off to our right on our way out, I hear the distinctive rhythmic sounds the swings make when they are being used. Looking over there, I see them swinging back and forth… but no one is on them! Mommy also notices this.

Stopping the carriage, she says with alarm, "Patsy, look at the swings, they're swinging all by themselves!"

Daddy looks over and says, "Obviously, the wind must be blowing them back and forth!"

"Wind? What wind?" Mommy scoffs.

There is absolutely no wind blowing, not the slightest breeze.

I turn just in time to see Daddy shake his head from side to side as he jokes, "Of course it can't be the wind; it must be some ghosts who have come here to ride the swings at night!"

Daddy's laughter annoys Mommy as she abruptly resumes pushing the carriage on our journey back home. Although he is obviously kidding about "ghosts" causing the swings to move, I believe an evil spirit is doing this, but not for anything good.

A quick left turn out of the park's exit on 84th Street, and we are now safely out of Carl Schurz Park. The utter darkness of the night, however, still leaves me feeling insecure. As we pass each corner on East End Avenue on our way home, I have a strong sense that something or someone bad is going to pounce out on us from the shadows. Each block is so long and is filled with countless doorways… and shadows.

As we walk in the utter darkness of the night, no one speaks. It is so quiet now; the only sounds filling the night air are the squeaking noises made by our wicker carriage, and our family's footsteps on the concrete pavement. No other people are out on the streets except us, and no cars drive by.

When we finally reach the block where we live, we make our way on the dimly lit street in the still of this balmy summer night. I recognize our building in the middle of the row of darkened brownstone tenements.

Ours is the one with a pitch-black image of the evil thing standing motionless inside the window of our apartment… waiting for me.

Chapter 4

THE GREATEST THING

March 1947

"Paddy, Kitty, and Bobby, come into the living room!" Mommy beckons us.

When we get there, she tells us to sit on the sofa so she can tell us something she says is very, very important.

Smiling from ear to ear as she stands in front of us and places her hand over her swollen tummy, she happily asks, "Has anyone noticed how big Mommy's tummy is getting?"

Paddy, Kitty, and I giggle and nod yes.

"And do you know why?" she asks.

We again laugh and shake our heads yes.

"Why? Who wants to tell me?" she asks.

Paddy is first to answer, "Because a new baby is coming!"

Wow, this is so exciting! There is a new baby in Mommy's tummy; we are going to have another brother or sister!

"As I wrap my arms around her legs, Mommy's tummy protrudes above my head. Mommy takes all our hands and places them on her rounded tummy, then places her hand over ours. Her tummy is very hard. I can feel the baby squirming around in there like he or she is doing somersaults!

"The baby just moved! Did you feel it?" Mommy asks.

Paddy, Kitty, and I joyfully nod our heads in unison.

Smiling, Mommy asks, "What do you guys think the baby will be, a boy, or a girl?"

Paddy and Kitty just smile and shrug their shoulders but I shout out, "It's a boy!"

Mommy giggles and says, "Oh, I see, Bobby. And how is it that you are **so** sure the baby is a boy, heh?"

I shrug my shoulders; "I don't know how… I just know."

Mommy explains, "Bobby, nobody knows whether the baby is a boy or a girl until the baby is born. So you should not say you know for sure; you should say that you **think** the baby is a boy."

"Yes, Mommy."

But I know it is a boy.

Paddy runs off to play in the other room as Kitty follows him. Mommy and I are left alone to revel further over this wonderful news. Mommy sits in her favorite armchair in the corner by the French door, and invites me to come and sit on the edge of the cushion next to her. Patting my head, Mommy smiles as she stares at me. It seems she is thinking about something else.

Daddy arrives home from doing food shopping at the A & P store on York Avenue and 80th Street.

Joining us in the living room, he asks, "Everything okay, Ellie?"

"Everything is fine, Patsy. I told the kids about the new baby."

Daddy looks pleased, "Were they surprised, excited to hear?"

"They were thrilled, of course."

Daddy nods and smiles with a look of great pride.

The following days fly by and soon it is Tuesday, May 14, 1947, a day that promises to be another glorious time in our family's life. Our home is filled with the sounds of joyful excitement and expectation of something wonderful that is about to happen.

Since we don't have a phone, Daddy quickly goes to get Aunt Marion to come over and watch us kids while Daddy takes Mommy to the hospital. It is fortunate that Aunt Marion lives nearby.

Daddy is going to take Mommy to Bellevue Hospital on York Avenue while Aunt Marion babysits us. We are very happy to have her watching us. Not only are we going to get a new baby in the family, we are also going to have Aunt Marion stay here with us! She is such a happy person, always smiling. Daddy says she is "happy-go-lucky."

Kind and attentive to us, she is always telling us how good we are. Her hugs are the tightest of any of our relatives, and her curly red hair always tickles my face when she kisses me. Yes, Aunt Marion's presence in our home today will make everything all the more exciting and joyful.

Aunt Marion lives with her husband, Uncle Saul Sullivan, and our cousins Edward, Mickey, Bunny, Maureen and the baby of the family, Donna Jean. They live nearby in a four-room railroad-styled apartment on the second floor.

Soon after Aunt Marion arrives, she tells us to sit still and pay attention so she can explain the "momentous event that is happening" as she puts it.

"Your Mommy and Daddy are going to the hospital so Mommy can have her new baby there. She will be there for about a week, and then she'll be coming home with your new baby brother or sister. And who knows, maybe both because twins run in the family!"

This amazes me because I have only sensed the presence of one baby in Mommy's tummy, a baby boy.

Mommy and Daddy say goodbye, tell us to behave for Aunt Marion, then rush out the door leaving Aunt Marion, Paddy, Kitty, and me standing there in the kitchen staring at one another. There is a brief pause before we all turn and run through the rooms to the left windowsill in the last room, the living room. Fortunately, it is wide enough for Paddy, Kitty, and me to sit together and look through the metal guardrail to see the street below.

Mommy and Daddy soon come out of our building and slowly walk over to a yellow colored taxicab that is waiting double-parked directly in front of our building as Daddy arranged. As Mommy, then Daddy, climbs into the back seat of the cab, I think how lucky they are to be going for a car ride. It must be so exciting. After Daddy pulls the back door of the cab closed, he looks up and waves to us as the taxi drives off to our right down the street.

Later, Aunt Marion sends us off to bed. Before I know it, the next morning arrives and I find myself jammed together on the windowsill with the others as if we are curious birds perched on a tree branch. We watch as cars go by, and people walk past our building. The only time we leave the window is to go to the bathroom.

Aunt Marion occupies herself straightening up the house. Every once in a while, she comes in to check on us to see what we are doing. When she is not watching, we have fun calling out to people walking below. There is a feeling of accomplishment when someone acknowledges us by looking up and smiling. Some people even wave and say something back to us!

We soon tire of greeting people so we decide to start a guessing game. Each of us guesses whether a car or a taxicab will be the next automobile to come down the street. Paddy suggests that we also guess what color the next car or taxicab will be. Much to Paddy and Kitty's annoyance, I often guess the type of car… and its color.

Paddy makes me switch places with him, thinking that my position on the right side of the windowsill affords me a view of the cars coming down the street. He thinks making me sit on the left side should take away my advantage. I still guess right most of the times.

The familiar sound of the "ice wagon" now fills the air. The ice wagon is an old wooden wagon, pulled by a horse, laden with blocks of dry ice.

As it slowly moves up the block, the iceman repeatedly shouts out loudly, "Ice for sale… ice for sale… ice for sale."

His shouting mixes with the rhythmic sounds of the horse's hooves that stomp up and down on the asphalt street, "clop… clop… clop… clop."

Stopping right in front of our building, the scruffy-looking iceman climbs down and walks over to the side of the ice wagon facing us. He lifts up a heavy tarp and pulls it to the side exposing large blocks of ice he is selling. One of our neighbors comes out from the building to our left. He is a short, stocky-looking man. Stepping up to the ice-wagon, he hands some money to the ice man and says that he wants to buy a block of ice. The

21

iceman nods, then grabs an ice pick and chops at a block of dry ice to loosen it from the surrounding blocks. Chips of ice fly off everywhere as he skillfully bangs away at the block. Once it is freed, he uses a two-pronged metal clamp, about two feet long, to pick up the block and place it in the waiting man's large metal bucket.

Aunt Marion joins us and explains that people buy blocks of ice for their refrigerators in order to cool the food that is stored inside.

"As the ice melts, cold water from the ice drips down to the bottom of the refrigerator where a pan catches it. You have to remember to empty the drip-pan every day; otherwise, it overflows onto the floor."

After the iceman and his horse-drawn ice wagon leave, the distinctive sounds of the fruit and vegetable wagon are heard coming down our street. This wagon is also made of wood, and is pulled slowly by a horse that looks even larger than the one pulling the heavy ice wagon. The hooves on this horse land more determinedly on the street making a similar pleasant sound, "clop... clop... clop... clop."

This mixes nicely with the singsong announcement of the fruit and vegetable man as he calls out, "Fruits and vegetables... come and get your fruits and vegetables!"

Since our building is located near the middle of the block, the fruit and vegetable wagon also stops in the street right below our window. In the back of the wooden wagon, two sides are slanted upward to form a peak in the middle. Each side has individual wooden crates filled with different kinds of fruits on one side, and different kinds of vegetables on the other.

The fruit-and-vegetable man climbs down, faces our building, cuffs his hands over his mouth, and calls out loudly, "Fruits and vegetables; come and get your fruits and vegetables! Fruits and vegetables... come and get your fruits and vegetables!"

He stands there repeatedly calling out his message and just when I think no one will come to buy anything, his patience is rewarded. Elderly sisters who live in a ground floor apartment nearby come out to buy some of his goods. The older looking sister carefully and examines some of the fruits while the younger sister does the same with the vegetables.

While this is going on, the Hungarian woman who lives in a ground floor apartment calls out an order from her first floor window to the fruit and vegetable man. After filling a brown bag with her order, the fruit-and-vegetable man walks over to her window, hands her the bag of food, then accepts the money from her.

Looking up and down the block, the fruit-and-vegetable man can see there are no other customers coming so he climbs back up on board, sits down and shouts out to the horse, "Giddy-yap," as he snaps the leather reins on the horse's back.

I am surprised to see the horse nod its head up and down as if it is acknowledging the man's command. The horse begins to move forward very slowly as it pulls the wagon away out of our sight.

Aunt Marion tells us that the fruit-and-vegetable man and his wagon often stop right in front of a grocery store where other women come out to buy some of his fruits or vegetables.

"When this happens," Aunt Marion tells us, "The owner of the grocery store, comes out and stands in front of his store with his arms folded with an angry scowl on his face glaring at the fruit-and-vegetable man. The grocer usually yells at the fruit-and-vegetable man who, in turn, yells something nasty back at him."

"Why?" Paddy wants to know.

"Because they are competing to sell fruits and vegetables to the same people on the block," Aunt Marion explains. "The grocer gets especially angry because the fruit-and-vegetable man purposely stops his wagon right in front of the grocer's store!"

A short time later, the sounds of excited children can be heard in the street below. We soon discover what is causing all the commotion as children begin to gather across the street anxiously looking up the block. Soon, a big brown horse pulling a red stagecoach with four large spiked wheels comes rumbling slowly down the middle of the street. Excited as I am to see this, I feel sad for the poor horse. It looks so tired as it slowly clops one hoof down after another as it struggles under the heavy burden to which it is cruelly fastened.

The horse and its stagecoach eventually come to a stop right across the street from us by the stubby, little fire hydrant. The stagecoach looks like a real, authentic one. The two rear wheels are larger than the two wheels up front. There is a railing around the entire top of the coach, and there are three small windows on each side.

The man driving the stagecoach is wearing cowboy clothes: a cowboy hat, dungarees, jacket and cowboy boots. He is sitting on a bench located high in the top front area, and he has a place to rest his feet. He is holding the leather reins that are attached to the horse in front of the stagecoach. A pony, with a big saddle on it, is tied to the back of the stagecoach. The man sitting on the very top of the stagecoach slowly ties the reins he was holding onto the handlebar by the side of his wooden seat.

Standing straight up in the air, he puts his hands around his mouth, tilts his head upward, and shouts loudly, "Stagecoach ride, five cents, pony ride ten cents. Come ride like cowboys on the frontier. Ride in a **real** stagecoach from the wild, wild West."

23

He is fat with a bushy mustache and dirty, disheveled clothing. His assistant walking behind the pony looks just like the fat man except that he is much shorter and thinner. The fat man turns his back to us as he climbs down the side of the stagecoach. His weight causes the whole stagecoach to tilt toward him as if it is going to topple over. Walking in front of the horse, the fat man pauses to say something to it and pat it on its head. He then continues over to where all the children are lined up anxiously waiting for him.

As he approaches, the children all start to speak at once. He shakes his head and smiles. Each of the children hands the fat man a nickel before he helps them climb up into the stagecoach. Soon, the stagecoach is filled to capacity. The fat man holds his hand up high in the air, and then turns to close the door. He says something to the remaining children still waiting on the sidewalk, then walks back with a boy to where the pony is standing in the rear.

The assistant helps the boy climb up onto the saddle, then stands by the side and holds the back of the boy's trousers so that the boy will not fall off the pony. The fat man climbs back up on top of the stagecoach causing it to lean back all the way over in his direction again.

Once seated, he unties the reins and snaps them as he yells out, "Giddy-yap!"

I watch as the wheels of the stagecoach gradually begin to turn. The stagecoach moves slowly down the street to the distinctive sound of the horse's hooves plodding on the street's pavement, "Clop.. clop... clop." By this time, the street is lined with children and adults everywhere watching the popular stagecoach roll down the street. After it has returned, the happy, carnival-like atmosphere fills the air, adding to my excitement.

Standing directly behind us, Aunt Marion asks, "How would you boys like to go for a ride in that stagecoach?"

After a disbelieving pause, we quickly tell her, "**Yes!**"

Aunt Marion tells Kitty that she has to stay with Aunt Marion because the ride is too rough for her. Kitty doesn't look disappointed; I think she is afraid to go in the stagecoach.

"Paddy Boo, you must hold your brother's hand all the time; you hear me?"

Paddy nods yes as Aunt Marion grabs her purse and escorts us out the kitchen door and slowly down the stairs. We are going slowly because Kitty can't move quickly. I am worried that we are going **SO** slowly that the stagecoach may leave before we get down to the street!

Bursting out onto the front stoop of our building, Paddy shouts at the top of his voice, "Don't leave! We are coming! Don't leave!"

Aunt Marion reminds us that we must always look both ways before crossing the street, even though she is crossing with us. Looking both ways, we carefully make our way across the street in time to come face to face with the big fat man by the side of the stagecoach. He looks much, much bigger up close, and so do the wheels. They are taller than I am, and the top of the stagecoach is much higher than it looks from our window.

Aunt Marion fumbles with her change, counting out the exact amount needed. I watch closely as she puts the coins into the fat man's chunky, outstretched hand where they disappear as he closes his hand and scoops them into his right pants pocket.

Aunt Marion says, "There now, there's ten cents for the two of them. Right?"

The fat man nods, "Yes, ma'am."

Aunt Marion turns and shakes her finger at us as she warns, "Now listen, I don't want any nonsense from you boys when you are in there! Do you hear me? Stay seated and behave yourselves! Paddy Boo, you are in charge in there."

Paddy hates to be called this; he says it sounds like a baby's name. I think Aunt Marion favors Paddy because he looks so much like Daddy, and as Aunt Marion has said so many times, Daddy will always be her beloved little brother.

"Now go have a good time!" Aunt Marion says.

The fat man helps each of us up onto a small step, then through the doorway. As the door slams and latches behind us, I look around the inside of the stagecoach. The seats are made of a coarse dark brown material and the walls are dark brown and dirty. There is a distinctive odor in here. I think it is coming from the two leather seats that are torn in places.

Looking out the window on my side, I can see Aunt Marion and Kitty smiling and waving to us. The stagecoach feels like it is tipping over to my side. I know right away that this must be from the fat man climbing up on top of the stagecoach.

Sure enough, I hear the snap of the leather straps as the fat man's voice booms out, "Giddy-yap."

The stagecoach suddenly lurches forward and rocks slightly as we roll on our way, accompanied by the distinctive, rhythmic sounds of the horse's hooves hitting the pavement, "Clop... clop... clop... clop."

I exchange smiles of satisfaction with Paddy and with the three other children riding with us. I see familiar faces outside - other children and their mothers standing along the sidewalk on both sides of the street.

"Look out for the Indians!" Paddy warns. "They may be sneaking up with bows and arrows and tomahawks to scalp us!"

His words alarm me out of my daydream. Daddy has told us stories about how Indians used to be all over the country. Then I remember that there are no Indians on our street. Just to be sure, however, I look out the window and canvas the street. Feeling safe, I allow myself to relax and enjoy these exciting moments.

All too soon, we are back to where we started. The door swings open to expose the fat man's hand extending into the carriage to help us out. Squeezing my hand, he helps me down to the small step on the side of the stagecoach, and then down to the street.

Paddy runs over to Aunt Marion and Kitty who have been waiting patiently for us by the fire hydrant, and begins to tell them all about our thrilling ride. Listening attentively, she occasionally raises her eyebrows feigning amazement to hear of our adventure.

Then, as usual, Aunt Marion tells us how proud she is of us for doing something that takes so much courage. She allows us to stay here with the other children watching the fat man as he climbs back up. The stagecoach again looks like it is going to tip over, causing us all to giggle.

The fat man waves and says to us, "So long, pardners. See yah next time we're 'round these parts. Giddy-yap!"

As he wickedly snaps the reins on the horse's back causing the horse to begin moving forward, we watch as the stagecoach slowly rolls on its way down the street until it reaches the corner where it turns and disappears.

Paddy continues to tell Aunt Marion all the details of our ride as we prepare to cross the street. Aunt Marion interrupts him to remind us to look both ways before crossing. Instinctively, I look up at our second floor window and see the dark shrouded figure glaring down at me from inside the right window!

Alarmed, I point up at the window and shout, "The 'bad thing' is by our window!"

This causes us to stop in the middle of the street and look up at the window.

Aunt Marion studies the window then admonishes me, "Bobby, there is nothing in the window! Now get out of the street before some 'car thing' runs all of us over!"

When we get to the sidewalk, Aunt Marion continues her scolding, "Bobby, I don't want to hear anything else about a 'bad thing,' 'a ghost,' or anything like it! Do you hear me?"

"Yes, Aunt Marion," I answer right away, more afraid of her at the moment than the bad thing.

I know I saw the 'bad thing' in the right window.

Climbing up the three sets of winding stairs to the second floor landing where our apartment is located, I stay close to Aunt Marion for safety. I guess she does not believe anything about the evil spirit.

As we approach the front door of our apartment, I watch Paddy turn the metal doorknob and push the door open to the left. I follow in after him and Kitty. Inside, I see the roaches scurrying everywhere. This time, they don't fall on us as we walk through the front door opening. I wonder if roaches purposely jump on people.

Aunt Marion, the last one in, goes directly to the living room and looks around as she mutters something under her breath. On her way back to the kitchen, she gives me a look that serves as a clear warning for me not to say anything more about what I saw. To make her point, she forces me to go with her into the living room where she tells me to sit by the window and watch for Daddy's return.

Stopping on her way out of the room, she stops to joke, "And don't be looking for anything else if you know what I mean!"

I feel safe at my position on the left windowsill looking up the block at the world outside. Determined not to look back into the room, I content myself to sit here until Daddy arrives.

Much later, I see him walking down the block toward our home so I turn and shout out to everyone, "Daddy's coming! Daddy's coming!"

Daddy is already looking up in my direction. I suspect he knew that I would be here waiting for him. Everyone else comes running in to look out the window with me. I also expected to see Mommy and the baby with Daddy but I remember now that they will be staying in the hospital for a few days. Daddy's happy demeanor indicates that everything is okay.

Smiling and brimming with pride and joy, Daddy, cuffs his hands around his mouth and shouts, "Mommy and your baby brother, **Larry,** are both doing fine!"

Baby brother! Baby brother! I was right. Mommy had a baby boy!

I am so excited, I jump down from the windowsill and begin jumping up and down with Paddy. Aunt Marion hugs Kitty and tells her that she now has a new baby brother. Paddy grabs my hands and we spin around in a circle as Aunt Marion and Kitty look on. Kitty looks so disappointed. I guess she wanted to have a baby sister... not a third brother.

Aunt Marion puts her hand on Kitty's shoulder and she tells her, "You know, if you don't stop frowning like that, it will freeze on your face! Someday, Kitty, Daddy and Mommy will have a little baby sister for you."

Soon, Daddy is outside in the kitchen hugging Aunt Marion and crying with joy.

Aunt Marion sobs, "I am so proud of you, my little brother. God bless you, the baby, and Ellie."

We come running out to Daddy to get our kiss and hug and to hear the exciting story of the day's great adventure.

Daddy's eyes are red and wet from tears of happiness as he tells us, "The baby is perfectly healthy, a good sized baby boy. He looks just like your mother! You should have seen your little brother when he opened his big blue eyes. He kept swinging his little fists around in the air like a boxer! He is the best looking baby in the hospital!"

"Of course, he is!" Aunt Marion agrees, "What do you expect? He's a Walsh!"

Daddy says, "When the nurse asked me what the baby's name will be, I could not remember what name Ellie and I had picked. It was not until later when the nurse was walking by that I finally remembered. I shouted out loudly so that everyone could hear, 'Hey nurse, the baby's name is Lawrence Anthony Walsh!"

Daddy wipes fresh tears from his eyes but when he looks at the clock he says, "Oh God, look at the time. It's almost three o'clock. I have to get going or I'll be docked for being late for work."

"Wait 'til my friend, Judice, hears it's a boy. He's so funny; he actually said he thought the baby was going to be either a boy... or a girl!"

Judice is one of the men who works with Daddy at REA, the Railway Express Agency at the West 16th Street branch between Tenth and Eleventh Avenues in lower Manhattan. REA is a company that delivers boxes by train and by trucks for people who ship things all over the country. Daddy is a "sorter" there; which is someone who marks a code on the boxes in chalk designating the city and REA branch where the boxes are to be sent.

Daddy gives some final instructions for Aunt Marion, gives each of us a quick kiss, one of his "smushkypops," and then rushes out the front door on his way to work. Aunt Marion steps over, closes the door, and turns the round knob on the door lock snapping the lock in place. This keeps burglars and other bad people out who might hurt us.

The evil voice whispers in my mind, "It cannot lock us out."

"Us!" It said, "us." The thought there might be several evil things scares me even more.

In the ensuing days, I feel so vulnerable without Mommy home. Our home feels so empty and it seems such a long time since I last saw her. Besides, Aunt Marion's cooking skills are not as good as Mommy's is. Aunt Marion forces us to eat everything she puts on our plates, even when I tell her I don't like what she cooked. I can tell she doesn't like to hear me say that.

Her usual response is, "Starving kids around the world would give anything to eat what you have. So eat up and be thankful to God you have something to eat!"

What Aunt Marion lacks in cooking skills, she more than makes up with her loving presence. She is always fussing over us and telling us how good looking we are, smart, and well behaved… most of the time.

Finally one day, Aunt Marion announces that today is the day that Daddy is going to bring Mommy and Larry home from the hospital. She asks us to help by keeping the house "straightened," then she busies herself getting the crib ready as she tucks a freshly cleaned white sheet on the mattress. I still feel nervous whenever I go near the crib because it reminds me of the night the evil thing first entered our home … and Blackie the cat attacked my feet.

I return to my perch on the left windowsill in the last room where I can wait and watch for Mommy, Daddy, and the baby. Wondering why Mommy and Daddy picked "Lawrence Anthony" for his name, I call out to Aunt Marion and ask if she knows.

"That's a good question, Bobby," she answers, "I have no idea. We will have to ask your father when he gets home with the baby."

From my seat by the window, I look across the street and study the brownstone tenement buildings as far as I can see them up and down our street. There are so many windows, so many lives, and so many stories.

A yellow taxicab comes rolling slowly down the street and stops right in front of our building. The right rear door opens and out steps Daddy. He looks straight up to where I am sitting, smiles and waves. I am so excited and happy to see him, I return his smile and wave back.

Daddy turns around and leans into the cab to help Mommy and the baby get out. Mommy is carefully cuddling a light blue bundle to her bosom. I know that little Larry is buried somewhere inside the blue bundle. When Mommy gets out of the cab, she doesn't look up. Looking down at where she walks very carefully, she steps between the parked cars and heads directly for our stoop with Daddy protectively supporting her left arm. Slowly, they climb the four concrete steps of our stoop and disappear into the front entrance of our building.

The ringing of the doorbell reminds me that I did not tell everyone that Mommy, Daddy and the baby have arrived! As soon as I shout this, Paddy runs ahead of Kitty and me as we hurry in toward the kitchen and the front door. Running past the French doors, I feel a cold air surrounding the area as the French doors slam closed behind me. I dare not look back since I know the French doors cannot close by themselves. It must be the evil spirit expressing its hostility at the arrival of a pure, new innocent life from God.

My ears fill with the joyful voices of family chattering away in the kitchen as I stand next to Mommy and my baby brother. Mommy has settled on a kitchen chair between the table and the old white gas stove. As I approach her, a gentle breeze swirls about the kitchen enveloping us in a delightful flow of air.

Aunt Marion is standing next to the stove made of white porcelain with black trim. It stands three feet high supported by four narrow legs. Our stove is one of those old-fashioned ones that Mommy says lasts forever. It has an oven door on the right side, a small broiler on the bottom left side, below it is a drawer where Mommy stores pots and pans. The section on top has four long porcelain handles to turn the gas on and off.

Resting on top of the stove is a shiny tin pot that Daddy says is an integral part of daily life for us Irish Catholics living on the east side of Manhattan. This simple pot is always perched on the stove filled with dark black tea leaves, Ann Page loose tea leaves, floating on the surface. Mommy buys the red distinctive box of Ann Page Tea each week when she does the food shopping at the A&P Supermarket located on York Avenue between 81st and 80th Streets.

Seeing my eagerness to see the baby, Mommy says, "Okay, Bobby, come here and take a look at your baby brother, Larry."

Stepping closer, I peer into the wiggling bundle on her lap. Mommy pulls back the crumpled blue blanket exposing a tiny pink face with piercing blue eyes. I am amazed to see how tiny and bald my little brother's head is. He has a small clump of black hair on top. Carefully leaning over, I gently kiss him on the cheek. This brings a slight frown as he turns his head toward me and seems to talk. Mommy explains that the baby turns his mouth toward me because he is hungry and that he is just looking for milk to drink.

Taking a cue from this, Aunt Marion walks over to the refrigerator and takes out a baby bottle filled with formula, and places it in a waiting pot of water on the stove. After carefully lighting a match, she turns the knob on the stove so that some gas starts coming out from the jet under the pot. I listen to the hissing of the gas as it comes out and watch as Aunt Marion's match ignites a fire under the pot. Mommy gets up and heads for her room hugging the baby protectively to herself. Paddy and Kitty follow closely behind her leaving Daddy, Aunt Marion and me in the kitchen.

Aunt Marion remembers to ask Daddy why they named the baby, Lawrence Anthony.

Daddy eagerly explains, "We actually couldn't decide on which of two great saints to name him after so we decided to name him after both of them, Saint Lawrence and Saint Anthony.

"We picked Lawrence as the first name because he was a courageous martyr of the faith in the year 258. The Emperor was so angry that St. Lawrence gave the church's money to the poor rather than to him, he had Saint Lawrence roasted on a grill over a slow burning fire. Before he died, Saint Lawrence said, 'I'm done on this side now, you can turn me over now!' We like to think that Saint Lawrence will bless the baby with courage and conviction of the faith ... and a sense of humor!

"We picked Anthony as the middle name because he's the patron saint for preaching ability and for finding things like his 'Book of Psalms' that was stolen from him. We like to think that Saint Anthony will help the baby find his way in life."

Turning to Aunt Marion, he says, "This is the greatest thing anyone can do in life!"

"Naming a baby after saints?" Aunt Marion teases him.

"No!" Daddy laughs. The greatest thing anyone can do in life is to bring a new soul into existence **for all eternity**. Catch wise, Marion, gazukstein, understand?"

"I agree with you, Patsy, enough with all the 'gazukstein' words," Aunt Marion laughs.

Daddy adds, "Money and material things are at the center of too many couples' lives today rather than having children, the very fruit of the vows they took before God when they got married.

"Don't get me wrong, it's okay to achieve financial riches… but not at the expense of not having children. They should realize they can't bring a single dollar, piece of jewelry, car, or any other material thing with them when they die and stand before God. All they bring with them is their record of how well they lived according to God's law. The greatest thing anyone can achieve in life is to bring forth new life, a new soul, into existence for all eternity.

"God said, 'be fruitful and multiply.' He **did not** say, 'get all the money and material things you can!"

Chapter 5

DEVILS AND ANGELS

September 1948

The two windows in our living room face the front of our building overlooking the street. The one on the right leads directly onto a metal fire escape in front of our building. Fire escapes like these are common throughout Yorkville. Daddy explained these fire escapes are there in case there is a fire so we can get out of the building.

The window on the left has a metal window guard on it so no one can accidentally fall out. That window is where I often sit on the sill in front of the window so I can watch people coming and going on the street below. That is one of my favorite things to do. I wonder where people are going, where they just came from, what are their families like, and why are so many people in such a hurry?

As some of the people pass my building, they recognize me when they look up and see me. I often get a smile or a nod hello. I never know who is going to come by next: a kind-looking person, a mean-looking person, someone who looks happy, or as happens so often, people who look sad and troubled. These appear to be deep in thought, and oblivious to their surroundings as they trudge along.

As usually happens when I sit here, I get the distinct feeling that someone – or something – is lurking right behind me. It is not a good feeling so I turn my thoughts turn to stories Mommy and Daddy have told us about their lives, our family's history, about God, the angels and the saints.

Recently, when our Walsh family uncles and aunts were visiting, I heard them talking about how everyone thinks I am a "special child." Daddy said he would not be surprised if one day I become the first priest in the Walsh or Sheridan families. Hearing this confirms what I feel deep inside.

Since Mommy taught me how to pray by simply talking to God, I talk to Him all the time. Besides telling Him things I think about, I ask Him to bless my family and relatives, and the people I see walking in the street past our building. Mommy says that God especially listens to the prayers of children, so I pray as often as I can. She says I should never doubt what God can do because Jesus Himself said that "With God, all things are possible!"

During the day, being near Mommy or others in my family gives me a wonderful feeling of security. She is my constant companion whose love and protection I know I can always depend upon. Her spiritual strength and faith in God are rock solid. I also feel secure in Daddy's presence because he is so sure of himself, and is so big and strong. He is usually working, sleeping, or talking to Mommy, but I am always happy to be near him, or hear his voice. I can always feel the love and affection he has for me.

Right now, Mommy is nestled comfortably in one of the two thickly upholstered living room chairs facing the front windows of our apartment. Beckoning me over, she tells me that although I am a big boy, I can still sit in her lap! Climbing up, I gaze into her beautiful hazel eyes, and recognize love and tenderness in her eyes.

Reaching out gently, she strokes my hair and asks what I am so busy thinking about. Looking up into her eyes, I tell her that I was just thinking about how I wish the black thing would stop bothering me!

Frowning, she snaps, "Bobby... I've told you not to talk about such things!"

"But you asked me what I was thinking."

Squinting, she asks if Daddy has been telling me "ghost" stories.

"No."

"No, heh. Tell me, where have you been seeing this 'black thing?'"

"In the dark."

"How can you see it in the dark if it is black?"

"It's darker."

Studying my face, she asks, "What does its face look like?"

"It does not have a face."

"It does not have a face!" she snaps incredulously.

After a pause, she asks, "Has it ever said anything to you?"

"Yes. It says bad things that scare me."

"Like what?"

"They say if I keep praying, they will take me far away from you and our family to a place where bad things will hurt me and no one can help me."

"You said, '**They** will hurt you,' Mommy says demandingly.

"What happened to there being only one bad thing?"

"There is one bad thing in charge... but there are many of them that sometimes come with it." I explain.

This answer disturbs Mommy even more.

"Bobby, do you ever see things that are good?"

"Oh, yes! There is a beautiful white light that comes to visit me often."

"Does this beautiful white light and the bad thing... ever come at the same time?"

"No, but the bad thing **always** leaves when the white light comes."

"I see."

Mommy continues, "You know, Bobby, it's a sin to make up stories

33

that aren't true. That's the same thing as lying. Do you understand that?"

"I know, Mommy, but I'm telling the truth. I really do see the bad thing and the white light."

My feelings are hurt. Mommy thinks I am making up stories about the bad thing and the beautiful white light.

Leaning closer, Mommy holds my face in her hands forcing me to look directly into her eyes. Looking away, she hugs me and gently rocks back and forth. I always assumed Mommy knew about the beautiful white light and the bad thing. I guess not.

She asks, "Do Paddy or Kitty see these things too?"

"I don't think so."

Mommy continues to study my face for reactions. She seems to be leading up to something she has difficulty talking about.

Finally, she surprises me, "Bobby, I do know something about this thing you call, 'the bad thing!"

Lowering her head as if cowering before a formidable opponent, Mommy says in measured words I can barely hear, "Bobby, **all** bad things come from a terrible, evil creature called, 'the devil.'

"It is a demon, the leader of all demons, the 'Father of all Lies.' The devil used to be in heaven where he was the greatest of all angels but he fought with God and was driven out of heaven into hell along with all the angels that followed him. The devil's name is 'Lucifer' which means light-bearer.

"He is the leader of all devils."

Mommy previously told me about God and His angels in heaven and how good and beautiful they are so I ask, "How could bad things, devils, come from something so good?"

"Lucifer was once second only to God, Bobby, but he was so proud that he could not accept that God created mankind and had the angels serve us! This so greatly offended Lucifer that he challenged God and fought Him. Many other angels who admired Lucifer agreed with him so they joined him in the fight against God! They thought they could beat God.

"Of course, they could not."

I ask, "Who are the bad angels who followed Lucifer."

"They were angels from each of the nine choirs."

"What are the nine choirs of angels?"

"There are nine different groups of angels, Bobby. They are called 'choirs of angels' because they sing beautiful songs of praise to God. Every angel in each of the choirs is entirely different from all the others. Although the bad angels were driven out of heaven, they retain their particular angelic powers and intelligence. One thing all the bad angels have in common, though, is that they no longer sing praises to God. In fact... they hate God!"

"That's terrible!" I protest.

"The names of the choirs of good angels are the Seraphim, Cherubim, Thrones, Dominions, Virtues, Powers, Principalities, Archangels, and Angels.

"The angels who love God and remained loyal to Him were led by Saint Michael the Archangel who was the next greatest angel after Lucifer. The bad angels and the good angels had a tremendous battle in heaven. The good angels won, of course.

"The bad angels then had to leave heaven and never come back. Saint Michael the Archangel and his army of loyal angels chased Lucifer and all the bad Angels out of heaven. They fell out of the loving light of God forever. That is why devils are called the 'Fallen Angels.' Some saints believe this is when God rewarded the good angels by bringing them into His full presence where they see God in all His splendor.

"The Fallen Angels are very, very bad, Bobby. They tempt people to do bad things so that when the people die they may go to hell rather than to heaven. Bad people go to the same terrible place where all the bad angels were sent, a place called 'hell.' It is a place of never-ending fire, pain and suffering, where all the devils and all the bad people must stay forever."

All this sounds so scary. It is frightening to think that I, or anyone I know, might be cast into such a terrible place forever so I ask what else is hell like besides having fire?

Her expression turns even more serious, "Oh," she says dramatically, "hell is filled with darkness, fire, smoke, pain, cursing, screaming, hopelessness, and suffering beyond all description where the devils and bad people constantly suffer from the fire and the torment in knowing that they can never escape. The bad people there are also called 'damned souls' because they can never, ever get out, and they are constantly tormented by the devils there.

"Lucifer is the leader of all the devils; he is the worst of them all. He is also called 'Satan,' 'the Evil One', 'the devil,' 'demon,'... or, 'the **Beast.**"

The **Beast**... how appropriate that sounds.

"Why does God let devils scare us?"

Mommy pauses before answering, "Nobody really understands why God allows such things to happen, Bobby. Perhaps it is to put us to a test as He did with Lucifer and the Fallen Angels. One thing is for sure, Bobby, God does not allow evil spirits to torment us by beyond our ability.

"How we live our lives in physical life will determine if we will go to heaven to be with God, His angels, and saints... or be cast into hell with all the devils and all the bad people."

35

"What are 'saints,' Mommy?"

"It's not '**what**' they are; it is **who** they are. Saints are good people who lived their lives well on Earth according to God's law, and are now enjoying their reward in heaven living with God and His angels in great happiness and joy."

After a pause, she adds, "God allows the devils to tempt us to do things that are displeasing to God, but the devils cannot **force** us to do something bad. It's up to us to decide whether we're going to be good or bad. The choice is ours. That's what we call 'free will,' Bobby. To help each of us, God gives us a good angel to guide us and influence us to do the right things in life. This good angel is called our 'guardian angel."

"Do I have my own guardian angel?" I anxiously ask.

"Yes, Bobby, you have had your very own guardian angel from the very first moment you were placed in Mommy's tummy by God. And you know what? Your guardian angel is with you your entire life, even after you die and go to heaven! In fact, I'm sure he's right here with you, right now!"

Wow, my very own guardian angel, by me right now!

With many beautiful images flashing across my mind, I ask, "What does my guardian angel look like, Mommy? Does he have wings? What clothes does he wear? How big is he? Does he fly?"

Mommy laughs, "Only God knows all this, Bobby. However, if I were to guess, I would say that your guardian angel is probably very large, has glowing white skin, powerful white feathery wings, wears a white robe, and is sparkling clean. And like all of God's angels, I suspect he's like a bright light who is very happy because he can always look upon the Face of God."

I can sense Mommy's guardian angel and mine standing right next to us, and I envision that they look much like Mommy describes, only more beautiful.

"Okay, enough talk about such things, Bobby. I want you to promise me something. Whenever you feel like something bad... something evil... is around you, I want you to say the name of Jesus over and over again. Okay?"

"Yes, Mommy, but why?"

"Because the devil can't stand to hear the name of Jesus, and when it realizes the result of its torments causes you to say the name of Jesus... it will stop."

Chapter 6

FATHER KELLY

September 1949

Over the past year since Mommy had that talk with me about the devil, things have gotten much worse. The demon still appears as a very dark, black shrouded figure, but I know there are different demons that come at times to intimidate me. Besides causing the French doors to violently open and close by themselves, religious pictures are knocked down, and terrible growling sounds often pierce the silence of the night.

Mommy and Daddy now realize that a malevolent entity not of this world is behind these disturbances. And so, Daddy recently went to see Father George Kelly at St. Monica's rectory to seek his advice and help. After Daddy told him all about what is happening in our home, Father Kelly said he is going to come visit us. Since then, the demon has become even more audacious.

The excitement of the telephone ringing in our home ignites a flurry of activity. Paddy, Kitty, Larry, and I run to where the telephone is located on the bureau in front of the catty-cornered window in the third room, the bedroom before the living room. Having a telephone in our home is so magical. Mommy tells us we are very fortunate to have such a modern device because not everyone in our neighborhood can afford one.

Daddy picks up the receiver, places it against his right ear, and politely says, "Hello, this is the Walsh residence. May I help you?"

Apparently, the person on the other end of the phone line is saying something that pleases Daddy because he raises his eyes, nods his head, and smiles.

"Oh, hello Father Kelly, how are you?" Daddy says cheerfully.

"I am fine, thank you. I know you are very busy, Father, but is it at all possible for you to come to our home... now... to bless it?"

After a pause, Daddy appears surprised and says, "Oh, thank you, Father, that's wonderful. Just ring the doorbell under our name on the mailboxes in the vestibule when you enter our building, and I'll ring the bell in return to allow you to enter.

"By the way, Father, there are two elderly ladies who live together on the first floor. If you let the door close too loudly when you come in, don't be surprised if they come out and yell at you... even though you are a priest."

Another pause, then Daddy says, "Thank you, Father. We'll see you in a little while. God bless you too, Father. Goodbye."

Carefully placing the telephone receiver back on the telephone base, Daddy turns and proudly announces, "Father Kelly is coming to our home right now!"

A low, distinct growl comes from the corner closet in the living room. The demon is infuriated that a priest is coming to our home.

Mommy smiles and tells us, "Quick, kids, pick up your toys and put them away so our home does not look like a pack of animals lives here!"

There is something far worse that lives here, I think.

As we scurry about putting things away, I realize why the demon is so angry that a priest is coming. Demons are consummate evil that follow Satan; priests are good and follow Jesus Christ.

Mommy tells us that it is a great honor to have a Catholic priest visit our home. Daddy explains that St. Monica's Roman Catholic Church is located only a few blocks away from us on 79th Street between York and First Avenues, so Father Kelly will be here soon.

"Father George Kelly is one of the best priests there," Daddy tells us, "He's Irish and was born right here in Yorkville. His parents immigrated here from the old country, Ireland."

Everyone who lives in St. Monica's parish in Yorkville on the east side of Manhattan knows Father Kelly. Greatly admired, loved, and respected, he is young and ruggedly handsome. He is five foot ten, thin but athletic, has jet-black hair, ruddy complexion, and a brogue that lilts his words in a pleasant way. And... he is always smiling.

Father Kelly also seems to be everywhere. He can be seen walking the streets of Yorkville chatting with mothers who routinely gather in groups with their baby carriages on the sidewalks outside the brownstone tenements where their families live. He is seen talking with workers and shoppers in the stores, greeting parishioners outside St. Monica's Church steps, and playing ball with the neighborhood boys. All too often, Father Kelly is also seen chastising boys he catches cursing, smoking, or otherwise misbehaving.

He is always dressed in his neat priestly outfit: black hat, black shirt with a white Roman collar, black suit, black socks, and black shoes. His happy, jovial appearance is one of the most common sights on the lively streets of Yorkville during these years in our parish life.

Soon enough, the doorbell in our kitchen rings announcing that someone has arrived in the foyer of our building and wants to enter. In my mind's eye, I picture Father Kelly downstairs in the foyer area of our apartment building. Since he will enter our apartment by the front door located in the kitchen, Daddy lines us all up to greet this very special guest to our home.

Daddy quickly reminds us that we are to address Father Kelly as

"Father."

This reminds me how I once asked Daddy why I should call a priest "Father" when he is not my father. When it comes to many things, especially religion, Daddy encourages us to ask questions.

Daddy explained that we Catholics call priests "Father" because they are our spiritual leaders, our 'fathers' in faith, who by their total commitment to Christ and the Church, are earthly reflections of God's commitment to love.

"As such, they provide spiritual guidance for us," he explained.

Daddy added that some other Christian faiths think it is wrong for us Catholics to call our priests "Father" because Jesus says in Matthew 23, Verse 9, "call no man your father!"

However, Daddy explained, "What Jesus means by that statement is that we should never put any one on the same level as our Heavenly Father. In the New Testament of the bible, there are 140 references of various people including Jewish patriarchs, Christian leaders, and physical fathers, being referred to as 'Father.' For example, St. Paul said in Acts 7:2 in response to St. Stephen, 'Brethren and fathers hear me. The God of glory appeared to our father, Abraham."

This led to a following question I had for Daddy on the subject of priests. Why do they wear black clothes? This confuses me because the demon I see has always been shrouded in total black.

Once again Daddy explained, "Our Catholic priests in North America and Western Europe wear black clothing to show that they are **'dead'** to the physical world in order to be 'fully alive' in service to God and His people.

"However, in hot places around the world," Daddy clarified, "priests often wear lighter colored clothing, usually white, because such clothing is cooler to wear in hot climates."

A loud, strong knock on the door interrupts my thinking to announce the arrival of our special guest. Daddy steps over to the door and opens it wide revealing a smiling Father Kelly, ruddy face, white teeth, black hat, Roman collar, black suit and all. I immediately sense a wealth of spiritual strength and goodness in this man of God. He is the same height as Daddy. His eyes are a remarkably soft blue color, framed within his handsome, ruddy Irish complexion. Walking briskly through the front door, he removes his black hat exposing wavy jet-black hair.

Daddy extends his right hand as he welcomes him to our home. Father Kelly quickly grabs Daddy's hand and vigorously shakes it. Turning to Mommy, he bows respectfully and politely greets her as "Mrs. Walsh."

I study his eyes as he quickly scans over each of us as Daddy introduces us. Father Kelly extends his hand to Paddy, to Kitty... then to me. As he stares intently into my eyes, he firmly shakes my hand but does not let go. His eyes suddenly move up to an area high up in the air behind me and to my left. I turn to discover what has caught his attention.

There, high above the stove is a hole in the ceiling where the hot water steam pipe goes up into the floor above us. Scurrying all over the area are clusters of brown roaches actively squirming in and out of the hole.

Turning away from this, Father Kelly soon has all of us laughing at funny remarks he makes in his voice spiced with a lyrical Irish brogue. I feel quite comfortable in his company. After a while, Father asks me to stay while Paddy and Kitty go inside to play. As soon as they leave, Father puts his surprisingly heavy hand on my shoulder and tells me to come sit by the kitchen table with him. Mommy and Daddy join us.

The seats of the chairs surrounding the kitchen table are covered with a thick plastic material. As we sit on them, they make a strange sound as the air is squeezed out of the cushion within.

Father Kelly, sitting next to me, leans over looking intently in my eyes, and says, "So now, you are the little Irishman known as Robert Walsh, are you?"

"No, Father!" I answer, "My name is Bobby Walsh."

Giggling, he looks to Mommy and Daddy, and says, "Right… Bobby Walsh it is. You know, Bobby Walsh… the name 'Walsh' is one of the proudest Irish names in the whole world. In fact, if I am not mistaken, Walsh is the second most common Irish name!"

Looking over to Daddy, Father smiles mischievously as he adds, "And don't be asking me what name is the first. We will be sure not to mention that family's name here in the Walsh home, right?"

Still looking over to Dad, Father continues, "And do you know now, what the motto of the Walsh clan is?"

I shake my head no.

"Well, then. The motto of the Walsh clan is, 'Wounded, but not dead!' That means no matter how difficult something may be, a 'Walsh man,' or a 'Walsh woman,' never, ever gives up!"

What Father says is exactly what Daddy and Aunt Marion have said numerous times before.

"Now that we have that important piece of business taken care of, do you mind if I ask you a thing or two, Bobby Walsh?"

I nod okay.

Staring directly into my eyes and placing his hands on my shoulders, he says, "Well now, your father here's been telling me some strange things have been occurring here in your home. Have you noticed that also?"

"Yes, Father. I see the 'bad things' here... and the bright lights too."

"You say the 'bad things' are banging on the doors, knocking pictures down, and things like that?"

"Yes, Father."

"Where do you see the bad things?" he asks as he studies my face.

"Usually in the dark but sometimes during the day too."

"I see," Father Kelly says.

"Do the bad things come to play with you when your brother and sister won't play with you?"

"No, Father…it doesn't play."

Father blinks again, clears his throat, glances looks over to Daddy then says, "You are saying 'it,' Bobby. Does that mean that you see only one?"

"Yes, Father, but sometimes it is a different 'thing' in the same black covering. There are a few of them."

Still staring intently in my eyes, Father asks, "Why do you think it, or they, are bad things?"

"Because I can feel how bad they are."

"I see. Has this bad thing ever said anything to you?"

"Yes, it tells to stop praying and do bad things, and that it is going to hurt me very badly."

"Has it ever hurt you?"

"Yes. There is so much badness in it that it hurts me to be near it, or see it. It's a horrible thing, Father."

Father Kelly looks over to Daddy again and says, "Bobby, your father tells me that you also see angels. Is that true?"

"Are angels made of bright lights, Father?"

Father smiles, "Well, it has been said that angels **are** made of bright lights. Is that what you think, Bobby?"

"Yes, Father."

"Do the bright lights ever hurt your eyes?"

"No, Father… they are so **beautiful!**"

"What color are they, white?"

"No, Father, they are far more beautiful than white."

"How do you feel when the bright lights come around you?"

"I feel **very** happy, and very safe."

"Do the bright lights come at night?"

"Yes, but they also come during the day."

"Have the lights ever said anything to you?"

"Yes, Father, very nice thoughts come from the lights."

What do you mean 'nice thoughts come to you?' How do they come to you?"

41

"The thoughts just come into my head."

"What are some of the nice things they've told you."

"Things like... God hears everything I say to Him, especially when I pray for someone who is sick.

Father smiles and says, "Tell me, Bobby, have the lights ever chased away the 'bad thing'?"

"Yes, Father, a few times."

Father, looking more serious now, says, "Bobby, you know it's important to tell the truth, don't you?"

I nod yes.

"And you know that making something up is like telling a lie which is a sin?"

"Yes, Father."

"And what is a sin, Bobby?"

"Mommy said a sin is when you do something bad."

"That's right. Your mother is quite right!"

My answer apparently impressed Father because he looks over to Mommy and Daddy with an approving expression, and says, "I can see that your parents are doing a fine job teaching you the faith."

Squeezing my shoulders a little firmer, Father says, "So you know that it is a sin to tell a lie, right?"

I shake my head yes once again.

"Right. Now, you wouldn't be telling us a lie, would you, about seeing a bad thing and bright lights?"

I shake my head no.

"That's good!" Father says and pats my head.

"Now, isn't it possible, Bobby, that you haven't **really** seen a bad thing... and bright lights? Perhaps you only see them in your mind. You know, they are not real. Your father, your mother, you, and I are real."

I feel intimidated that Father Kelly obviously thinks that I am making everything up. I look to Mommy and Daddy but they appear unsure.

Despite how I feel, I look directly into Father's eyes and tell him, "Father, they **are** real. The bright lights are good... like Mommy, Daddy, you and me. But the bad thing is **very** bad."

Why don't they believe me? I am suddenly afraid realizing that I must be the only one who sees the demon and the beautiful bright lights. I remember how Mommy once told me that most people don't believe that bad things like devils exist, and some don't believe that angels exist either! I can sense that Father Kelly is one of the few people who knows that devils and angels exist. He just doesn't understand that both appear to me.

Father Kelly asks, "Does this 'bad thing' have a name?"

"Yes... the devil!" I tell him.

Father Kelly moves backward hearing these words from me.

"**The devil!** You shouldn't say that word!" he snaps at me.

The mere mention of this word has an immediate and disturbing effect on Father Kelly. Leaning even farther back away from me, he now has a troubled expression. His demeanor has changed.

Mommy and Daddy also notice Father Kelly's reaction. They look concerned. The word, "devil," is obviously something that scares and concerns everyone, not just me. Father's ruddy complexion looks even more ruddy now.

"Where did you hear that name?"

"Mommy told me; she told me all about the devil," I explain.

Father looks rather sternly at Mommy as he removes a black book from his right jacket pocket. Clenching it, he says, "Mother... you shouldn't be speaking of such things to your children!"

Mommy and Daddy look surprised at how Father Kelly has chastised Mommy for telling me that the evil thing's name is the devil.

"I never speak of such things in my home, Father," Daddy blurts out in his own defense.

Mommy looks very annoyed and agitated. Uh, oh.

Recovering from Father's righteous reprimand, Mommy says in a raised voice, "With all due respect, Father, Jesus Himself warned us about the devil so I don't think there is anything wrong with my warning my children about the wiles and wickedness of the devil. And whether or not **you** believe it, Father, I believe there **is something very evil** in our home... and I think it **is** the devil!"

Father Kelly looks surprised and taken back by Mommy's combative comments.

"For Christ's sake, Ellie, calm down. Don't be so disrespectful to Father Kelly!" Daddy chides Mommy. "After all, he is a priest."

"I don't care if he is the Pope! No one tells **me** how to protect my kids... especially when it comes to the devil. That's our faith, and it is my responsibility as their mother to warn them, to protect them."

"All right, all right, Ellie, please calm down," Daddy pleads with her, "Don't make a federal case out of this."

Turning to Father, Daddy apologies, "I am so sorry, Father."

"There is no need to be apologizing to him," Mommy snarls.

Daddy shakes his head and shoulders toward Father Kelly but doesn't dare say another word to draw more of Mommy's ire.

Father Kelly's reprimand ignited Mommy's Irish temper. Looking at Father Kelly, however, it looks like his Irish temper is also aflame as he snaps back.

"Mrs. Walsh, with the same due respect, it is **my** priestly duty to tell you when I believe you are doing something that may be harmful to the spiritual well-being of your child."

"You let me worry about that, Father. I am the one who carried him in my belly for nine months, not you. I know what is best for him."

"Ellie, please!" Daddy begs her to stop to no avail.

Ignoring Daddy's plea, she adds, "He's not like any other four-year-old child, Father. From the day he was born, we could tell that he was a special child of God... a 'blessed child!' And you know what, he understands quite well what we are talking about!"

Mommy is right... I do understand.

Stopping to get her breath, Mommy continues her ranting at Father Kelly, "You need to take more seriously what is going on here, Father. The devil knows Bobby is one of God's special children, and so it is doing everything it can to hurt him.

"We need you to do **your** job as a priest! You need to help us... not reprimand us. You should bless every corner of our home with Holy Water. That is what we need!"

"Ellie, please!" Daddy begs her once again.

Father Kelly's countenance softens now as he bows his head and says, "I'm terribly sorry, Mrs. Walsh; I did not intend to offend you. Of course, you're right. If I had understood how strongly you yourself feel about these things, I certainly would have been more sensitive. Please accept my apology. And, of course, you should... you must... follow your maternal instincts to protect your children especially in spiritual matters such as this."

"Okay," Mommy says as tears flow down her face.

Wow. Look at what just happened at the mere mentioning of the devil... angry words, Father Kelly yelling at Mommy, Mommy yelling at Father Kelly, Daddy caught in the middle, tension, tears, and unhappiness. The devil must be pleased.

It looks like Father Kelly does not know what to say or do now. Staring at me, he is in deep thought. Reaching into his right pocket, he pulls out a small bottle of holy water. Opening it, he whispers a prayer and swings the holy water bottle in the air splashing it around me and each wall of the kitchen.

"Let's bless your home," Father Kelly says with resolve as he rises to walk through the rooms and splash holy water everywhere.

"Paddy, Kitty, and Larry," Mommy calls out through the rooms. "Come out here right now and join us! Father Kelly is going to bless our home."

A nasty-sounding growl comes from the living room. Although there is a light on in each room, Father gives Mommy a blessed candle to carry. Reaching in his pocket, he retrieves a small book of matches, strikes a match, and lights the candle.

We follow Father Kelly into each room where he splashes holy water in four different directions and says prayers from his little black book. As he does, the light in the room flickers, and the light on the candle Mommy is carrying also flickers even though there is no wind blowing in our apartment. The demon is showing its disdain for what we are doing, and especially does not like Father Kelly.

What Father Kelly is doing is very holy... and very effective. As soon as we reach the last room, the living room, Father turns around and begins to go back out toward the kitchen blessing each room one more time. Walking through the rooms, we hear the French doors behind us open and close by themselves as a strong gust of cold air blows at our backs.

A menacing growl comes from the kitchen and reverberates through the rooms. I have the impression the demon is doing this to convince Father Kelly that his prayers and holy water have no effect on it. It is waiting for us in the kitchen.

Kitty begins to cry as Mommy says, "Did you hear that?"

Father Kelly responds by telling us not to be afraid, ignore what is happening, and concentrate on praying.

When we reach the kitchen, I sense the presence of the demon lurking right here in our midst. It is a proud, audacious, combative devil. As we huddle around Father Kelly, the upper section of our large kitchen corner window falls violently straight down creating a loud crashing noise! Mysteriously, no glass is broken in this four-foot wide window, nor is there any damage to the lower window or the windowsill.

Mommy cries, "What in God's name happened to the window?"

Daddy makes a hurried sign of the cross, and Father Kelly looking quite startled does the same. Standing together in the middle of the kitchen, we realize that the room has become so cold, we can see our breath!

Daddy tells us to stay right where we are as he walks over to the window. Pulling mightily, he tries to lift the upper window section back up to where it belongs... but he can't move it!

"I can't budge it!" he tells Father Kelly. "It feels like it weighs a ton! I lift large heavy cartons for a living, but I can't lift this. **It is as if something is holding it down!**"

Not something, I think. It is the demon.

I am worried that Daddy might slip... or be pushed through the glass window by the demon and fall to his death.

"This has **never** happened before, Father!" Daddy protests.

The wind swirling in the room becomes stronger.

Sensing things are about to get worse, I close my eyes, raise my right hand toward the window, and pray, "Dear God, please send St. Michael the Archangel to cast the demon out of here!"

A brilliant white light fills the room as the rank air disappears... and Daddy easily raises the window back up to its proper position. The sense of danger is gone; the crisis is over.

After composing himself, Daddy says, "Ellie, please get the kids off to bed."

But looking at me, he adds, "Bobby... you stay right here."

As Mommy ushers them off to bed, Paddy's protests, "That is not fair, I am the oldest, how come Bobby gets to stay up?"

"Never mind," Mommy says, "your father and Father Kelly need to talk to him. Now get yourself off to bed... **now!**"

As I sit, I notice how nervous Father Kelly looks now. His whole demeanor has changed so much from earlier when he appeared so self-assured and confident that nothing sinister was going on here... only the vivid imagination of a young boy. Witnessing the unmistakable presence of a malevolent entity in our home, he is now faced with a terrible reality few priests experience.

"Now that I have blessed your home with holy water and prayed for your family's protection against evil, I must be going," Father says. "I am on duty back at the rectory."

Daddy says, "Have your prayers and holy water cast it out?"

Looking pensive, Father answers, "Mr. Walsh, there appears to be something evil in your home. Sometimes prayers and holy water are not enough to cast it out. Even greater prayers may be needed."

"What kind of greater prayers?" Daddy asks.

"They are called 'Deliverance Prayers,' Father says softly.

"What are they, and how are they any different from regular prayers. I thought all prayers are the same," Daddy says.

"Well... sometimes evil spirits retreat when a priest comes to a home to bless it. After the priest leaves, however, the demon resumes its diabolical activities. When that is the case, Deliverance Prayer is a more specific, powerful prayer to cast it out."

Daddy worries, "So how can we be sure if your prayer cast out the evil spirit?"

"If there **is** an evil spirit present, Mr. Walsh, you will know it especially after our attempt to drive it out. In many cases, its activities become even worse than before."

Turning to me, Father Kelly says, "if you see or hear anything you think is bad, Bobby, I want you to tell your father and mother right away so they can call me. Do you understand?"

"Yes, Father, I understand."

Softening his appearance, Father says, "I have a **very** good sense about you, Bobby Walsh. I would not be at all surprised if you grew up to become a priest someday. Did you ever think about becoming a priest?"

"Yes, Father, I often think of becoming a priest when I grow up. I would like to be a priest like you, Father."

Smiling broadly, Father says, "Well, thank you, Bobby, thank you for saying that."

Giving way to his Irish humor, he laughs, "I must say, Mr. Walsh, your son has excellent judgment."

Daddy laughs, "I couldn't agree more!"

"Thank you, Father, for coming here and blessing our home. I will call you and let you know how things are going."

Father Kelly nods in acknowledgment as he puts his black hat snugly on his head, grabs the doorknob, and gives it a quick turn to open our front door.

Before he walks out, I ask, "Father, can I visit you in church?"

Smiling, he answers, "Bobby, you can visit me anytime. I will be happy to show you where I live in St. Monica's rectory and tell you all about what we priests do."

"I know what priests do, Father," I tell him.

"And what is that? he chuckles.

"Priests help people go to heaven!"

Father smiles again as he nods his head and raises his eyebrows, "Praise the Lord, that is **exactly** what we priests are called to do! Out of the mouths of babes; heaven be praised!"

Then he adds mischievously, "You might wish to share those thoughts with your mother!"

He and Daddy enjoy a good laugh at that suggestion.

Father says, "God bless you!" tips his hat, and steps out into the darkness of the hallway outside our apartment. I listen carefully to the sounds of his footsteps maintaining a steady pace in the hallway downstairs leading to the exit from our building. He must be relieved to be leaving and happy to be going to a holy, safe place like St. Monica's Church.

I can't wait to go there and visit **Him**... and Father Kelly.

Chapter 7

ST. MONICA'S

July 1950

"Hey, Bobby, for Christ's sake, what're you doing? Hurry up, or we'll be late for Mass!" Daddy calls out from the kitchen.

The humidity has me sweating profusely as I struggle nervously to get my striped polo shirt over my head. Our apartment is always so hot during the summertime despite the fact that Mommy keeps the windows open in the front and rear to "get a cross-breeze" as she says. I wish she did not do this because keeping the windows open also allows all the annoying flies to get in… and they have a nasty bite! Besides that, it is very rare that I feel a cross-breeze.

My shirt is so tight on me that my ears get pinched as I wiggle my head from side to side and pull the shirt downward.

As I struggle, the demon taunts me, "You're stuck in the shirt; you'll never get out. You're going to suffocate!"

I fight even more and until finally, my head pops free through the opening and I take a deep breath of relief and tuck the edges of the shirt into my trousers.

"Do you know what today is?" Daddy asks.

I shake my head no, and wonder why he is asking.

"Today is July 9, 1950. I want you to remember this date because it's the day you attend your very first Mass at St. Monica's."

I am so happy that Daddy is taking me to my first Mass. Mommy and Daddy have told me all the wonderful things that happen during Mass, and now I am going to see for myself!

Daddy comes over and crouches down, "It's swell how much you care about going to your first Mass. I am very proud of you."

Relishing the moment, he stares admiringly at me, but then remembers the time, "Holy God, it's getting late. We'd better hurry or we'll be late for your first Mass!"

Paddy and Kitty had declined Daddy's offer to take them to Mass with us; they prefer to stay home playing. Daddy says Larry is too young to join us.

"He'd only make a 'commotion' being there."

Mommy gives us a kiss goodbye before we hurry out into the cool, dark hallway outside the front door of our apartment. We quickly descend the three sections of winding stairs to the ground floor. At the end of the long

48

hallway on the ground floor, I see the door that leads to the bright light outside our building. Daddy turns the doorknob, and for what seems like an eternity, he slowly opens the door. I burst through the door then push past the double swinging doors leading to the front stoop and the bright daylight.

"Whoa, slow down, Bobby!" Daddy calls out, "Hold your horse. it's not **that** late. Take it easy, we have plenty of time to get there."

Walking briskly, we pass a group of mothers gathered as usual with their baby carriages in front of one of the buildings on the street.

Daddy nods to them and politely says, "Good morning, ladies."

They pause from their chattering only long enough to return his greeting before resuming their frenetic exchange of words. I wonder how they can hear each other since it sounds like they are all talking at the same time! Mommy says these ladies meet like this every day.

Along our journey, we pass the gigantic all-girls public school on the corner of 82nd Street and York Avenue. This school building occupies about one-quarter of 82nd Street leading up to York Avenue. The building is made of red brick, and is six stories high. It has a four-foot high black wrought iron gate all around its perimeter except for its entry doors. This school occupies all of York Avenue between 82nd and 81st streets.

As we approach 81st street and York Avenue, I hold tightly onto Daddy's big strong hand as I observe all the people and places around us.

At the corner, Daddy tightens his grip on my hand and as he tells me, "Bobby, always look both ways before you cross the street even if the light is green. You know... the light will not run you over, the cars will! Catch wise? Understand?"

"Yes, Daddy," I answer, grateful that he shares such important things with me for my safety and well-being.

Carefully looking both ways, we hurriedly cross the street to the other side where my attention is drawn to the A&P Supermarket located to our left in the middle of the block between 81st and 80th Streets on York Avenue. I remember once before being with Mommy when I saw women entering and leaving the store, carrying bulging brown paper bags filled with groceries. Some of them had their groceries in bags in metal shopping carts on two black wheels that allowed them to pull the carts behind them.

Daddy tells me this is where Mommy always goes to do her food shopping. He points up at the large red A&P sign hanging high above the entrance of the store. We continue to walk along York Avenue passing countless large brownstone apartment buildings on both sides of the avenue.

Daddy says, "We have a lot of praying to do today, Bobby."

"Why, Daddy?"

"Well, besides praying for our family, we have to pray that God prevents another world war. Our soldiers just got back from World War II, fighting the Nazis and the Japs, and now it looks like they may have to be fighting the Koreans. This is terrible, Bobby. In a war, any war, thousands of people are shot, stabbed, beaten to death, starved to death, crippled for life!"

This is terrible.

"Who are 'Koreans,' Daddy?" I ask with difficulty pronouncing the word, Koreans.

"They are people who live on the other side of the world between Germany and Japan," he explains. "You see, there are bad people over there called 'Communists' who live in the upper half of Korea. Last Sunday they invaded the lower half of the country and killed people, and stole their food and belongings."

This greatly disturbs me. People are supposed to love and help one another, not hurt each other, "If it's their country, why do they hurt each other?"

Daddy smiles, "You'll understand when you grow up, Bobby. For now, let's just say it's because the Communists want to force everybody to live their way."

Daddy stops walking and looks to me, "For one thing, they don't believe in God, and they don't let people go to church like you and I are doing right now. They are afraid that people will have greater allegiance to God than to their Communistic way of life. We live in a great country, Bobby, where we can go to church and worship God without worrying about someone putting us in prison for the rest of our lives, or even killing us. Don't ever take our freedom for granted, son."

I nod in obedience and promise never to take our religious freedom for granted.

As we resume walking, Daddy adds, "On Tuesday, President Truman announced on the radio that he's sending our troops, ships and planes to South Korea to help the people there protect themselves. The President and Vice President Barkley have a tough job ahead of them. God help us, it looks like there may be another war."

Daddy interrupts his story at the northeast corner of 79th Street and York Avenue where we stand silently facing the traffic. As we stand looking west up 79th Street, Daddy's hand protectively clasps my left hand. The traffic is flying by in front of us. I think about what Daddy said about war in a place far away from where we live. I'm relieved that it's not happening here. War sounds so terrible and frightening.

"Daddy, will you have to go there to fight the bad people?" I worry out loud.

"No, son. Fathers of families like ours have to stay home and take

50

care of their families," he assures me. "That's how we fulfill our obligation to our country. Somebody has to take care of things here at home during wartime."

This is comforting to hear. I don't want Daddy to go to some faraway place on the other side of the world where bad people would try to hurt him and possibly kill him.

My thoughts are rudely disturbed by the deafening sound of a gigantic bus passing right in front of us. Daddy pulls me back a step as I look in amazement at the bus's huge wheels turning around and around. I am awed by the tremendous size of the wheels; they are as tall as I am! The roar of its engine located in the very back of the bus is so loud! This is quite an experience for me because I never see buses on the street where I live; they only travel on Manhattan's avenues and major crosstown streets like 79th Street.

Exhaust fumes from the bus envelope us causing us to cough as we wave the smoke away from our faces. It's a good thing Daddy is still holding my left hand because I am disoriented within the poisonous cloud of smoke. Fortunately, the traffic light finally changes so we quickly hurry across York Avenue and continue on our journey westward up 79th Street toward St. Monica's Church.

Gazing straight ahead toward the other end of the block, I can see a high, black wrought iron gate that encloses a long set of stairs going up to what I know must be the church. The stairs jut straight out beyond the line of the long row of three-story brownstone tenements that line the right side of 79th Street from York Avenue all the way up to the black gate.

"That's St. Monica's up there, Bobby, by the gate and the stairs," Daddy points out.

My heart starts to beat rapidly.

"That's God's home," I say, "We're going to visit God in His home, just like we visit Nana in her home!"

Daddy chuckles, obviously amused by my comparison.

Suddenly, the sound of ferocious growling fills the air behind me. Even though I am still holding onto Daddy's hand, I am terrified by this unseen menace. My whole being focuses on what sounds like a fierce creature, a predator of some kind that has just cornered its prey, a tasty meal… me. My heart and mind explode with fear as razor-sharp teeth clamp on the back of my right leg above my ankle.

Sharp pain radiates from there all the way up my leg as I scream out in horror, **"Oooow!** Daddy, help me; something is biting me!"

Daddy's hand tightens like a vise over my left hand as he swirls around to confront the beast that is attacking me. With another scream swelling in my throat, I turn to discover that the fierce creature attacking me is a small but very angry, curly-haired dog! It is moving its head from side to side and backing up while its teeth are clamped on my leg! My eyes quickly follow upward along the dog's leash to where it is held by a well-dressed woman who looks startled by what her dog is doing to me.

As I try to pull away from the dog, I see Daddy's leg come swinging into view as his foot lands directly under the dog's belly making a loud "thump" sound. Daddy's leg continues upward thrusting the dog, leash and all, high into the air as the dog's sharp teeth let go of my leg! When the dog lands a few feet away, it is stunned and hurt.

As the dog whelps in pain, the lady is outraged by Daddy's attack, "Oh, my God, you terrible man! Why did you do that? My poor baby! Somebody call the police!"

The lady's shouting further alarms me. For the moment, I feel guilty that I have caused Daddy to hurt the dog in defending me. Now I am worried that the police will come and arrest Daddy for kicking the dog. Daddy surprises me by angrily shouting right back at the lady.

"Why don't you control your goddamned dog, lady! It bit my son! You go ahead and call the cops; I'll have **You** arrested for not controlling your dog!"

Daddy moves forward to kick the dog again, but the lady and her dog seeing Daddy charging, turn and run down 79th Street toward York Avenue. Daddy stands there glaring as the dog races ahead of the lady so fast that the leash is strained tight as an arrow.

Daddy is so upset saliva drips out of the corner of his mouth as he angrily shouts after them, "You'd better keep running. Son of a bitch! She cares more for her freaking dog than she does my kid!"

Cupping his hands around his mouth so his voice will carry farther, Daddy thunders, "You and your goddamn dog better keep running!"

The lady and her dog reach the corner of York Avenue where they turn left and disappear from view. This is so uncharacteristic for Daddy to be so impolite and aggressive toward a woman, especially such an impressive-looking lady. He is usually very courteous. His actions demonstrate quite dramatically how much he loves me, and how protective he is of his family.

Daddy turns back to me and bends down to check my leg and my slightly torn trousers.

"Are you all right, son?" he asks still quite agitated, "Are you cut? Let me see."

I look down at the area above my ankle and am greatly relieved to discover I am not cut or bleeding. It just looks red, and throbs painfully.

Although Daddy can see I am not seriously injured, he mutters,

"Dog-loving, wacko woman!"

"I'm okay, Daddy," I say bravely even though I am still shaken by the dog's attack. I throw my arms around his neck and cling to him for reassurance. It occurs to me that this terrible thing happened to me on my way to church.

"Everything's all right now, son, the dog is gone. You're safe," he reassures me as I relax safely in his powerful embrace.

I hear the familiar growl of the demon as it lets me know that it followed me and agitated the dog into attacking me. I don't wonder why... I am going to my very first Mass. I remember that Mommy once said that the devil can use animals to hurt and intimidate people. This attack was especially upsetting since I am deathly afraid of dogs.

"Can we please go to St. Monica's now, Daddy," I plead.

Looking in my eyes, Daddy says, "Just a minute, son, hold your horses; I have to tell you something first. Listen to me and pay attention."

Daddy points his finger in my face for emphasis, "Never, ever, go near any dogs... even if they are with their owners. Do you hear me? They are ALL vicious. Dogs can bite you and hurt you and if they have Rabies disease, you will have to get eight giant needles right in your stomach! That is very, very painful! Do you hear what I am telling you? Understand? You stay away from dogs, okay?"

"Yes, Daddy, I will."

He continues, "One more thing, if you are ever attacked by a dog like that again, you kick the dog as hard as you can right in its nose or in its stomach, and then keep kicking it until it runs away. You yell at it too, loudly. Sometimes screaming at a dog can scare it away. Catch wise?"

I nod in agreement. My eyes wander over Daddy's shoulder to the front of St. Monica's Church where I see people climbing up the long stairs into the church.

Daddy also looks over and says, "Okay, let's go before we miss the beginning of Mass."

As we approach the church, it seems to get larger and larger until we are finally standing right in the very front by the center of the long stairs. My eyes scale up the long steps that span the entire front of the church. In front of the stairs to the right and left is a tall black wrought iron gate with long, sharp points along the top. When the gate is closed it extends across the entire front of the stairs. The gate is about one foot higher than Daddy and gives the impression that its purpose is to lock out unwelcome things. Especially bad things, I think.

I bend my head all the way back so I can look straight up the front of the church. The church is so high that it seems to reach into the clouds and heaven itself! Just beneath where the church comes to a pointed top, I notice there is a stained glass window that is difficult for me to see because of the bright sunlight glaring off the golden colored brick front of the church.

Rising above the top of St. Monica's Church are spires on either side of the top center area. These spires rise even higher into the sky than the center peak. I wonder about the significance of these spires. They are probably intended to point toward heaven where God lives. Daddy once told me that the spires are decorative but they also help people recognize where the churches are located in the city because the churches stand out clearly in the skyline thanks to the spires.

I know what Daddy said is true, but I also think the spires are intended to point upward toward God in heaven.

There are three sets of doorways leading into the church. At the top of the stairs directly in the center of St. Monica's Church, the entrance is comprised of two large red doors facing us. Each door has a half-panel of glass in the top section. The doors are set inside two other outside doors also red in color. These doors are wide open in a welcoming gesture. Similar sets of doors stand at each of the two side entrances at the top of the stairs in front of St. Monica's Church.

I feel so small and fragile compared to the church's mighty structure of brick, concrete, steel, and glass, but I am thrilled to see a small window at the very top of this mighty structure. In a similar way, I reason, although I am small in terms of physical size, I know that I am far more important than any buildings no matter how big or grand they may be because I am one of God's children.

God gave me a soul enabling me to live, think, breathe, choose, see, hear, and to do things for myself which a building can never do. As one of God's children, I can also feel His love for me... something non-living things like buildings can never enjoy.

People scurry past us on the right and left as we climb the stairs, and quickly disappear into the church through the two swinging red doors at the top. I count each step as we make our way up, eleven steps in all. Daddy and I then pass through the large red doors and enter the cool, dark area on the other side.

I immediately sense the presence of a magnificent, all-consuming entity that is gentle, loving, and kind. This presence is everywhere filling the entire church, transforming it into a deeply hallowed, holy place. From what Mommy and Daddy have told me in the past, I know that what I sense must be the presence of God in here.

"This area of the church is called the vestibule, Bobby. You were Baptized right over there," Daddy says as he points to a small room off to our far left.

We walk over to the small room and peer through its two full glass doors. I can see a large white marble Baptismal font standing prominently in the center of the room. A smaller font is connected to its right side.

"You know, that's where everyone in our family was baptized over the years," Daddy says sounding emotional, "That includes Mommy and me!

"Your godparents, Aunt Flo Porter, your mom's sister, and her husband, Vinny Porter, held you right over there, Bobby, only a few years ago. How do you like that, heh?"

There is a special kind of beauty in this holy place where I, my brothers and my sister, my parents and so many others became Christians. Right here! I can envision my godparents holding me over the larger font while the priest pours the holy waters of Baptism over my head. I can almost feel the cool water flowing gently over my forehead... cleansing my soul of the original sin all of us are born with.

Sadly, that was the last time my godparents saw me. Aunt Flo and Uncle Vinny, and their daughter, Barbara, have never visited us at our home. I wonder why.

"Look at the floor tiles, Bobby. They're made of marble bordered with 'quatrefoils' which symbolize the four Gospels."

Daddy turns and leads me by my left hand through the set of glass doors to our right bringing us into the center rear area of the church. A sense of awe fills me as I gaze in wonderment about this cavernous, colorful structure inside St. Monica's Church. The sweet scent of incense delights my nose while hushed tones about me create an appropriate atmosphere of holiness and reverence for the presence of God in here.

Straight ahead of us is the front of the church. I recognize the large, white marble altar Mommy described so many times. She explained that this is where Jesus comes to be among us during each Mass when the priest lifts the white round host of bread and the cup of wine high into the air and offers them up to God the Father. A miracle takes place as the Holy Spirit of God descends upon the bread and wine transforming them into "the Body and Blood, Soul and Divinity of Jesus Christ" which we then receive in Holy Communion.

Mommy also told me that when Holy Communion is not distributed, it is stored in a sacred box behind the golden doors in the center of the altar. This sacred place is called the "Tabernacle."

To my right and left, I see dark wooden panels behind the last pew where people are sitting as they wait for Mass to begin. The panels are four feet high, about one foot higher than me. At the end of each panel, there is a golden font attached right by the aisle. Each font contains holy water for people to bless themselves as they enter and leave the church.

Daddy dips his right hand into the font on his right then makes the Sign of the Cross inadvertently splashing me with the holy water in the process. Using his right hand, he first touches his forehead, then his heart, then his left shoulder, and finally his right shoulder. Daddy nods to me to follow his example. Slowly, I repeat what Daddy did... carefully avoiding spilling any of the holy water.

We make our way over to the left side of the church where we turn right by the last pew, and walk up toward the front. At the tenth pew from the Communion rail, Daddy stops and genuflects. I imitate him as best I can by bending my right knee until it touches the ground; then I stand up. We enter the pew to our left, kneel down on a padded kneeler, and say a 'prayer of hello,' as Daddy calls it, to God. After our prayer of hello, we sit down.

I look around these hallowed surroundings while my hands examine the pew I am sitting on. The pews all look the same; they are shiny, hard to the touch, and made of dark brown wood.

To my right, I notice a small group of nuns sitting together in the front-right center section of the church. They are dressed the same in long black robes covering their entire bodies from head to toe. A white cloth is wrapped around their heads framing their faces, and a large, stiff white collar covers the upper chest area. Each nun has a large-silver colored crucifix hanging in front over their hearts and brown rosary beads hanging down the right side of their bodies from the waist to just below the knee. Most of the older-looking nuns, the ones with lots of wrinkles, are wearing eyeglasses.

Mommy once told me that nuns are called "Sisters" because they live together most of their lives just like real sisters growing up together. She also explained that nuns live in the same home called a "convent." Like priests, nuns consecrate their entire lives to God, and so, they don't marry or have children.

"Look up there," Daddy says as he turns toward the back of the church and nods at the choir loft located high above the pews in the back of the church.

"There's Mr. Hughes and Mr. Kuebler at the organ. They play the music during Mass. Mr. Hughes usually plays the organ and Mr. Kuebler sings. That organ was built in 1906 but it still sounds like new."

My eyes sweep past them to study the gigantic golden-colored organ pipes occupying the entire width of the loft's center section. The pipes stand out brilliantly in front of the dark brown wooden panels behind them. They glisten in the bright sunlight pouring in through the large, colorful stained-glass windows above them.

As Mr. Hughes begins to play the organ, beautiful, lilting sounds flow together and resonate throughout the church. Easing back against the pew, I am filled with a great sense of peace and belonging, the kind Mommy has told me about. She says we should enjoy such times because the bad times inevitably also come to all people, times of sadness and hardship. Mommy said this is what life is all about… happiness and goodness, grief and sadness… and the eternal struggle between good and evil.

I study the altar area in the front center of the church. First, there is a set of three steps leading up to the Communion rail. This rail separates the Sanctuary from the rest of the church. The top step has a padded kneeler where people kneel when receiving Holy Communion. The rail itself is about three feet high and is made of white marble. In the center of the Communion rail, there are two golden gates that can be swung open when necessary.

About ten feet from the Communion rail are five marble steps that lead up to the center altar that is made of white marble. There are three shelves above the altar itself. Pretty flowers rest on the shelves. At the very center of the altar is the golden door of the Tabernacle where Holy Communion is reserved. Above the Tabernacle is a three-foot high golden crucifix with the figure of Christ hanging on it. To the far right and left of the crucifix, there are white marble statues of an angel. Daddy tells me that the angel on the right is the Archangel Michael standing on top of the fallen angel, Lucifer.

A few feet above the golden crucifix, there is a five-foot white marble statue of St. Monica holding a cross. Above this statue is a spire that rises about ten feet higher. It has a plain white cross at its very top. Just behind this is a colorful, twenty-foot stained glass window that depicts Jesus hanging on the cross. Pictured at the foot of the cross is Mary, the Apostle John, and one of the holy women. To the left of this stained glass window, there is another stained glass window showing the nativity scene with angels floating in the air above the Holy Family and two shepherds. To the right of the center stained glass window, there is another stained glass window that shows Jesus ascending into heaven with the apostles looking on.

A bell rings from somewhere up front. Everyone suddenly stands up. Off to the right side in the very front of the church, there are two altar boys walking out with their hands folded in a praying position. Walking right behind them is a priest who is carrying a chalice covered by an ornate cloth. The altar boys are wearing white surpluses over long black cassocks. The surpluses look like baggy shirts with short sleeves but no collars. The cassocks look like snug dresses buttoned up the middle from around the ankles all the way up to the neckline.

The priest is wearing a colorful, loose fitting garment. They pause at the side altar where the altar boys genuflect and the priest bows. They now proceed to the center altar where they repeat the same actions. After making the Sign of the Cross, the altar boys kneel down. The rest of us in the church kneel down and listen to them praying.

I hear them praying certain words but they don't make sense. I can't understand what these words mean. It sounds like they are saying, "Ad Deum qui lae ti fi cat iu ven tutem me am."

Seeing my confusion, Daddy leans down and whispers, "They're praying in Latin, Bobby. The Mass is said in the Latin language."

This is confusing. Why is the Mass said in another language? I tug on Daddy's hand, and forgetting that I should speak softly, I ask in a loud voice, "Do you speak Latin, Daddy?"

Daddy quickly puts a finger to his lips and whispers, "Shush, don't speak so loudly, Bobby. Nobody here understands Latin except maybe the nuns and priest. The rest of us follow along in this Daily Missal which covers the entire Mass."

He nods to the black book he is holding. Looking around, I notice how most people are in fact also using a similar looking book. But I still do not understand why Latin is used rather than English, so I ask again, "Why don't they say Mass in English so we can understand what they are saying?"

Daddy looks annoyed now as he snaps impatiently, "Shush! That's just the way it's always been, that's all! Latin is the language spoken around the world. Now stop asking so many questions and pay attention to the Mass. We'll talk about it after Mass."

I still don't think they should be saying Mass in a foreign language that no one understands.

Daddy shakes his head in annoyance and turns his attention back to the Mass up front. At different times, the organ plays very solemn but beautiful sounding music. This adds a special feeling of reverence to what is happening. I wonder if Jesus had music playing when He prayed in the temple. I bet He did.

Everyone stands up now as the priest walks up a winding staircase that leads to an all-white marble pulpit about eight feet high up above everyone in the pews. We make the Sign of the Cross with our right thumb on our foreheads, our lips, and our hearts. Mommy told me that we Catholics do this whenever the priest is going to read the Gospel so that God's words that he reads will bless our thoughts, our words, and our hearts.

I listen as the priest reads the Gospel, the living Word of God. When he finishes reading, we sit down and listen to what Daddy said is called a "homily," or a "sermon." That is when the priest explains what the scripture readings mean, and he gives us a special message to live by. His words sound impressive but I really don't understand what they mean to me.

When he finishes, the priest turns and climbs back down the stairs from the pulpit and returns to the center altar. Just now, a man serving as an usher comes down the aisle carrying a wicker basket attached to what looks like a very long stick. The usher reaches into each pew holding the basket in front of the people who put money in it. When he comes to our pew, Daddy digs into his right pocket and retrieves a dime that he deposits in the basket on top of other coins. Daddy whispers that this is how we help to support our church so it can pay its bills.

"What bills, Daddy?"

"The electricity, the… never mind!" he says annoyed, "it's just to help pay whatever bills the church has. Everyone gives whatever they can afford. Now please be quiet and pay attention to the Mass."

The sound of a loud bell clanging up by the altar fills the church and draws my attention to the priest who is now standing at the top of the steps in front of the altar with his back to us. He has his hands extended over the bread and wine as he is praying words in Latin too low for me to hear. Everyone in the church is kneeling.

A tingling sensation ripples all over me as I realize there is something quite extraordinary happening up at the altar. There are lots of angels and people in white gowns now surrounding the altar. I feel so much joy listening to the faint sounds of beautiful voices singing a glorious song of love to Jesus. The song doesn't have words, just sounds of love and praise.

I can hear each voice, and yet they blend together forming one beautiful voice. They must be the angels and holy people Mommy said come to every Mass when the priest extends his hands over the bread and wine and says a special prayer. There is an ever-expanding sea of these holy spirits filling the church.

Daddy whispers, "Watch closely, Bobby, the priest is going to raise the little white host of bread that has become the Body of Christ."

An altar boy, kneeling just behind the priest to his left, holds the bottom of the priest's garment so it doesn't touch the ground. The other altar boy rings the bell as the priest stands up and raises the consecrated white host high in the air. The priest returns the Eucharist to the altar, genuflects, and says another prayer, then holds up high the chalice containing the wine that has become the precious Blood of Jesus. The other altar boy again rings the bell.

I feel light-headed so I slump back onto the pew. The cool feeling of the wooden pew is helpful but I feel so weak. Daddy tells me to get up and kneel down but I tell him I can't because I feel dizzy. I am relieved that he allows me to continue sitting.

Daddy whispers that he is going to go receive Holy Communion so he tells me to stay in the pew and watch what he does. He gets up and stands in line behind other people in the aisle. Gradually, he makes his way up to the front where he waits behind people kneeling down at the Communion Rail. As soon as these people receive Holy Communion, they rise and return to their pews. Daddy walks up the three steps to the Communion Rail and kneels down becoming part of a long line of people kneeling at the Communion Rail waiting to receive the Eucharist.

Slowly and reverently, the priest distributes Holy Communion to each person by directly placing the consecrated Host onto each person's outstretched tongue. An altar boy accompanying the priest extends a gold plate under each person's chin to catch the Holy Communion if it accidentally falls.

The priest is now standing in front of Daddy. Reaching into the Ciborium, the priest carefully selects one of the consecrated Hosts and places it on Daddy's tongue. Daddy makes the Sign of the Cross then rises to return to our pew. His hands are folded together, palm to palm, in reverence to the presence of God within him.

I am happy I have seen Daddy receive Holy Communion. He looks so reverent and solemn as he kneels down next to me and buries his face in his hands. The organ is playing in the back of the church leading the congregation to sing a beautiful song, "Jesus, My Lord, My God, My All."[3]

"Jesus, my Lord, my God, my all;
How can I love Thee as I ought?
And how revere this wondrous gift,
So far surpassing hope and thought?
"Sweet Sacrament! We Thee adore,
O make us love Thee more and more,
O make us love Thee more and more."

With Daddy in silent prayer, I feel so happy being here with him and so many other people who are praying, singing, and celebrating the presence of God and the angels and saints among us.

Sometime after everyone has received Holy Communion, we all sit down. Another collection is being taken up now while more nice music is played on the organ. After the music stops, everyone in the church stands up. Facing the congregation, the priest gives us his blessing as we make the Sign of the Cross. He then turns and bows before the Tabernacle as the two altar boys genuflect. The priest turns to his right and follows the altar boys as they

---

[3] "Jesus, My Lord, My God, My All" was written by Father Frederick William Faber (June 18, 1814-September 26, 1863.)

walk toward the sacristy off to the right side of the church. They pause before the altar on the right side and genuflect before the Tabernacle there.

I follow Daddy out of the pew, genuflect in the aisle as he did, turn, and walk away from the front of the church where the Tabernacle is located. As we walk toward the rear of the church to leave, Daddy asks what I think of my first Mass.

"It was wonderful, Daddy!"

"What about what the priest had to say, were you able to follow and understand what he was saying?"

"Not so much," I answer honestly.

"What did you like best about the Mass?"

"I liked everything… especially the beautiful singing," I tell him.

Daddy laughs, "Beautiful voices! What beautiful voices? Some of the people I heard singing sounded more like alley-cats than they did people!"

Daddy laughs at his own joke, and is joined by an elderly couple walking behind us who apparently were listening to our conversation.

Obviously, they did not hear the same heavenly voices I heard. I guess they also did not see all the angels and holy people dressed in white robes either.

Chapter 8

KINDERGARTEN

September 1950

I am shocked bolt upright out of a sound sleep with a strong sense of danger, the worst kind of danger. The demon is nearby.

I can't focus my sight in the darkness where I am sitting on the bed in the third room. The sounds of Daddy's snoring breaks through the utter silence of the night. It is amazing that everyone can sleep with such noise. I am alone, isolated, and feeling vulnerable. The lights are off in our apartment as usual during the night. This only adds to my sense of dread.

A feeling of being scanned, intimately examined, comes over me. The demon is probing every cell of my being as if searching for something in particular. What is it looking for? Why is it doing this? Although it is pure spirit, it occupies the area directly behind me in the room radiating its pure hatred and wickedness at me.

It hates me because it recognizes I am a child blessed by God with the gifts of healing and evangelization. It wants to stop me, hurt me, and ultimately, carry me away into the abyss where Satan and its demons torture damned souls forever.

My heart pounds with fear as my eyes gradually become accustomed to the darkness. Peering about the room, I see Paddy and Kitty sleeping at the other end of our bed. Larry is in his crib against the wall. Mommy and Daddy are sleeping in the next room, the one between mine and the kitchen.

I sit up near the outside edge of the bed and cross my legs under me as I pull the big woolen blanket over me. Only my upper torso is exposed to the cool night air since the heat is off as usual during the night. Where is the demon lurking in my room?

"Dear God, please protect me."

After nothing happens, I decide to lie down and close my eyes and continue praying for God's protection as Mommy taught me.

She told me, "We all have a free will to choose between being afraid and **not** being afraid, being good, and **not** being good. The devil can tempt us and do terrible things to frighten and intimidate us, but it can **never** force us to do something against our will. So, whenever you sense the presence of evil nearby, pray, 'Dear God, please protect me!"

Lying on my right side on the edge of the bed, I sense the demon is close, very close. Opening my eyes, I see an odd, round surface, dark charcoal in color, five inches from my face. As I watch, this rounded thing begins rising from the floor! It is the demon! My heart jumps with fear as I close my eyes and turn my head away from this diabolical entity. A foul, rank odor fills the room.

I cry out, "Dear God, please help me, please protect me; please protect me; please protect me; please protect me; please protect me!"

A frightening thought invades my mind... the demon is going to attack me tomorrow when I am isolated in school! I ignore this threat and refuse to open my eyes again. Soon, my fear gives way to exhaustion as I sink into the welcome world of sleep where the demon cannot follow me.

Hours later, I awaken to the first sounds of morning accompanied by bright, beautiful sunlight streaming throughout the rooms of our apartment. The sounds of steam heat can be heard sizzling through the radiators and pipes making their distinctive hissing noises as they warm the cool morning air.

I recall the horrifying encounter with the demon last night. Thank God, I don't sense its presence nearby now. I hear the footsteps of the family living in the apartment above us scurrying about their morning activities. I study the familiar curls of dried paint peeling from the ceiling and watch a solitary roach slowly travel across the ceiling from one side to the other. I keep my eye on it because I know they sometimes position themselves right above you then float right down on you. This has happened to me many times before.

Mommy walks into the room and says cheerfully, "Good morning, Bobby. Did you have a good sleep?"

Before I can tell her what happened last night, she continues, "Please get up now, honey, and get ready for the day. Today is a very special day; it's your first day of school!"

These are painful words that strike immediate fear in my heart. Mommy is going to take me to kindergarten in the public school located on the north side of 86th Street between York and East End Avenues.

"Don't look so concerned, Bobby. There's nothing to be afraid of," Mommy encourages me as her eyes search mine for agreement.

"School is a wonderful place where they sing songs, play games, and teach you interesting things."

Her comments only add to my growing sense of panic because I know she just does not understand. I am **not** afraid of school itself, I am afraid of the demon and the possibility that it will follow me to school where I will be away from Mommy and the rest of my family. Besides, this will be the first time in my life that I will be by myself away from my family. What if I get lost? How would I ever find my way home?

Mommy is determined that I am going to start school today, no matter what I tell her about these fears. She says that I will be fine and will like school. I don't know what is going to happen to me. I am so afraid but I know that I must control my fears and be brave. Daddy's advice comes to mind. He said that I should pray to Jesus for courage whenever I am afraid, and so, I call to God for help to be brave.

Time races by before I find Mommy holding my hand as we rush out the front door on our way to school. We walk to York Avenue where we turn and head toward 86th Street where the public school is located.

Normally, I would be thrilled to go for a walk with Mommy along York Avenue. But I can't enjoy any of the sights today because I know she is going to leave me alone in a strange school where I have never been. Soon we reach the corner of 86th Street and York Avenue. There across the street to the right in the middle of the block is the dark, ominous looking school building. It looks like such a terrible place. The very sight of it causes me to freeze perfectly still.

Mommy looks down at me with a frown, "What are you doing, Bobby? Come on, let's go before you miss the beginning of school."

I refuse to budge.

"Bobby, do you hear me? I said let's go!"

I resist her pull on my hand; I am determined not to move an inch closer to that dreadful looking place.

"Mommy, please don't make me go into that school!" I beg her. "A demon came after me last night, and I am afraid it is going to come after me in school when I am alone. Please don't take me there, Mommy. Please!"

Mommy surprises me with a look of annoyance as she yanks on my shoulders practically knocking me off my feet.

"Now look, Bobby, no more talk about demons! There are no demons in school, and you are certainly not going to be alone there. You will have plenty of classmates. Now that's all there is to it! You are going to school so stop acting like a big baby and get going! School is a wonderful place. You will see. Let's go!"

I have no choice but to start walking. At the moment, I am more afraid of Mommy than I am of anything else. I know when Mommy gets angry she can be quite scary. So I keep my mouth shut and hurry along with her as she practically drags me into the school.

There is a blur of students, noise, and long discussions Mommy has with different people in the school's main office. Finally, I am taken up a flight of stairs by Mommy and some other lady. We walk along a long corridor of classrooms until we enter one on our right. The classroom is filled with many noisy children sitting at their desks. A stern, older-looking woman greets us at the door.

She has an ominous, black shadow surrounding her head. Before I

64

can say anything to Mommy, the teacher grabs my hand, and pulls me over to the front of the class. Her hand is very cold.

She shouts in a gruff voice for the students to listen. The children stop talking and look at her. They all afraid of her.

"Children," she says loudly, "this is another classmate; his name is Robert... Robert Walsh. Please welcome him."

The boys and girls look at me and smile as they slowly call out, "Welcome, Robert."

A wave of giggles follows as the teacher brings me to the third row from the door then walks me down the aisle to a seat located near the back of the class. Practically shoving me into the seat, she tells me to wave goodbye to Mommy who is standing in the doorway. Panic erupts within me as a painful lump swells in my throat.

I wave weakly to Mommy realizing she is leaving me here.

The sense of the demon's presence grows stronger. Just as I feared, it is here.

As Mommy waves and walks away out of my sight for the first time in my life, the demon's voice fills my mind, "She's left you here, you'll never see her or your family again! Now you're ours!"

A quick look around does not show where the demon is located. I feel defenseless, like an innocent creature about to be viciously attacked and mauled by a fierce, powerful predator. Tears flow; I am so afraid. How can Mommy ignore my pleadings and leave me here in this strange, scary place with the demon?

The scary-looking teacher is standing over me to my right shouting something at me. Her face looks so twisted, I cannot look at her anymore, and her voice is so hurtful, I place my hands firmly over my ears. My God, she is trying to pull my hands off my ears! Now she is grabbing my shoulders and violently shaking me! As my head snaps upward, I see the black shrouded figure of the demon suspended above the teacher!

I must get out of here but the teacher has me pinned down in the seat with her hands painfully pressing against my upper arms. Suddenly, a sharp, wicked pain rips across the left side of my face. The teacher slapped me! She slapped me!

I sense the demon is rejoicing and urging the teacher to hit me again, and harder! A hot, stinging sensation swells along the left side of my face. The teacher looks enraged, out of control. Salvia spills out of her mouth as she screams madly at me. I must get out of here before the demon descends upon me and carries me off. The teacher has me pinned down in the seat.

Fear and desperation, anger and indignation, overwhelms me. I realize I must escape from this wicked teacher who seems to be holding me down for the demon. I call out to God to save me.

Just when it seems all is lost, a thought comes to mind showing me how to escape. I place my hands over the teacher's hands, slip down slightly in my seat, and move my body slightly to the right. Bracing myself, I bring up my feet up and kick her with both feet as hard as I can! The teacher cries out as she goes reeling backward with her arms flailing and a look of astonishment on her wicked face! Only the desk and a student behind her prevents her from falling to the floor.

This gives me just enough time to bolt out of my seat and run to my left away from her before she can grab me and hold me for the demon. Running as fast as I can toward the front of the classroom, I turn right at the front row of desks, and in a flash I am out the door of the classroom. Freedom! Safety!

Blindly running out into the corridor, I turn left and speed wildly past students and adults in the hallway bumping into many of them as I scramble to safety. I hear shouts behind me that I assume are directed at me. Everyone must think I am a wild, misbehaving student running to avoid punishment for something bad I did. I later learn that in my frantic run to freedom, one of the people I ran past in the hallway was Mommy! I never noticed her! She had paused to talk with one of the other mothers she knows who also has a child here in kindergarten!

My heart is pounding wildly as I burst through the front doors of the school and run straight out onto 86th Street where I turn right toward York Avenue and continue to run as fast as I can to escape. I must keep running as fast and as far as I can. If I stop running, I will get caught and be brought back to that wicked teacher… and the demon.

My lungs feel like they have turned to stone! I can hardly breathe; my chest is so tight it hurts badly as I gasp for air. I never realized that I cannot run very far without my lungs hurting like this. But I must keep running until I reach the sanctuary of my home on the street where I live.

I am sure someone must be chasing after me but I don't hear any footsteps behind me. Turning left at the corner, I run out into the intersection of 86th Street and York Avenue without looking to my left at oncoming traffic.

This nearly costs me my life.

I get half way across when I hear the sound of screeching tires to my left and the shocking appearance of the front grill of a car hurtling right at me! I am so startled I can't move! In the next instant, powerful arms lift me high up and sweep me out of harm's way! Some strong person has saved me from getting hit by the onrushing car!

I am carried in this position over to the sidewalk so easily I feel like I am flying. There are some adults standing there with a look of amazement at what just happened.

"Isn't it terrible how kids misbehave today?" An old lady complains. He almost got himself killed! If that nice young man wasn't there, that boy would've been killed!

"You shouldn't be running out into the street like that!" she scolds me as she shakes her finger at me.

She said a nice young man saved me but I didn't see anyone in the street when I ran out into traffic. There was absolutely no one in the intersection, and I didn't hear anyone behind me. So, where did he come from? Whoever he is, he must be very strong to pick me up like I was a feather and effortlessly carry me over to safety.

I turn around to see him but I am blinded by a blazing white light in front of me. Before my eyes can acclimate to the light, I sense his spirit is one of profound goodness. When I can see him, I am taken back by the remarkable appearance of his dazzling blue eyes. His smile is in keeping with the joyful spirit I sense within him. He is tall and powerful looking. The outfit he is wearing is very odd. All his clothes are white, even his shoes!

"You escaped the 'dragon,' Robert," he says. "You must be watchful of what comes your way… and what follows you!"

He knows my name!

"Now you know how Daniel felt when **he** got out."

He must be referring to Daniel who was kept in the lions' den overnight but God protected him by keeping the lions from eating him. He is an angel! God sent this angel to save me!

"Thank you for saving me. You're an angel, aren't you?"

His only reply is a smile.

Mommy suddenly appears sounding out of breath from running after me. She bends down and hugs me. All is well now; Mommy is here. But is she going to take me back to that terrible school?

The old lady tells Mommy, "If it wasn't for that nice young man, he would have been run over by the cars!"

Pulling back from me, Mommy looks very frustrated as if to say, "What am I going to do with you?"

Shaking her head, she says to the young man, "Thank you so much for saving my son. Today is his first day in school, and he was upset about going. I never dreamed he'd run away from the school!"

The young man just smiles. He understands why I ran away.

Mommy says, "I'm going to take him back to school now. Come on, Bobby, let's go."

Oh, my God, no! The thought of going back into that school with the demon and the wicked teacher terrifies me. I pull away, and plead with her not to bring me back there. I tell her about the demon and how the wicked teacher slapped me in the face.

Mommy looks at the side of my face and sees the nasty red welt where the teacher slapped me. Now Mommy's face gets red... with anger.

"She hit you! Why in the world would the teacher hit you? You're a good boy."

"I don't know, Mommy; I wasn't doing anything wrong. She has a black area around her head, she's wicked. When she slapped me in the face, I kicked her and ran away from her as fast as I could."

"Good! You did the right thing, Bobby!" Mommy says emphatically.

"Wait 'til I talk to that teacher and the principal of the school. I'm going to give them both a piece of my mind. That's terrible."

As an after-thought, she adds, "I'm not sure I want you to go to that school now… but where can I send you then?"

The young man smiles and says, "Where I come from, 'Father' always knows best."

I know he is referring to God the Father but Mommy thinks he is referring to Daddy.

Mommy says, "You're right; that's good advice. Thank you. I'll talk with Bobby's father; he'll know what's best to do. For now, Bobby, let's go home."

We take a few steps toward home before Mommy turns to thank the young man again, but he is gone. He has vanished!

"What in God's name? Where did he go? He was right here a second ago!"

"He went back to heaven, Mommy. He's an angel God sent to save me."

Mommy keeps looking around; she is really amazed.

"God sent him to save me!" I repeat. "He even knew my name and why I ran away from school."

Tears well up in Mommy's eyes realizing that the young man in white really was an angel in disguise who saved me.

Mommy does not say another word all the way home; she apparently is greatly moved by this experience.

After we arrive at home, I tell her, "I don't want to go back to that school. If the angel didn't save me, I might be dead right now! If you take me back there, I'll run away again!"

My audacity in speaking to Mommy this way surprises me.

She just shakes her head and says, "We'll see what your father has to say when he wakes up later. You can go inside and play until then, Bobby."

Later, I listen to Mommy and Daddy in the kitchen discussing what happened. Daddy is greatly impressed to hear about the angel who saved my life, and then just disappeared.

Mommy tells him that the angel knew me by my name. Daddy says this is just another sign that I am called to be a priest when I grow up.

"The angels can tell he is a 'blessed child of God,'" he states.

Mommy adds that the angel said, 'Fathers know best.'

Daddy chuckles and jokes, "That's what I like, an angel with a high IQ!"

When I am called to join the conversation, I am relieved to see they both appear to be at ease.

Mommy smiles and puts her arm around me and says, "Daddy and I have decided that it will be better for you to wait until next year to begin school. Is that all right with you, Bobby?"

"Yes," I answer enthusiastically.

What a relief. I don't have to go to school until next year!

Mommy continues, "You can skip kindergarten this year, and start school next year in the first grade. Okay?"

I nod my head yes repeatedly to make sure Mommy and Daddy know that I agree.

Daddy adds, "Also, we think it would be best if you, Paddy, and Kitty go to the Catholic school, St. Monica's, instead of going to the public school. You'll get a much better education there. The teachers there are Franciscan nuns so you'll also be taught about our faith at the same time. And the school is on 80th Street between York and First Avenues, right around the corner from the church on 79th Street."

Mommy says, "If God can send an angel to save you, Bobby, the least we can do is send you to a Catholic school. What do you think about that?"

"Do I have to wait until next year?"

Chapter 9

NANA

November 1950

It is Thanksgiving Day, a day for happiness, reflection, the Thanksgiving parade... and turkey!

As he so often does, Daddy is talking about **his** Mommy, "Nana." Occasionally, he speaks of his other Walsh family relatives but strangely, he doesn't speak about his father, Grandpa Edward John Walsh.

I sit down on the kitchen chair across from Daddy and drawing his attention, I seize the moment to ask him to tell me about my Nana. Calling her **my** Nana obviously pleases him as he smiles and takes on a far-away look.

"**Your** Nana's full name is Catherine Marie Clarke Walsh. She was born in Freeland, Ireland on June 28, 1893. When her family immigrated to America, they settled on the East Side of Manhattan where so many Irish located. She was Protestant in faith but converted to Roman Catholicism when she met and married my father, Edward John Walsh. His family also lived on the East Side."

"Please tell me about your father, my grandpa."

Daddy's happy appearance becomes less happy looking as he just stares.

After a pause, he finally speaks, "My father, Edward John Walsh, was born in America on October 25, 1887. His father, my grandfather, your great-grandpa, was John Patrick Walsh, a stonecutter and builder who came to America in 1879 with his wife, my grandma, your great-grandma, Mary Durkin Walsh. You know, they were only 21 years old. In 1920, they lived at 156 East 84th Street near Lexington Avenue in Manhattan."

Daddy pauses, apparently deep in thought once again.

"My grandpa, John, passed away on May 10th, 1922. He died from pulmonary tuberculosis."

Daddy looks so sad.

After a while, he continues, "My grandma, Mary, lived in that same apartment on 84th Street until the day she died."

"What about their parents, Daddy? Tell me about them."

"Well, I am afraid I don't remember too much about them, Bobby, except that their names were Michael and Alice Walsh, my great-grandparents. They both lived and died in a part of Ireland called Gutermore in County Sligo. That's where our Walsh family roots come from. All I remember is that they were good and faithful Catholics who greatly loved and cared for their family."

Daddy excuses himself and walks off inside. I look over to Mommy where she is doing the dishes. Always understanding me, her glance confirms she can tell I am sad because Daddy became sad.

Speaking softly as if to avoid being heard by Daddy, she explains, "Daddy is sad, Bobby, because a lot of sad things have happened to his family... and he just remembered some of those sad things."

"Did something sad happen to his mommy?"

"Well, not directly. You know that Daddy greatly loves and admires his mom. Like so many women of her day, she is strong, incredibly resourceful, self-sacrificing, and fiercely dedicated to her family... and her heritage.

"Your Daddy is much like her in many ways. Not only do they look alike, they are they both five feet, ten inches tall, very intelligent, and they are not afraid to stand up for what they believe. Thank goodness Nana was strong and self-sufficient because, like so many women of her day, Nana had to raise her family of six children all by herself due to a terrible family tragedy."

Mommy pauses to look inside to see if Daddy is nearby to hear what she is about to say. She comes over to sit right next to me to tell me something she obviously doesn't want Daddy to overhear.

Speaking very softly, she says, "Daddy's father, Edward John Walsh, died of a fractured skull when he fell out the fifth story window of the apartment they lived in on Second Avenue near the corner of 74th Street in Manhattan. Grandpa Edward Walsh was only 33 years old at the time. No one in the Walsh family talks about this terrible tragedy because it is too sad and painful."

Pausing once again to make sure Daddy isn't coming our way, she continues, "It happened around 1:40 in the morning on December 12, 1920. Grandpa Walsh had just arrived home following a night of beer drinking with his friends in one of Yorkville's many pubs. Drinking beer, sharing news, and storytelling with fellow Irishmen is a common custom here in New York as it is over in Ireland.

"Nana told me what happened. She said she was walking into the room with your father when they saw Grandpa Walsh leaning out the window shouting back and forth with his friends who were still down at the front of the building. Nana was about to tell Grandpa Walsh to stop yelling out the window when a black shadowy figure suddenly appeared outside the window directly in front of Grandpa! Nana swears she clearly saw it floating outside in mid-air gesturing to Grandpa to come out! She doesn't know if Daddy also saw it.

"Grandpa started yelling at it and then he leaned out the window and threw a punch at the black figure. His fist went right through the evil thing causing Grandpa to lose his balance and fall straight out the window to his death five flights below!

"Nana swears that the black figure was a devil!

"Grandpa landed in such a way that his head smashed on the concrete sidewalk so hard it cracked open his skull instantly killing him."

Mommy pauses and appears to be considering whether or not to tell me more. I ask her to continue.

"You must not discuss this with your father; it breaks his heart to think about what happened."

"I promise."

"And you must not talk about this with any of your uncles or aunts either. This is not something they ever talk about. Okay?

"Do you understand, Bobby?"

I again give my promise.

"Your Daddy was only four years old at the time this happened. He was awake... and sadly saw it all. He was devastated. He and his father were very close. Your Daddy greatly loved his father... just like you love your Daddy.

"When Daddy saw his father slip out the window, he yelled to Nana telling her what happened and he ran down to the street to where Grandpa Walsh was lying motionless with his eyes and mouth open and blood spilled all over the sidewalk from his head. Your Daddy kept crying out to him to wake up, but of course, he could not."

While Mommy is telling me this terrible story, I can picture it happening in my mind. I feel so sad for Daddy and my grandpa and grandma. Mommy wipes away a tear before continuing.

"When Nana came down, she pulled Daddy away from Grandpa and tried to help him herself. Daddy grabbed onto Nana and begged her to help his Daddy get better. But Nana could see by Grandpa's eyes, and the condition of his injury, that there was nothing anyone could do to bring him back.

"To comfort Daddy, Nana told him that his father would be all right. When the police and an ambulance arrived, Nana told them that Grandpa had slipped out the window. She didn't tell them why. Nana took Daddy aside while the ambulance workers put Grandpa's body in a body bag, placed him in the back of their wagon, and left."

Mommy pauses again, and swallows hard before continuing. "Grandpa Walsh's father, John Patrick, went to the morgue and identified the body of his son. He then made all the funeral arrangements and took care of notifying relatives with the terrible news. The funeral Mass was held for

72

Grandpa Edward in St. Monica's Church on East 79th Street, and he was buried in Calvary Cemetery in Queens on December 14, 1920.

"Your father never really recovered from that terrible tragedy. That is why he never talks about his father, and, in fact, rarely talks about his childhood either."

"Please tell me about Daddy's brothers and sisters."

"Well, Daddy has five brothers and two sisters. The oldest brother is Uncle Eddie, then there is Uncle Buddy whose real name is Francis but he doesn't like to be called that because he says it sounds like a 'sissy's name.' The youngest brother is Uncle Donny, your godfather. The other two brothers are with God. One brother, John Walsh, died from illness on April 13, 1915; he was only six months old. The other brother, Joseph, also died from illness when he was three years old. Daddy's two sisters are Aunt Marion, the older sister, and Aunt Dotsy. Your grandpa Edward was thin and short, only about five feet, six inches tall. Despite being small, he had such a large family.

"Without Grandpa Walsh around to help, Nana had a very difficult time supporting and raising her family of five children. You see, in her day during the 1920's, women were expected to stay at home and take care of the family. However, with no money coming in because her husband died, Nana **had** to go to work. But the only work she could get was cleaning the hallways of buildings on the block where she lived. So that is what Nana did to support her family. That kind of work does not pay much, so the family had things very hard.

"I think that's all for now, Bobby. Now remember, don't talk to Daddy about any of this; it makes him very sad. Okay?"

"I promise."

I feel so sad to hear all this, but I also feel proud to hear how my Nana was so strong and courageous in facing such hardships alone. Poor Nana, poor Grandpa Walsh, poor Daddy, and my uncles and aunts!

It has become a joyful family tradition for us virtually every other week to visit Nana in her apartment. Mommy and Daddy are planning such a visit again today. Fighting against the cold, brisk air, we are quite excited and filled with expectations of another happy family time. It is wonderful that Nana lives on First Avenue between 81st and 82nd Streets, not far from us.

Larry, Kitty and I are close to Mommy holding onto her coat. Paddy is walking independently by himself next to us. Daddy is puffing away on his Chesterfield cigarette and occasionally telling us to watch where we are walking. Mommy and Daddy are afraid that one of us might run into the street without looking and get hit and killed by crazy drivers.

Along the way, we pass St. Stephen of Hungary Church and School in the middle of 82nd Street between York and First Avenues. There are a lot of people coming out of church. That is because today is Thanksgiving Day. I imitate Daddy as he makes the Sign of the Cross as we pass the church. This is done in reverence to the presence of Christ that is inside the tabernacle in the church… as in most Catholic churches around the world.

Even though St. Stephen's Church is located near our home, Mommy and Daddy do not consider it to be our church since Mommy and Daddy's families have always been members of St. Monica's Church. Mommy once told me that she and Daddy were both baptized at St. Monica's, as were all of us children. Mommy was baptized on December 24, 1922, and Daddy on July 16, 1916.

Whether Mass is said at St. Monica's or St. Stephen's, I still don't understand why Mass is said in a foreign language, Latin, which no one other than the priests and nuns understand.

At the corner of 82nd Street and First Avenue, the light is red so we stand back from the curb and wait for the light to change to green. Nana lives on the other side of the street, the west side of First Avenue, just to the left of the small bakery shop where Daddy buys the best rolls, jelly buns, and sliced sour-rye bread for breakfast. The sour-rye bread is one of Mommy's favorite foods. The rolls at this bakery are indescribably delicious, even better than the rolls we get at the German bakery on York Avenue between 80th and 81st Streets.

The traffic light finally changes and Daddy cautions us with his usual warning, "Look both ways, kids; the light won't hit you, the cars will!"

Having heard this countless times before, we make sure to look both ways before proceeding into the street. Daddy once told us about a boy who used to run across the street as soon as the light turned green. One day, however, he was hit by a car that was speeding to beat the light. He was thrown far into the air and killed when his body smashed against the ground.

After cautiously looking both ways, we cross First Avenue. When we get to the other side, Daddy tells us we can run ahead to Nana's building near the other end of this street.

"But I want to see you at all times, so all of you wait there in front of Nana's building!"

Paddy, being the fastest runner, is the first to reach Nana's building. I am second, and Kitty is a distant third. As soon as Mommy and Daddy arrive with Larry, Daddy tells us to ring Nana's bell. He says we can run up to her apartment on the fifth floor, the top floor in the building.

"Remember, no noise in the hallways and make sure you wish your grandmother a happy Thanksgiving!"

Paddy rings the bell and races up the stairs ahead of us and quickly disappears from sight. Only the sounds of his feet charging up the stairs give evidence of his presence. There are so many steps it seems that they will never end. And it is so tiring. Each new set of stairs and new landing presents a sense of satisfaction that I have made it this far. Climbing all these stairs is worth the effort because my Nana awaits us on the top floor.

As I finally reach the top floor landing, I see Nana standing by her front door on the right side of the hallway. She is crouched over hugging Paddy. Her light brown hair is tied up in a bun on top of her head, and she is wearing a light lavender dress with tiny white flowers. Her eyes are tearful as she rises up and greets me with a loving, magical smile that only grandmothers can project.

I return her loving message as best I can as I run over to her and bury my face in her loving embrace. The three of us stand there clinging silently to one another until Kitty arrives then Daddy, Mommy and Larry.

"Hey, hey, what's going on here?" Daddy yells kiddingly drawing our attention to him. "Happy Thanksgiving, Mom!" he says as he steps over to Nana and wraps his arms around her.

"Give Nana a 'schmushkypop', Daddy," I suggest to everyone's amusement.

"A 'smushkypop!" Nana says in amazement. "I can't believe you taught the kids about 'smushkypops!"

Daddy smiles proudly. A "smushkypop" is Daddy's name for the biggest, most loving kiss you can give someone. Daddy follows my suggestion and plants a drawn-out kiss on Nana's cheek. As Nana chuckles, I see her eyes glistening with tears of joy.

Mommy steps up to Nana and teases Daddy, "Hey, Patsy, stop hogging Nana all to yourself. Let Larry and me get a chance too!"

Mommy and Nana hug each another with poor Larry stuck between them. Nana peeks at Larry and says, "Oh, he's so handsome; he looks just like you, Ellie!"

Mommy smiles proudly and hugs Larry who seems quite pleased with all the attention.

"What do you say we all go inside," Nana encourages us as she escorts Mommy and Larry into her apartment. Daddy and the rest of us eagerly follow behind in single file. Entering the apartment, I find myself standing in Nana's kitchen. Her home is filled with the delicious aroma of stuffing and turkey Nana has prepared for us. To my left there is a simple table with a large brown, scrumptious-looking turkey resting majestically at the center of the table.

Folding her hands maternally, Nana says, "Now why don't you children go inside and play while your Daddy carves the turkey for Nana."

"And don't make a mess either, or I will tan your hides!" Daddy warns.

Nana's apartment is railroad style like ours. The rooms are lined up in a straight line. I am fascinated by the white cotton doilies Nana has on the arms of her furniture and on all the end tables. Sitting on her old couch, I hold one of the doilies up to the light, and run my fingers along and through the doily's woven pattern.

It feels so soft and delicate, I decide to try it on Larry's head as a hat for him. This brings hearty laughter from Paddy and Kitty, and a quick swipe from Larry as he removes it from his head. Putting it back on his head brings a different response from him. This time he seems thrilled with this new object of curiosity that makes everyone laugh. Now he pulls on it and runs his fingers through its open weave, and to our great amusement, puts it back on top of his head!

Our laughter brings Mommy into the room with a puzzled expression on her face, "All right, what's going on in here. What's so funny?"

After Paddy explains what Larry is doing, Mommy chuckles, shakes her head, then removes the white doily from Larry's grasp and returns it to its rightful place on the arm of the sofa. Mommy then leads us in a game of "Ring around the Rosies," then "Hide and Seek." After this, Mommy sits us down and tells us a story about how the pilgrims first came to America many years ago. She says they were the ones who started the tradition of Thanksgiving after coming to America from across the Atlantic Ocean from a place far away called Europe.

"They gave thanks to God for all the food and good fortune they had. That is what we do now," she explains.

After Mommy tells us more about the pilgrims, Nana calls out, "Come and get it, you hungry pilgrims. Supper's ready!"

Daddy is just now finished carving the turkey. We scramble out to the kitchen and sit around the table in our respective chairs. Nana and Daddy are sitting at either end. Mommy places Larry in a high chair next to where she is sitting. Larry immediately begins to bang his spoon on the empty tray creating a loud annoying noise.

"Ellie, please take that spoon away from him," Daddy pleads, "you know Larry will keep pounding it until his arm falls off!"

"That will only upset him and make him sad. I will just hold onto it with him so he can't bang it," Mommy says.

Nana's smile indicates her agreement, but Daddy looks frustrated.

"Why don't you say grace, Pat," Nana requests.

Daddy makes the Sign of the Cross by first touching his forehead, then his heart, his left shoulder, and finally his right shoulder as he prays, "In the name of the Father, and of the Son, and of the Holy Ghost. Amen. Bless us, O Lord, and these Thy gifts which we are about to receive from Thy bounty through Christ our Lord. Amen!"

Daddy ends the prayer by making the Sign of the Cross once again.

Nana joyfully says, "Thank you, Pat. Now, everyone dig in!"

I am so hungry, I can't wait to eat. The food smells so delicious. Having so many different foods is a real treat. It is only on holidays like this that we get to enjoy such a fantastic feast: turkey, stuffing, sweet potatoes, turnips, creamed cauliflower, peas, cranberry sauce, carrots, and lots of different nuts. Nana and Mommy fill everyone's plate with a little of each type of food.

"Dig in, dig in," Nana urges us.

As I begin to eat, I look around the table. Daddy is munching voraciously on a large drumstick. Soon, all that is left is the white bone. Mommy is enjoying Nana's stuffing. That is my favorite too. Paddy, Kitty, and Larry are chomping away. Nana looks pleased as she looks around the table at her family enjoying her cooking. Nana looks so thin; she should eat more.

Paddy says something to Kitty causing her to giggle.

Daddy looks annoyed, "Hey, how many times have I told you kids, no fooling around at the table! Children are to be seen and not heard! Remember? Now be quiet and eat!"

This quiets all of us for the rest of the dinner. I am pleased; it is easier to hear what Daddy, Mommy, and Nana have to say. Daddy talks about his job, Mommy and Nana talk about cooking and family news.

After dinner, everyone helps clean up by putting the dishes in the sink. Mommy says she will wash the dishes so she orders us to go inside to spend time with Nana and Daddy. I follow the others into the living room where we gather around Nana. Paddy and I sit on the floor by her feet as she rests comfortably in her favorite thickly upholstered chair. Larry sits in Nana's lap much to her obvious delight.

After a while, Mommy comes in and sits next to Daddy on the sofa facing us, and says to Nana, "Okay, Mom, we are all here to hear you sing for us."

I look forward to hearing Nana sing, especially her favorite song, "Because of You."[4] She begins by telling us that she liked this song so much when it came out in the early 1940's that she wrote down all the words while listening to it on the radio. With a big smile, she sings for us.

---

[4] "Because of You" was written by Arthur Hammerstein and Dudley Wilkinson in 1940.

"Because of you, the sun will shine,
The moon and stars will say you're mine,
Forever and never to part.
I only live for your love... and your kiss,
It's paradise to be near you like this.
Because of you, my life is now worthwhile,
And I can smile, because of you."

Mommy and Daddy tell her what a nice voice she has. Paddy urges her to sing another song.

Stroking Larry's hair and gently rocking him, Nana now sings one of our favorite songs,

"Rock a bye baby, on the tree top;
When the wind blows, the cradle will rock;
When the bow breaks, the cradle will fall;
And down will come Larry, cradle and all!"

This wonderful Thanksgiving Day comes to an end listening to Nana's soft, lilting voice sings one beautiful song after another. How I wish such moments could last forever.

"Someday they will.

Chapter 10

MISERICORDIA

February 1951

Mommy and Daddy are in the living room watching television while Paddy and I are having a great pillow fight on the bed in the second room off the living room. It is early evening now.

The lights are off in our room, and it is difficult to maintain my balance because the bed is so bouncy. As I swing the pillow at Paddy, he hits me with his pillow knocking me off my feet. I quickly scramble up and am about to regain my balance facing the headboard when Paddy wickedly falls into me driving my face into the sharp metal edge of the headboard.

Owwww! My forehead instantly hurts and throbs as my eyesight is temporarily blinded. Rising up away from the headboard, I turn around to face Paddy but feel something wet flowing down my face into my eyes.

Although my vision is clouded, I recognize the unmistakable form of the demon behind Paddy. It pushed Paddy into me.

Paddy's eyes bulge as if he sees a ghost, "Oh, my God, Bobby, your head's bleeding! Alarmed, he shouts, "Mommy, Daddy, come quick; Bobby's head is bleeding real mad!"

Hearing this, Mommy comes running in and when she sees my thoroughly bloodied face, she faints on the floor!

Daddy comes in, and seeing me, he says, "Jesus H. Christ, what the hell have you boys been doing! Don't move! Stand right there, I'll be right back! Kitty, quick, see if you can get your mother up!"

Now I am really scared. The demon is in the corner of the room but I obviously am the only one who can see it there.

Kitty rouses Mommy as Daddy comes running back into the room with a towel and presses it roughly onto a bleeding cut on my forehead.

"Here, hold this on the cut," Daddy instructs, "and... and... remain calm!"

I don't know about remaining calm.

I can't see past the towel on my face. Daddy steadies me as I stand next to Mommy who is just now getting up. Kitty is standing there with her mouth hanging open and a worried expression. The towel is now thoroughly soaked with my blood. I am really scared.

Daddy says, "Paddy, what in God's name happened?"

"We were having a pillow fight when somebody pushed me real hard into Bobby knocking him into the head-board of the bed."

"But everybody was in the living room; there was no one else who could have pushed you," Daddy says.

Paddy replies, "Well, somebody pushed me, somebody very strong because I went flying into Bobby!"

"The next thing you're going to tell me is a ghost pushed you," Daddy snaps.

"It wasn't a ghost, I tell Daddy, it was the demon that pushed Paddy!"

Hearing this, Daddy looks frightened.

"Paddy, keep an eye on things while your Mother and I take Bobby to the hospital," Daddy directs.

"You're the man of the house while I'm gone. Keep the door closed and don't open it to any strangers. And don't worry... Bobby will be all right."

I don't know if I believe that, considering how badly my head hurts and seeing how much blood I have lost. Daddy picks me up and with Mommy close behind, we are quickly out the door and down the stairs leading to the first floor.

"Say a prayer we can get a taxi," Daddy says to Mommy.

"Please, God, I pray, send us a taxi... and please don't let the doctors give me needles."

Mommy rushes ahead and opens the front doors of our building allowing us to step out onto the stoop. I can't see anything because Daddy has the towel draped across my eyes and entire face.

"Oh, I can't believe our luck," Daddy cries, "Here comes a taxi! **Taxi! Taxi! Wait right there!**"

I hear Mommy open the door of the taxi for us as Daddy bends down and practically dives into the back seat of the taxi. It felt like he lost his balance. Mommy comes in and closes the door.

"Misericordia Hospital," Daddy shouts to the driver, "and hurry, we have an emergency."

Daddy asks, "How do you feel, Bobby?"

"It stings and hurts. I'm afraid of what they're going to do to me at the hospital."

"Don't be afraid; it's no big deal," he reassures me.

"Do you know what Jesus says? Jesus tells us in Mark 5:36, 'Don't be afraid, just have faith.' So don't be afraid, just have faith that everything is going to be okay."

Daddy's words are comforting. If Jesus tells me not to be afraid, then I will try to be brave.

I like the sound of the taxi's engine and wheels as we drive through the streets of Yorkville on the way to the hospital at 531 East 86th Street between York and East End Avenues.

I say, "Paddy was telling the truth. It was the demon that shoved him into me."

Hearing this, the cab driver looks surprised and interested but Mommy tells me, "Just rest, Bobby, no more talking!"

At the hospital, I am quickly taken into the Emergency Room where Daddy puts me on a table as he explains to a doctor and a nurse what happened to me. The nurse tells me that she has to clean off the area where I am cut so the doctor can see it better.

The light overhead is blinding!

She asks, "What's your name?"

"Bobby, Bobby Walsh."

"How old are you, Bobby?"

"I just turned six."

"Oh, you sure are a big boy."

"This may hurt a little," she adds, "so be a big brave boy for me and keep your head as still as you can."

Hurt a little? Oh, my God, the pain is terrible as she rubs hard around the area that is cut!

As she cleans my forehead and face, the pain around the cut hurts even more! Soon she is finished, and I hear the doctor come back into the room.

Lifting the gauze pad off the wound, he says, "This is going to take a few stitches to close! I'll give him a needle to dull the pain before I stitch him up."

Oh, my God, no! A needle right into my cut! I tell the doctor, "I don't want any needles or stitches! I'll be okay."

Ignoring my words, the doctor asks, "What's your name?"

"My name is Bobby; the Bobby who doesn't want any needles or stitches."

Chuckling, he says, "It's okay, Bobby. It'll only sting for a second. We need to do this so you can get all better. Mommy and Daddy are staying right here, okay? Now it's very important that you stay perfectly still. I need you to be a big boy and hold still. Do you think you can do that for me?"

"Okay," I answer reluctantly.

"I'm going to give you a needle or two to dull the pain so I can stitch up the cut you have. It'll only hurt for a second, then you won't feel any pain at all. Okay?"

"Is there any other way you can fix it?" I ask.

Chuckling, he says, "No, this is the only way, Bobby. We have to do this but it won't be as bad as you think and before you know it, we'll be all done. Right now, I have to put a cloth over your face except for the area of the cut. Mommy and Daddy are staying right here by your side while I make you all better. Okay, Bobby?"

"Okay," I whisper.

I am really **not** happy about all this. How I wish Paddy and I didn't have that pillow fight.

The nurse puts a thick white cloth over my face. It has a hole in it where the doctor will be stitching my cut.

The doctor says, "Now keep your eyes closed, Bobby, and think about something really nice."

I call out, "Mommy and Daddy, are you still here?"

I hear them giggle as they both assure me they are still here.

The doctor asks, "Bobby, do you know the name of our hospital?"

"Misericordia," I answer.

"Very good," he says, "Do you know what that stands for?"

"No, I don't."

"Misericordia is a Latin word that stands for mercy," he tells me.

"Do you know what mercy means?" he asks.

"No."

"Well, mercy means being very kind and helpful to others," he explains.

This is comforting to hear because I need lots and lots of mercy and comfort now to avoid needles and more pain. Owww, oh, my God, there goes one really, really painful needle right into my forehead! It hurts and stings so badly but he just keeps pushing it into the cut and moving it around. Be brave, be brave, I think.

I can't think of anything right now other than what the doctor is doing to my head. Owww, there goes another needle! Oh, my God, I feel like turning away and screaming. Mommy must know what I'm feeling because I hear her crying.

" It 'l l be over soon," Daddy assures me.

After a while, th e doctor asks, "Bobby, can you feel this?"

I feel a tugging on the injured area but surprisingly the pain is gone so I answer, "Everything feels numb and tingly."

"Good!" he says loudly, "Now you'll feel a little tugging as I fix everything so you'll be good as new. This will only take a minute. Okay?"

"That's swell," I tell him trying to sound brave.

My words bring some laughter. I said "swell" because that's one of Daddy's favorite words. He says that whenever he thinks something is especially good. I certainly think it's **swell** that the doctor said this will only take a minute!

The doctor asks, "Are you thinking of something really nice, Bobby?"

I tell him, "Yes, I remember after Mommy told us to offer all our sufferings up to God for the poor souls in purgatory, two of them came to visit me. They asked me to pray for them."

The doctor stops what he is doing and says, "Wow! Now that's **very** interesting!"

"Do you know about this?" he asks Mommy and Daddy.

"Yeah," Daddy responds, "Strange things like that happen with him all the time," Daddy explains. "He's a very special child."

"I'll say," the doctor politely replies.

Turning his conversation back to me, he says, "Tell me more."

"They told me prayers would help them get out of purgatory sooner so I promised to pray for them. Then they left."

"Where did they go?" the doctor asks as he continues working on my cut.

"They went back to purgatory."

"Well… that's certainly a nice story. Thank you for sharing it," the doctor says. "Did you ever see them again?"

"Yes. They came back another time to thank me and tell me they were in heaven, and were going to pray for me now until I get to heaven."

"Wow! How nice of them," the doctor says dramatically.

I can tell he doesn't believe what I am saying actually happened. This is annoying but that's the reaction I usually get from people when they hear something beyond their understanding of God and how God may choose to work.

Now I feel the presence of the two good spirits here with me right now! They apparently have come to comfort me as I once did for them! One of the good spirits tells me not to get upset when people don't understand.

The doctor surprises me by saying, "There, now that wasn't so bad, was it? We're all finished, Bobby! The nurse is going to put a nice big white bandage on your head so you can go home with Mommy and Daddy. Okay?"

"Yes, doctor, thank you for stitching me up," I tell him.

As the doctor prepares to leave, one of the good spirits tells me, "Tell the doctor after watching him work, we think he made a good choice becoming a doctor… rather than a… far… ma… cist."

Before I can say this, the other good spirit adds, "And tell him that **prayer** really is the best medicine of all!"

So I tell the doctor, "The good spirits told me to tell you that after watching you work, they think you made a good choice becoming a doctor rather than a pharmacist, and that **prayer** really is the best medicine of all!"

The doctor stops dead in his tracks and looks bewildered.

"How did you know that? Only my wife and parents know what a tough time I had deciding between the two. And what you said about prayer, that's what I used to say when I first became a doctor!"

"Well, that's what the good spirits told me to tell you."

"Holy God," he says.

Standing there stunned, this man of science couldn't quite understand what just happened.

Eventually, he says, "Well, next time you see your 'good spirit friends,' tell them thanks for the compliment... and for the reminder about prayer."

I tell him, "I don't have to tell them; they hear you themselves."

How appropriate it is that those two good spirits came here to comfort me and to bless the doctor here in this particular hospital, "Misericordia," a place of mercy.

Like purgatory.

Chapter 11

JIMMY'S BOY

March 1951

On this wonderful Saturday afternoon in late March, the sounds of an infant's cry once again graces our home filling our hearts with the joy and magic of new life. Mommy and Daddy brought home the newest addition to our family, my second sister, Geraldine Frances Walsh.

Geri, as Daddy has nick-named her, was born a week ago in a most auspicious way on Saturday, March 10, 1951, in the psychiatric emergency room at Bellevue Hospital on York Avenue.

Mom's water broke while she was shopping in the Mays Department Store on 14th Street and Union Square. When the police arrived to help, the cop on duty was a rookie who was so nervous he didn't listen to Mommy telling him to take her to Lenox Hill Hospital. Instead, he took her to the Psychiatric Emergency Room at Bellevue where within minutes of arrival Geri was born!

Daddy found out about this when he got a phone call from a nurse in the emergency room telling him that Mommy just delivered a healthy, ten-pound baby girl in the Psychiatric Emergency Room!

When Aunt Marion heard about this, she could not resist saying, "Well, they either thought Ellie should have her head examined for having a ten pound baby... or because she's a Brooklyn Dodgers fan!"

As usual, Aunt Marion is always here to help when something special is going on in our family. This time, Uncle Saul Sullivan, her husband, has joined her. He has a gravelly-sounding voice that matches his deeply wrinkled, red face. Mommy and Daddy like him; they say he is a good man.

He is only five feet, ten inches tall, thin, and very muscular. Mommy says he is very muscular because he works in "construction" for a living. She said Uncle Saul has a ruddy complexion because he is Irish and works outdoors all the time in the sunshine.

Although Geri is tiny and fragile, Mommy is going to let me hold her. Sitting down next to Mommy by the kitchen table, she carefully places the baby in my arms, and cautions me to make very sure that I support the back of the baby's head at all times which, of course, I carefully do.

The baby feels so warm and soft. I hug little Geri close to me and kiss her on her cheek. During these precious first moments, I feel a special bond with my tiny little sister. Her little blond eyebrows frown as I whisper to her. She must be concerned about what is going on around her. The sound of my gentle voice appears to reassure her against all the other noises.

Daddy is busy telling Uncle Saul and Aunt Marion how Grandpa James Aloysius Sheridan, Mommy's father, is coming to see the new baby. Daddy says that Grandpa Sheridan has not seen any of us kids yet!

I detect a sound of indignation in Daddy's voice, "He should have come to see the kids a long time ago!"

Aunt Marion chastises him, "Jesus Christ, Patsy, just be happy he **is** coming! Don't be making any trouble now. He's an old man, and he's your wife's father. Give him some respect! Some day you may be in the same position as he is today, coming to visit your daughter after many years. How would you like it if your son-in-law treated you with an attitude, heh?"

"In a pig's tit," Daddy snarls. "I would never stay away from my daughter the way he did just because he didn't approve of the man she married. Not me! Not ever! And no daughter of mine will ever marry the wrong man to begin with! I'll see to that!"

"Stranger things have happened in life, Patsy. Just mind your manners," Aunt Marion says.

"Of course, I'll be polite to him, Marion. What kind of a man do you think I am? Mom raised us to be polite, civil people, didn't she? Well, that's what I am. I always conduct myself properly... even if my father-in-law **is** an old pig-headed, self-righteous, and proud Irishman!"

Aunt Marion glares at Daddy with an expression that indicates she's heard enough, and he had better listen to his big sister!"

Uncle Saul recognizes that look and chimes in, "Oh boy, you'd better listen to your sister, Pat. I know better than anyone, once she digs her heels in on something, that's the way it is going to be... like it or not!"

After she and Uncle Saul leave, Mommy and Daddy discuss Grandpa's upcoming visit. They sound happy he is coming, and appear anxious to show the family they have formed. Daddy says he can't wait to "show us off."

"Please dress the kids in their best clothes when your father comes," Daddy requests.

Then he tells us children, "And you kids mind your manners when you are around your grandfather."

Mommy tells Daddy not to worry about what we wear, "My father is a good man who will see the goodness in the kids no matter how they are dressed... or how mischievous they may behave!"

As Mommy speaks of Grandpa, I envision him in my mind's eye, and sense the extraordinary goodness in him. I can't wait to meet him in person and spend time with him.

The days leading up to Grandpa's visit drag by slowly. The joyful activity at this moment involves hovering around Mommy in the kitchen as she feeds Geri a bottle of prepared baby milk she calls "formula."

Mommy is also excited about Grandpa's visit but for some reason she appears to be hiding her anticipation. Over the years, she has told us stories about Grandpa Sheridan, describing him as a loving father and family man who has lived a good, noble, and interesting life.

"He is a man of great faith who has been involved in all kinds of miracles," Mommy says. "Many of the miracles took place in St. Jean the Baptiste Church on Lexington Avenue and 76th Street in Manhattan."

Now with a faraway look, she tells us, "Your Grandpa has a special devotion to the 'Good St. Anne,' Jesus's grandmother. There is a special shrine in St. Jean's that is dedicated to St. Anne. The shrine consists of a statue of St. Anne and her daughter, Mary, the mother of Jesus. A relic of St. Anne's arm is there. This is a very holy place where many miracles have taken place when your Grandpa has prayed over sick people there. People were healed of physical, emotional, and spiritual disorders.

"Your grandfather is also blessed with the gift of evangelization as evidenced by the fact that he personally has brought over one hundred people to the Roman Catholic faith. He has dedicated his life in service to God and family at great expense to his own physical and emotional peace. Because he is a holy man who turns people to God, the devil has done terrible things to discourage him."

"Like what?" I ask.

"Well, probably the worst thing to ever happen to Grandpa happened years ago when he was working as a roof-repairman. He and a co-worker were called to do repair work on the damaged roof of a building in Brooklyn. Grandpa was working on the lower side of the slanted roof just below his co-worker. The other man, working a few feet above Grandpa, was heating the tar needed to repair the roof.

"Something happened that caused the man to lose his balance and kick over the red-hot pot of tar. It tipped over and poured scalding hot tar onto Grandpa positioned just below it! The man was able to gain his balance and avoid falling off the roof to his likely death.

"Grandpa was not so fortunate. The red-hot tar poured down over his shoulders and back, and seeped right through his shirt scorching his skin and flesh underneath. Fortunately, Grandpa was able to cling onto where he was despite being in excruciating pain.

"His co-worker kicked the cauldron away and used a 'rescue rope,' to hook Grandpa to himself, and helped Grandpa down off the roof. Grandpa was in so much pain he thought he was going to die so he asked God to forgive the sins of his life.

"At the hospital, the doctors worked on Grandpa for hours removing the tar from his shoulders, upper arms, and back. Unfortunately, since the tar had already bonded to his body, much of his skin and flesh were ripped off as the tar was surgically removed!"

Mommy concludes this terrible story saying, "Grandpa was in the hospital for weeks, horribly scarred for life, but he said, 'at least I am alive.' His courage and strength up there on the roof when the red-hot tar poured down on him saved his life."

I think there was more involved. For all the people Grandpa has helped, I suspect God allowed Grandpa's guardian angel to help him avoid falling off the roof when he was so terribly burned. Besides, I am sure that God still has much that Grandpa can do in physical life in ministering to others.

Mommy adds more to this remarkable story, "Grandpa later understood how guilty his partner would feel for causing the terrible accident. Grandpa forgave him, and he told us to do the same. He was offering his suffering up to God in the hopes that others might be spared such agony.

"Rather than focusing on his misfortune, Grandpa chose to forgive his partner, and to thank God for sparing his life. This he did sincerely even though he realized he was going to suffer excruciating pain the rest of his life. Despite how his deformity diminishes his physical abilities, Grandpa continues his ministry of healing."

"Mommy, why hasn't Grandpa visited us?" I ask.

Mommy stares with a blank expression. It appears she can't form the right words to answer. Her mind has apparently switched to another place and time. Soon, she hurries me along telling me to get dressed. I detect a look of sadness on her face as she turns to prepare breakfast for us. As I obediently go about getting ready for the day, I feel badly that my question took her out of a happy mood and saddened her.

Later at the kitchen table, Paddy, Kitty, and I discuss what we are going to tell Grandpa. Larry is kneeling in his chair so he can reach the table as he listens to our chatter. Mommy puts thick oatmeal cereal in our bowls then places eight pieces of white bread in the broiler in the bottom section of our oven. That is how she makes toast for us. Sometimes she leaves the bread in too long and it comes out burned. When this happens, Mommy just scrapes the burnt layer off the top of the bread then smothers the toast in salted butter.

The tin pot on the top of our stove is filled to the brim as usual with steaming hot tealeaves floating across the top of the water. The strong aromatic scent of the tea blends with the unique smell of the oatmeal and toast. This provides a familiar and welcome treat for us on most mornings throughout our childhood.

After I finish eating, I join Paddy, Kitty, and Larry huddled around Mommy as she holds a milk bottle for Geri to drink. I watch as the baby guzzles down the milk, and then look around at Mommy, my brothers and my sister, Kitty. I feel so much love for them. Moments like these are so precious. I absorb every bit of it with a great sense of personal joy and appreciation. I wish we could be happy like this always, but I know that the nature of life does not permit such uninterrupted peace and happiness. There will always be some sadness and stress intermingled throughout our lives.

As Mommy says, it is only in the next phase of life when we cross the lifeline and live in heaven with God, His angels and His saints, that we will enjoy total peace, happiness and love forever.

Following breakfast, I rush inside to the last room, our living room, where I climb up to my usual place on the left windowsill overlooking the street below. Since today is Saturday, I expect to see some children playing games in the street in front of our building. The street below, however, is deserted. Perhaps it is because it is very cold out today, and looking up, I can see the sky is darkened signaling that wet weather may be on the way too.

Leaning my right cheek against the windowpane, I am surprised to discover how cold it is. I breathe on the window causing it to fog up. Fascinated, I wipe it away then blow my warm breath on it. The closer I am to the window, and the harder I blow on it, the wider the area that fogs over. Staring at it, I envision it as a barren hill. Reaching out with my right forefinger, I draw the shape of a cross at the peak of the hill, then a cross to the right and another to the left. Easing back, I study what I have drawn.

I know from Mommy's stories this scene represents the crucifixion of Jesus Christ on Calvary. Even though he is the Son of God, he was crucified with two men who were criminals. A deep sorrow forms in my heart and engulfs me in a shroud of grief. A painful lump throbs in my throat.

I recall the terrible things Mommy said were done to Jesus. Roman soldiers viciously beat Him, mocked Him, put a crown of thorns on His head, made Him carry a heavy cross through the streets where people yelled at Him as He made His way to a desolate hill where they nailed Him by his hands and feet to the cross.

I can't imagine how people could do something so cruel, so merciless to a fellow human being. And why? Mommy explained that Jesus died for us to make up for the Original Sin we are all born with because of Adam and Eve's sin against God in the Garden of Eden. Only Jesus as God and as Man could make a supernatural sacrifice to make up for the supernatural offense against God.

In terms of the cruelty done by the people who crucified Jesus, Mommy said there are many people in the world today who are capable of doing terrible things like that to others. She calls this capacity to hurt others, "man's cruelty to man."

It is so heart breaking to realize that people crucified Jesus in front of His mother and others who loved Him. I am surprised no one tried to help save Jesus, no one tried to stop the people from hurting Him. If no one helped Jesus, the Son of God, what would happen to me if I needed help? I feel so vulnerable.

I notice a large black car is moving slowly down the center of our street. It passes our building and continues down the block until it comes to an open parking space on the other side of the street several buildings opposite our building. The car backs into the space then maneuvers back and forth until it is properly parked next to the curb.

The rear door on the street side opens slowly and out steps a husky old man whose bright white hair stands out from under the rim of a light brown hat he is wearing. His thick overcoat is a stark black color. With the car door still open, the old man turns in the street and looks right up in my direction. Our eyes meet, and I am filled with a sense of great joy and recognition. My Grandpa has arrived.

He raises his right arm and waves so I promptly return his greeting. The people walking with him must be Uncle Emil, Aunt Vera, and their two daughters, my cousins, Margaret Mary and Flossy. Now they are all b oking up at me, smiling and waving as they approach our building. Boy, my aunt and girl cousins are some of the biggest people I have ever seen! Mommy did warn us that they are "very large people," but they look even larger than "very large."

Quick as a flash, I jump down off the windowsill and run toward the kitchen shouting, "Grandpa is here, Grandpa is here!"

Mommy stands frozen in the middle of the kitchen holding Geri in her arms. Geri looks alarmed at the sudden burst of excitement. Paddy, Kitty, and Larry jump down from their kitchen chairs and dart madly toward the front door to greet Grandpa and the other family members.

Standing there anxiously waiting, no one says a word. Mommy looks back and forth from us to the door, then back again. Our doorbell explodes with its distinctive ringing sound officially announcing the arrival of Grandpa and the family, "Bbrring, bbrring, bbrring!"

Paddy reaches up and pushes in the small round buzzer-button located on the wall to the right of our front door in the kitchen. This allows the locked front door downstairs to be opened so Grandpa and the others may enter.

90

Bursting with excitement, we stand together facing the door and listen to the distinctive sound of many footsteps lumbering along in the hallway corridor downstairs. As they now climb the winding staircase that leads up to our apartment on the second floor, the steps of the stairs squeak loudly under the tremendous weight of our visitors. I hope the stairs are strong enough to carry all their weight on the stairs at the same time.

The loud squeaking of the stairs gives way to the sound of heavy, plodding footsteps approaching our apartment on the left side. For a fleeting moment, there is no sound. We exchange nervous glances wondering what they are doing.

Suddenly, from the hollow sounding hallway outside our front door comes a mellow voice, "Vera, which door is it? There are two of them! Is Ellie on the right or on the left?"

"We are in here, Grandpa, we are in here!" we all shout in unison.

"Hey, Ellie, open up. It's me, Pop," Grandpa pleads as he taps on our door.

Mommy has an anxious look on her face. Her eyes are glistening with tears as she shifts Geri over to her left arm. Holding the baby securely, she steps over to the door.

"Step back, kids," she commands as she turns the knob opening the bolt-lock on our door.

The door swings wide open to disclose Grandpa Sheridan standing right there in the doorway! His shocking white hair frames sparkling blue-colored eyes with a broad smile gracing his deeply wrinkled face. He is a handsome, chubby, rugged-looking man with an unmistakable air of confidence.

I feel a natural, comfortable familiarity with Grandpa as though I have known him all my life. As he looks at me, he nods his head as if to signal that he knows some secret about me.

Stepping into our apartment, Grandpa reaches out to hug Mommy as he says, "Ellie, my sweet little Ellie."

Grandpa wraps his arms around Mommy and Geri. Mommy is crying because she is so happy to see her father after such a long time.

I recall how Mommy told us she and Grandpa had a terrible disagreement years ago. It was when she told Grandpa that she wanted to marry Daddy. She was seventeen at the time and Daddy was six years older at twenty-three. Grandpa told her she should **NOT** marry Daddy because he was one of those "Wild Walshes" from 75th Street in Manhattan!

Grandpa said he knew the Walsh Family quite well before he moved the Sheridan Family to Brooklyn, New York. For years, the Sheridans lived at 418 East 76th Street, and Daddy's family lived at 408 East 75th Street between

First and York Avenues. For a while, both families attended St. Jean the Baptist Roman Catholic Church right on Lexington Avenue between 76th and 77th Streets in Manhattan.

Mommy told us how she tried to convince Grandpa that the Walshes were not "wild," they were just active, fun-loving people. She explained how Daddy in particular was very well liked and admired by everyone in Yorkville. He was a gentleman, a good athlete, and could sing and whistle as good as Bing Crosby. Unfortunately, Grandpa's mind was made up at the time and he simply was not going to change his mind. He would not allow Mommy to marry Daddy!

Mommy told him that she loved Daddy and was going to marry him whether or not Grandpa approves. When Mommy went to leave, Grandpa stood in her way and would not let her pass so Mommy shoved past him and left. Before Grandpa could stop her, Mommy was out the door, not to return again! It was her eighteenth birthday, December 4, 1940.

Mommy and Grandpa have not seen nor spoken to each other since.

After leaving home, Mommy stayed with Daddy's mom, Nana Walsh, until she married Daddy… without Grandpa's blessing. It was on a quiet evening on January 27, 1941, that Mommy and Daddy got married in St. Ignatius Loyola Church on Park Avenue and 84th Street in Manhattan. Mom wore a navy blue dress with white pokadots. Since Daddy didn't have more money at the time, he gave Mommy a cigar-band for a temporary wedding band.

Only a handful of people were present including Nana Walsh, Aunt Marion, and a few other Walshes. Sadly, none of Mommy's family was present for her wedding. After the ceremony, everyone went back to Nana's apartment and celebrated. That is all we ever heard about Mommy and Daddy's wedding day.

Suddenly the doorway is completely filled with Aunt Vera Wolf, a giant of a woman much larger than anyone I have ever seen. She appears to be close to six feet tall and very, very… chubby. Everything she is wearing is black. Her bright auburn colored hair is flying about her large round face as she stands there with her arms stretched out toward us kids. Her large double chin and big cheeks jiggle wildly like Jell-O as she moves her head.

The joy of finally meeting our jolly Aunt Vera is disrupted by the evil one as it conveys a mysterious message, "Watch this."

My attention is drawn to a movement above Aunt Vera's head. There is a large brown roach floating down from the overhead doorway descending right in front of Aunt Vera's face! The roach drifts before her eyes causing her to cross her now widened eyes as she focuses on the descending roach. The roach lands on Aunt Vera's large protruding bosom then scurries down into the space between her enormous breasts. As it disappears, Aunt Vera's eyes bulge even wider as she explodes in terror screaming so loudly people across the street must hear her!

Frantically flailing at her bosom, Aunt Vera darts past us and stampedes in through the rooms screaming as she goes, "My God, somebody help me; there's a giant bug running on me! Aaaahhhhhhh! Oh, my God, someone help me!"

Mommy gives the baby to Paddy telling him, "Paddy, take the baby. Everyone stay right here; I have to help Aunt Vera."

With that, Mommy runs through the rooms after Aunt Vera who is already in the last room, the living room.

Aunt Vera is turning in a circle as she wickedly hits her breasts and screams, "It's in my brassiere, it's in my brassiere! Get it out, Ellie, get it out!"

Aunt Vera struggles mightily as she pulls her full-length dress up and over her head in a frantic attempt to get at the bug. I watch in amazement as all Aunt Vera is wearing is her white brassiere, white panties, stockings, and shoes! Mommy shoves Aunt Vera forcing her to the side of the living room out of sight from us children. All I can hear is Aunt Vera screaming and Mommy laughing and telling Aunt Vera to calm down.

"There it is," Aunt Vera shouts, "It's running on the floor! Quick, get it before it gets way!"

All of a sudden, I hear a thunderous sound as the floor throughout our apartment vibrates under us. Aunt Vera has stomped on the roach she knocked off her onto the floor!

"There, you goddamn bug, there!" Aunt Vera screams as she again violently stomps on the roach that caused her to strip down half-naked in front of all her family.

Mommy says, "Vera, please watch the language... and get your clothes on!"

I can hear Mommy laughing over Aunt Vera's mumbled words of anger and relief. Soon, Aunt Vera joins Mommy in the laughter. The two of them stand there in the middle of the living room, Aunt Vera in her underwear, hugging each other and laughing like two little girls. Sisters forever, I think.

After Aunt Vera composes herself, she complains, "I don't know how you can laugh at that, Ellie, seeing me attacked by that terrible creature. It is **not** funny; I was terrified. You wouldn't like it if a roach ran down your dress."

"Don't be such a big baby, Vera," Mommy teases, "What can a little bug like that do to such a large person like you? You are a million times bigger than that poor little thing! Look what you did to it."

"I can't believe you are saying that to me, Ellie, after what I just went through! Please keep the kids outside while I get dressed."

"Well, I can promise to keep the kids outside... but I can't promise I can keep all the roaches outside too," Mommy teases.

"Stop it, Ellie! That is not funny!" Aunt Vera bellows.

"You'd better shake out all your clothes just in case another roach got in," Mommy advises.

"Ellie!" Aunt Vera thunders.

After a pause, Aunt Vera worries, "You don't really think there is another roach that got into my clothes, do you?"

"I told you what I think, Vera. If I were you, I would shake out that dress until my arms fall off," Mommy laughs.

As I listen to the sound of Aunt Vera violently snapping her dress about in the air, I realize how lucky it is that none of us children were in her path when she panicked and stampeded through the rooms. We could have been trampled under her enormous weight, and would now be on our way to Lenox Hill hospital!

Looking quite embarrassed, Aunt Vera walks back out into the kitchen where we are waiting to hear what she has to say about her ordeal.

Aunt Vera's cheeks shake as she shouts at Daddy and Uncle Emil, "Don't you guys say a word if you know what is good for you!"

Hearing that, I wouldn't dare tell her why I think the roach fell down onto her and ran into her bosom.

I can understand that she wants to ignore what has happened, perhaps even make believe nothing happened. It will be interesting to see how Daddy and Uncle Emil handle this. Faced with such a large, powerful, angry woman as Aunt Vera, they simply smile and turn away from facing her and appear to be fighting the urge to scream out in laughter.

Turning to us children, Aunt Vera booms out, "Ohhhhh, now look at these beautiful children. They are so adoooooorable!"

"You must be Paddy," she says as she swoops down surprisingly fast for such a large woman. Scooping Paddy up like he is a mere feather, she gathers him in her huge arms. After a loud demonstrable kiss and a smothering hug, she returns a dazed Paddy to the floor where he almost falls down as she lets go of him. There is a startled look on his face as he looks up at Aunt Vera. I feel intimidated by her size, loudness, and bold actions. I wonder what she is going to do next.

No sooner have I thought this, than she turns her attention to me and booms out, "And you must be Bobby! Come to your Auntie Vera, you cute little pumpkin."

Suddenly I am flying high up into the air in her powerful hands. She hugs me so tightly it is difficult to breathe, and she is hurting my ribs.

Thrusting me backward as she holds me suspended in mid-air, she examines my face then announces at the top of her voice, "Papa... Papa... look. This boy has your eyes!"

Apparently noticing that I am wincing because she is squeezing me so hard, she puts me down.

"Ellie, I think I may have squeezed him too hard," Aunt Vera says.

"Poor baby, Aunt Vera is sorry. Please don't be afraid of your Aunt Vera, I am just a little loud, that's all."

"Yeh, that's like saying the sky is a little high," Aunt Vera's husband, Uncle Emil, laughs at his own wise crack.

"Hey, you'd better watch it mister, or you will be seeing first-hand just how high that sky really is," Aunt Vera half-seriously warns him.

Suddenly, I feel Grandpa's hand encircle mine creating a sense of warmth, safety, and strangely... understanding. His eyes sparkle with kindness, inner joy and celebration. His appearance is of one of kindness and love, but there is also the aura of a powerful, seasoned warrior who is confident of his knowledge and ability, and who is unafraid to engage the enemy in battle.

I look over at Uncle Emil and his two very large daughters, my cousins, Margaret Mary and Flossy. Uncle Emil is not smiling; he looks quite grouchy. Margaret Mary, although she is only a teenager, is almost as big and chubby as Aunt Vera. Cousin Flossy looks shy but mischievous, and is always smiling. She is not as large as Aunt Vera and Margaret Mary. I have a strong sense that these beautiful ladies from the Sheridan side of our family are good, loving, God-fearing people.

Uncle Emil, however, has a grouchy look on his face, and I have yet to see him smile.

While the adults are busy talking, Uncle Emil leans down to us kids and whispers, "If any of you kids misbehave while I am here, I will rip your eyes out!"

I think he is kidding but he looks so serious saying this. He scares us.

Grandpa squeezes my hand twice then releases it so he can take off his overcoat.

Handing it to Aunt Vera, he says, "Here, Vera, please find a place for this old coat while I rest my weary bones inside with this young fellow."

Paddy, Kitty, and Larry run off to the next room chattering with Margaret Mary and Flossy while Mommy proudly shows baby Geri to Aunt Vera and Uncle Emil. Grandpa steps over and announces that he thinks Geri looks just like Mommy when she was a baby!

"Let's hope she turns out half as nice as my little Ellie," Grandpa says sweetly.

This greatly pleases Mommy as she smiles widely.

Looking down to me, Grandpa smiles and says, "Come on, little man; you and I have some things to talk about."

As we leave the room, Aunt Vera says, "There he goes. I tell you, that boy is all Poppa has talked about since Bobby was born."

"Yep," Uncle Emil adds, **"He is Jimmy's Boy!"**

Looking up at Grandpa, I ask, "Grandpa, is that your real name... Jimmy?"

Grandpa answers with a twinkle in his eyes, "Yes, it sure is. My name is James Aloysius Sheridan, but my family and friends call me Jimmy. You can call me 'Grandpa' which is far more special."

I can't conceal my pride and joy at this great discovery. They call me, **"Jimmy's Boy!"** That is, "Grandpa's Jimmy's boy!"

I try to imitate his smile and that look of determination he has. As we proceed to the last room, I notice that the curtains and drapes in the living room are wildly gyrating from left to right and back again. Since the windows are closed, this can only mean that the demon is displaying its hostility to Grandpa's presence.

Grandpa pauses as he walks slightly ahead of me with me in tow. Reaching the entrance to the last room, he stops and surveys the right French door and the living room beyond it. Clearly, he must sense what I do.

"This door opens and closes by itself I hear," Grandpa says.

"Yes, Grandpa. The demon does it."

This comment doesn't seem to bother Grandpa.

The drapes framing the two windows suddenly stop waving back and forth; they are deadly still now. There is a total absence of sound or motion in the room but I can tell that the demon is lurking nearby.

A loud, ominous banging noise comes from inside the corner closet of the living room.

Looking over at the closet door, Grandpa shouts in a surprisingly powerful tone of voice, "Coward and bully, in the name of Jesus Christ, I command you to be still and cease all disturbances!"

I am surprised that Grandpa is insulting and ordering the demon to stop... and it is not doing anything in response.

Taking my hand, Grandpa steps firmly into the room and continues over to the thickly upholstered armchair stationed in front of the left window. Grandpa grunts as he eases himself down into the chair, still glaring at the closet door facing him. I position myself on the floor by his shiny black shoes. His white hair glistens brilliantly in the sunlight pouring in through the window. The sun warms me and complements the feeling of security and goodness I experience in Grandpa's presence.

Smiling down on me, he says, "Your mother told me on the phone all about you. She says you see angels... and... the 'bad things.' Is that true?"

"Yes, Grandpa."

I am surprised to hear that Mommy told him about me.

"I understand, you know," he says surprising me yet again.

After a thoughtful pause, he asks, "How old are you now, Bobby?"

"I am six, Grandpa," I tell him proudly.

Leaning forward, he smiles and gently pats my head.

"Bobby," he says deliberately choosing his words, "I know all about these things, you know. Many years ago when I was about your age, I also saw angels and 'bad things."

This is amazing to hear!

Grandpa adds, "The bad ones still bother me, but the angels keep them from harming me."

"Did your Mother tell you what the 'bad things' are?"

"Yes, she said they are devils."

"That's right, they are devils," he says raising his eyebrows apparently impressed that Mommy told me about them.

Turning toward the window, his eyes take on a far-away look as he appears to be remembering something that happened a long time ago.

"I was also called a 'blessed child'... as you are. At first, I did not understand all the strange, unnatural things that I saw and heard – both good and bad. I soon enough realized that I was, indeed, a 'blessed child' and that the devil knew it too. Do you understand what it means to be a blessed child of God, Bobby?"

"Yes. Being a 'blessed child' means that God has blessed me with special gifts to use in helping people turn to God."

"That's right. You know, I had no one I could talk to about this. No one could help because no one understood. Even **I** did not understand what was happening at first, or **why** these things were happening. It wasn't until I was about fourteen years old that I finally discovered what it was all about.

"I was in St. Jean the Baptist's Church in Manhattan before the Blessed Sacrament on exposition. I remember begging God to help me understand. That is when I got a strong urge to open and read my bible. Figuring this urge may be God's answer for me, I decided to open my bible to wherever it opened and read what was there."

Leaning over to one side, Grandpa digs into his right jacket pocket and pulls out a badly worn black book. It is so old, its pages are wrinkled and yellowed with age and use.

97

"This is that bible, Bobby. The same one I had that very day so long ago."

Grandpa flips through the stiff pages until he arrives at a certain destination.

Placing a finger on a page, he says, "I had randomly opened the bible and wound up at the Gospel of John 15:16. Let me read what God says to both of us here. God says, 'You did not choose me; **I chose you,** and I appointed you to go and bear fruit, fruit that will last, so that the Father will give you whatever you ask Him in My Name."

Grandpa gently closes the bible, leans toward me, and dramatically looks into my eyes and asks, "Do you know what this reading means?"

Replaying these words of John in my mind, I think about their meaning. Christ's message through John seems perfectly clear to me.

So I tell Grandpa, "It means that God has chosen me to do something for Him, and that He will give me whatever I need to get it done."

A smile graces Grandpa's face as he nods approvingly, "Very good, Bobby, very good. That is **exactly** what it means. I, too, realized its meaning the first time I read it."

Grandpa continues, "I believe that God in His infinite mercy and love for us all, blesses some people in every age with special gifts to lead others toward heaven. When I realized that I was one of those special people, I cried for joy, and asked God to give me extra graces to always do His will."

Looking to the window again, his eyes take on that faraway look one more time.

"God certainly answered my prayer that day and every day since. Whenever I have needed wisdom, courage, or strength, He has always provided the graces needed."

"Like what? What did He give you, Grandpa?"

"He gave me graces to carry on a ministry that led people back to God. The gift of healing is probably the most effective gift of all because through the healing of mind, body, or spirit, a great many people turned to God. That, of course, is the greatest healing of all, and it is the only one with lasting value because it can last forever.

"What a joy it has been over the years to feel God's healing graces flow through my hands onto the people I prayed over. There is no other feeling like it. So many, in so many remarkable ways, right in front of me."

"So many people, so many faces, so many souls. Thanks be to God."

After a while, Grandpa's countenance takes on a serious, troubled appearance as he leans forward in his chair, and warns me.

"Bobby, the devil knows **all** the people whom God has blessed with such gifts. Everyone like you and I are recognized by the devil from the day we are born.

"Knowing that our mission in life is to turn everyone we can toward God, the devil does everything it can to disrupt our lives. It knows full well that physical healings can lead to spiritual reunions with God for the people who are healed ... and sometimes for the people who witness the healings too.

"Yes, that is why the devil does what it can to disturb those of us who are blessed with healing ministry. It tries to cause confusion, create doubt, disturb our dreams, threaten and intimidate us, affect our health, interfere with our personal relationships with others, and more. Literally, anything and everything it can.

"The worst torment for me has been when the devil attacked me through my family. It flooded their minds and hearts with falsehoods and misjudgments about me. The devil tried to wear me down by discouraging me and breaking my spirit. That has been the hardest thing for me to cope with and endure.

"Since God has entrusted these special gifts into your care, Bobby, you must always use these gifts for His greater glory. To do so, you have to keep your heart and mind fixed on serving God, and do not allow anything to prevent you from helping others. As simple as all that may sound, it is the very heart and soul of ministry.

"And remember that Jesus said, 'To those whom much is given, much is expected.' We are accountable to God for how well, or how poorly, we use the gifts He entrusted into our care. Do you understand what I am saying?"

"Yes, Grandpa, I understand."

"I must confess, in some situations... and with some very difficult people... the only way I could pray over them was to remember Christ's words that He came for the sinners, and He came to serve, not to be served!"

Grandpa expands, "The devil is second only to God in intelligence, and as such, is a formidable foe. It knows all our weaknesses and uses them against us. Before I discovered this, the devil had a field day with me. But once I realized that the devil knows Christ's words in John as well as I do, I was able to manage so much better. The saying, 'knowing the enemy is half the battle,' is so true."

His eyes squint slightly as he adds, "As soon as I heard the stories going around the family about you, stories about ghosts and angels..., and the visit by that priest... I recognized exactly what was happening.

"I remember how on the day you were born, I felt something very special about your arrival. I think it was God's way of letting me know that He had blessed someone else in my family with similar gifts of healing and spiritual ministry.

"You can be sure the devil is behind the kinds of things I hear going on in your young life. It is the 'Father of Lies' and will do anything it can to turn you away from your calling.

"In many ways, the older we get, the more difficult it becomes to cope with the devil's assaults. It's something like the saying, 'When we are young, we live to eat, but when we get older, we eat to live!"

"So don't ever let your guard down; stay close to God. Speaking of being close to God, I don't know when Our Lord is going to call me home… but I sense it won't be too long now. That's why I was so anxious to see you today. I knew I had to talk to you about being blessed, and to warn you about the devil."

Grandpa turns his hands upward in front of me. As I place my hands on top of his, he enfolds them. Looking directly up into his eyes, I am blinded by the bright sunshine pouring in over the two of us. What a beautiful moment this is.

Grandpa invites me to pray with him, "Let's thank God for the blessing of life, for the gift of one another, for the gift of our family, for the gift of salvation, and for the special gifts He has given us to use and to enjoy."

I close my eyes, open my heart to God, and pour out all the love and appreciation I can. A gentle wave of peace and exhilarating joy flows over me as we sit in silent prayer, basking in the warm 'Sonlight' of God. I, Jimmy's Boy, am in a beautiful, serene place.

Grandpa looks greatly pleased as our hands part and he rests back in the chair. His puffy eyes are moist as tears well up and flow down over the crevices of his deeply wrinkled cheeks. Wiping them aside, he tilts his head back and gazes out toward the brilliant sunshine.

"God loves you very much, Bobby, so pray to Him, talk to Him, go to Mass often, and when you are old enough, go to confession and Holy Communion regularly.

"God likes it when we praise Him and thank Him for all He does for us. Do you remember the story of the ten lepers who Jesus healed?"

I shake my head no.

"Jesus healed ten lepers but only one came back to thank Him, the Samaritan. Jesus made a **big deal** about the fact that only **ONE** leper came back to thank Him! In so doing, Jesus tells us that it is important to thank Him, God the Father, and God the Holy Ghost for all that God does for us. So make sure you thank God often for all the good things in your life."

"Yes, Grandpa."

"By the way, did you know that tradition tells us the one leper who came back to thank Jesus had everything restored to him that the leprosy took from him! Can you imagine? All the skin, all the flesh that was destroyed

100

by the leprosy was completely restored!

"Remember all these things, Bobby, and please pray for your Grandpa whenever you can. Okay?"

"I promise, Grandpa."

Grandpa is such a wonderful, holy man. He looks quite happy now that he was able to tell me these important things. I feel so content sitting here with him, basking in the sunlight streaming in through the window. As I rest my head against his leg, I find myself drifting off to sleep.

Hours later, I awake alone on the sofa in a cold, dark living room. It is nighttime now. I wonder where Grandpa has gone. I jump up and run out through the rooms toward the light in the kitchen where Mommy is cooking dinner on the stove on the right side of the room.

"It's about time you woke up, Rumpelstiltskin!" she teases, "I hope you can sleep later when you go to bed."

"Where is Grandpa?" I ask.

"Grandpa left a while ago with Aunt Vera and her family," Mommy giggles, "You slept right through their visit!"

My heart sinks with profound sorrow; Grandpa left.

"Why didn't he wake me up?" I cry.

Mommy shrugs her shoulders and continues looking at the food she is cooking on the stove.

"Did Grandpa say anything before he left?" I want to know.

"Yes. He said to make sure I tell you goodbye for him, and to tell you to remember what he told you about using your gifts. He made a 'Sign of the Cross' on your forehead and gave you a kiss before leaving."

I am so sad that Grandpa left before I could spend more time with him, and say goodbye when he left. I may never see him again before he dies and goes to heaven. A painful lump swells in my throat.

Why didn't he wake me up? In my sadness, I am comforted with the strong sense that Grandpa will, in fact, come back someday to say goodbye.

After all... I am **"Jimmy's Boy!"**

Chapter 12

SCHOOL DAYS

September 1951

Telltale coolness in the air these last few days signals the approach of autumn... and school days. Mommy promised me that going to school this time will be pleasant and enjoyable because I am going to go to the Catholic school, St. Monica's. She told me that Catholic schools are much better than public schools... like the one she tried to get me to attend last year.

She explains, "First of all, St. Monica's school is run by the Franciscan nuns who have dedicated their entire lives to God by teaching children. They are excellent teachers who do a far better job than the public school teachers. In addition, they don't allow any wild stuff in their classrooms like public school teachers do. If you behave yourself, Bobby, there's nothing for you to worry about.

"Besides," she adds, "the school is much closer to home so it's a shorter walk for you, Paddy, and Kitty. You'll appreciate that in the winter time when it's freezing cold outside, believe me!"

"Where is it, Mommy? Is it near our church?"

Smiling, she answers, "Yes, the school is right around the corner from our church. In fact, you can even walk through the backyard of the church and go right into the backyard of the school! Paddy and Kitty's classes did that last year. The school itself is located at 416 East 80th Street right in the middle of the block. You will see it yourself today, Bobby, when we go there to see the principal. We are going to get you registered."

"You are not going to leave me there like you did last year at the public school, are you Mommy?"

Mommy assures me, "No, honey. I promise you. I will not leave you there today. **However, you will have to stay there** at school without me when school begins in a few days. Now do not worry, Bobby, you will not be alone there. Your brother and sister and Sullivan cousins are going there, and what's more, there are many nice kids there from Yorkville who will become your friends. You'll see, you're going to be very happy there, Bobby."

I believe her and sense that everything she says about St. Monica's is right. It must be good...it is a Catholic school run by Catholic nuns.

Most importantly for me, since the school is located right next to the church where God is in the tabernacle, the demon is not likely to want to follow me too closely there.

"Today we're just going to visit Sister Evasia to talk about getting you into the first grade class which starts soon. Then we can see if we can find Paddy and Kitty playing with their classmates on the playground outside the school at lunchtime. We'll walk around the school itself so you can see for yourself how nice it is. You may even see your cousins, Aunt Marion's girls, Maureen and Donna Jean. You know, they go to St. Monica's too."

All this is so soothing to hear. Although the thought of going to school still scares me, it is not as upsetting as last year. Daddy said that I was just too young to start school last year. He also thought Mommy did not properly prepare me for what to expect before leaving me there as she did. In addition, of course, there is that mean, wicked teacher who hit me. Mommy assured me that none of the nuns would hit me because I am a good boy who listens, obeys, and cooperates. But what if they mistakenly think I am a bad boy?

My comfort is in knowing that St. Monica's school rests on hallowed grounds buttressed by the mighty fortress of God's home right behind it. I can picture the nuns and priests as God's soldiers scurrying all over His property guarding against the forces of evil. I also imagine the devil stays away from holy places like St. Monica's because they are spiritual sanctuaries where God's people can find refuge from the devil and its torments.

Before long, Mommy and I are walking up our street in bright sunshine.

As we pass the large girl's school that takes up all of York Avenue from 82nd Street to 81st Street, Mommy says, "Look, Bobby, God is sending His sunshine down especially for you to let you know He's happy you are going to St. Monica's Roman Catholic School."

What a beautiful thought, God is happy I am going to Catholic grade school!

The sunlight blankets me with a feeling of comfort and reassurance. As we walk along York Avenue, I see the A & P Supermarket on the east side of York Avenue between 81st and 80th Streets. On the west side of the avenue, there are several small stores. The German bakery catches my eye, then next to it is "Bills candy store" where Daddy told me the school kids stop to buy a piece of candy for only a penny.

As Mommy and I walk toward 80th Street, I can hear happy, exciting sounds of children playing. When we turn the corner onto 80th Street, I can't believe what I see. There is a sea of boys and girls running around, jumping rope, playing tag, hundreds of them filling most of 80th Street from one end of the block to the other!

Interspersed among the children I see nuns watching the children in their classes. Mommy and I make our way toward the school building in the middle of the block. It extends out from the row of brownstone tenement

103

buildings on the left side of the street. The top of the school can be seen from anywhere on the street because it is one story higher than the other buildings on that side of the street, and it has a unique pyramid shaped top!

The school's stairs jut far out onto the sidewalk. A six-foot high black wrought iron spiked fence surrounds the steps, just like the church. The fence begins in front of the school and continues up 80th Street enclosing the one level school gymnasium and the nuns' four-story convent building close to First Avenue.

When we are a little way up the left side of the block, a familiar voice calls out to us from a crowd of girls playing in the street to our right, "Aunt Ellie, Bobby, hello!"

I turn to see a beautiful red-haired girl running toward us. It is my beautiful cousin, Maureen Sullivan! She is such a sweetheart as Daddy says. She is always smiling, kind, vivacious, and quite Irish looking. Clearly, she is the prettiest girl I have seen in Yorkville.

When she reaches us, she is excited and a little out of breath. She gives Mommy and me a kiss hello then asks if I am going to St. Monica's this year.

Mommy says, "Bobby and I are going to see the principal, Sister Evasia, right now to register him for the first grade. Tell Bobby, isn't this school wonderful and don't you like going to St. Monica's?"

Maureen enthusiastically shakes her head yes as her eyes dart from Mommy to me.

"Tell Bobby how nice it is," Mommy encourages her.

Still smiling, Maureen's eyes open wider for emphasis as she excitedly tells me, "Oh, Bobby, you are going to love it here. It's so much fun, you won't believe it."

Gesturing with her right arm in a sweeping motion toward the street of boys and girls playing behind her, she continues, "Just look at all the kids playing here. Each day after we have lunch in the school, the nuns take us out here to play!"

"But what is school like on the inside?" I ask.

"Oh, you get your own desk and books, you learn how to read and write, and sometimes they play records on a Victrola in the classroom. You also get to go to plays in the auditorium, there is a recess every morning during which you can buy cookies, and they even let you take a nap on your desk sometimes!"

Wow!

It seems like Maureen has a lot more to say but Mommy interrupts her, "Thank you, Maureen. We have to get going now, or we will be late for our meeting with Sister Evasia."

Maureen quickly gives me a kiss, kisses Mommy, and says, "Have fun, Bobby. See you soon."

Off she runs back into the crowd as quickly as she came. I will always remember this brief encounter with my beautiful cousin, Maureen, her red hair, her cheerful encouragement about the school, her pretty smile... and the kisses she gave me too!

Although I do not see Paddy or Kitty anywhere, seeing Maureen has lifted my spirits about being among so many strangers here. Everyone appears to know everyone else. As we approach the school building, I begin to feel that everything is going to be all right. I know that Paddy, Kitty, Maureen, and my other cousin, Donna Jean, are all here at the school. Moreover, their friends will probably become my friends.

Mommy and I enter through the two large metal doors guarding the front of the school. Once inside, I listen to the now cushioned sounds of the children playing outside. Before us on our right are six steps leading up to a landing. To our left, there are six steps leading down to the basement floor where, Mommy tells me, the lunchroom is located where I will be eating lunch every day.

"You get a delicious sandwich and cup of soup for lunch every day. You are going to like it here, Bobby."

We start up the stairs on our right to continue our journey to the principal's office. Looking down at the steps, I notice that the top of each step is covered with a dimpled metal plate across the entire width of every step. On the landing we turn right and pass through two large double doors and see the nurse's office facing us directly across the hall only a few feet away. Mommy smiles and says hello to the nurse sitting at her desk facing the open door. The nurse looks annoyed; we must have startled her.

"Can I help you?" she snaps.

"No thank you, I know where we are going; we are going to see the principal," Mommy says confidently as we turn left through yet another set of double doors.

We cross a large open area that has a light colored wooden floor and a high ceiling. We proceed toward the principal's office on the other side. The floors echo the sounds of our footsteps throughout this hollow area announcing our presence. There is a classroom to the left ahead of us, and another classroom to our left behind us. There is a winding staircase to our right which I assume leads upstairs to other classrooms on the higher floors.

All around this wide-open hall are thin wooden slats that run about three feet straight up the walls perpendicular to the floor. They are dark brown, the same color as the benches located right against the walls. Hanging just above the wooden slats are pictures of student classes that have previously graduated from St. Monica's over the years. There are so many that virtually every space on the walls is occupied.

I wonder about all these people. Where are they right now, and what they are doing? How did attending St. Monica's grade school help all these people to live better lives? I know that someday I will also be in a picture hanging on the wall… silent evidence of so much life shared by so many children, so many souls growing up together.

Straight ahead and to our right at the far end of this open area is a dark brown wooden door with beautiful molding around its frame. This, I know instinctively, leads to the sacristy where the altar boys and priests get ready to celebrate Mass. In my mind's eye, I can picture the church on the other side of the sacristy. My nose can even pick up the strong scent of incense reminding me that I am in a holy place, a sanctuary from the pain and suffering of the outside world.

The principal's office is nearly opposite the door that leads to the sacristy so Mommy and I turn left there and bump right into Sister Evasia! She is very thin and short. This is pleasing to me; I feel more comfortable with people who are not much bigger than me.

Sister is wearing a long flowing black robe that extends from her shoulders down to her black pointed shoes. An opening along each side discloses a thick white rope around her waist with one long section that extends down her right side. It has several knots tied into it so that it serves as rosary beads for when she prays the rosary while walking, standing or sitting.

A large crucifix with a silver figure of Jesus on it hangs on a chain in front of her heart. Just above it is a stiff white cardboard that is shaped like the bottom half of the moon. It reaches up and around her shoulders.

"I thought I heard someone out here," Sister says. "Now who is this handsome young man I have standing here before me?"

"My name is Bobby, Bobby Walsh, Sister, and I am here to go to school," I answer respectfully.

"Well, that makes me very happy!" Sister says.

"Do you mind if I call you Robert? It is such a special name and it seems to fit you so well."

"Yes, sister, you can call me Robert because that is also my name," I tell her wisely.

Sister smiles and adds, "You must be wondering what my name is. My name is Sister Evasia so you can call me 'Sister Evasia." Now Robert, would you be so kind as to introduce me to this lovely lady you brought here with you?"

"Sister, this is my mother. Her name is Mommy, Mommy Walsh. I didn't bring her here today though, she brought me."

106

Smiling, Sister says, "Oh, I see. Well, how do you do, Mrs. Walsh. Won't you please come in and sit for a while?"

Sister Evasia allows us to go in her office ahead of her. Mommy tells me not to sit down until Sister Evasia sits. Sister sits bolt upright and folds her small hands neatly together on top of the green desk pad in front of her. Her half smile never fades and her eyes twinkle joyfully under her thin silver framed glasses. She has a special grace and peace about her. It must be because of her great love for God and for what she is doing in life.

As Mommy tells her about me, I watch Sister Evasia's eyes move back and forth between Mommy and me. Her demeanor projects authority but her face displays a wealth of gentleness and understanding. I am comfortable in her presence. I like her.

A white cloth is wrapped around the sides of her head and neck entirely covering her hair and skin except for the very front of her face. Just above her eyebrows, there is a stiff white cardboard that wraps around her forehead and extends two inches above her head where the top of her black cape rests. This all looks very strange to me. I wonder why nuns dress this way.

Sister says, "Thank you, Mrs. Walsh, for taking the time to tell me what a special boy Robert is. That is useful for us to know."

Slowly turning to me, she asks, "Well, Robert, how do you feel about going to school here at St. Monica's."

I tell her how eager I am to go to St. Monica's School.

"Well, that is very good, Robert" she says.

"Do you mind if I ask you an important question?"

"No, Sister, I don't mind."

I feel grown up that Sister Evasia, the principal of this big, beautiful Catholic school wants to ask me a question.

"Will you run away from this school when Mommy leaves you here?" Sister asks me.

Her bluntness surprises me.

I quickly look over to Mommy then back to Sister Evasia, and answer, "No, Sister, I will **not** run away from here; I already like it here. This is a much better place than that public school."

This brings a full smile to Sister Evasia... and Mommy.

"Well then, it is settled," Sister says with a sound of finality.

Turning to Mommy, she hands Mommy papers and says, "Here are some papers we need you to fill out, Mrs. Walsh. It also contains information telling you more about the school."

Turning back to me, Sister asks, "How would you like to take a quick look at your classroom before you leave, Robert?"

"Oh yes, I would love to, Sister!" I tell her as I jump up out of my seat ready to go.

"Very good," she says as she rises from her chair. "Why don't you and I go for a walk up one flight up the stairs to see your classroom while Mommy stays here to fill out your enrollment forms. Is that all right with you, Robert, and is that all right with you, Mother?"

Mommy smiles and nods okay. I am suddenly alarmed by what appears to be a planned form of deception to get me away from Mommy, to see how I will react alone. I am a little nervous, but not frightened. I feel perfectly capable to leave Mommy's side for a while... especially since I will be with Sister Evasia.

"Let's go see my classroom; we will be right back, Mommy. Don't worry," I tell her proudly.

As Mommy giggles, I follow Sister Evasia out of her office and walk over to the staircase which winds up to the right. Each wooden step creaks loudly under our footsteps. I can only imagine how loudly they would creak if some of my aunts and cousins were here.

I follow closely behind Sister Evasia. When we reach the top of the stairs, we turn to our left where there is another set of stairs. I am surprised to see how quickly Sister Evasia is able to climb all these stairs. She looks like she is very old, but she moves like a young person.

At the top of these stairs, there is another landing that leads to another set of stairs to our right going up now in the opposite direction. We quickly scale these and arrive at the second floor landing practically running the last few steps. It sounds like Sister Evasia is laughing.

There is a classroom immediately to our right, but we turn to our left instead, and then a few feet later, we make a quick right. Practically jogging, we go all the way to the other side of the floor, about twenty-five feet, passing two more classrooms that are perpendicular to each other in this corridor. Finally, we turn right at the end of the long corridor and walk six feet into what is my first grade classroom.

Stepping into the classroom after Sister Evasia, I stop next to the teacher's desk and look around. In front of me, I see four rows of desks going straight back toward large rear windows. Each row has eight wooden desks supported by black wrought iron metal legs. The utter silence and stillness here betrays what I sense is normally a very active classroom.

"Sister, why is there a hole in the top of all the desks?" I ask.

"Where, Robert?"

"Over there," I say as I point to a hole on the right side of the desk in front of her.

"Oh, I see," she says smiling, "That is an ink-well where the ink

108

bottle is kept. Upper grade students need that for their fountain pens. If you look closely, you can see a slight indentation just to the left of the inkwell. Can you guess what that is for?"

"Is that where the pen is kept when it is not being used?" I ask.

"Yes. That's very good, Robert!" she praises me.

Behind me, I see a large console piano made of dark brown wood. Next to it is the entrance door to the classroom. Its' top half has four glass sections. I look around the room and observe oak wood flooring, wooden slats going up the bottom half of the walls, and the same plain cream-colored wall above. From everything I have seen of the school so far, it seems that it is built the same way throughout the school building.

The teacher's desk is positioned directly in the front-center area of the classroom, just two feet in before a gigantic, shiny blackboard that spans the entire width of the classroom. A narrow wooden ledge at the bottom of the blackboard holds chalk and erasers. High above the center of the blackboard is a crucifix with the figure of Jesus on it. Seeing this, I feel secure and comfortable here.

"This is a very nice classroom, don't you agree, Robert?"

"Yes, Sister, I do."

"You'll have your very own desk to sit in, you know, and I think you'll enjoy learning many interesting things here with your classmates. You have a special teacher in this class, Sister Pascaline. I am sure you will like her **very** much."

Sister is closely studying what I say and do. Tilting her head, she asks, "Is there something you wish to ask about your classroom... or school, Robert?"

Before answering, I gaze at the other long blackboard running down the entire left side of the classroom. There is nothing unusual there. But on the opposite side of the room, I see something that puzzles me. There is a board positioned on a small section of wall between two of the windows on the right side of the room as I look back from the front of the classroom. The windows are unusually large, practically reaching the ceiling.

Pointing to the board, I ask, "Sister, what is that board used for with all those badges on it?"

"I am glad you asked, Robert. That's one of the very special activities here at St. Monica. That picture over there of Jesus is when He was a young boy, just about the age you are right now. When Jesus was on earth, He tried to do His very best all the time. He was kind, loving and respectful to everyone. When you imitate Jesus by behaving like Him, Sister Pascaline will make you a member of the `Boy Savior Club.

"That's quite an honor, Robert. Your name is placed on the board and you get to wear one of the Boy Savior badges with a blue ribbon on your shirt every day. I bet you can become a Boy Savior if you try real hard."

I resolve that I will work as hard as I can to become one of the Boy Saviors in my class. I can't wait to start.

On our way back to her office, Sister Evasia walks much slower than when we went up. Also, she is walking alongside me with her right arm across my shoulders.

"Well, Robert, what do you like best about your school?"

Searching my mind, I think of the crucifix on the wall in front of my class, and the crosses worn by all the nuns. This gives me a feeling of safety because I assume the devil stays away from holy places like St. Monica's and therefore will not likely bother me here.

"Robert, did you hear my question?" Sister Evasia asks.

"I am sorry, Sister, I was thinking of what I like best."

"And what is that?"

I look straight up into her eyes and tell her, "There are crosses all over the school!"

Sister Evasia stops and says, "Robert, what a wonderful thing to say! That also is one of the things I like most about our school. You are going to be happy here at St. Monica's, and I know that we are going to be happy to have you here with us!"

Sister quickly adds, "Now I will race you back to Mommy. Ready, set, go!"

Before I can start running, Sister is already on the go down the stairs! She is not running very fast. I think she is keeping pace with me so she can let me win. As I suspected, I arrive at the bottom of the steps just ahead of her.

"Now, Robert," she playfully admonishes, "don't tell any of the Sisters in our school about our race… and how you won! We did this for fun now because everyone is outside now on recess. At all times, Robert, there's **NO** running allowed inside the school.

Just as we arrive back at her office where Mommy is patiently waiting, she asks, "Have you thought about what you would like to do when you grow up, Robert?"

"Yes, Sister, I have," I start to say but Mommy interrupts, "Well, how do you like your school, Bobby?"

"Oh, it's so nice, Mommy. I am going to have my own desk with an ink well for a fountain pen!" I answer excitedly.

Sister quickly assures Mommy, "Yes, but he won't be using any ink this year, Mrs. Walsh."

Mommy chuckles, "Well, I guess I don't have to ask what you like best about your classroom then, do I?"

Sister Evasia and I exchange knowing glances as I tell Mommy, "The cross, Mommy, I like the cross. It's beautiful, and it's high on the wall where I can always see it."

Mommy and Sister Evasia are obviously pleased to hear this. Sister Evasia gently pats me on the back of my head, and says, "Very good, Robert."

After a pause, she asks, "Well, are you going to tell us, or not?"

I am puzzled by her question so she clarifies, "You were about to tell us what you would like to do when you grow up."

I look at her, then Mommy, then back again to Sister.

"Well, go on, Bobby, tell us," Mommy orders.

"I would like to become a priest."

Chapter 13

GIANTS AND DODGERS

October 1951

The man in white is furious!

Picking up the closest thing to him, a large white vase, he raises it high above his head then throws it across the room at two men! These two men on the television show are dressed in Alpine clothing and are wearing what looks like false mustaches. Amazingly, one of the men, the thin one, catches the vase and throws it right back at the man in white hitting him solidly on top of his head smashing the vase into pieces! To my surprise, he starts running after the two men! The fat man is the first one out the door followed closely by the thin man, then the angry man in white close behind.

Daddy walks in the room joining Paddy, Kitty, Larry, and me.

Sitting down he says, "Oh, you are watching Laurel and Hardy, heh? They are hilarious! Hey, look at them running in and out of those closets. Now watch, Hardy is going to get stuck in one of them because he is so fat."

Daddy laughs again enjoying what he calls "the shenanigans" of these two funny men in the television movie. I am surprised to see Daddy become so quickly engrossed and amused.

"Your mother loves them, too, you know," he tells us. "They are her favorite comedians, but mine are the Marx Brothers."

He could have fooled me judging by how hard he is laughing.

I do not pay attention to what Daddy is saying right now because there is a big hairy gorilla chasing Laurel and Hardy on the show now. The gorilla must have been in some accident because it has bandaging around the top of its head and its lower right leg, and it is using crutches! The gorilla is angry at Laurel and Hardy who must have had something to do with the gorilla's injuries.

Daddy gets a big kick out of this kind of comedy. He calls it, "slapstick comedy," that is, when people do wild, crazy things. Daddy laughs even louder as Laurel and Hardy run down the road with the gorilla on crutches chasing them. The gorilla, seeing that it cannot catch them, stops, and flings one of its crutches at them. I watch in amusement as the crutch hurtles high in the air and comes down right on top of both Laurel and Hardy knocking them to the ground! The movie ends with the gorilla happily jumping up and down... and Daddy laughing uproariously.

While I can see the obvious slapstick humor intended, I do not like the fact that it is at the expense of showing people and an animal getting hurt.

I wonder how many people watch, and perhaps even act out slapstick humor in real life and do not see anything wrong with it.

A few days later while watching cartoons on television, Daddy walks into the living room and says, "Mark the date, Bobby, October 3rd, 1951, the day the Giants are going to win the National League Pennant against the hated **"Bums,"** the Brooklyn Dodgers!"

"We are going to watch the Giants-Dodgers playoff game. Today is the final game of the special playoff for the National League Pennant, you know. They are playing at the Polo Grounds, the Giants ballpark."

This is bad news for me because I want to watch more cartoons or a cowboy story. However, I can see that Daddy is intent on seeing this baseball game. He is already setting up the big armchair for himself, dragging it from its place by the left window in the living room, and positioning it three feet directly in front of the television set which is now on a table between the two living room windows.

Sitting down, Daddy then places his cup of tea in its usual place on the floor by his right foot. Then reaching over, he changes the channel to the New York Giants baseball game. Settling back in his chair, he makes a loud slurping sound as he takes a sip out of his cup of tea. Still disappointed that I cannot watch something more interesting than baseball, I ask Daddy if I can watch just one more show before his ballgame starts.

Huffing, Daddy snaps, "You gotta be kidding! Didn't you hear what I said? This is **THE** game of the year; it is the final playoff game! The winner takes the National League Pennant and goes on to play in the World Series against the New York Yankees. There is no time to watch another show; I can't risk missing the beginning of the game. Understand?"

"Yes, Daddy," I answer, but I feel very sad that Daddy is choosing to do something he wants rather than doing something for me. I just do not understand what the big deal is about watching little figures on the television screen as they play baseball. I really wish Daddy would change his mind and let me watch some cartoons. Maybe he will stop watching the game after a while. Just in case he does, I am going to stay right here on the floor right next to his chair.

I have to learn what there is about baseball that so engrosses Daddy.

"Daddy, please tell me about your baseball team."

"Sure," he says eagerly, "You mean **OUR** team! Well, for beginners, I grew up rooting for the New York Giants. They're in the National League, and they play great baseball... most of the time."

"What is their ballpark like, Daddy?" I want to know.

"The Polo Grounds was built during the 1890's, Bobby, about sixty years ago. It's a rectangular shaped park located by a small cliff called

'Coogan's Bluff' on one side, and the Harlem River on the other. As a matter of fact, just across the river is 'Yankee Stadium' in the Bronx. That is where the New York Yankees play American League baseball. Unfortunately, the Yankees usually have good teams too.

"You know, as much we Giant and Dodger fans don't like each other's teams, we have one thing in common…**we all hate the Yankees!"**

As Daddy chuckles, I ask, "Why does everyone hate the Yankees?"

"Just because that is the way it has always been. If you root for the Giants or the Dodgers, you just naturally hate the Yankees!"

"Oh, I see."

"Where are the Polo Grounds from here?" I ask.

"The Polo Grounds are north of us in upper Manhattan on 155th Street and Eighth Avenue. About 56,000 people can fit in the park at one time because it has a double deck that runs all around the park, except for the bleachers in centerfield. There is only one high set of stands in centerfield because there is a thirty-foot high scoreboard located in the center of the bleachers.

"The walls around the ball field are green and they are about twelve feet high except in center where it's only six feet. It is pretty easy to hit a home run in the Polo Grounds because right field is only 257 feet long and left field is only 279 feet. If you hit it straight away, however, you are in trouble because the centerfield wall is a whopping 483 feet away from home plate! To hit a home run there, you have to really belt it."

"Who are the players on the Giants, Daddy?"

"Well, let's see… there's Whitey Lockman at first base, Eddie Stanky at second, Alvin Dark at short stop, Bobby Thomson at third, Don Mueller in right field, Monte Irving in left, Willie Mays in center, and Wes Westrum catching. Our starting pitchers are Sal Maglie, Larry Jensen, Jim Hearn, George Spencer and Koslo. Irving, Mays and a third baseman, Hank Thompson, are the first colored guys ever to play on the Giants. And you know, they are all damn good players."

"Who is the best player on the Giants?"

"Hmmm, that is a good question. Right now I would have to say it's Willie Mays. He is the most exciting player on the Giants… maybe in all baseball. He is a great fielder, hitter, and base runner. Even though he came up from the minor leagues just this year, he already has become a star ballplayer. If it wasn't for him, I don't think the Giants would be where they are today!"

"How old is he?"

"He's only a kid, eighteen, I think. I will bet you anything, Bobby, the 'Say Hey Kid' as he is called, will go on to become one of the greatest players ever to play the game of baseball. You mark my words, someday he will be inducted into the baseball Hall of Fame.

"I almost forgot to mention the Giants' manager, Leo 'The Lip' Durocher. He is called 'The Lip' because he is always arguing with the umpires. You know, he was once the manager of the Brooklyn Dodgers, our archrivals. Unlike the guy who manages the Dodgers now, Charlie Dressen, Durocher has done a fabulous job managing the Giants this year.

"If the Giants' manager is good because the Giants tied for the Pennant, then the Dodgers' manager must also be good because he got his team to tie for the Pennant," I rationalize.

Daddy does not respond; he just looks annoyed to hear my logic.

"It doesn't work that way, kid. Let me explain how Durocher did a much better job than Dressen. Back on August 12, the Giants were thirteen and a half games behind the first place Dodgers, but the Giants went on a tear, winning thirty-eight of their last forty-seven games including six out of seven over Brooklyn. The 'Bums' played only .500 ball during the home stretch. That is how the Giants caught up to the Dodgers and tied them on the second to last day of the season, setting the stage for an exciting end on the very last day. With the National League Pennant at stake, all New York was going crazy. Giant and Dodger fans and people all over America were following both teams as they played their last game of the season."

"Please tell me what happened, Daddy," I beg.

"Well, on the very last day in September, the Giants were playing the Boston Braves while the Bums went up against the Philadelphia Phillies. The Giants won their game easily, but the Dodgers had to struggle over 14 innings in Philadelphia before Jackie Robinson, the first colored guy ever to play in the majors, hit a home run against Robin Roberts to win it, nine to eight. I really thought the Giants were going to win the Pennant when I heard the Dodgers had gone into extra innings.

"Too bad," he sighs, "Do you know the Dodgers blew the Pennant last year to the Phillies on the very last day of the season? Yep, and five years ago it was even worse. In 1946, they tied St. Louis for first place but went on to lose the very first playoff ever played for the Pennant in National League history. You can see why the Dodgers are called the 'Bums.' It is because of the way they play baseball; they stink! I will not be surprised if they never win a World Series!"

I am surprised by the level of emotion Daddy displays. He genuinely does not like the Dodgers.

"Daddy, why do you dislike them so much?" I ask.

"Hey, listen, they come from Brooklyn first of all, that's reason enough! People from Brooklyn think they are better than everyone else in

New York. And that includes our teams, the Giants and the Yankees. You know, even their ballpark is small and ugly. It is called 'Ebbets Field.' It is in Brooklyn and can seat only 32,000 people. And the outfield walls are ridiculous, they go ALL the way up in the air.

"Dodger and Giant fans have only three things in common: we live in the same city; we love baseball; and we all hate the 'Bronx Bombers,' the New York Yankees," Daddy laughs heartedly.

"Why are the Yankees called 'the Bronx Bombers?'"

"Because they have had so many great hitters who hit home runs, they can bomb any pitcher right out of the game... which is what they usually do. Guys like Babe Ruth, Lou Gehrig, Joe DiMaggio and others, have consistently been among the best hitters in baseball. The 'Babe' still holds the record for hitting the most home runs in one season, sixty, and the most home runs in a lifetime, 714! Can you imagine that! 714 home runs. That is amazing!

"It may be possible for someone to come along and hit more than sixty homers in one season, but I have to tell you, I don't think anyone will ever hit more than 714 home runs in a lifetime. That's why Babe Ruth is called the 'Sultan of the Swat,' the home run king of all time."

As the pre-game dialogue starts on TV, Daddy's mood begins to change. He is now nervous and fidgety, constantly shifting about in the armchair as he puffs away madly on his Chesterfield cigarettes. He is totally engrossed in watching and listening to the television to the exclusion of everything around him. I think I could climb up the corner steam pipe to his right and he would not notice... or care. Clearly, this baseball game right now is the single most important thing in his life.

The ashes from his cigarette silently flick off and land all over his pants, his shoes and the floor. He has smoked the cigarette down to a tiny butt that looks like it is going to burn his fingers as he pinches it between his thumb and forefinger. At the very last moment, however, he reaches down with it still between his fingers and places it under his right shoe and then squashes the lit butt out on the floor by twisting his shoe from side to side! As he moves his shoe away, I can see an ugly black mark left on the floor... next to the others he has made. Mommy is going to be infuriated when she sees this. She has asked him so many times in the past to stop putting his cigarettes out on the floor like this, but he does it anyway... especially when he watches baseball on TV.

Daddy now lights up yet another Chesterfield filling up the living room with the acrid smell of sulfur fumes from his small book of matches. Observing how engrossed Daddy is in this game, I decide that it may well be worth watching after all, so I remain stationed on the floor to the right of

Daddy's chair to watch the game with him.

The announcer is giving the background to today's final playoff game. He explains how the Giants' pitcher, Jim Hearn, won the first game by the score of three to one. Then the Dodgers came right back to win the second playoff game by a lop-sided score of ten to nothing. Clem Labine was the winning pitcher for the Dodgers.

And so, it has come down to this final game of the season for the Giants and the Dodgers at the Polo Grounds. The winner takes all! Both teams have their best pitchers ready for today's game, Don Newcombe for the Dodgers, and Sal 'the Barber' Maglie for the Giants. Maglie is called the Barber because he is notorious for throwing fastballs so close to batters' chins that they will be shaved if they do not jump back out of the way! He has won 23 games this year, the most in the National League.

The stage is set for a great game. The ballpark is jammed to overfilling with crazed Giant and Dodger fans cheering wildly while millions of baseball fans all over the country follow the game on radio and on television.

My interest wanes as the announcer's voice describes the action on the field. I find myself thinking about experiences in school over the past first weeks. For the most part, they have been very pleasant. Each morning Mommy walks Paddy, Kitty, and me off to school, and then picks us up promptly at three o'clock when school is over. I can see her standing there on the corner of 80th Street and York Avenue waiting for us as each of us marches down 80th Street in single file with our classmates. One class after another marches in single file from St. Monica's school in the middle of 80th street all the way down to the corner of York Avenue.

This daily marching routine actually begins in the classroom. Sister Pascaline, my first grade teacher, always reminds us that no talking is allowed, and that we have to stay strictly at our place on line. She reminds us how we are an example of what Catholic children are like to other people in the neighborhood who observe how we behave. Once we get outside the school entrance, we have to walk along the centerline in the cement sidewalk until we reach our mothers waiting at the corner. And there's no stopping or talking allowed during our march!

Sister Pascaline accompanies us along the way, constantly looking up and down the block to make sure everything is okay... and everyone is behaving. I get the feeling that the nuns are also watching for danger. As Daddy has said a million times, there are a lot of bad, sick people in the world who can hurt us.

The seventh-grade school monitors also accompany us. They make sure nobody bad does hurt us, or tries to take us away before we get to our mothers at the corner. The monitors also help us students safely cross the intersection of 80th Street and York Avenue when some of the students have permission to walk home alone by themselves.

My school days are pleasant because Sister Pascaline is a gentle, loving and motherly woman of God. She hugs us, strokes our hair, asks how we are doing, and is always telling us how good we are. All of us in my class know that she loves us and cares for us... like she is one of our aunts. We love her and trust her.

Each day Sister brings eight of us at a time to the front of the classroom where we sit on small wooden chairs in a circle and learn how to read by listening to her read as we point to the words on the page with our right forefinger. I remember the day I read an entire page! Sister Pascaline was so impressed, she said that I did a very good job reading. I felt so proud, I could not wait until I got home to tell Mommy.

My classmates are very nice, especially those who sit around my desk in the back of the classroom on the right side. All the boys sit on the right side of the classroom; the girls on the left. I feel close to all my classmates as if they are my brothers and sisters. I have a crush on one of the girls, Judy. She is so pretty and is always smiling and pleasant.

Each school day begins with our class saying prayers together. I really like this. Later on, Sister Pascaline plays large black records of classical music on the old Victrola record player she keeps up in front of the classroom on the right side. In order to get the Victrola to work, Sister has to crank it up with an L-shaped metal handle. She inserts it into the side of the unit, then turns it around and around before she places the arm with a needle on the end on the record. Everyone laughs when Sister does this because she then acts like she is exhausted after cranking up the Victrola.

My school days have already been filled with many precious moments because of my wonderful classmates and so many interesting things to do and to learn. My cousin, Maureen, was right that I would love St. Monica's school.

While daydreaming about my days at St. Monica's school, the Giant-Dodger game has moved far along with Daddy alternately cheering and shouting, and at times, pounding his right knee and shouting in frustration.

I can tell when the Dodgers are doing well because Daddy shouts things like: "goddamn it," or, "what the hell is going on," or, "for Christ's sake!"

When he says, "For Christ's sake," he usually throws his right hand up into the air and looks skyward. He acts so strangely when he watches baseball on TV.

As the game wears on, Daddy intermittently gets up and nervously paces back and forth, looking very worried as he puffs on one cigarette after another.

Curious to know how our team is doing, I ask, "Daddy, are the Giants winning?"

"No!" he angrily snaps, "they are **not** winning! They're losing four to one. I can't believe it. Don Newcombe is pitching the greatest game of his life, and now the Giants have their backs to the wall. It is the bottom of the ninth inning, and we have only three outs to tie the score. If we don't, the Dodgers will win the Pennant and go on to play the 'damn Yankees' in the World Series!"

Daddy looks like he was going to have a heart attack… as Mommy often says.

"I can't believe this!" he complains again, "I can't believe this! Sal Maglie, the Giants' best pitcher, gives up eight hits and four runs in the most important game of the season. How do you figure it?"

Alvin Dark leads off the ninth inning for the Giants and as he steps into the batter's box, Daddy yells out to him as if Alvin Dark can hear him, "Come on, Alvin, you can do it; start off the rally!"

To my amazement, Alvin Dark does! He hits a single and stands at first base with the crowd on television, and Daddy, cheering wildly. The next batter, Don Mueller, steps up to bat and Daddy exhorts him to get a hit like Alvin Dark did.

As I watch the screen, I see the pitcher wind up on the pitcher's mound and throw the ball very fast toward home plate. Don Mueller swings his bat at the ball and hits it for another single giving the Giants two men on base now!

Daddy is screaming and yelling as he jumps out of his chair and punches his fist wildly in the air. His yelling causes Mommy, Paddy, Kitty, and Larry to come in to find out what all the commotion is all about.

Daddy excitedly tells everyone, "The Giants have two men on base and nobody out with the tying run coming up to the plate!"

"All right, all right, Patsy; you don't have to shout," Mommy complains. "We are all right here."

Mommy looks so annoyed. Stepping over to the left window, she adds, "Calm down, will you!" she admonishes him. "You've got the whole neighborhood looking up at our window from the street wondering who's getting killed!"

Daddy looks up at her and sneers before returning his attention back to the game on TV. He abruptly shifts from one side of his chair to the other, then leans forward toward the screen as he squeezes his hands so nervously together they look discolored.

"Here's Monte Irving at bat," he announces excitedly. "He's the league leader in runs batted in this year with 121."

Daddy really knows his baseball.

"Big deal!" Mommy surprises me with a sarcastic remark. "He's going to hit into a double-play!"

Daddy bites his tongue in anger as he sneers at her.

I understand what is going on between them. Mommy lived for a long time in Brooklyn, and so she is a Dodger fan even though she doesn't follow baseball with the same fervor as Daddy.

Daddy's hopes and expectations are suddenly crushed as Monte Irving pops up for the first out of the ninth inning. Two outs left, I think. Daddy looks instantly depressed, as he stares down at the floor in front of him and shakes his head from side to side mumbling something. I can't believe how upset he is; it looks as if he is going to cry!

The next batter is Whitey Lockman who steps confidently into the batter's box. He has to get a hit to keep the Giants' hopes alive. Daddy sits up staring intently at every motion on the screen. Lockman suddenly hits the ball to the outfield for extra bases! Daddy's eyes bulge wildly as he jumps up and watches Alvin Dark come around to score while Don Mueller makes it to third and Whitey Lockman goes into second base with a double!

Wow! Oh, my God, the Giants are rallying!

Daddy is jumping up and down, screaming and cheering! The score is now four to two in favor of the Dodgers. With two men in scoring position, the Giants actually have a chance to tie the game!

"A base hit here now will send both men home to tie the score, and send the game into extra innings!" Daddy says breathlessly.

Reaching over to me, he messes up my hair and says, "Now you see why I love the Giants; they never give up. A single now will score two runs and tie the score. Just one hit away, Bobby, just one hit away!"

Mommy smirks and says, "You think so, eh? You ever hear the saying, 'so near, yet so far?' Well, I have news for you, Patsy; the next two batters are going to go down swinging!"

I suspect that Mommy really doesn't care if the Dodgers win or lose; she is just having fun teasing Daddy. He will be crushed if the Giants lose so I decide that I also want the Giants to win.

I surprise everyone by saying, "Come on, Giants, hit a home run!"

Daddy laughs and says, "That a way, Bobby! Say a prayer for the Giants, will ya! Say a real good prayer for them!"

Mommy laughs, "Ha! He'd better say a prayer for them because the Giants are going to need a miracle to win this game! There is no way the Dodgers are going to lose!"

I don't think it would be right to ask God to arrange it so that the Giants will win the game, but I do pray that the they will use all their talents… and win this game on their own merits.

Oh, no! Don Mueller twisted his ankle sliding into third base so he has been replaced by Clint Hartung as the base runner. The Dodger manager, Charlie Dressen, walks out to the mound and stands there talking to Don Newcombe and the catcher, Roy Campanella. They decide to bring in a new pitcher, Ralph Branca, a thirteen game winner this year, to try to end the Giants' rally and preserve the win, and the Pennant, for the Dodgers.

Ralph Branca walks all the way in from the 'bullpen' all the way out in centerfield. It's a long, long walk in to the infield.

As Branca warms up, Daddy says, "Bobby Thomson is up next; he has hit thirty-two home runs this year, and he's the one who hit a home run off Branca in the first playoff game. Can you imagine if he hits another one now to win the game!"

Mommy steps over to Daddy and pats him on the shoulder as she teases, "It's almost four o'clock, Patsy, only a few minutes left in the Giants' season! Branca is going to strike out Bobby Thomson… and the next batter too! I told you, the Dodgers are going to win the Pennant. They are the better team."

Once again, Daddy wickedly bites his tongue in anger as he pulls his shoulder abruptly away from Mommy and snaps, "Don't jinx them, Ellie. Don't jinx them! The Giants are rallying and can win it all right now!"

"Keep on dreaming, Patsy. This is the playoffs and there's no way Branca is going to give Bobby Thomson, or the next batter, something good to hit. The Giants are as good as dead! They will probably walk him to load the bases so the next batter can hit into a double-play and end the game!"

Daddy is a complete nervous wreck while Mommy appears quite calm standing there leaning against the mantelpiece as she watches the game on TV. Paddy, Kitty, and Larry are stationed between her and Daddy. Having grown up in Brooklyn Dodger country, she learned the game from her father including how to love the Dodgers, and to Daddy's dismay… how to tease Giant fans!

Daddy sits bolt upright again, and leans toward the television screen as Bobby Thomson steps into the batter's box on the left side of the plate. His number, 23, looks enormous on the back of his shirt. He is a powerful right hand slugger up against a very fine relief pitcher in an incredibly tense drama pitting the fortunes of both teams and millions of their fans heavily upon both their shoulders.

The scene is set: the 1951 National League Pennant is on the line. It is the bottom of the ninth inning at the Giants' Polo Grounds with the score four to two in favor of the Dodgers. There is one out but the tying runs are on second and third base, and the winning run is the batter at home plate. A single now ties the game. The crowd sounds like it is going crazy with noise as Giant and Dodger fans cheer for their respective teams.

The pitcher, Ralph Branca, looks at the runners on second and third, goes through his deliberate wind up, then fires the ball toward home plate. The ball flies by Bobby Thomson as he just stands there and looks at the pitch. The umpire throws his right arm high up into the air signifying strike one! The crowd screams in response. I can't believe that Thomson just stood there looking at the pitch as it zipped past him into catcher Roy Campanella's mitt!

Daddy shifts backward in his chair as he moans and grimaces while Mommy giggles mischievously. Making the Sign of the Cross, Daddy squeezes his hands so tightly together that his fingers appear swollen and bright red.

Daddy begs loudly, "Come on, Bobby, get a hit! Slam that goddamn ball! Please, if ever you got a hit, get one now!"

Mommy continues to giggle as she stands by the mantelpiece looking quite relaxed despite all the tension and excitement. She is obviously quite sure the Giants are going to lose.

Ralph Branca looks in toward the catcher, Campanella, for a sign as to which pitch he should throw now. Apparently getting the sign, Branca looks at the runners, then winds up and fires the white ball straight down the middle toward home plate. This time, Bobby Thomson wickedly swings his bat at the ball and there is a distinctive "crack" sound as the ball flies high up in the air toward the left field side of the ballpark.

As the ball travels up and out toward the stands, Daddy's mouth drops open and his eyes bulge. The players on the field are frozen in disbelief with the realization of what is happening as the ball sails over the left field wall into the lower deck of the stands for a three-run home run winning the ballgame and the Pennant for the New York Giants!

In that instant, the Giants have won... and the Dodgers have lost!

Pandemonium sets in at the Polo Grounds. I am stunned as I watch Daddy leap straight up so high that his head nearly hits the ceiling. He is screaming at the top of his lungs and jumping up and down like a man possessed. The floor shakes every time he lands!

Now he runs over to the left window, throws it open and screams at the top of his voice to no one in particular, "The Giants won the Pennant! The Giants won the Pennant! The Giants won the Pennant!"

This is such a remarkable moment. The clock on the mantelpiece reads 3:58pm. Mommy was wrong.

It turns out it is the Dodgers who are dead before four o'clock! Mommy is so shocked she is still standing there with an expression on her face as if she just saw a ghost. Staring at the television screen with her mouth hanging open, she is in shock... I imagine like Dodger fans everywhere.

The Giants' television announcer, Ernie Harwell, is shouting, "The Giants win the Pennant! The Giants win the Pennant! The Giants win the Pennant! The Giants win the Pennant! The Giants win the Pennant!"

I can't believe what I am witnessing! Baseball history just unfolded right in front of me.

As Bobby Thomson rounds the bases, he is jumping up and down. Eddie Stanky runs out of the Giants' dugout and jumps on the back of the manager, Leo Durocher, who was coaching at third base when Thomson hit the home run. They both fall to the ground ecstatic over what has happened! Bobby Thomson nears home plate, jumps up in the air, lands on the plate, and is immediately mobbed by all his Giant teammates waiting there for him. Mayhem has set in everywhere for the Giants and their fans.

Sadly, very sadly, shock and heartache have brutally fallen upon the Dodgers and their fans. Their archrivals, the Giants, have defeated their beloved "Bums." They came so close, so very close. One pitch, and they lost it all.

I wonder who will be blamed for that one pitch. Will it be the manager, Charlie Dressen, who called Branca to come in to pitch to Thomson? Or will it be the catcher, Roy Campanella, who decided what kind of pitch Branca should throw to Thomson? Or will it be Branca himself for throwing the pitch the way he did? I wonder. In the final analysis, I think no one was at fault; everyone did what they thought was best.

After all is said and done, it wasn't a question of who caused the loss; it was a matter of who did something right at the right time to make the difference. Bobby Thomson did something right, something very right, indeed!

There are players and fans massed all over the field jumping and cheering wildly. The excitement of this moment is something I will always remember.: the noise on the TV, Daddy jumping up and down, and the sounds of cheering from people all over our street. Yes, this is one of those remarkable moments in life, and I am part of this magic. I have just fallen in love with baseball and the New York Giants. They just won the National League Pennant!

Seeing the tears of joy streaming down Daddy's red face, I feel like I am also going to cry with happiness. Seeing that I am also emotional, Daddy comes over and hugs me so tight I can't believe it!

In the midst of all this excitement, I feel so sorry for Ralph Branca and the rest of the Dodgers... and their fans. This loss is a terrible, heart-breaking experience. They came so close to winning the National League Pennant against their archrivals, the Giants, but lost it all on that one pitch, that one swing of the bat, that one moment in time. To lose that way, seems so unreal, almost unfair. But then, the best teams don't let it all come down to one pitch.

I can just imagine what it must be like at this moment in the homes of Dodger fans all over Brooklyn. I hope that someday the Dodgers will win the Pennant, and maybe even the World Series so they and their fans can be happy like we Giant fans are today. Right now, that seems like it would take a miracle for the Brooklyn Dodgers to win a World Series.

But then... I know that miracles can and do happen.

Chapter 14

BLESSED VISION

December 1951

It's cold, dark and dreary outside... matching the atmosphere inside our home recently.

Mommy and Daddy are deeply troubled over something. Curious to discover what's wrong, I make my way out through the rooms until I am right in front of the kitchen table where Daddy sits to my right, and Mommy to my left. They are so involved in their discussion they don't acknowledge my presence.

Daddy pleads, "I see nothing wrong with my mother coming here to live with us for a while so we can help take care of her. She's worked hard her whole life taking care of our family, raising six kids on her own after my father died during the depression!"

I remember that Daddy's father died after falling out a fifth story window. Daddy looks like he is going to cry.

He continues, "There were many times when she didn't eat so we kids could have more to eat. Now she's old and sick and needs us to help take care of her."

Mommy, also looking upset, replies, "Patsy, this has nothing to do with how hard your mother worked to raise your family. I know what she did was wonderful, but it has nothing to do with her coming to live with us."

As their discussion goes back and forth, my thoughts fade to Nana. Daddy once told me how when he was growing up, they were so poor they didn't have money to buy wood or coal to burn in the kitchen stove for heat when the cold weather set in. In order to heat the apartment to keep her children warm, Nana used to rip the wood up from the floors in the apartment, from the moldings, and even from inside the walls. She did this to get wood to burn in the stove for heat, and to cook. When she got close to running out of wood in the apartment, she would find another apartment in the neighborhood then move out in the middle of the night when no one was around to see her and her brood of children slipping away. She was able to do this because in those days, people didn't have to pay security money before they moved into an apartment.

Nana moved her family very often.

Mommy's voice abruptly interrupts my thoughts of Nana.

"I know how much you love your mother and I want to help her too, Patsy. We may have our backs to the wall in our small four room apartment, but you and I and our five kids can always make room for Nana if no one else can help her."

Daddy looks so sad but somewhat relieved at the possibility that we will take Nana in if no one else can. I am thrilled to hear this!

With tears in his eyes, Daddy says, "Thank you, Ellie, I don't know what I'd do without you. You're wonderful!"

Hearing this, I interject, "I will help by saying a prayer, Daddy."

This brings a smile to his face, "Yes you can, Bobby; praying definitely helps."

Giving me a kiss, he adds, "Why don't you go inside right now and say that prayer."

In the living room, I lie down on the sofa and call out to God and implore Him to send His graces to resolve Nana's dilemma. As always, I have the distinct feeling that God hears my prayer but I can never tell what He may do… or when He might do something.

Throughout the night, Mommy and Daddy ponder how things can work. Eventually, they agree to wait and see how other choices work out. They decide that all of us should go visit Nana as often as we can. That way, Mommy reasons, we can see how well she is doing and at the same time, we can help her while we are visiting.

Mommy and Daddy plan to take us to visit Nana in her apartment in the top floor of a brownstone apartment building on the west side of First Avenue between 81st and 82nd Streets in Manhattan. I am so happy we are going to spend time with her. I enjoy walking to Nana's, and once we get there, I enjoy climbing up all those stairs that seem to go on forever. Daddy always says it is well worth climbing up all those stairs because they lead up to a place like heaven. Mommy explains that Daddy says this because at the top of those stairs is his beloved mother, Nana.

It is wonderful to spend time with her because she is so kind and gentle, always fussing over us. Surprisingly, this time when Paddy, Larry, and I get up to her landing on the top floor, Nana is not standing there waiting for us as she usually does by her door on the right side of the hallway. Since her door is open, we quickly rush in and look for her. There she is… sitting at the kitchen table smiling.

"Well, well, well, what have we got here?" she says playfully. "Three handsome Irishmen. Oh, you boys are gonna drive the girls crazy. Come over here and give your Nana a big hug and kiss, you handsome little leprechauns!"

There aren't too many places in the world I would rather be than in Nana's wonderful embrace. I love her so much, I wish we could see her every day. Soon Mommy and Daddy arrive with Kitty and Geri, and the happy visit commences. While the others go inside to play, I stay outside with Nana, Mommy, and Daddy.

I listen as Nana explains, "I'm so tired all the time, Pat. I just couldn't get myself untracked to cook dinner today."

Looking over to Mommy, Nana adds, "I hope you don't mind rustling something up, Ellie. There's some food in the refrigerator that Dotsy and Frank brought up here for me."

Mommy smiles and says, "I'll be happy to cook dinner, Mom; it will only take a second."

Daddy looks concerned as he sits at the table across from Nana, and asks, "How are you feeling, Mom?"

"Oh, all right, I guess. You know, aches and pains all over, but that what's to be expected at my age. There's nothing to worry about, Pat, I'm fine. Now tell me how life is treating you. I want to hear everything."

As Daddy begins to tell Nana how things are doing with his job and family, I study Nana's reactions. She has a look of pride and admiration for her son. Mommy has said that Daddy is Nana's pride and joy. I don't think Nana is really listening to much of what Daddy is saying... but Daddy doesn't seem to notice.

Later after dinner, we relax in Nana's living room while we listen to Daddy discussing things with Nana and Mommy. Nana's radio on the corner end table is playing some beautiful-sounding music. All too soon, the time approaches for us to end our visit and head to our home nearby. My heart aches to see Nana's look of sadness.

I want to cry, "No, Daddy, no, we can't leave Nana now. You were right, we must take her home with us and take care of her."

I say nothing, though, because I know such words will only bring more sadness to Daddy and Nana. She knows we must return to our home, and she also understands that we cannot take her with us. Oh, how I wish I could do something to take away her sadness.

Why is it that she is left here all alone like this after having taken care of so many others in her large family? How painful her suffering must be to live in solitude after a whole life filled with the constant companionship of many children and a home filled with so much joy and activity. There is no one left now for her to take care of... or, to share life with her in her older years.

It hurts me so much to see this; it just doesn't seem fair. But I remember Mommy once said that we are never alone because Jesus said "He is always with us."

This is comforting... but I still feel sad. Nana walks over and kneels down on the floor by me. It is almost as if she knows what I am feeling. I must try not to show her how sad I am for her. When our eyes meet, the unspoken language of love between us is conveyed. Fussing over my hair and clothes in her grandmotherly way, I think she is letting me know that she understands how I feel, and that she will be all right.

I ask her, "Nana, are you going to go to heaven soon?"

Looking surprised at my question, she says, "Bobby! You shouldn't ask such questions. Your Nana doesn't mind, you know you can ask me anything, but most other people wouldn't like you to ask them that. Okay?"

I nod my head yes, but ask, "Why?"

"Well, some people don't like to think about dying."

"But why, Nana? You have to die before you can go to heaven."

Nana laughs, "How true! Well, let's just say that some people are afraid to die; that's why."

"Are you?" I ask.

Nana smiles but looks a little more serious.

"No, Bobby, I'm not afraid to die. In fact, I'm actually looking forward to it because in heaven I'll get to be with my family members who are already there. Now isn't that wonderful!

"You see, Bobby... Jesus tells us that death is not an ending, it is only a beginning. Just imagine what a glorious moment it will be for your Nana when I get to be with my husband again, your Grandpa Edward John Walsh. With him will be our two boys who died when they were little babies. And there will also be my mommy, my daddy, my nana, my grandpa, and all my other family members! And don't forget, there will also be lots of angels. They will all be there to welcome me and escort me to see God. Now can't you just imagine that!"

"Yes, Nana, I can imagine all that, and it sure looks beautiful."

Stroking my hair, she says, "I'm sure you can, Bobby. I know you're a very special child of God, and you're much like your father was when he was your age. I'm sure when you grow up, you're going to be like him... big, strong, and good... very good. He tells me you want to become a priest someday when you grow up. Is that right?"

"Yes, Nana. I want to be a priest."

"Well, you know you will then be the **very first** priest ever in our family!"

Nana pauses moving her loving eyes over to study Daddy as he walks past us gathering things up for our return home. He appears to be unaware of her attention to him.

With a look of relief and tranquility, Nana looks back to me and says, "When your Nana goes to heaven, I want you to promise me that you will pray for me every day. Will you do that for your Nana?"

"Yes, Nana, I promise… but I don't want you to go for a long, long time."

Nana laughs, "I understand, but that is entirely up to God. There's so much I want to say to you, but so little time. There's never enough time for the things we want to do, is there? We'll just have to do all our catching up when we're all in heaven where we'll never run out of time, and we'll never have to leave to go home… because we will be home.

"Now remember that God listens well, but He can only hear you if you talk to Him! You be the best person you can be, and never ever give up on anything, no matter how difficult things may be. You come from a long line of strong, courageous people, Bobby, so live your life with courage, honesty, and goodness. And look after your brothers and sisters. Will you do that for your Nana?"

"Yes, Nana."

"Promise?"

"Yes, Nana."

"Honest, Injun," she says playfully poking me in my tummy.

"Yes, Nana."

"That makes me very happy, Bobby. And you **will** remember to pray for me, right?"

"Yes, Nana, I promise, and when you go to heaven, you can pray for me, too."

She chuckles, "Oh, you're something else. What a beautiful thought. Of course, I'll pray for you while I am in heaven."

Gently pulling me to herself, she whispers, "Come now, Bobby, bless your Nana with one more big hug before you go."

I melt in her arms, saddened with the thought that my Nana may soon be going home to God where I will not see her for a long, long time. Nestled in her embrace, I enjoy that special closeness that exists between family members. My physical life comes from her through her son, my Dad. And now, I may not see her again until we meet in heaven someday far in the future.

Soon after leaving Nana's arms, I find myself descending the seemingly endless stairs of Nana's building, one flight after another, holding Larry's hand.

Nana's final words reverberate down the hallways throughout the building, "Look after one another; remember your Nana. I love you."

Paddy has already made it all the way down and outside Nana's building. I wonder if he heard Nana's final words. Her words remind me that Daddy told me to hang on to Larry's hand as we descend the long flights of stairs, and to wait outside the front door. Just as I am thinking this, Larry pulls his hand out of mine and bolts quickly down the stairs ahead of me!

My heart beats wildly as I run as fast as I can trying to catch up to Larry.

"Larry, wait for me!" I cry out as loudly as I can. "Larry, please stop running! **Larry, please wait for me!**"

As I race down the old wooden stairs, the sound of the front door downstairs opening and closing brings panic to my already frenzied heart and mind. Will he wait outside the building? Paddy is there and may be able to grab Larry as he comes out. But what if Larry doesn't stop? What if Paddy can't get him? What should I do if he is running wildly down the street? I am afraid he will get lost because he is not familiar with the neighborhood. He may never be able to find his way home. I may never see him again!

I finally reach the bottom and run outside to discover that my worst fears have come true. Only Paddy is standing there looking up the avenue. There in the darkness of the night to my left, I see Larry running away along First Avenue heading toward 82nd Street. I call out to him again at the top of my voice but the noise of the traffic on First Avenue drowns out my words. I watch in horror as he reaches the corner then turns right without hesitating and races out onto First Avenue in front of onrushing cars barreling toward him.

My heart feels like it is going to explode from fear that my little brother may be run over and killed by one of the cars. I am overwhelmed with a profound sense of fear, desperation, and helplessness. Realizing there is only one thing I can do, I concentrate all my consciousness into a soulful plea to God. I feel detached from my physical surroundings as I cry out to God to protect my baby brother from harm.

Frozen in fear, Paddy and I watch as Larry speeds halfway across without being hit but there is a long tractor-trailer thundering along the far side of the avenue heading directly for Larry. With wheels that look as tall as me, the tractor-trailer roars ahead without a break in speed. The driver apparently does not see Larry!

I pray, "Please, God, don't let the truck run him over!"

The cab of the trailer passes right in front of Larry who continues to run and bending over, he runs under the mid-section of the long trailer section! After the tractor-trailer continues up the avenue, I look on in great fear to see if Larry's body is lying in the street all mangled and lifeless in the wake of the truck.

I focus through the darkness of the night aided only by the light cast on the area by the corner lamppost. Larry's body is **not** lying there in the street! Other worries quickly flash through my mind. Is his body being dragged along First Avenue under the huge truck? Or, he is caught up in the undercarriage of the trailer?

It is also possible that God heard my cry and spared Larry.

A visual inspection of First Avenue farther on discloses that Larry is **not** lying in the street, and common sense tells me he probably is **not** stuck underneath the trailer. This can only mean that he miraculously made it safely across by running under the long section of the tractor-trailer without getting run over!

Tears flow down my face as I thank God for protecting my little brother from being killed by the mighty truck. I know that God heard my cries and answered my prayer. A feeling of relief and gratitude wells up within.

"Where is Larry?" Daddy shouts angrily as he arrives and looks up and down the street.

"Where is he? Why the hell are you boys just standing there? Answer me, where is your little brother? Did he run away?"

Before I can answer, Daddy slams me across the back of my head practically knocking me over as a sharp pain cascades throughout my head.

"What did I tell you about holding his hand? Didn't I tell you not to let go of him, to hold his hand? Which way did he go?"

"He pulled away from me, Daddy, and ran down the stairs. I couldn't catch up to him. He was too fast. When I got outside, I saw him run across the avenue but the truck didn't run him over! I think he continued running down 82nd Street."

"Jesus Christ almighty! Can't I depend on you boys to do anything right?" Daddy complains.

"Why the hell didn't **you** stop him, Paddy?"

"I couldn't. He ran right past me," Paddy answers looking worried that he, too, might get belted by Daddy.

"Why didn't you run after him?" Daddy asks.

"You told me to stay by the front of the building, Daddy," Paddy explains.

"Jesus Christ, I can't believe you kids."

Staring out into the dark of the night, Daddy says, "Where could he be now? Son of a bitch. I'm going to give him the beating of his life when I get my hands on him."

Mommy comes out of Nana's building with Geri in the carriage she just retrieved from the back of the hallway. She looks terrified hearing that Larry ran away.

"Patsy, please run ahead and see if you can catch up to him before he gets too far," Mommy suggests.

"You're right," Daddy answers, "Keep an eye on the rest of the kids."

I watch as Daddy quickly walks out between the parked cars,

carefully looks both ways, then begins to run very fast across First Avenue. At the corner, he turns right onto 82nd Street, and disappears. Mommy instructs us to gather close to her and to hold onto the handlebar of the carriage as we start our worried journey home.

Mommy asks me to explain what happened, so I tell her how Larry ran away from me, ran past Paddy, and then ran under the gigantic tractor-trailer.

Mommy has a horrified expression as she snaps, "That's it! Don't tell me anymore; I don't want to hear any more of this."

Off we go, heading toward home. Mommy is walking so fast we can barely keep up with her. As we hurry across First Avenue at 82nd Street, I look ahead and see Daddy and Larry in front of St. Stephen of Hungary Catholic Church in the middle of the block on the right side. It looks like Daddy is holding onto Larry and hitting him! He is also shouting but I can't hear what he is saying. Suddenly, Larry breaks free and runs off into the darkness with Daddy in hot pursuit after him once again.

The rest of us quickly walk down 82nd Street. As we pass St. Stephen's Church, I am comforted because Jesus is there in the tabernacle. I ask Him please to help us find where Larry has gone.

A feeling pours over me indicating that God will help me find Larry so I tell Mommy and Paddy, "Don't worry, God is going to help me find Larry!"

Wiping away her tears, Mommy says she hopes so.

Passing each of the darkened hallways, I peer in to see if Larry is hiding there from Daddy. He is not. I realize that there is no telling where Larry and Daddy have gone. I can only hope that Larry has run safely back to where we live and is waiting there for us. I also hope that Daddy gets over his anger.

We reach York Avenue and wait for a green light. It seems like a long, long time before the light finally turns green. After crossing, we soon come to a street where halfway down the block there is a lamppost stationed in front of a building. It sheds light on the immediate area showing a solitary figure walking in front. It is Daddy pacing back and forth as he peers out into the darkness of the night looking for Larry.

"I wonder if Daddy found Larry and made him go home already," Paddy says hopefully.

"I don't think so," Mommy says dejectedly, "It looks like Daddy is still looking for him."

When we catch up to Daddy, I can see he is visibly upset and worried. Together, we all continue our worried journey toward home.

Daddy confesses, "I caught him by St. Stephen's Church, and gave

132

him a good whack on the head, but the son-of-a-bitch ran away down the block somewhere."

"You hit him?" Mommy says incredulously, "What the hell is the matter with you? Why did you hit him, Patsy? Didn't you realize he would run away again?"

"I don't want to hear it right now, Ellie. I chased him down here but he disappeared in the dark. I asked the old lady if she saw anything from her ground floor window, but she said she just got there and didn't see anyone."

I turn to see the old lady still peering out shyly from behind her shade in the ground floor window to the left of the stoop.

Mommy is crying.

"Don't worry, Ellie, we'll find him," Daddy assures Mommy.

"I am worried, Patsy, it's dark out and there's no telling where he is now. He's probably lost and scared to death, and doesn't know his way home. Who knows what perverts may be out tonight! Why the hell did you hit him?" Mommy bitterly complains.

"All right, all right, please stop, will you. We'll find him," Daddy persists.

"Let's get the baby and the carriage up into the apartment, then I'll go out looking for him. Kitty you come upstairs with Mommy. Paddy, you and Bobby stay down here and keep your eyes peeled out for Larry. If you see him, don't chase him. Just tell him to stay put until I get back."

Paddy and I look up and down the street straining our eyes in the hopes of seeing Larry, but he is nowhere in sight. Except for an occasional person walking here and there, the streets are deserted, dark and quiet. Overwhelmed with guilt and despair, I sit down on the ice-cold concrete steps of my front stoop and call out to God once again and beg Him to let me know where my little brother Larry has gone.

My angel's familiar voice fills my mind, "He is down by the river."

This is immediately followed by a vision of Larry sitting on top of a large, curved concrete structure down by the East River. He appears to be relaxed enjoying a panoramic view of the East River. The sound of Daddy's heavy footsteps behind me disrupts my vision. As Daddy appears by my side, his face displays fear and concern, so uncharacteristic for him. I don't recall ever seeing him like this.

"Did you boys see Larry?" Daddy asks.

"I saw him, Daddy," I say with certainty as if Larry was standing right here in front of the building with us.

Daddy quickly asks, "Where? Where did you see him?"

I realize that Daddy probably will not understand that my angel just told me where Larry is right now… but I decide to tell him anyway.

"My angel told me that Larry is down by the river. Then a picture appeared in my mind showing him on top of that big concrete thing that is down by the East River."

As I answered, I pointed off in the distance toward the river.

"What are you talking about? You can't see that area from here; it's too far away," Daddy says incredulously. "It's physically impossible to see that area by the East River from here!"

"But I can see him, Daddy; Larry is down there right now. We should go get him before he runs off again," I say with a sound of urgency.

Paddy's eyes dart back and forth from Daddy to me while Daddy stares at me then looks again toward the river. It is clear from his expression that he doesn't understand but he is so desperate to find Larry, he is willing to try anything... to believe anything.

Turning in the direction of the East River, he says, "You can see him down by the river, heh?"

"Yes, Daddy, I see him there in my mind. He's down there right now."

"Well, miracles do happen with you, kid, don't they? Let's go!" Daddy says hopefully.

"Let's pray he's there," Paddy says.

We practically trot down toward the river, Daddy in between Paddy and me. It is interesting how a little hope can so quickly lift your spirits and your attitude. There is a feeling of confidence and eagerness about us now as we reach East End Avenue and look both ways before quickly proceeding across the intersection. Soon we are close to where I see Larry in my mind's eye.

Paddy says excitedly, "There he is, Daddy, Larry is sitting on top of that concrete thing."

Paddy is pointing toward the other end of a short street between us and the wide promenade walkway that overlooks the East River.

Daddy says in a low voice, "Shhhh, be quiet! If that's him, we don't want to scare him off. Let's walk up to him nice and easy. Don't say anything to him. If he starts to run, though, we've got to run as fast as we can to get him. Okay, boys?"

"Yes, Daddy," Paddy and I whisper together at the same time.

Calmly and quietly, we proceed up the street that is about one hundred feet long. I turn in time to see Daddy's face transform from one filled with fear and distress, to one of great relief as he apparently can see that Larry is sitting there... just as I said.

Larry smiles widely as he watches us approach. Saying nothing, he just sits there calmly with his knees pulled up to his chest and his arms wrapped around his legs. Strangely, no one says anything as we stand there together looking back and forth at one another.

Daddy, with his hands on his hips, and a smile of relief on his face, asks Larry, "What're you doing up there, 'LaLa?"

"LaLa" is Daddy's affectionate name for Larry whenever Daddy is happy about something involving Larry. I guess he is happy Larry has been found safe and sound.

Larry shrugs his shoulders and answers, "Just watching things."

"Just watching things, heh," Daddy says, "Come on down, son; I'm not going to hit you. I promise. I just want you to come home with us now."

Daddy encourages Larry to come down by extending his hands outward to help him climb down. I am surprised to see Larry eagerly grab Daddy's hands and stumble awkwardly down the rounded structure to the safety of the ground where Daddy gives him a big hug.

I am so happy we found Larry safe and sound. Paddy and I go over and put our arms around Larry's shoulders. The look on Larry's face tells us he is quite pleased with all the attention he is getting.

"You scared the hell out of us, Larry!" Daddy states, "I didn't know where you ran off to. When did you tell Bobby you were going to come down here?"

Looking up at Daddy, Larry frowns and says, "I didn't tell Bobby."

"Then how did Bobby know that you were down here, heh?"

Larry looks at me with a surprised expression, and shrugs his shoulders.

Daddy must realize that this is another miracle because he knows no one can see all the way down here in the middle of the night from our front stoop. It is physically impossible.

"Your mother is worried to death by what you did, Larry. We'll continue this conversation at home."

At the corner, Daddy asks Larry, "Weren't you afraid you were lost?"

"A little... but I knew Bobby would find me."

"Why do you say that? Because Bobby knew where you were going?"

"No, he didn't. I know that God tells Bobby things, so I knew that God would tell him where to find me.

"Oh, I see," Daddy chuckles. "You really didn't tell Bobby where you were going?"

"Nope."

"By the way, why **did** you run away? What possessed you to go down there by the river to sit on that thing?"

Larry doesn't answer so Daddy repeats his question in a more demanding voice, "LaLa, did you hear me? I asked you why you ran away from Nana's and came down here?"

Larry looks up at Daddy and answers, "I don't know; I just felt like it!"

Daddy bites his tongue in anger, "You just felt like it, heh? You just felt like it! You had us all worried to death, but **you** just felt like it! Larry, I want you to promise me that you'll never, ever do this again. Do you hear me? Never!"

Larry shrugs his shoulders as he marches along and says matter-of-factly, "Okay."

Relieved to hear that Larry promises not to do this again, I relax and enjoy the unplanned pleasure of walking home in the utter stillness of the night with Daddy, Paddy, Larry... and our guardian angels.

Chapter 15

NIGHT OF THE BABYSITTER

February 1952

"Children, wake up, wake up! Please get up and come out here. Mommy has something important to tell you."

Mommy's words awaken me after a restless night. Now I know why I could not sleep; someone very close to us has died.

Reluctantly, I slip out of bed and slowly walk into the kitchen and look at the calendar hanging on the kitchen door to my left. It shows that today is February 25, 1952, a day I can sense I will long remember.

The expression on Mommy's face confirms my fears. She has been crying and her face is blotchy. Now she directs us all to join her in the first room I just came from.

As we sit together on the bed facing her, Kitty asks, "Mommy, should I wake up the baby, and bring her here too?"

Mommy laughs and says to let Geri sleep.

Paddy anxiously asks, "What is the matter, Mommy?"

She doesn't answer. This raises our level of anxiety.

I snuggle between Paddy and Larry and look over to kitty who is sitting close to Paddy. This reflects the closeness among us. Paddy and Kitty are very close, just as Larry and I are very close... and we all love the baby. We hold hands and wait for Mommy to tell us what is wrong.

Mommy's voice quivers with sadness, "I have something very sad to tell you."

I don't recall ever seeing her look so upset. I expect this is bad news about Nana because a vision of her fills my mind. She looks different... in a good way. She doesn't look old and weary now; she looks much younger with a great joy, peace, and happiness about her.

My vision of Nana is interrupted by Mommy's solemn words, "You all know that your Nana has not been well lately... and she's been in the hospital. Well... "

Tears flow from Mommy's eyes as she struggles to finish.

After a deep breath, she continues, "Nana won't be suffering anymore. You see, she's gone to heaven to be with God and the rest of the family who went to heaven before her."

Mommy's words race to the center of my being and confirm my feelings. A great sadness comes over me as the realization sinks in that my beloved Nana has left this physical world and gone to heaven. We will no longer be able to go for those wonderful walks to her apartment on First Avenue. Now we must wait until we get to heaven to see her again.

Tears stream down my face. I wish there was some kind of mistake, and Nana is still alive so we can visit her again. But I know she has gone where we must all go someday when God calls our name. All I can do now is talk to her through prayer.

"Dear God, I know you love Nana more than I do and will take good care of her. Please tell her how much I love her, and will miss her but I'm happy she won't suffer any more."

Paddy, Kitty, Larry, and I surround Mommy and hug together.

Larry looks confused and disturbed by all this.

"Can we go visit Nana in heaven?" he asks.

This brings welcome relief as Mommy says, "No, Larry, I'm afraid we can't visit Nana in heaven, but we'll see her again when we go to heaven."

Mommy pulls us all together in her loving embrace where we cuddle and cry together. The realization that I can't see Nana again until we meet in heaven is so painful. Burying my head in Mommy's arms, thoughts of Nana flood my mind. She looks so vibrant, so young, filled with more joy than I have ever seen. Surrounding her are many other happy people who I sense Nana knows and loves. By them are angels of all sizes with white feathery wings. Nana is in good company... and she will never again be lonely or sad.

While Nana is now perfectly happy, Daddy is not. He is grieving terribly, devastated at the loss of his beloved mother. Normally very talkative, he hasn't said a word to anyone. Nana's death has cast a heavy, morbid pallor of grief and darkness over our family and our home. In keeping with our Irish tradition during a funeral wake, no radio or television is played, family members dress in black, no one speaks unnecessarily, and our relatives are expected to come to our home before or after the wake each day. This means we will be seeing many family members during the traditional wake of three days and nights followed by the funeral Mass on the fourth day at Nana's church, St. Monica's.

Since Nana is on Daddy's side of the family, members of Mommy's family are expected to come over to help with babysitting, cleaning the apartment, doing the laundry, shopping for food, cooking, and whatever else is helpful. And so, Mommy has arranged for her sister, Aunt Vera, to bring her sixteen-year-old daughter, Margaret Mary, to come babysit us. That will make it possible for Mommy to go to the funeral home each afternoon and evening with Daddy and the rest of Daddy's family.

Earlier, Mommy reminded Larry that Aunt Vera is his godmother who sponsored him at his Baptism in St. Monica's Church. Mommy has never mentioned who Larry's Godfather is. I wonder why?

Daddy's brothers and sisters are now somberly gathered in our kitchen consoling one another with pleasant stories of Nana. Aunt Marion, Aunt Dotsy, Uncle Eddie, Uncle Donny, and Uncle Buddy are taking turns sharing something special they remember.

Poor Daddy. He is just sitting there by the kitchen window alternately looking out the window then back down at the floor. His heart is broken with the loss of his beloved mother. His eyes are puffy and red. Tears flow down his face in a continuous stream. I feel so sad watching him suffer like this that a painful lump forms in my throat.

"Bbrring, bbrring," the front door bell rings bringing a welcome feeling of relief as it announces the arrival downstairs of new family members. This seems to lift everyone's spirit's a bit. I guess we all feel more secure when we have lots of people around us in times of personal loss and crisis like this.

Silence falls upon our household as Daddy slowly gets up and trudges over to push the buzzer to the right of our front door. Ringing this bell, as usual, allows the entrance door downstairs to be opened by whoever rang our bell in the ground floor foyer. Daddy opens the door and stands there. Everyone is quiet as we all join him in listening to the footsteps in the hallway downstairs. Judging by the sound of many heavy thunderous footsteps, it is clear to everyone that our large Aunt Vera, skinny Uncle Emil, and our girl cousins, Margaret Mary and Flossy, have arrived. Everyone knows that this part of Mommy's family is quite large.

A smile graces Daddy's face as our eyes meet and we communicate without saying a word. We are amused that we can tell who is coming simply by the sound of their footsteps… their very heavy footsteps.

Soon, greetings and condolences are exchanged among the adults. I am surprised that no one offers condolences to me or to the other children of our family. I have also suffered a terrible loss. My Nana has died and I miss her so badly. When we children are finally greeted, it is subdued compared to what we are accustomed to receiving during happier times. Margaret Mary assures Mommy and Daddy that everything will be fine while they are at the funeral home. Daddy cautions us to behave, to remain respectfully quiet, and to go to bed when we are told.

Without wasting any time, Mommy and Daddy put on their coats, and give each of us a kiss goodnight. Our uncles and aunts do the same before marching out the kitchen door, one at a time. Soon, they are all gone, and the door closes behind the last one out, Daddy.

Standing in silence, we listen to the sound of their many footsteps echoing in the hall until the door downstairs opens then closes confirming their departure from the building.

Margaret Mary gathers us together in the kitchen to give us a little talk. Sitting around the kitchen table, we look up at her as she stands there smiling. She is in her mid-teens but looks much older. Mommy told us earlier not to talk about Margaret Mary's weight because she weighs about four hundred pounds, and is very sensitive. Despite this, Margaret Mary is very pretty, kind, and loving to us.

"Now listen, kids," she begins, but Paddy interrupts her to register a complaint.

"Don't call us kids, Margaret Mary, we're grown-up too, you know!"

Margaret Mary looks surprised and laughs, "I'm sorry, Paddy, I know you're grown-up too! I was a kid once too, you know. The word, 'Kids,' is just a term for people your age, that's all. But I promise, I won't call you 'kids' any more.

"Now, what was I saying? Oh, I started to say that I understand that you must be feeling very sad about your Nana dying, but there is something you should realize. Your Nana has gone to heaven where all of us will be going someday... if, of course, you are good and live a good life.

"Up there, Nana is very, very happy because she is with God, the Blessed Mother, all the angels and saints including her own mother and father and all the other people she loves who died before her. There is no pain or suffering in heaven, you know... only happiness and joy. Isn't that wonderful?"

"I know," I tell her, "I saw Nana and all those beautiful people with her!"

"Wow, that's wonderful!" Margaret Mary says.

"God lets Bobby see things like that," Kitty explains.

Paddy asks, "Do the people in heaven have bodies?"

"No, Paddy, their bodies stay down here on earth when they die. Only their soul goes to heaven."

"What happens to Nana's body then?" Paddy follows up.

"Well, her body is put in a coffin which they keep at home or at a funeral parlor for three days so that family and friends can come to see her one more time, one last time, before she is buried. This also gives everyone a chance to console one another. Your Nana Walsh is being 'waked' at Connolly's Funeral Home on 79th Street right across from St. Monica's Church."

"What do they do with Nana after that?" Kitty asks before Paddy can ask another question.

Margaret Mary, pauses before answering.

"They drive her body in the coffin in a long, black car called a 'hearse' to church where the family prays for her soul during a special Mass for people who have died. The Mass is called a 'funeral Mass.' After the Mass, the priest goes with everyone to a cemetery where the people who have died are buried. There, gravediggers have already dug a hole for her grave. The hole they dig is six-feet deep."

"Who carries Nana and her coffin to and from the funeral parlor, and is Nana's funeral Mass going to be at St. Monica's?" Paddy asks.

"Our Irish tradition is that the men in the family carry the coffin into and out of the church. After Nana has her funeral Mass at St. Monica's, her coffin will be driven in the hearse to First Calvary Cemetery in Queens where she will be buried. The family goes along with her on this final journey."

"How do you know where her body is buried in the ground after they cover it up?" Kitty wonders out loud.

"There's a white stone with her name on it that is placed right above her grave. It is called a 'headstone' because it is positioned right above where Nana's head is located in the ground," Margaret Mary explains.

Margaret Mary, appearing anxious to move on to other topics, says, "Enough of this talk for now, kids. What do you say we play some games in the living room?"

We follow her walking through the rooms in single file as Mommy taught us to do with our hands on the person's shoulders in front of us. I turn back to see little Geri thoroughly enjoying this as she crawls along after us. Looking straight ahead, all I can see is Margaret Mary because she is so tall and wide. The floors strain under her enormous weight creating a chorus of squeaking noises.

In the living room, Margaret Mary eases herself down onto the couch and encourages us to play "Ring around the Rosie" in the middle of the floor. Hurrying to accommodate her, we form a circle holding hands then circle to our left as we sing,

"Ring around the rosies,
A pocket full of posies,
Ashes, ashes we all fall down!"

At this, we all fall down throwing ourselves to the floor as we giggle loudly. Geri, naturally much slower at this than the rest of us, is the last one to throw herself down after which she proudly claps her hands heartily congratulating herself. After repeating this routine several times, I remember that Daddy said we are not supposed to play games or laugh during this time of mourning in respect for Nana's loss.

I remind Margaret Mary of this but she shrugs and says, "I know, honey, but a little fun isn't going to hurt anyone. We'll keep this as our secret, okay kids? Don't tell Mommy or Daddy about playing games otherwise they'll be angry with me and won't let me stay with you again. You don't want that to happen, now do you?"

After quick mischievous glances to one another, Paddy, Larry, and I tease her by shouting together, **"Yes!"** After pretending that we are going to tell on her, we finally assure her that we'll keep it a secret.

"Margaret Mary, what does "Ring around the Rosies" mean? Where does that game come from?" Larry asks.

Margaret Mary, looking surprised by the question, pauses before answering, "That's a very good question, Larry."

Thinking she has the answer, Kitty blurts out, "It's probably just a song for singing around a circle of roses. That's all."

Margaret Mary says, "That's a good guess, Kitty, but here is the answer. This song was sung by people during the 'Black Plague' in Europe that killed thousands of people. The ring is a red circle around each sore, and the pocket full of posies is what the people believed would keep the Plague away. The expression, 'ashes, ashes all fall down,' refers to what they thought was going to happen to all of them anyway, sooner or later."

"All right, enough of this," she continues, "how about playing 'Hide and Seek' with me?"

Margaret Mary volunteers to be "it," and tells us that the home base of safety will be the living room couch where she is sitting. While Margaret Mary covers her eyes with her hands and counts to ten, we run through the rooms seeking places to hide from her.

Paddy hides somewhere in the room right next to the living room where Margaret Mary continues counting slowly. Kitty takes Geri with her to hide in the bathroom. I am sure they will get caught because Geri constantly giggles. As usual, Larry runs with me so we can hide together. I want to hide in the kitchen under the table because I know Margaret Mary will never see us in the dark.

Looking to the kitchen, however, I see the familiar ominous black figure of the demon standing in front of the window! I stop next to the bed in the room before the kitchen, and look to see what it is doing. It just stands there radiating hatred at me. I grab Larry's hand and pull him down under the bed with me. This feels like a safe place away from the demon… and a good place to hide from Margaret Mary since she is far too big to get down on her knees to look under the bed.

"Here I come, ready or not!" Margaret Mary calls out loudly.

The sound of the couch moving under her enormous weight indicates she is rising to search for us. There is very little light for Margaret Mary to see anything because all the lights in our apartment are off, and it is very dark outside now.

I can hear her heavy footsteps lumbering slowly through the rooms

142

as she searches for us. When she reaches the bed where Larry and I are hiding, she pauses and stands quietly listening for telltale sounds to detect where we are hiding. Quietly chuckling, we look out at her enormous feet bulging out of her shoes only two feet from our faces!

Suddenly Margaret Mary shouts triumphantly, "Tap, tap, Larry standing by the kitchen window, one, two, three! You're caught, Larry. Now go to home-base and stay there until somebody frees you!"

Since Larry is right here next to me, and I know Paddy, Kitty, and Geri are not in the kitchen, I realize that Margaret Mary must be seeing the demon! This is very bad that it is showing itself to her.

"Where did you disappear to, Larry?" Margaret Mary asks as the demon apparently vanishes.

"You know, when you're caught," she continues, "you're supposed to go to home-base. You are **not** supposed to go hide somewhere else. That's cheating! Now come on, Larry, do what you are supposed to do."

Margaret Mary knows for her to catch someone, she must correctly name who she sees. Unfortunately for her, she doesn't realize that what she saw wasn't one of us, it was a demon lurking in the shadows by the kitchen window.

When there is no answer, she deducts, "Perhaps that wasn't Larry; perhaps it was someone else... like Paddy... or Bobby. It's too dark for me to tell from here, but when I get closer... someone is going to get caught!"

The sounds of hushed words and giggling can be heard coming from the bathroom.

"Ah, ha! I hear some noisy little people in the bathroom," Margaret Mary announces.

Opening the bathroom door, there is an outburst of laughter from Geri.

"Tap, tap, Kitty and Geri sitting in the bathtub. You two have been caught; now you have to go to home-base on the couch to see if anyone can free you," Margaret Mary says victoriously.

I lay my right cheek against the ice-cold linoleum floor with my face turned toward the open area next to our bed so I can watch when their feet pass by.

Suddenly, the French doors by the living room violently slam closed creating a thunderous sound. That's a very bad sign. The demon does things like this to challenge and frighten us. We are all in extreme danger. Margaret Mary rushes out of the bathroom, and stands in the doorway of the room we are in.

Looking in the direction of the French doors, she says, "I see someone has beaten me back to home-base. Who is that I see standing there in the middle of the living room? Hmmm, judging by that height, that must be you, Paddy. Is that you, Paddy?"

There is no answer. Margaret Mary is in mortal danger.

When no one answers, she calls loudly out through the rooms, "Well, ready or not, here I come!"

I watch as Kitty, carrying Geri, follows her as captured prisoners. Standing in front of the French doors, Margaret Mary finds that she cannot open the French doors. They appear to be jammed or locked... but I know that the French doors do not have locks. Grunting loudly and using her enormous weight and strength, Margaret Mary pushes hard against the doors as she turns the knobs of both doors.

The doors don't budge!

Exasperated, she shouts, "All right, who's the wise guy in there who locked the doors? Come on, answer me!. If that's you, Paddy, quit fooling around and open these doors right now!"

Again, there is only silence in the last room beyond the French doors.

"All right, now I'm **really** getting mad. Paddy, I can see you in there! Open these doors!" Margaret Mary angrily demands again.

Larry and I crawl out from under the bed and go stand behind Margaret Mary as she stands in front of the glass-paneled French doors. Geri, looking scared, clings onto Kitty.

Paddy now comes out from under the bed to our right unnoticed by Margaret Mary who remains engrossed in getting the French doors open. She bends over and peers into the living room through the sheer curtains on the right French door.

As she does, I realize what she sees once again is the demon.

"Paddy, I can see you standing in there, now quit fooling around and unlock these doors! When your parents get home, you're going to be in real trouble!" she threatens.

Still there is no motion or sound coming from inside the living room so Margaret Mary again violently pushes and pulls on the glass knob handles. Despite her massive size and strength, the doors still do not open.

"Paddy, open these doors," she thunders, "Do you hear me?"

I pull on Margaret Mary's dress, and tell her, "Margaret Mary, Paddy is right here with us!"

Her head snaps over and sees Paddy standing with us in the darkened room. Looking confused, she quickly looks over the rest of us and realizes that all of us are here. Instantly, she realizes that the black shadowed figure she sees in the living room is not one of us!

With eyes bulging, Margaret Mary turns and looks once again into the living room through the curtains of the French doors. Just then, the right

French door slowly creaks open by itself, and cold, musty air blows out from the living room and passes right over us!

Margaret Mary's hands begin shaking as she turns toward the kitchen and tells us, "Quickly, come with me, kids."

Walking in single file, we follow her through the rooms to the safety of the kitchen far away from the French doors… and the demon in the living room. Margaret Mary gathers us close to her and puts her arms around us for safety. I sense this is as much for her comfort as it is for ours. Everyone is frightened, myself included, so I call out to God for His protection against this powerful, audacious demon.

Margaret Mary sits down on a chair by the kitchen closet. Shaking and crying, she realizes that what her family calls "a ghost" is in the living room, and she doesn't know what to do about it. I recall now how Mommy once told me that Margaret Mary and her sister, Flossy, are deathly afraid of "ghosts." Moonlight pours in through the Venetian blinds silhouetting her large trembling body in the darkened kitchen. We stand in silence by Margaret Mary as she wonders what to do. Considering her vulnerability, I realize that I must help my teenage cousin.

Terror still glistens in her eyes as she gasps, "I'm afraid of ghosts, kids, and I'm afraid there's one in that last room. Let's stay out here where it's safe. Whatever you do, do not leave this room, kids; stay right here with me. Tell me if you see anything moving around anywhere!"

I tell her, "Margaret Mary, do you remember how you earlier thought it was one of us in the kitchen by the window? It wasn't us. Larry was next to me under the bed, and Paddy was under the other bed in the room next to the living room."

She looks befuddled, "Well, Kitty and Geri were hiding in the bath tub, so who did I see in the kitchen?"

Paddy says, "It must have been the same ghost; Bobby sees them all the time."

Something Mommy once told me comes to mind, "Mommy told us that God lets people who are stuck in purgatory appear to us as ghosts so they can let us know they need prayers to get out of purgatory and go into the paradise part of heaven. They're allowed to appear as ghosts to family members. The ghosts can move doors as a sign that they need help to pass through the door between purgatory and paradise."

Margaret Mary snaps, "I don't want to hear any more talk about ghosts. Be quiet! No more talk!"

"Okay, Margaret Mary," I answer.

The only sound in the apartment now is the ticking of our Big Ben alarm clock. It's loud, familiar cadence is comforting to hear as we huddle anxiously by Margaret Mary. After a while, everyone starts to relax… except me.

Margaret Mary is trying to maintain her fragile control, but noticing my uneasiness, she asks, "What's the matter, Bobby? Do you see something?"

Sensing that something unusual is about to happen, something unpleasant, I tell her, "We have a large black cat that's crazy, Margaret Mary. Its name is Blackie. I call it a 'demon-cat,' a creature of the night, because it runs wildly through the rooms all night long until it gets tired. Sometimes, it runs sideways on the walls and even jumps on the windows without getting hurt! Mommy tells us if we get up during the night and Blackie sees us, he'll attack and scratch us badly! I'm afraid that Blackie is going to come out soon and start running crazy."

Margaret Mary sobs, "You stop that! Don't you be telling me such crazy, scary things! There's no such thing as a 'demon cat!'"

Margaret Mary hasn't seen Blackie yet because he stays hidden under the bed in the second room until late at night when he comes out and goes crazy. During the day, he sneaks out to eat his food in the kitchen, then runs back under the bed. He gets water by perching himself on the toilet seat and leaning down to drink from the toilet bowl. He really is a crazy cat.

It is strange to see such a large, grown person so frightened like this. I know I shouldn't talk about Blackie any more, however, I sense that Blackie is about to do something scary. I also have the feeling something sinister and dangerous is high up behind us. Slowly, I inch away from the corner closet and move toward the doorway to the next room.

Margaret Mary, noticing what I am doing, snaps, "What're you doing, Bobby? Why are you backing away? Do you see something bad? Tell me!"

I am too frightened to answer or look up at the top of the closet in the corner behind where she is sitting. Everyone else joins me in backing away and stands now in the eerie moonlight streaming in through the kitchen window on the right side of the room. I summon the courage to look up to where I sense danger.

There, perched high on top of the closet is our crazy family cat, Blackie. He is frozen still with his body arched as if in a state of rigor mortis. Its hair is standing outward like porcupine needles, its tail pointed is upward at a forty-five degree angle, and its sharp white teeth are menacingly braced as if it is going to bite. Blackie's eyes pierce the darkness with a fiery orange glow. It really is like a 'demon cat.'

Following the direction of my eyes, Margaret Mary looks up to see the distorted condition of our crazy black cat. She instantly explodes from her chair in a mad dash to safety. Her face has become a mask of sheer terror as she runs wildly… right in my direction! Her uncontrolled stampede leaves me little choice but to dive out of the way to avoid being trampled by her. I can understand the panic she feels after seeing the hideous appearance of Blackie exuding the very appearance of evil.

I jump on the bed in the second room and settle in the welcome sanctuary of this familiar bed. I watch in horror as Blackie in his diabolical condition chases after Margaret Mary who is now screaming as she rambles madly through the rooms.

"Help me, somebody, help me!" she screams.

Running after Margaret Mary, Blackie leaps onto the bureau in the second room then leaps forward onto the bureau in the next room. I listen to the sounds of Margaret Mary throwing herself heavily onto the couch in the living room as she alternately cries and screams for help. A metallic crashing sound from inside the living room evokes another blood-curdling scream from Margaret Mary. Blackie has catapulted himself from a dead run onto the middle ledge of the right living room window... through the metal Venetian blinds!

I can never understand how Blackie, a large cat running at great speed, can do this without breaking the window.

In her desperate attempt to evade the marauding cat that is now perched perilously by the right living room window, Margaret Mary bolts up from the couch and runs back out through the rooms toward the kitchen. Out there, she stands looking back through the darkened rooms and sobs pitifully. Paddy, Larry, and Kitty holding Geri, rush onto the bed next to me.

"Quick, get under the covers before it comes back," Paddy orders us.

Does Paddy mean Blackie, or our large rampaging cousin? I quickly deduct he must mean Blackie. Each of us scrambles to get under the covers as quickly as possible, and huddle together. There is a distinct feeling of security that comes in numbers.

Curious to watch what happens next, we peek out from the covers and lean over the bed to see what happens. Soon we hear Blackie burst out from where he is positioned on the inside window creating another crashing noise from the blinds in there. He lands hard upon the floor with his claws making their distinctive sound. Then he springs up onto the arm of the armchair by the left French door, leaps down onto the floor of the next room, and continues his mad dash.

Horrified to see the crazy black cat bounding out through the rooms heading directly at her, Margaret Mary screams again. We see Blackie leap madly onto the top of the bureau in the next room, then, in a maddening jump, leaps into our room landing squarely on top of the dresser right across from us.

Margaret Mary has collapsed into a sitting position on the kitchen floor facing the rooms. Good thing she did. In a flash, Blackie leaps out onto the kitchen floor right in front of her then springs high up in the air over Margaret Mary's left shoulder! Crashing into the kitchen window blinds once again, Blackie has once again landed safely on the tiny ledge between the upper and lower windows without breaking the window! One of these times, he is going to crash through the closed window and fall down to his death in the yard below.

Margaret Mary, crazed with fear, struggles to her feet and stumbles mightily through the rooms returning to the living room couch again where she throws herself down crying and praying.

From where I am, I can see Blackie poised perfectly still on the ledge, positioned as if it is ready to pounce on anyone who enters the kitchen. His eyes glow ominously through the darkness with a threatening glare in my direction. For a moment, it seems as if the demon has taken control of Blackie.

Margaret Mary calls out, "Children, where are you?"

"We're in here, Margaret Mary, on the bed by the kitchen," I answer.

"Please come in here and keep me company 'til my parents come back," she begs.

Her words echo strangely through the rooms sounding as if she is in a cave.

"We can't," I answer for all of us. "The cat is watching us from the kitchen window. If we get up, it will chase us and attack us with its claws and teeth. I told you it is a 'demon-cat."

Blackie moves about as I speak, apparently positioning itself to spring at any moment if one of us gets up.

"Don't talk about that cat, Bobby! I want you to stop it right now, do you hear me? You're trying to scare me. You just wait 'til your father gets home; he's going to give you the beating of your life when I tell him what you've done to me!"

After a pause, she asks, "Did any of you see where the ghost went?"

"I don't know," I answer. "But if I were you, I would keep my eyes closed and pray!"

"Stop it! Stop it!" she screams. "I don't want to hear another word from you!"

A low, menacing growl rumbles through the rooms from the kitchen causing us all to scurry under the sanctuary of our covers. It didn't sound like Blackie's kind of growl.

Margaret Mary calls out, "Very funny, Bobby. You just wait 'til your parents come home and I tell them what you've done. I thought you were a good boy; I can't believe how mean you are."

"That's not me who growled," I warn her. "It was the demon or Blackie that did it. If anything comes in there after you, close your eyes, make the Sign of the Cross, and pray to God."

"Stop it! Stop it!" she screams again. "Now look what you've done; you made me wet myself!"

After I pray again for God's help, peace and silence descend upon our home. No one speaks as we snuggle securely together under the covers. Eventually, sleep mercifully falls upon us... and apparently upon Blackie as well... but not poor Margaret Mary.

We are asleep when Mommy and Daddy finally arrive home from the funeral parlor with Aunt Vera, Uncle Emil, and Flossy. They are all speaking loudly as usual. Margaret Mary is practically hysterical as she tells them about how she saw a ghost, and how the 'demon-cat' terrified her as it ran back and forth through the rooms all night.

Aunt Vera is very upset, "Oh, my poor baby. This is terrible."

Aunt Vera hugs her sobbing daughter and strokes her hair and tells her that everything is all right now. She is safe.

"Mommy and Daddy are here now; no ghost or crazy cat is going to hurt you."

It is beautiful how Aunt Vera still regards Margaret Mary as her baby. That is the way I think God feels about each of us. No matter how big or old we get, God still loves us as His little children.

Unfortunately, Uncle Emil is not as sympathetic, "Ghost, 'demon-cat,' my foot! You're a 'big baby!' Uncle Emil chides her. "Your little cousins tell you some ghost stories and a little black cat runs around, and you pee all over yourself and the couch. You should be ashamed of yourself!"

Judging by what Uncle Emil said, I am guessing there is urine all over the couch and the floor inside.

"There really was a ghost here, Pop; I saw it! And that is no little cat; it really is a 'demon-cat!'"

Uncle Emil scoffs, "demon-cat, ghosts. Phooey! The only thing running around here is your imagination! You're beginning to sound just like your mother... believing in ghosts and goblins!"

My God, Uncle Emil doesn't believe in the existence of ghosts and evil spirits! He doesn't realize how terribly wrong he is. I pray he is never put to the test.

"All right, all right, that's enough!" Aunt Vera yells at him. "You leave Margaret Mary alone! She's your daughter, remember? I'd like to see how you'd react if the same things happened to you, you old grouch. You'd probably go running out into the street crying for help!"

Ignoring what Aunt Vera said, Uncle Emil snaps, "We gotta get going. I'm sure Ellie and Pat can use some time alone together, and we have a **long** trip home to Brooklyn."

"Talk about being a big baby, there he goes complaining about taking a few trains," Aunt Vera chides him.

Since Aunt Vera is quite combative right now, Uncle Emil lowers his head and sulks over to the front door without saying another word.

"I love my little cousins, but boy am I glad I didn't stay here with you tonight," Flossy says to Margaret Mary.

"I wish you were here, Flossy. I was so scared. It was terrible!" Margaret Mary confesses.

"Aunt Ellie, I'm sorry but I can't come back here again to babysit tomorrow night… or ever! I'm too scared."

Aunt Vera jumps right in before Mommy can say anything, "That's all right, honey. I'm sure Aunt Ellie and Uncle Pat understand."

"Ellie, it sounds like your kids could have been a lot kinder tonight, especially Bobby. After all, she **was** here to help out by babysitting so you and Pat could go to the wake. Teasing her and scaring her about a ghost and a 'demon-cat,' is way out of line. I am very disappointed. You have to do a better job with the kids, Ellie. What they did was cruel."

Daddy, trying to lighten the moment, says, "The only cruel thing in this house is Ellie's cooking!"

Over Daddy's laughter, Aunt Vera quips, "Oh, yeah? Looking at your size, buddy, your wife must be a world-class chef! You look **pretty well** taken care of."

Daddy suddenly gets emotional, "Yeah, that's true, Vera. That's true… in more ways than one. I don't know what I'd do without my Ellie."

Teary-eyed, Daddy steps over to Mommy and puts his arms around her, and buries his head on her shoulder. I am so sad to see Daddy heart-broken like this, but I am comforted in knowing he has another mother figure, Mommy, to offset the terrible loss of Nana.

Thank God for the gift of all the mothers in our lives.

Chapter 16

FOREVER SCARRED

May 1952

Larry and I have become very close this past year spending virtually all our free time together.

It is bedtime now so we are in bed together in the room off the kitchen. All the activities in our home have quieted down except for the sound of the television blaring in the living room where the rest of our family is gathered. Although Larry is only five years old, he is quite precocious and highly-intelligent. And so it is that he listens attentively and understands what I tell him about the strange things that have happened to me since that first terrifying experience in the crib when I was only a baby.

"The demon scares me just being around," I tell him. "It knows when I sense that it is present. When Blackie the cat attacked me when I was in the crib, it was in the room. There was also the time that a dog attacked me on my way to my very first Mass at St. Monica's. I'm sure that Blackie was encouraged by the demon to attack me. Blackie and the demon were chased away by a beautiful bright light that came when I cried out to God for help."

"What about the dog?" Larry asks.

"Daddy saved me from the vicious dog when he kicked it high in the air and yelled at the lady who owned the dog. You should have seen how the two of them ran down the street!"

"Bobby, how do you know when the demon is around if you can't see it?"

"I can only see it when it shows itself to me... but I can always feel its presence when it is near me. There's something deep inside me that warns me. It is as clear as hearing a big truck roaring up behind me. I don't have to see it to know when it's nearby."

"Is there a demon around us right now?" he asks obviously concerned.

"No."

Larry asks if I will let him know if I see one so he could try to see it also, or at least to sense its presence. I tell him that I do sense something high above us where we are on the bed. I can see something in my mind's eye. It looks like a giant cockroach up on the ceiling with it back to us.

"It's about as big as me, Larry, and it's just staying up there. It looks very brown and disgusting."

Pointing up in its direction, Larry asks, "Right up there?"

151

"Yes," I tell him.

"I don't see any roach, Bobby. Maybe the demon is trying to trick you."

"Yes," I assure him.

But then the vision of the giant cockroach appears to start descending. In my mind's eye, I see the roach's hair-thin legs wiggling down closer and closer to us.

Alarmed, I shout, "The roach is coming down on us, Larry! Quick, let's get out of here!"

In a flash, Larry climbs over me and jumps out of the bed on the run as he quickly disappears out of the room with me only half a step behind him. In the next room, we dive onto the safety of the bed and bury ourselves under the soft, woolen blankets.

After a few minutes, we decide it is safe to poke our heads out to see if the roach, or anything else, has followed us. There are no roaches, real or imaginary, that can be seen anywhere. Only the sounds of the television can be heard blaring away in the next room where the rest of the family is gathered unaware of our dilemma.

I realize now that the devil placed the image of the giant roach in my mind's eye to scare us.

Larry asks, "Do you see anything in here, Bobby?"

I cast my eyes cautiously about the room hoping **not** to see anything sinister. Unfortunately, I see the dark ominous shadow of the devil stationed right in front of the left French door! It is posed perfectly still, facing us, emanating pure hatred at Larry and me.

I whisper this bad news to Larry who squints his eyes and stares intently at the doors before saying, "I don't see anything over there, Bobby."

I can see it standing perfectly still facing us. Its appearance is familiar - a dark, black shrouded figure about four feet tall with no distinguishable facial or other features.

Larry leans over and cups his hand around my ear as he whispers in barely audible words, "What do you think will happen if I go over there and punch it as hard as I can? Do you think it will go away?"

This sounds so ridiculous, I tell him, "You can't punch a demon, Larry; demons don't have bodies. They are spirits so you can't hit them."

"Well, maybe it will get annoyed and go away," Larry reasons, "I'm going to give it a real good punch."

Before I can say anything, Larry jumps off the bed and hurries over to the left French door, and in one flashing motion, wickedly swings his left arm at where he believes the devil is standing! I watch in horror as Larry's arm passes right through the demon and crashes through one of the small

152

glass panes on the left French door! As he pulls his arm back out across the broken glass, blood suddenly spurts out of the middle of his left arm!

Shards of glass fly everywhere covered with blood from his arm. Larry turns and looks at me with shock and fear on his face. I don't know what to do as he walks over to me and sits on the bed.

The devil, having accomplished its goal, has now vanished.

Mommy and Daddy come quickly running into the room. As soon as Mommy puts the light on and sees Larry's arm bleeding profusely, she cries out and collapses onto the floor with a loud thud! She is unconscious.

Daddy's eyes are bulging as he grabs a pillow from the bed and shakes it upside down until the pillow falls out. He nervously rolls the pillowcase into the shape of a large rectangular bandage that he wraps tightly around Larry's entire forearm to stop the terrible bleeding. Larry winces as Daddy tightly wraps the injury hoping to stop the bleeding.

Larry looks so scared. His eyes are filled with fear, panic and tears. My heart aches as if it is going to explode from fear and grief as I watch the ominous appearance of blood begin to seep through the white pillow case around my poor little brother's arm. Daddy also seeing the blood appear begins to look scared himself.

"Please take Larry to the hospital, Daddy," I plead.

"I am, I am. Take it easy, everyone. Everything's going to be all right. Just relax. It's only a small cut, no big deal. He'll be all right," Daddy reassures us all.

Mommy has composed herself and risen from the floor.

"Patsy, keep your hand on the wound to stop the bleeding. Pick him up and carry him, and make sure to hold onto his arm. Let's get a taxi on York Avenue and take him to Misericordia Hospital on 86th Street."

Daddy tells us, "Say a prayer, kids, and keep the door locked until we come back home. Paddy, you look after the family while I'm gone."

The fact that Daddy is speaking so loudly tells me that he **really is** greatly distressed by Larry's injury but he is trying to act calmly to reassure us... and Larry.

The three of them quickly disappear out the front door with Larry cuddled securely in Daddy's powerful arms. Paddy, Kitty, Geri, and I are left standing there numb and frightened as we listen to the sound of their footsteps hurrying down the stairs and finally out the building's front door.

We stand together hugging and crying. I am so shocked and mesmerized by this terrible thing that has happened to my little brother. The trail of red blood spots on the floor by the front door leading back to the left French door graphically remind me of the serious nature of Larry's injury.

Marshaling all my spiritual resources, I beg God to help my little brother, "Please God, please heal Larry's arm."

"Who are you talking to, Bobby? Are you crazy?"

I look up to see Paddy hovering over me.

"I was praying for Larry," I explain.

"Praying for Larry, heh? You're always talking out loud like that to yourself; someday you're going to wind up in one of those crazy houses for loonies!"

"I was **praying**," I correct him.

"What happened to Larry? Why did he put his arm through the glass door like that? Did you have something to do with that?"

Under the circumstances, I know it is best not to tell Paddy what happened. I don't think he, Kitty, or Geri would understand... or forgive me.

So I simply answer, "I don't know what happened; I turned around when I heard the crash and saw Larry standing by the French door bleeding."

They look skeptical, apparently suspicious that I know more about what happened than I am sharing. Paddy reminds us that he is in charge now, and suggests that we all should sit together in the living room and say a prayer for Larry. Once we are settled, I ask God to heal Larry's arm.

Paddy tells us we can watch television until Larry, Mommy and Daddy return. Geri is tucked comfortably between Kitty and me on the sofa while Paddy sits in an armchair facing us at an angle. Kitty tells us that tonight reminds her of the time Larry had to go the hospital to have his appendix taken out.

"Mommy told me he almost died then; that is why they kept him in the hospital so long."

"Yeah," Paddy chimes in, "I remember that he waited too long to tell Mommy that his tummy was hurting."

I think back to that evening when all our uncles and aunts had gathered at our home, just as they have every time something bad has happened in our family. Aunt Dotsy had come into the bedroom off the kitchen where we were jumping up and down on the bed. She scolded me, grabbing me by the shoulders as I stood on the mattress.

I felt so sad when she admonished me saying, "What's the matter with you, Bobby? Don't you know how to obey? Don't you realize your baby brother is in the hospital being operated on right now, and may die! I can't believe how naughty you are! Now you stop jumping on the bed, lie down, and say a prayer that your little brother will be all right!"

I remember how shocked and frightened I was to hear this at the time because I had not realized that Larry was so sick that he might die and not come home! I only knew that Mommy and Daddy had to rush him to the hospital because his tummy hurt, and that it was hard and swollen. I remember seeing his tummy like that when he was lying on the bed just before Daddy carried him out to the hospital. Aunt Marion had come over to watch us then and told Paddy, Kitty, and me to pray that the doctors would make Larry all better.

Larry later arrived home with a long, thick scar on his right side. At the time, the family spoke about how the doctors at the hospital were amazed that Larry' appendix had not burst… it was at the point of bursting only moments away.

I am so frightened as I crawl under the covers and pray fervently for his healing. I ask God to send His healing graces down upon Larry in the hospital. A tingling sensation pours over me. That usually indicates that God is answering my prayer. I picture Larry resting on a table with a bright light above him as the doctor and nurses work on his injured arm.

Much later, Larry arrives home with Mommy and Daddy. He has a large white bandage covering his entire forearm. Paddy asks him what the doctor did to fix his arm.

Larry says, "He gave me some needles in the arm so I didn't feel any more pain; then he fixed the cut."

"Were you scared?" Kitty wants to know.

"Yeah, I was very scared, Kitty, until a big white light appeared above me. Then I felt okay."

Chapter 17

THE POLO GROUNDS

June 1952

Since Larry's terrible injury early last month, and Nana's death four months ago, our home has not been the same. Daddy is so sad looking all the time, and hardly ever talks to Mommy... or to any of us children. Sometimes he just stands at the front left window looking out at nothing in particular. There are two things he still does regularly, however: smoke Chesterfield cigarettes, and drink A & P tea.

I guess if my Mommy just died, I, too, would be very sad.

In an effort to try to cheer Daddy up, Mommy told Paddy and me she is going to get Daddy to take us to a New York Giants baseball game at their ballpark, the Polo Grounds. She said if anything could take his mind off losing Nana, it would be his Giants... especially if they beat their archrivals, the Brooklyn Dodgers!

"They are playing each other at the Polo Grounds this coming Thursday, the 26th, and that is Daddy's day off. Let's see what I can arrange … and pray that the game is not rained out," Mommy says hopefully.

I ask God to keep the rain away from New York City this Thursday.

Thursday quickly arrives and Mommy's plan looks like it is going to work! It looks like our prayers have been answered for good weather since the sun is shining brightly this morning. Brilliant light streaming in through our kitchen window has set our entire apartment ablaze with glorious sunshine. In the living room in the front of our apartment, there also is a bright, almost blinding, sunshine coming in from a reflection off the glass windows of the buildings directly across the street from us.

"Well, God has done His job, now it is up to you boys... and the Giants... to cheer up your father," Mommy tells us.

Daddy has agreed to bring Paddy, Larry and me to see the Giants play baseball at the Polo Grounds in uptown Manhattan. This is our first trip to the ballpark ever and we are thrilled at the prospect of seeing our team in person especially since they are playing their archrivals, the Brooklyn Dodgers today.

Mommy has packed some sandwiches for us and tells us, "Stay close to your father at all times, boys, and hold each other's hands so you don't get separated and lost. Remember, if you do get lost, look for a cop and tell him your address where you live in Manhattan. He will get you home. Also, remember what I've said about talking to strangers, too. You don't talk to

156

anyone you don't know. Understand?"

"Yes, Mommy," we answer in unison before giving her a kiss goodbye.

"Oh, and Larry," she adds as an afterthought, "try to keep that bandage wrapping over you arm."

Larry agrees. He has not always been too careful about keeping that bandage in place especially when he plays.

When Daddy finally comes out of the bathroom, he heads for the front door where we boys are anxiously waiting for him.

"Oh, and one other thing," Mommy adds, "Don't be stupid like your father thinking the Giants can beat my Brooklyn Dodgers! They haven't got a ghost of a chance of winning!"

Mommy's remark is good-natured in its intent but she did grow up in Brooklyn and loves the Dodgers like most Brooklynites do. We understand this and take special enjoyment in teasing her whenever the Giants beat the Dodgers.

"We'll see who is laughing after the game is over," Daddy challenges her. "Meanwhile, you ladies take care of the roost while we 'men of the house' are out."

Daddy gives Kitty, Geri, and Mommy a big kiss, his famous "smushkypop," and off we go. Down in the street, East End Avenue is where we walk to then on to 79th Street where we board the cross-town bus. Daddy puts some coins in the fare box for himself and Paddy then tells the bus driver that Larry and I are under seven years old, and Daddy then gets some free transfers from the bus driver. Kids under seven ride for free.

We sit all the way in the very back of the bus where there is one long bench-like seat that goes from one side of the bus to the other. The bus's engine is so loud back here. I enjoy looking out the window at the many people and buildings as we pass by. Soon, Daddy announces that our stop is next so we should get up and stand near the rear exit from the bus. The bus is bouncing around so wildly I have to hold onto the back of a seat to avoid falling.

Daddy reaches up and pulls on a cord up near the ceiling. This causes a loud bell to ring up front by the bus driver.

"That's to let the driver know that we want to get off at the next bus stop," Daddy explains.

When the bus stops, we carefully climb down three steps leading out of the bus onto the street next to the curb. We follow Daddy over to join the back of a long line of people who are standing near the corner.

Daddy explains, "It's a good bet that everyone here is going to the Giant/Dodger game at the Polo Grounds. This bus will take us right to the

157

Polo Grounds where the game is going to be played today."

The man in front of Daddy turns around and says, "It's also a good bet that the Dodgers are **not** going to win today!"

"Are they all Giants fans like us, Daddy?" Larry wants to know.

"Only if they are smart!" Daddy laughs.

This sets off a chorus of cheers from several people on line who quite apparently are hearty Giants fans. Now it seems that they are competing to see who can say the most impressive thing about the merits of this year's Giants team.

Once the bus arrives, it is so crowded we are lucky to get on. We stand together jammed in the middle of the bus holding onto the back of the seats for balance as the bus bounces wildly making its way uptown over the city's bumpy streets on our way to the Polo Grounds. All the adults on the bus are in a happy mood.

The driver calls out, "If anyone needs to get off between here and the Polo Grounds, ring the bell, otherwise, I'm not going to make any more stops because the bus is already too full."

I notice now that there are a few colored men on the bus standing right next to us. They sound so happy, constantly laughing and smiling. Come to think of it, this is the closest I have ever been to a group of colored people in my whole life!

I don't recall ever seeing a colored person anywhere in Yorkville. There are no colored students or nuns in St. Monica's school, no colored priests or parishioners in church, no colored workers in local stores, in Carl Schurz Park, John Jay Park, John Jay Pool, the library, RKO or Loews movie theaters on 86th Street, no cops or firemen. In fact, there are no colored people anywhere in Yorkville. How strange.

Some of the men on the bus are smoking smelly cigars, others are smoking cigarettes. I hate the smell of thick, acrid tobacco smoke in the air. People should not be allowed to smoke around other people. Breathing in smoke has to be very harmful to our health.

Soon Daddy tells us we have arrived at the Polo Grounds on 155th Street and Eighth Avenue.

"Hold each other's hands real tight and stay close to me," Daddy tells us as we follow the crowd off the bus and join an even larger crowd walking quickly to the back of long lines of people in front of the ticket sales booths at the ballpark.

While waiting on line, Daddy strikes up a conversation with men on the other lines.

"I think the 'Bums' stink and belong in the minor leagues."

Daddy obviously says this to instigate playful debate among the

158

many Giant and Dodger fans standing on the lines. It did not take long to work.

Within seconds, several Dodger fans begin shouting, 'Then how come the Giants are always trying to play ball like the Dodgers?'

Giant fans respond by reminding them that the 'Bums' lost to the Giants last year in the playoff for the National League Pennant!

This brings momentary silence from the Dodger fans until one of them calls out, "Well how about our Carl Erskine pitching a no-hitter against the Chicago Cubs last week? I don't remember reading about any Giant pitcher throwing a no-hitter like that in a long, long, long time!"

Now that comment silences the Giants fans... for a while.

Now Daddy asks me a leading question, "Bobby, who do you think is going to win the National League Pennant **this year**?"

The men around us await my answer.

"That's easy," I say, "The best team is going to win!"

My comment unites Dodger and Giant fans together in a good laugh.

"Your kid is going to be a politician when he grows up," a Dodger fan quips.

Daddy corrects him, "Even better... he wants to be a priest."

That brings a truce between the warring fans until one says, "Oh, that's good. That way he can pray for the Giants to play like the Dodgers!"

Even Daddy laughs at this witty comment.

Once inside the ballpark, I survey the surroundings. The walls around the ball field are a dark green color and they're about twelve feet high except in centerfield where there are only about six feet high. I am impressed with the smell of beer and cigarette smoke everywhere. It seems that everyone around us is smoking and drinking beer out of white cardboard cups.

Our seats are very hard and uncomfortable. They're made of wooden slats. We are located in the lower deck in left field. From here, I can see the Giants players during batting practice. The Giants uniform is bright white with black and orange colors around the Giants name and the players' numbers. Their caps are black with the letters, NY, in orange on the front.

Daddy appears to be showing off his knowledge for the benefit of people sitting around us as he tells Paddy what he has told us at home a thousand times before, "The Polo Grounds were built during the 1890's, about sixty years ago. The park is located by a small cliff called 'Coogan's Bluff' on one side, and the Harlem River on the other. Just across the river is 'Yankee Stadium' in the Bronx. That is where the New York Yankees play in the American League. They usually have pretty good teams. You know, as much as we Giant and Dodger fans don't like each other's teams, **we all hate the Yankees!**

"For big games, 56,000 people can fit in the Polo Grounds because we have a double deck. It's pretty easy to hit a home run in the Polo Grounds because right field is only 257 feet long and left field is only 279 feet. If you hit the ball straight away, however, you are in big trouble because the centerfield wall is 483 feet away from home plate! To hit a home run there, you really have to belt it."

The players are running on the beautiful, green grass field throwing the baseball around, hitting the ball, and chasing bright white baseballs. Every time a player hit's the ball, it makes a "crack" sound which doesn't reach our ears until a second or two later.

"There's Bobby Thomson!" I shout at the top of my voice as I point at him catching a long fly ball hit right near the wall down below from where we are sitting! He looks the same as he does on television except that he is in color here.

Daddy meanwhile is busy telling us how he, Daddy, was once a security guard here at the Polo Grounds years ago.

"There were many times when I and the other 'bulls,' as I call them, had to break up fights in the stands when people had too much beer to drink and began fist-fighting. It was a dangerous, low-paying job so I quit and went to work as a 'Sorter' at the Railway Express Company, REA.

"You know," he continues, "when the football Giants were practicing here at the Polo Grounds during the football season, I was patrolling along the sideline when the football came bouncing over to me. I picked it up and realized this was my chance to get discovered so I took the ball and kicked it back to the players. Well, the ball must have gone over sixty yards in the air, a tremendous punt! When the coaches saw this, they called me over and told me to do that again, so I took the football and kicked it again. This time, it went even farther. Right then and there, the coaches wanted to sign me up to be the Giants' punter! All I had to do was pass a physical exam and sign a contract."

With sadness on his face, he adds, "Unfortunately, I had a scar from a knee injury from playing sandlot football so the Giants' doctor wouldn't pass me! The team wouldn't listen to anything I said about it being healed. They just wouldn't listen. What a shame... I came so close."

"The Giants were stupid not to sign you, Daddy," I tell him.

"If you kicked the football that far, didn't that prove your leg was okay?"

Daddy just nods his head but still looks sad as he relives that missed opportunity.

Fortunately, the ball game begins. Despite the action on the field, I am intrigued with the vendors walking in and about the stands selling hot dogs, peanuts, and ice cream. I find this as intriguing as the screaming crowd and the game on the field. In particular, it is interesting to see how easily and freely these vendors move about everyone in the stands relatively unnoticed by anyone.

This is similar to how the devil moves in and around people virtually unseen and undetected. The devil also tries to sell us things, only the things it sells are not good for us, and, in fact, can actually be spiritually lethal. Anything we buy from the devil comes at a very, very high price.

I notice a father sitting behind us one seat to our right who is buying just about everything for his son from the vendors who come by. This time, as the ice cream vendor passes, he calls out to him for two ice creams. I turn around and look at the man and think about how much I would enjoy eating some ice cream. Daddy earlier said we can't afford to buy anything because the food they sell in the ballpark costs way too much money.

An interesting thought crosses my mind. If Larry and I stare longingly at the man as he eats his ice cream, he might just feel sorry for us and buy some for us! I tell Larry my idea, and he agrees that it might work. So both of us turn around in our seats and stare longingly at the ice cream the man is eating. We are trying, if it is at all possible, to make it obvious that we are begging for him to buy us ice cream.

Finally, the man notices that we are staring at him. Shifting uncomfortably in his seat, the man looks quickly at his ice cream and realizes why we are staring at him.

"Hey, kids," he says to us, "if you want some ice cream, ask your old man to buy you some."

Without hesitating, I answer, "He can't. We're too poor."

Then remembering what Daddy says so often, I add, "There are seven mouths to feed at home, so he can't afford to buy luxuries like ice cream!"

The man looks sad for us so I ask him, "Can you buy some for my two brothers and me?"

Now the man looks annoyed. I am lucky that Daddy is busy discussing baseball with Paddy and the man sitting to Paddy's left, and doesn't notice what I am doing.

The man looks up at the roof, leans over, reaches for his wallet, and says, "Sure, kid."

"Hey you," he shouts at the ice cream vendor in the aisle, "three more over here please."

The man passes the money for the ice cream to the boy next to him telling him to pass it along to the vendor in the aisle. Meanwhile, the vendor retrieves three ice creams from the silver metal container hanging on his shoulder. Then he throws one at a time through the air to the man behind us. After the man catches each one, he hands them to me.

I give Larry one of the ice cream sandwiches, and tell him to pass the other one to Paddy. Larry interrupts Daddy to ask him to pass the ice cream along to Paddy.

When Daddy sees Larry and me already holding ice cream, he says, "Hey, where did you kids get that ice cream?"

"From that nice man behind us," Larry tells him.

"What! Why did he do that?" Daddy asks further.

"It's all right," the man behind us says, "the treat's on me. Your kid explained."

Daddy's eyes quickly shoot from the man to me, then again back to the man.

Frowning, Daddy asks, "What do you mean, he explained? What did he tell you?"

The man doesn't answer, so Daddy asks me, "Bobby, what did you tell the man?"

"I just told him we are too poor to buy ice cream, that's all. You have too many mouths to feed at home!"

Laughter cascades all around us as Daddy bites his tongue in anger looking like he wants to hit a homerun with me as the baseball!

Turning back to the man, Daddy says, "Do me a favor, buddy, don't buy anything else for my kids. I have plenty of money to buy my kids things. Okay?"

"Sure, no problem," the man answers.

After a brief pause, Larry innocently asks, "Daddy, since you have plenty of money, can Bobby and I have another ice cream sandwich?"

This evokes even more laughter from those around us… even Daddy!

Mommy was right. Taking his sons to see his beloved Giants play at the Polo Grounds… and beat their archrival Dodgers 3-0 has taken Daddy's mind off Nana's passing.

Chapter 18

THE "GHOST"

September 1952

The atmosphere in our home is filled with tension and unhappiness since Mommy and Daddy had a big disagreement over his beer drinking and gambling. I suspect the devil has something to do with it all.

As Mommy says, "The devil does everything it can to turn people away from God, and sometimes that includes turning family members and friends against one another. The devil knows our weaknesses and uses them against us... especially pride and unforgiveness."

It is scary to know that the devil does this and is so cunning, the father of all lies, second in intelligence only to God. Lately, it appears my parents have unknowingly fallen victim to the devil's evil influence. I never dreamed there could be so much tension between Mommy and Daddy who greatly love each other. In addition to being uncharacteristically hostile toward one another, they have also been short-tempered with us kids.

Each day brings new, increased tension as they continue their petty bickering. At the heart of their difficulties is the fact that Daddy continues drinking beer with friends after work. He has also been gambling some of the money he earns at Railway Express Company. Mommy complains to us about him coming home drunk after, as he says, he has had a "night out with the boys."

She adds, "Your father is a good, hard-working man but he is **terribly** misguided about drinking and gambling. He does not understand how destructive these can be. You kids make sure when you grow up that you do not follow Daddy's example. There is nothing good or noble about drinking and gambling!"

Daddy shrugs off Mommy's complaints and says there is nothing wrong with this; that this is what all hard-working men do. Mommy reacts by telling him that "real men" don't waste money on beer and gambling rather that spending it on their kids' food and clothing! Daddy just shakes his head as he leaves for work.

After a while, Mommy orders all of us to put on old torn clothing. She says she is going to take us to Daddy's job! Uh, oh! Why is she doing this? Why are we dressing in rags? I am afraid that we will find out we are NOT going there for a good reason.

After the bus ride across 79th Street in Manhattan, we then climb onto another bus going downtown. Soon we get off and walk a few blocks to where Daddy works at Railway Express Agency, REA, on West 16th Street. Paddy, Kitty, Larry and I walk next to Mommy as she carries Geri.

Soon we follow her into a large, unheated building through one of the big open bays where large REA delivery trucks are being loaded with large boxes. I remember Daddy once told me this is the area where men load the trucks with boxes of things that are shipped all over the country.

As we walk along, Mommy asks different men working there if they know where "Patsy Walsh" works. Finally, Mommy finds Daddy working with several other men near the back of the building. They are marking large numbers on cartons that roll past them on a long, metal roller. When Daddy sees us, he looks surprised and bewildered.

"Ellie, what're you doing here? Is everything all right?"

Mommy has a very unpleasant expression on her face as she snarls, "What am I doing here? I'm here to beg for money from your drinking and gambling buddies so I can buy your kids the food and clothing they need! That's what I am doing here!"

Daddy is stunned.

"Obviously **you** don't give a damn about them since you keep on pissing away what little money we have on beer and gambling. You want to be a big shot with the 'boys,' and don't give a **goddamn** what it costs your wife and kids! That is why I'm here!"

The workers around us have stopped working and are listening to what is happening. Daddy's face is bright red; he looks so embarrassed.

"Ellie, please!" Daddy begs.

But Mommy taunts him further, "What's the matter, Patsy? Don't you like your buddies to know how your beer-drinking and gambling affects your wife and kids? Why don't you tell them how you lost our rent money last week on Jersey Joe Wolcott who you **'just knew'** was not going to lose the heavyweight championship to Rocky Marciano!"

Daddy savagely pushes one of the cartons nearby knocking it to the floor as he shouts, "Stop it, Ellie, please stop it!"

I feel so badly for Daddy.

Her mission accomplished, Mommy turns and begins to walk away with us kids as she says, "Let's go kids, I think your father got the message."

What Mommy has done is mean. She is usually loving and kind, but in doing this, she has shown how mean she can be. I know we are all called to solve our problems with one another in peaceful ways, not like this.

Mommy has a sad expression on her face now as we make our way out passing many of Daddy's co-workers who look on in amazement. I can hear the hollow sounds of Daddy's voice speaking back inside the building as we exit and turn up 16th Street heading toward the bus that will take us home.

"Mommy, why did you do that?" Paddy asks.

"I did it because your father has been drinking too much lately and gambling his paycheck away with all those morons he works with. Nothing I said made a difference, nothing. So I thought embarrassing him in front of his co-workers might do the trick!

"The last thing your father wants is to be humiliated in front of the men he works with so he is going to think twice before he drinks and gambles again. He won't want to risk having me come back to his job again!"

"But what if that doesn't work?" Paddy asks.

"Well, then Daddy's co-workers are going to be seeing a whole lot of us because I'm going to keep coming down here until your father stops. People who drink too much wind up hurting themselves and those they love. I am not going to stand by and allow that happen to him and to us."

We sit quietly on the way home, saddened and worried about what just happened. The ride home seems much longer than our journey going to Daddy's job. When we finally reach home, Mommy looks very nervous as she paces back and forth through the rooms and occasionally peeks through the venetian blinds in the living room window. Looking to see Daddy when he comes down the street below, she is worried about what Daddy is going to do when he gets home. He must be so mad at her. I, too, am worried about what Daddy is going to do when he gets home tonight.

Since it is Saturday and there is no school on Sunday, Mommy says we can stay up late tonight and watch television with her. At nine o'clock, "Your Show of Shows"[5] goes on with Sid Caesar and Imogene Coca doing silly, funny things that make us laugh.

At 10:30, we watch "Your Hit Parade,"[6] a show where all the popular songs in the country are sung. Mommy and I like Gisele MacKenzie's singing best; Daddy favors Dorothy Collins and Snooky Lanson. Larry has fallen asleep on the couch so Mommy picks him up and carries him off to bed while Paddy, Kitty, and I listen to the closing song, "So Long for a while." When Mommy returns, she chases us off to bed with a kiss good night.

"Is Daddy going to come home and start yelling, Mommy?" I ask.

"I don't know, Bobby; I hope not," she says.

"I want you all to say a prayer before you go to sleep. Ask God to give Daddy the graces he needs to stop drinking and gambling... and to be nice when he comes home."

I know God always hears our prayers so I wonder why it is taking so

---

[5] "Your Show of Shows" was a live 90-minute variety show broadcast weekly on NBC, from February 1950 to June 1954, featuring Sid Caesar and Imogene Coca.

[6] "Your Hit Parade" was a music program televised from 1950 to 1959. Each Saturday evening, the program offered the most popular and bestselling songs of the week.

long for Daddy to stop drinking and gambling. I remember the last time he came home drunk. Daddy had awakened all of us from a sound sleep by arguing with Mommy. He made so much noise, the neighbors called the police. When the cops came, they told Daddy that if he did not stop making so much noise, they were going to arrest him for disturbing the peace. That worked.

However, as soon as the police left, Daddy stormed over to the kitchen window, threw it wide open, leaned out, and shouted, "Hey, all you nosey bastards who called the police, you should know that they just left after having a nice cup of tea with me! Next time, mind your own goddamn business and leave us the hell alone!"

No one responded. Not a peep was heard in the alleyway. I think our neighbors are afraid of Daddy because he is such a big, strong man.

Now we wait in fear and dread for what Daddy is going to do when he comes home after Mommy embarrassed him so badly today at his job in front of his co-workers. I try to think of something I might do to calm him down. The only thing I can think of is to pray.

As I lay on the bed next to Mommy, she continually moves nervously about by the edge of the bed. Kitty and Larry are asleep at the bottom of the bed. Geri is sound asleep in the crib at the foot of our bed, and Paddy is in the next room off the kitchen. I think he is asleep also. We are in the room next to the living room. Mommy and I have our heads at the end of the bed closest to the French doors.

Having all the lights off, casts our apartment in total darkness adding to my sense of dread. Right now, everything is dead quiet in our home but I feel a strong sense of impending danger. It doesn't take long to find out why.

Daddy arrives home at 1 A.M. banging on the door downstairs and ringing our doorbell. Mommy gets up and buzzes him in through the return bell in the kitchen. I can hear Daddy shouting in the hallway downstairs then mumbling something as he stumbles up winding the stairs. He has obviously had too much to drink once again.

Shouting as if it is the middle of the day, Daddy complains, "What took you so long to ring that goddamn bell, Ellie?"

My heart pounds as he arrives in the kitchen. An eerie silence sets in as he and Mommy glare at each other. Daddy, as expected, is wickedly biting his tongue in anger as he is apparently thinking about what Mommy did to embarrass him in front of his co-workers at his job today.

"After all we've been through over this," Mommy complains, "you have the goddamn nerve to come home again with drink on your breath! What is it going to take, Patsy, to get you to stop? Don't you realize how serious this is?"

166

"I will tell you what is serious. Going to my job and humiliating me in front of the men I work with… now **THAT** is serious! Having one or two beers with the guys… **that is <u>NOT</u> so serious!**"

Everyone is awake now including the baby who is crying. Mommy comes in, picks up Geri and tries to soothe her. Daddy meanwhile continues complaining at the top of his voice to no one in particular out in the kitchen.

Opening the kitchen window, he leans out and shouts, "My wife has no respect. She thinks it is okay to disgrace and humiliate her hard-working husband in front of his co-workers!"

Mommy sits on the edge of the bed quietly crying as she rocks back and forth with the baby held securely to her chest. I am so sad to see Mommy suffer like this.

"Please don't cry, Mommy," I plead, "Daddy will stop soon."

"Hey, Ellie," Daddy calls out, "How do **you** like it now that all your neighbors hear your private business? It's not too nice now, is it? Maybe the next time you will think twice before going to my job… **and humiliating me in front of the men I work with.**"

Mommy calls out, "You are not hurting me, Patsy. You are just disgracing yourself with our neighbors so they can join your co-workers in feeling sorry for me and the kids."

Mommy tells us kids, "Lie down and try to sleep, kids; don't pay attention to what Daddy is saying."

Mommy puts the baby in the crib then returns to bed with us. The tension in the air is unbearable as we listen to Daddy's ongoing loud rantings in the kitchen. One of our neighbors yells out his window for Daddy to stop making so much noise in the middle of the night.

"Nights are for sleeping, Mr. Walsh, not screaming out the window!"

Another neighbor complains, 'Knock it off!"

Daddy shouts back, "Why don't **you** mind your own goddamn business!"

"It is my own goddamn business when I can't sleep because of your screaming!" the neighbor yells back.

Daddy responds by challenging all the neighbors to "come down to the street and settle things like real men!"

Mommy warns him, "Patsy, if you don't stop, the neighbors are going to call the cops and have you hauled off to jail!"

The sound of the window slamming down tells us that Mommy convinced him to stop. Unfortunately for us, he is coming our way muttering something under his breath.

"Patsy, it's late and the kids are trying to go to sleep. **Please** stop shouting and go to bed," Mommy begs him.

I look up to see Daddy biting his tongue indicating he is still very angry. He sticks his tongue out over his lower lip, places his upper teeth over his tongue, and then clenches it all together. Everyone in our family knows that he only does this when he is very, very angry.

A moment later, his grimace fades as he shakes his head from side to side. Walking into the living room, he violently pushes the French doors open, then slams them closed once he is inside. I hear him lie down on the couch on the right side of the living room. That is where he usually winds up when he comes home after drinking too much.

Judging by the sounds of him tossing and turning repeatedly, he is having trouble going to sleep. Feeling secure that his rampage is finally over, the rest of us settle down and try to sleep… except Mommy and me. She is worried about Daddy starting things up again so I ask God to please help Daddy go to sleep… and to quit drinking and gambling!

My thoughts are disturbed by a breeze that suddenly whips through the rooms of our apartment. The air feels noticeably different. An extraordinary spiritual activity has begun… and I feel that it is not good.

An unholy disturbance fills the air by something that is outside the natural boundary between physical life and the spiritual plane. All of us are exposed. Nestling up as closely as I can beside the protective wall of Mommy's back, I wait in dreaded anticipation for what is about to descend upon us.

I don't have to wait long to find out. From a distance far beyond the kitchen window, I sense the approach of an evil spirit heading directly for our home. A demonic entity is heading directly toward us.

It is coming after Daddy, and for him alone.

Soon the evil thing is near. Leaning over Mommy, I look toward the kitchen and see a demon gliding slowly in our direction! It's outline is a dark shade of charcoal that stands out crystal clear in the darkness of our apartment.

It is about four feet tall with a rounded head, no neck, and sloping shoulders. No eyes, no ears, and no hair is distinguishable. It appears to have a heavy cloth draped over its head and body.

As it slowly approaches the entrance to my room, I lean back on my right forearm. Apparently everyone else in our room also senses the presence of this spirit. Geri stirs in her crib, Mommy snaps her head up in the direction of the evil spirit, Larry and Kitty sit up and look at this spirit as it floats slowly into our room through the open doorway.

We watch in horrified silence as the spirit glides slowly and methodically heading straight ahead toward the living room where Daddy is lying on the couch unaware that a spirit is coming his way. This evil spirit apparently wants us to see it and to observe what it is doing.

Slowly gliding without any motion whatsoever up or down, or side to side, it proceeds perfectly straight ahead in a determined, very slow, unstoppable march toward the last room where Daddy is resting. As it passes us, the air about us gets icy cold.

The spirit passes one foot in front of Mommy and me without pausing as it steadily glides straight ahead for the living room. Mommy makes the Sign of the Cross and I follow her example. As we do, I watch the spirit enter the living room by passing right through the closed right French door as if the door was made of air!

Now the spirit is in the room with unsuspecting Daddy.

"Mommy, did you see that?" I whisper, wondering if she also saw the spirit and how it just glided through the rooms and then through the right French door.

"Yes, Bobby," Mommy whispers in return, "It's a ghost. Say a prayer!"

Apparently not hearing our conversation, Kitty asks, "Mommy, did you see the ghost?"

"Yes. Don't worry, it's gone now," she reassures her, "There is nothing to worry about. Make the Sign of the Cross and lie down and go to sleep. Everything will be all right."

Kitty and Larry scurry under the sanctuary of the blanket as I burrow as close as I can to Mommy's back for safety.

"Do you think it's going to come back this way, Mommy?" I ask.

"I don't know, Bobby. Watch and listen… and keep praying."

I call out to God for protection from the evil spirit.

"What's the commotion in there? What the hell is going on?" Daddy shouts loudly from what now sounds like a hollow-sounding cave.

Mommy answers, "Patsy, I know you are not going to believe this, but a ghost just floated right through the French door into the room there with you! I am not kidding. You'd better get out of there… right now!"

A heavy silence follows as we wait for Daddy's response… and listen to hear if he sees the spirit in there.

"You're sick, Ellie, goddamn sick, just like the rest of your family... a bunch of freaking whackos!" he snarls.

"Patsy, I'm not kidding. Some black thing, a ghost, just went in there a minute ago. You'd better be careful because whatever it is, it is **NOT** human, it's a ghost, something very bad, I swear!" she warns.

"For Christ's sake, Ellie, cut out the bullshit. What do you think I was born yesterday? You get pissed off at me, and now all of a sudden there's a goddamn ghost floating through the door. Very cute, Ellie, very cute."

Once again a deadly silence falls upon our home as I sense something else unnatural is about to happen. My attention is drawn to the right French door and I watch it slowly open by itself! That is, it appears to be moving by itself. For sure, the spirit is moving the door. After a momentary pause, the door now swings back closed in the same slow, eerie way it had opened. The latch of the door clicks into place sending a loud metallic sound reverberating through the rooms.

"Patsy, did you see that?" Mommy asks.

"Yeah, real scary, Ellie. Grow up, will you. Leave the goddamn door alone!" he fumes angrily.

"I didn't touch the door, Patsy; honest to God."

"Sure, sure you didn't. It was the ghost right?" he taunts.

The spirit again causes the door to swing open ever so slowly. After a brief pause, it again slowly closes with another resounding "click."

"For the love of God, Ellie, leave the freaking door alone!" Daddy shouts. "Stop playing games, I want to sleep; I am tired."

"Patsy, I swear to God I am not touching the door," Mommy answers sounding more alarmed. "It is moving by itself... the ghost is moving it. You can ask Bobby, he can see my hands right here in front of him. Tell Daddy, Bobby, have I been touching the door?"

"No, Daddy," I yell out, "Mommy has not been touching the door! And I also saw the ghost go through the door!"

"That's nice," Daddy snaps, "now you've got the kids lying for you."

I watch Mommy's hands and look beyond them to see the right French door once again slowly open... then close. The curtains on the door sway gently back and forth as the door is moved by the evil spirit. Why is the demon doing this? What is it trying to accomplish?

"That's it, that's it; I've had it!" Daddy bellows angrily, "This horse shit is going to stop right now!"

Daddy gets up, turns on a light, then storms over to the French doors where he stations himself in front of the left French door and stares at us through the translucent curtains hanging down the full length of the doors. This is all so disturbing.

I can make out the ugly look on Daddy's face projecting anger as he sneers at Mommy... and wickedly bites his tongue.

"All right, now let's see the freaking door open, Ellie," he snarls, "Now that I am standing here watching you, let's see it open."

As soon as these words leave his mouth, the right French door once again opens in a slow, purposeful way. Through the now open doorway, I can see the expression on Daddy's face instantly change to one of shock and confusion. His mouth drops open as he stumbles backward and falls awkwardly into the armchair directly behind him. The spirit violently slams the door closed with a thunderous noise accompanied by an air of defiance and finality.

"Jesus, Mary and Joseph!" Daddy cries as he repeatedly makes the Sign of the Cross in rapid succession, rolls out of the chair, and frantically crawls away on his hands and knees away from the French doors.

"Oh, my God!" Mommy cries as she also makes the Sign of the Cross, "God, help us and protect us!"

The right French door again flies violently open but this time Daddy comes running madly through the opening and runs out to the kitchen where he grabs the straw broom from the right corner between the refrigerator and the wall.

In a flash, he comes thundering back through the rooms with a fierce, combative expression on his face as he continues to bite down on his tongue. Thrusting himself headlong past the French doors into the living room, he is swinging the broom wildly in the air from one side of the room to the other!

"Come out and show yourself, you goddamn coward!" he shouts at the invisible spirit!

"Come out and fight me like a man, you goddamn no good son-of-a-bitch!" he curses not realizing the nonsense of what he is saying.

I can't believe Daddy is fearlessly confronting the spirit… and it is not responding!

Paddy, Kitty, and Larry join in watching Daddy use the broom to wickedly pound the chair by the left window. Shouting one curse after another, he challenges the spirit to fight him! We huddle closely together and peer through the glass French doors as Daddy repeatedly swings the broom through the air in futile attempts to hit the spirit that is somewhere in the room with him!

Moving in our direction, Daddy beats the armchair in front of the left of the French door. Dust goes flying in the air after each powerful whack from the broom. Daddy now focuses his anger on the open space between the two doors and violently punishes the air there. This final effort leaves him gasping for air as he staggers backward, totally exhausted, and collapses into the left armchair by the left window. As he sits there perfectly still, the only noise in the house now is his labored breathing.

He says, "I don't know what's going on here, Ellie, but I can tell you one thing for sure, a door does **not** open and close by itself. It must be a ghost!"

"Patsy," Mommy says, "Bobby and I saw that ghost glide into the room before it started playing around with the French door. This is very bad.

171

None of us are safe now with a ghost thing in our home. You've got to call St. Monica's and get a priest to come right away to bless our home."

Daddy nods in agreement as he sits slumped in the armchair. He has instantly sobered up. It is amazing to see what a visit by a ghost can do.

Mommy adds, "Meanwhile, what are we going to do tonight?"

"Don't worry," Daddy says calmly, "I'll sit up tonight with the lights on and keep watch. I have a feeling there won't be any more trouble tonight. Perhaps that thing accomplished what it intended and left. You can go back to sleep now; I'll keep watch. Everything will be all right."

Feeling more secure knowing that Daddy is going to keep watch to protect us from the devil if it returns, I climb back onto the bed and snuggle closely as I can to everyone else for reassurance.

Larry asks, "Bobby, did you see the ghost?"

"Yes, I did. It floated right past us and went through the door, then started swinging the French door back and forth."

"Do you think it is going to hurt us?" he worries.

"I don't think so, Larry. I am pretty sure it came after Daddy because of his drinking and gambling!"

Mommy says, "Patsy, maybe the ghost was your father coming to let you know that you have to stop the drinking and gambling!"

No response comes from Daddy.

Directing her comments to the rest of us, she adds, "I think it was Grandpa Edward Walsh because the ghost was the same size as him, and Grandpa had the same problems that your father is struggling with now. Because Grandpa Walsh drank too much, he fell out a fifth floor window one night and died. If you ask me, I would not be surprised if God did allow Daddy's father to come back to warn Daddy to stop drinking before something terrible happens. Do you hear me, Patsy?"

It sounds like Daddy is crying.

Mommy says, "We should pray for Grandpa Walsh because he may be stuck in purgatory."

"Why do you think that, Mommy?" I ask.

Mommy reminds me of what she told us once before, "Our church teaches that sometimes family members are stuck in purgatory and need our prayers to help them get out, so God allows them to come back and give us a sign that they need prayers… like the opening and closing of a door!"

"Why?"

"Because a door here on earth symbolizes a passageway… like a door between purgatory and the paradise parts of heaven. Once souls are in purgatory, they cannot help themselves other than enduring great suffering there. We on earth can help them by praying for them so they can get out of

172

purgatory sooner and enter the fullness of paradise. And the greatest prayer of all is the Holy Sacrifice of the Mass."

Larry says, purgatory is a kind of washing machine for souls."

"I think they can only see the bright light of paradise through the door, but I don't know if they can see any of the people there including God. They are eager for us to help them open that door."

"We've got to be careful; that ghost can also be the devil!"

"How can we tell, Mommy?" Larry asks.

"You can tell by how you feel when a ghost is around you, and you can also tell by what the ghost does. Finally, you can tell by the results of its visit. If you feel good and good things follow, then it probably is a good spirit. But if you feel in danger and bad things happen instead, then it is probably an evil spirit."

"I had bad feelings when it passed us, Mommy," I tell her.

"Me too," Larry says.

"I did, too," Mommy says.

"What if it was a bad ghost?" Larry asks.

Looking very concerned, she says, "Then God help us!"

Chapter 19

JINGLE BELLS

December 1952

"That is one of the scariest movies I have ever seen! Larry says.
"I thought it was funny," Paddy responds.
I thought it was scary, funny and very entertaining, and I especially like the music. Kitty is not here to tell us what she thinks... she left the room as soon as she saw the 'Bogeymen' appear. She is staying out in the kitchen with Mommy.
We are talking about the movie, "The March of the Wooden Soldiers,"[7] which we just finished watching on television. It is a story about life in Toyland where nursery-rhyme characters come and go, do funny things, and sing beautiful songs.
Daddy tells us, "The two funniest actors are Stan Laurel and Oliver Hardy who play the toyshop workers, Stannie Dum and Ollie Dee. They live in a shoe house with Widow Peep, her daughter, Bo Peep, and eleven other children. Charlotte Henry is the actress who plays 'Bo Peep.' She was born in Brooklyn and was a popular child star during the 1930s."
I think Daddy likes the movie more than I do.
The three little pigs are cute, and the little mouse that runs around chased by a big, silly cat is hilarious. At one point, Bo Peep loses her sheep and is very sad until the people of Toyland find them for her. Bo Peep and Tom-Tom, her boyfriend, are in love and want to get married.
There is an evil villain by the name of Mr. Silas Barnaby who threatens to evict Widow Peep from her shoe unless Bo Peep agrees to marry him. Mr. Barnaby is very dislikeable. He is a tall skinny man who wears a tall black hat, eyeglasses, and has sideburns and a small goatee. He walks with a cane and is always looking like he is up to no-good.
Stannie Dum and Oliver Dee trick Mr. Barnaby into canceling the mortgage on the shoe house so Bo Peep does not have to marry him. Barnaby then frames Tom-Tom for a crime that never happened, the eating of the three little pigs. As a punishment, Tom-Tom is exiled to Bogey-land where all the monstrous Bogeymen live.
Stannie and Ollie expose Mr. Barnaby's lies so Mr. Barnaby is then sent to Bogey-land himself. Evil Mr. Barnaby then brings all the Bogeymen

---

[7] "The March of the Wooden Soldiers" is a Stan Laurel and Oliver Hardy musical film released on March 10, 1934. Based on Victor Herbert's popular 1903 operetta, "Babes in Toyland," the film was produced by Hal Roach, directed by Charles Rogers and Gus Meins, and distributed by Metro-Goldwyn-Mayer.

into Toyland where they attack the innocent men, women, and children. Just when it looks like all is lost, Stannie and Ollie activate the one hundred six-foot tall wooden soldiers they earlier built in error. They were supposed to build one hundred six-inch-tall wooden soldiers for Santa Claus!

The wooden soldiers chase off all the bad Bogeymen and send them back to Bogey-land where they belong. At the end of the story, a canon is set off in celebration but the canon barrel flips around and shoots Ollie in the back with hundreds of needle-like darts!

Daddy told us that "March of the Wooden Soldiers" was actually made many years ago in 1934, and the beautiful music played in the movie is based on a musical composed by Victor Herbert called, "Babes in Toyland."

The television stations considered some scenes in Bogey-land too grim for young kids so they cut them out of the movie.

From the living room, Mommy's happy singing can be heard throughout our apartment. She is hanging Christmas cards we received on a long string she has draped from one end of the mantle-piece to the other as she sings, "Santa Claus is Coming to Town."[8] That song has become so familiar and so much a part of our Christmas celebration every year.

> "You'd better watch out, you'd better not cry,
> Better not pout, I'm telling you why,
> Santa Claus is coming to town.
> He's making a list and checking it twice,
> Gonna find out who's naughty and nice,
> Santa Claus is coming to town.
> He sees you when you're sleeping,
> He knows when you're awake,
> He knows if you've been bad or good,
> So be good for goodness sake."

Paddy, Kitty, Larry, and I are sitting on the couch in the living room watching Mommy and enjoying her wonderful singing. Suddenly, she whips around and faces us as she playfully wags her finger at us as she sings her version of the song,

> "**Momma** knows when you're sleeping,
> **Momma** knows when you're awake,
> **Momma** knows if you've been bad or good,
> So be good for goodness sake,
> Oh, you'd better watch out, you'd better not cry,
> You'd better not pout, I'm telling you why,

---

[8] "Santa Claus is Coming to Town" is a Christmas song written by John Frederick Coots and Haven Gillespie and was first sung on Eddie Cantor's radio show in November 1934.

Santa Claus is coming to town!"

Now in a solemn tone, Mommy says, "You know Santa Claus can see you at all times, so you should always be good. Otherwise, you might get pieces of coal from him as your Christmas gifts!"

Daddy enters the room singing,

"Jingle bells, jingle bells, jingle all the way,

Oh what fun it is to ride in a one horse open sleigh!"

As soon as he stops singing, he asks invitingly, "Okay, who wants to come with me to pick out our Christmas tree and carry it home?"

Naturally, we all jump up at once and volunteer to go with him.

Mommy, however, chides Daddy, "You always wait 'til the very last minute on Christmas Eve to go out and buy our Christmas tree. One of these years, you are going to go out and find that all the trees have been sold. Then what will you do?"

"Nonsense!" he snaps, "Christmas Eve is the **best** time to buy your Christmas tree because the sellers are anxious to get rid of any trees they have left over. That is how you get a nice tree at a bargain price, and this year, I assure you, will be no different."

"So what do you say, Paddy and Bobby. Do you guys want to come with me to get our Christmas tree?" he asks.

"Yes, Daddy," we answer eagerly.

"What about me?" Larry says, "I want to go too."

"I'm sorry, Larry, I'm afraid not. I can't be worried about you running off. I'm going to be busy looking at trees and won't be able to keep an eye on you. Remember how you ran away from Nana's? I'm sorry; it's your own fault that you can't go. Case closed, case dismissed, that's the end of it; not another word out of you!"

Larry looks so sad as he slumps back onto the couch and looks over to Mommy. His eyes plead for help hoping she might feel sorry enough for him and tell Daddy to let him go with us on the hunt for our Christmas tree. I expect Mommy to come to Larry's aid and try to convince Daddy to let Larry go with us, but she surprises us all.

"Daddy is right," Mommy says, "You have to learn to listen to what you are told to do, Larry, especially when it comes to running away. You almost got yourself killed last time!"

Larry turns and buries his face in the cushions and cries. I feel sorry for him but I understand how important it is that he learns to obey for his own safety.

Turning her attention to Paddy and me, Mommy advises us, "You boys better bundle up, it's below freezing out there, and your father likes to shop all over the neighborhood before he buys a tree. You may be frozen to death before he finds a tree he likes enough to buy!"

Within minutes, we are out the door, down the stairs and out into the shockingly cold air of the night. The ground is covered with frozen slippery snow making it very difficult to walk. With the wind howling about us driving the cold air up my trousers and coat sleeves, I already am very, very cold and uncomfortable. Every breath I take brings in piercing cold air hurting my mouth, nostrils, and throat. As I breathe out, a cloud of steam billows out of my mouth as my warm breath escapes. After walking only a short distance up the street, my legs and arms are already freezing cold as shivers cascade throughout my body. I hope that Daddy finds a Christmas tree he likes enough to buy... soon... very soon.

At the corner of York Avenue, there is the first group of Christmas trees to inspect leaning at an angle upright against the school railing. The trees give off a distinct delightful scent from their pine needles, and they serve as a barrier to block the wind from whipping us. Daddy pulls out a tree and shakes it so its branches fall out so he can see the tree's shape better. He looks carefully at its height as he turns it around to see how full it is from top to bottom. This one he says is not good enough. He then selects another tree nearby and repeats the process... unfortunately with the same results.

The man selling the trees has been watching Daddy. Now he steps over and says, "Merry Christmas, pal. See one you like?"

"Well, not really; they are all pretty scrawny looking!" Daddy answers. "What are you asking for these... leftovers?"

I am amused by the clouds of steam swirling from their mouths as they speak.

"Only ten bucks," the man says as he shifts from one foot to the other and continually rubbing his arms in an attempt to stay warm.

"Ten bucks," Daddy says incredulously, "You gotta be kidding. These look more like twigs than they do Christmas trees! Five bucks maximum, that is all they are worth, and at that I am being generous!"

"Well, see if you can do better elsewhere because I can't let them go that cheap. Sorry."

Daddy shrugs his shoulders, and off we go along York Avenue heading downtown to continue our hunt for a Christmas tree. As we trudge along, I look off in the distance and see the 59th Street Bridge. Daddy, seeing me looking in the direction of the bridge, assures us that there are many more good Christmas tree stands we can visit before we reach the 59th Street Bridge.

My God, I think to myself, he may actually go as far as the bridge before he buys a tree! Paddy gives me a worrisome look apparently thinking the same thing. We both know how particular Daddy can be. We may freeze to death out here on the streets of Yorkville by the time he finally settles on a tree!

"That last tree looked pretty good, Daddy," Paddy says, "Why didn't you buy it?"

"That tree was fine, Paddy, but the price wasn't," he explains.

"We can't afford a tree that expensive. Don't worry boys, we will find a tree for five dollars or less. You will see. You have to learn how to bargain and chisel down the price. Everybody expects you to do it. It is called the 'art of negotiation.' Just be patient and learn from your old man how it is done."

The howling wind whips mercilessly around my ears causing them to sting and ache in this bitterly cold night air. I am more worried now about how far we will have to walk from home and the comfort and warmth of our steam-heated apartment before Daddy finally finds a tree he likes enough to buy... at a low enough price!

Our next opportunity comes at the corner of 79th Street and York Avenue where Daddy goes through the same bargaining routine, with the same results. No sale, shrugging shoulders, piercing wind, freezing cold, and a heightening sense of desperation swelling in my frozen body and mind as we continue on our way even farther south along York Avenue. My feet are so cold now they hurt badly.

"How much longer, Daddy?" I beg him, "My face and feet are freezing!"

"Soon, Bobby, soon. Let's go to the next tree stand," he says.

Blasts of bitter cold wind whip against my unprotected face as we turn west onto a darkened 78th Street. I think of how lucky Larry is to stay home where it is warm and comfortable, and there is no brutal wind whipping against his face, and no slippery ice under his frozen feet. But then, I look up to see 78th Street filled with windows brightly decorated with colorful Christmas lights. And there are sounds of Christmas music playing everywhere. Perhaps I am the lucky one to experience this beautiful Christmas moment.

I wonder if it was bitterly cold like this when Joseph and Mary were trying to find a place to stay on the night Jesus was born. At least I know I will eventually get indoors at home, but they did not know where they would stay that night, and they knew that the Baby Jesus was going to be born soon! I pray to God the Father who is time eternal and Who can reach back in time, to protect Mary, Joseph and Baby Jesus from the elements and from fear of the unknown.

The sound of a ringing bell now fills the air. I turn to see a man dressed in a Salvation Army uniform standing on the corner methodically swinging a bell up and down with his right hand. I don't know how he can stand out here on this terribly cold night doing that. He must be freezing. To do this, he must really believe in what he is doing. Mommy once told me that the Salvation Army is a group of very special people who collect money like this so they can help poor people.

A man passing us in the opposite direction calls out to us, "Merry Christmas, and happy new year!"

Daddy shouts a quick reply, "The same to you, Buddy!"

A man and a woman come rushing along in the opposite direction fighting against the wind and the slippery ice all over the sidewalk call out, "Merry Christmas!" to us. Paddy and I join Daddy in shouting the same greeting back to them over the howling wind. The streets are filled with people rushing about their business carrying packages. I am thrilled by all this, the music and excitement in the air, people hustling by, Christmas trees and wreaths everywhere, snow on the ground. This is all part of what makes Christmas so very special in Yorkville.

"Keep moving your arms, boys, to stay warm, and don't think about the cold," Daddy advises us. "We are almost there."

"Where is that, Daddy?" Paddy asks.

"The guy on the corner of second Avenue and 78th Street always has good trees at reasonable prices. That is where I buy our Christmas tree every year."

"Why didn't we just go there in the first place?" I ask.

"Part of the great joy of Christmas is hunting for the Christmas tree itself. This is a Christmas tradition for our family, you know. When you are older, you will understand."

Yeah, if I don't freeze to death before then, I think to myself.

Just as Daddy said, a short distance before the corner of second Avenue and 78th Street there are several people looking over trees lined up against the side of the building there. Daddy walks right over to the last one on the left side and wrestles it out to inspect it. It is a very tall tree standing about seven feet, and it is wide and full. The sweet pine smell coming from all these Christmas trees blends deliciously with the cold air filling my nostrils with a delightful treat. Hundreds of pine needles crunch under everyone's feet creating a unique sound as people move around the area inspecting the trees.

"What'd you think, boys?" Daddy asks.

"It is beautiful, Daddy," Paddy says.

I am too cold to do anything except nod my head in approval.

"Let's see what we can get it for," Daddy whispers as he drags the tree over to the man who is only wearing a red and black plaid shirt. He is swinging his arms around himself, and jumping up and down to keep warm.

His thick gloves and funny looking cap apparently don't help very much in warding off the brutal cold. I wonder why he isn't wearing a jacket.

Daddy chides him, "What're you crazy out here dressed like that? You can get your death of a cold."

"I know but to tell ya the truth, I didn't know it was going to be **this** cold tonight," he explains. "You want that tree? I can give it to ya for eight dollars. That is a bargain for a big tree like that."

Daddy looks sadly at the tree then at Paddy and me before saying, "The tree really is beautiful; but we can't afford that much money. I have a lot of mouths to feed back at home. Times are really tough for large families like mine."

Slowly dragging the tree back toward the wall and looking sad, Daddy turns and blinks to us as he motions for us to follow him away. We don't get more than a few feet away when the man comes up quickly behind us and taps Daddy on the shoulder.

"Wait a second, buddy. This is Christmas Eve; I will never be able to sell that tree to anyone at that price. How does five bucks sound? What do you say?"

Even though Daddy is bargaining with the man, I can tell that Daddy is genuinely touched by this man's kindness.

"Gee, that's swell," Daddy says sincerely, "That is really nice of you. Thank you very much. God bless you for your kindness."

The man smiles and nods his head as he says, "Don't mention it. It is Christmas, right? This is a time to help one another, and hope that better days are coming."

The man quickly ties the tree with a cord made of straw-like material. Daddy gives him a five dollar bill then vigorously shakes his hand, and says, "Thanks again, and Merry Christmas to you and yours."

"Merry Christmas!" the man calls out joyfully.

Wow, little kindnesses like that make Christmas so special. That is the true spirit of Christmas … kindness and giving.

With the tree hoisted up on our shoulders, the three of us anxiously start off on the long trek back home with our prize tree. Daddy is in front carrying the heaviest part of the tree, the base. Paddy is barely visible, buried somewhere in the middle of the tree. I bring up the rear holding the top of the tree that keeps bouncing up and down as we slowly trudge along… one staggering step at a time. Every time the tree wiggles, my hands, face and neck get scratched with what feels like hundreds of pine needles!

Carrying this tree is like carrying a giant porcupine.

I am happy but I feel so miserable. I can't see where I am going, and the wind feels like it is blowing twice as hard now as it howls fiercely around my ears. The ground is so slippery and difficult to walk on. My extremities are so numb I am afraid I might get frostbite. Please God ease my pain, and PLEASE make the wind stop blowing so hard! It seems like we are never going to get home! All we keep doing is walk, walk, walk. When are we going to reach home? Just when I think I can't take another step, we finally arrive in front of our building.

"We are here, boys," Daddy announces to my great joy and relief.

Oh, thank you, God, I think as Daddy drags the tree up the front stoop and squeezes it through the double-door entrance to our building. Inside the hallway, the tree scrapes the walls leaving a trail of Christmas tree needles all along on the floor. Somehow Daddy maneuvers the tree up the winding stairs to our second floor apartment leaving behind a long trail of tiny pine needles on the stairs as well. When we get to our front door, it does not look like Daddy is going to get the tree inside, but he just keeps pulling it until the tree is in. Now there are pine needles all over the kitchen floor.

It is so good to be back in our warm toasty home. Everyone follows Daddy as he drags the big tree through the rooms. Now there are pine needles on the floor of each room.

In the living room, Daddy cuts away the cord from around the tree, and obviously not worried about the mess pine needles make, he violently shakes the tree back and forth. The living room floor is now also covered with pine needles.

He explains why he shakes the tree, "This helps the tree to open up its branches."

Surprisingly, Mommy doesn't seem to mind the mess Daddy is making even though she is the one who will be cleaning up all the needles. Now using a saw, Daddy cuts off four inches from the bottom of the tree so that it will fit in the room without hitting the ceiling. Mommy cautions all of us to stand safely back from where Daddy is working. Raising the tree straight up into the left corner of the living room by the window where the armchair is usually stationed, Daddy mutters to himself as he struggles to position the tree securely into the tree-holder.

Mommy and Paddy step over and help him by holding the tree steady. To our amusement, we watch as Daddy gets down flat on his stomach under the tree so he can tighten the tree-support bolts into the trunk of the tree. Then he takes a hammer and drives long nails through the tree-support, the linoleum, and into the wooden floor. After he gets up, he tells us this was necessary to anchor the tree-support to the floor so the tree won't tip over.

Now that the tree is in place, Mommy takes over. She first lights two candles that are set in a wooden holder that is shaped like a white birch tree log. Next, she turns on the radio so we can listen to Christmas

181

music as we decorate our Christmas tree. Then she goes to the corner diagonal closet of the living room, opens the door, reaches in, and takes out boxes of Christmas decorations stored there.

Moving quickly, she places the boxes of ornaments on the sofa and removes the boxes of Christmas lights. She and Daddy go about wrapping the sets of lights around the tree. I especially like the bubble lights, the ones that have bubbles flowing up inside a thin glass tube attached to a ball-shaped bottom.

Mommy now turns to the boxes of colorful glass balls and other ornaments. Each year, I look through these boxes to find my favorite ornament, a dried-up lemon that Mommy varnished in order to preserve it. It has a tiny green artificial leaf glued on its top to make it look more realistic. I find this precious ornament near the bottom of a box, carefully pick it up, and admire it. Although it is somewhat ugly and funny looking, I consider it a priceless treasure because it reminds me of past Christmas times filled with so much love and happiness. Mommy made it herself during Christmas 1941.

Studying where I can hang it on the tree, I finally decide to hang it on a branch in the middle-front section of the tree. Soon, all the ornaments are on the tree so Mommy puts thick garland around the entire tree. Tinsel is always the last to go on, so Mommy gives each of us some strands to throw on the tree branches. This is fun throwing tinsel strands as high up on the tree as we can.

Now comes the final touch, the placing of an angel ornament at the very top branch of the tree. Standing on a kitchen chair, Daddy ceremoniously places it there as we cheer and clap. Christmas has now once again officially arrived at the Walsh home.

We children sit on the sofa and watch Mommy and Daddy hugging each other in front of the mantelpiece and join us in silently admiring our beloved Christmas tree. Adding to the special joy of this moment, we hear Bing Crosby singing the song, "White Christmas"[9] on the radio. My heart is bursting with happiness as I look around the room at my family. No one speaks and yet so much is said with looks of love and togetherness. We are bonded so closely together at this moment, made from the same flesh and blood, sharing life and the same Christian faith and family love. What a blessing it is to be part of our family This moment is so beautiful, so sacramental, exemplifying what Christmas is all about, what being a family is all about.

---

[9] "White Christmas" is an Irving Berlin song that reminisces about an old-fashioned Christmas setting. It was sung by Bing Crosby. Accounts vary as to when Berlin wrote the song but it is believed he wrote it in 1940 while staying up all night. He then told his secretary that he felt he had just written the best song anyone had ever written!

I can imagine it being like this on the night Jesus was born. Mary and Joseph looking at their precious child, loving Him and loving each other in the quiet peace, joy and happiness of that very first Christmas.

The sudden ringing of our doorbell intrudes upon this special moment.

"Santa Claus!" Larry shouts out excitedly!

"No, Larry. Santa Claus doesn't come ringing the doorbell," Mommy laughs, "he comes riding in his sleigh pulled by reindeer onto the roof."

Mommy's words were too late because we are running out to the front door in the kitchen already. After our mad dash through the rooms, we wait for Mommy to come to push the doorbell located to the right side of our front door. Mommy looks to Larry and reminds him that this bell allows the door to our apartment building to be opened downstairs so people who ring our doorbell can get in.

I wonder who it is. Carefully listening to the voices of people coming up in the hallway, I recognize the voices of Daddy's sister, Aunt Dotsy, her husband Uncle Frank Sisto, Daddy's younger brother Uncle Buddy, his wife Aunt Josie, Uncle Donny, and his wife, Aunt Terri. They are very happy, kind, fun-loving people. I am so thrilled they have come to visit us. They usually come to see us on holidays; Aunt Marion Sullivan comes more often than the others because she lives nearby.

They enter our apartment with a chorus of, "Merry Christmas!"

"Look at these beautiful little angels! Aren't they adorable?" Uncle Frank Sisto says as he looks at us. As he steps over to us, Kitty backs up and ducks behind Mommy. I guess she is afraid because she is not familiar with him.

"Don't be afraid, Kitty, I'm not a big, bad Bogeyman. I am your Uncle Frank Sisto," he says reassuringly.

Kitty allows him to give her a kiss. After a flurry of hugs and kisses, and compliments about how cute we children are, Mommy takes out cold cuts and bread from the refrigerator then puts a big pot of water on the stove to make A & P loose tea for our guests.

I remember to be careful with Uncle Buddy because he always chases us and tickles our tummies too hard. Right now he is just smiling at me and nodding his head. I suspect he is thinking about chasing us even though Daddy is busy telling him things.

Just when I think Uncle Buddy may not have remembered, Larry asks, "Uncle Buddy, when are you going to chase us and tickle us?"

"Right now!" he shouts as he explodes out of his chair and runs right at us setting us off on a wild scramble squealing through the rooms. Uncle

Buddy is fast but he does not catch us until we are on the living room couch. Paddy, Larry and I are trapped underneath Uncle Buddy's strong hands as he alternately tickles each of us. I know he is playing with us but his fingers really hurt when he digs them into my stomach as he tries to make me laugh.

"Hey, would you guys like to see a trick?" Uncle Buddy entices us.

I don't trust him. He seems to be up to something else, but I'll go along with it because we're having fun and I'm sure whatever he does, we won't get hurt.

"I'll bet I can make water wet something after I've spilled it... without touching the water! Want to see me do it?"

Paddy, Larry, and I look at each other and agree that we would like to see how he can do this. Uncle Buddy then goes to the kitchen and returns with a glass of water.

Sitting down opposite us, he says, "Okay, sit closely together on the floor, put one foot out front so that your feet touch each other's, bend your knees, and leave a little room in the middle under your knees."

Looking devious, Uncle Buddy pours a little water on the floor directly underneath our bent knees then says, "Okay, you can see that I am spilling a little water on the floor wetting it, right? Now, you see that I am putting the glass of water down out of the way, right? Now, I am going to show you guys how I can make the same water I spilled onto the floor wet something else without my ever touching it. Are you ready?"

Giggling, we tell him yes and watch closely. Grabbing our feet, Uncle Buddy quickly pulls the three of us forward right into the puddle of water as he laughs uproariously!

He yells out toward the kitchen, "Hey, Pat, I told you they'd fall for it!"

Laughter now comes from the kitchen where the rest of the family is gathered. Uncle Buddy planned this trick on Paddy, Larry, and me! We are laughing, too, because what he did to us really is funny.

Fortunately for me, I did not get as wet as Paddy and Larry who are now jumping on Uncle Buddy's back and shouting, "You tricked us, now you have to give us a horsey ride! Giddyap, horsey, giddyap!"

I join them as Uncle Buddy crawls around the living room a few times then throws us off his back telling us that he is going to tickle us again. We dart out toward the kitchen with him in hot pursuit. He can't catch us because we are too fast... and he is too slow. We dive under the bed in the room next to the kitchen knowing that he can't get us here.

Acting as if he is frustrated, he says, "I'm going to wait all night if I have to until you come out. Meanwhile, I'm going to go out to the kitchen to hang out with your **old** relatives."

"Hey, I heard that!" Aunt Dotsy kids him. "I'm the young one here!"

This leads to more good-natured comments about who is older. I know Uncle Buddy was only kidding about coming back so I go out to ask Uncle Donny and Aunt Terri to come to the living room to play some game with us, or to tell us a story. Kitty joins Paddy, Larry, and I as we lead Uncle Donny and Aunt Terri to the living room. They sit on the couch while we sit on the floor. It is beautiful how both of them continually smile at us.

Uncle Donny directs his attention to me first by asking, "Bobby, do you know who was the first president of our country?"

"George Washington," I tell him.

"Very good. Now, do you know what the color of George Washington's white horse was?"

What a strange question, I think.

"I don't know. How can I know the color of George Washington's horse? He lived a long time ago before I was even born."

Uncle Donny and Aunt Terri laugh as he says, "Didn't you hear my question? Listen carefully. Do you know what the color of George Washington's **white** horse was?"

Again, I tell him I have no idea what color George Washington's horse was. This is puzzling. How can Uncle Donny expect me to know this?

Laughing, he explains, "It's white! The correct answer was within the question I asked you. I asked if you knew the color of George Washington's **white** horse!"

I feel so embarrassed. They must think I am not very smart. I can feel my face turning red. I must pay **very** close attention to what they say to me so I won't be embarrassed again by not listening carefully.

Uncle Donny and Aunt Terri now tell us how Santa Claus lives in the North Pole with lots of elves who help him make toys all year long. Uncle Donny stresses how they also help Santa Claus keep records showing who has been good... or bad... during the year. Aunt Terri says those who are good get nice gifts, and those who are bad get pieces of coal for gifts!

Leaning forward, Aunt Terri says, "By the way, you know that Santa Claus will not come until you are all fast asleep, and if you don't go to sleep early enough, he may not come at all! He has so many children to bring Christmas toys to tonight that he might have to skip you all together if you're still awake when he comes."

We all agree that it is time to take our bath and get to bed. I am very tired anyway from the evening's events, and Mommy woke us all up very early this morning. After our baths, we crawl into bed under the covers and remind one another how important it is that we ALL go to sleep right away.

"But what if I can't go to sleep?" Larry worries. "If I can't sleep, Santa Claus will know that I am awake."

Mommy hears what Larry is saying so she comes in and says, "Larry, all you have to do is think of sheep jumping over a fence, and count them as they jump. Before you know it, you will fall asleep."

"But I don't like to see sheep jumping over a fence," Larry protests.

"That's all right, Larry, just try."

Nestled closely together, one by one we fall asleep wondering what presents Santa Claus is going to bring us this Christmas Eve. I feel warm, secure, and happy snuggled against my two brothers and one sister, Kitty, on this very special night. Geri is close by in her crib. Sleep soon overtakes me.

I am awakened by Mommy's whispered words to Daddy, "Patsy, the kids are asleep now; let's get the toys out of the closet before they wake up."

Wow, I realize right away what this means. Just as I have suspected, Santa Claus really does **NOT** exist, nor does his flying reindeer, elves, or home in the North Pole where all the gifts are made. It is all make-believe. I am bewildered and feel greatly disappointed.

I make believe that I am still asleep as I listen to Mommy and Daddy taking our Christmas gifts out of the corner closet in the living room. I am so sad to hear this.

A loud voice booms out from the hallway of our building, "Ho, ho, ho, Merry Christmas, everyone, Merry Christmas! Ho, ho, ho, Merry Christmas!"

Mommy and Daddy shout, "Wake up; everyone wake up! Santa Claus is coming down the hall stairs from the roof right now!"

In a flash, everyone is up out of bed running in our pajamas toward the kitchen. I follow, confused about what is happening. When we reach the kitchen, we hear a loud crashing noise like someone falling down the stairs with lots of things. Daddy looks startled as he opens the door and hurries out into the hallway followed closely by the rest of us.

Looking down the stairs, I see Uncle Frank Sisto sprawled on his back... dressed in a Santa Claus costume. Next to him is a ripped bag with toys scattered all over him and the stairs.

"Are you all right, Santa Claus?" Daddy calls out barely able to control his amusement.

"It is **not** funny, Pat!" Uncle Frank snaps, "I am all right."

Aunt Dotsy rushes past us down the stairs to help him as Larry asks, "Daddy, are those our toys... and are the reindeer up on the roof?"

"Yeah, those are your toys."

He then hurries us all inside as he says with a big smile, "Why don't you kids go wait in by the tree while we help Santa Claus bring them inside.

Okay?"

Our family tradition is to receive gifts by the Christmas tree on Christmas Eve. Although the mystery and fantasy of Santa Claus has been spoiled for me, I still feel the thrill of anticipation over what gifts I will be getting. It is quite a while before Mommy and Daddy return.

Daddy tells us, "Santa Claus told us to say goodbye for him because he has to rush off to bring toys to so many other children. He said his sleigh is still full of toys."

Larry wants to know if it is possible that Santa Claus forgot to leave some of our toys. Laughter fills the room as Mommy assures him that Santa Claus has indeed left all our gifts with Mommy and Daddy to give to us.

The opening of the gifts is one of the high points in our Christmas celebration. This year, Paddy and I got great gifts. Each of us got a toy tractor-trailer! Kitty and Geri got cute looking dolls, and Larry got realistic-looking rubber cars.

Withdrawing into a corner of the room away from everyone, Paddy and I play together with our beautiful trucks. Larry soon joins us with his rubber cars. The three of us make believe we are driving around the city by crawling after one another across the living room floor then back to the right corner. We pause only to say goodbye to our relatives.

All too soon, Mommy announces, "Okay, guys, it is time for bed. It's very late, and you need your sleep. When you get up in the morning, you can continue your playing. Put your toys down now and come give Mommy and Daddy a big kiss goodnight."

After kissing them goodnight, we start off to bed carrying our toys with us. Mommy, however, calls out, "Hey, hey, you guys can't sleep with your trucks and car in bed. You can get hurt rolling over on top of them in your sleep so let's have them right here, please."

She sticks her hands out toward us and receives each one of the toys.

"But Mommy," Larry protests, "you let the girls go to bed with their dolls; why can't we go to bed with our toys?"

"There's nothing wrong with the girls sleeping with their dolls, Larry. Unfortunately, your toys have sharp edges that can hurt you while you are sleeping. You can play with them to your heart's content tomorrow, boys. I'll leave them right here under the tree for you, okay?"

We reluctantly hand our toys over to Mommy but I still feel we are not being treated fairly. I often feel that Mommy and Daddy treat the girls better than us guys.

"What if we wrap them up in the blanket?" I ask.

Mommy smiles but shakes her head no.

Snuggling under the blanket together, there is a flurry of giggles as we seek shelter from the chilly night air. The exciting events of this Christmas Eve swirl about in my mind. I wish Nana was still alive and could have joined us tonight. A part of me senses her presence here in spirit along with other relatives who died before us. As sleep begins to overtake me, I ask God to give Nana and my other relatives a hug and tell them how much I love them and wish them Merry Christmas.

Early next morning, seemingly only moments after falling asleep, I awake to the sound of loud crashing noises. Daylight floods our home as a flurry of activity instantly materializes around me. The covers are whipped off in a flash as everyone scrambles madly out of bed and runs into the living room to see what caused the crashing noise. There sprawled before my startled eyes is our Christmas tree lying down stretched grotesquely across the length of our living room floor!

Glass from broken Christmas balls is scattered all over the floor, and the tinsel that was draped so beautifully over the branches is now cast all over the room, hanging in ugly, twisted curls on the mantle-piece and the lampshades. It looks as if a hurricane blew through the living room. As we stand there looking on in disbelief, the middle of the tree begins to move, its branches wiggling. I take a step backward along with the others. It is frightening to see the branches moving all by themselves!

All of a sudden, a black furry head pops up through the branches. **It is Blackie, our family cat!**

"Meow," Blackie cries as if greeting us! He is tangled in the midst of all the decorations as he struggles unsuccessfully to free himself from the middle of our fallen Christmas tree.

"That goddamn cat!" Daddy snaps angrily, "look what he did. I am going to kill that cat when I get my hands on him!"

While the rest of us laugh at our incredibly mischievous cat, Mommy says, "Patsy, there is no way the cat could have knocked that tree down. Something else must have happened."

Mommy is right; the cat could not have done this. Daddy ignores what Mommy said, hurriedly puts his shoes on, and wearing only his boxer shorts, walks gingerly into the room crunching glass under his heavy feet everywhere he steps.

Reaching in, he grabs Blackie by the scruff of his neck and despite Blackie's squirming and crying, Daddy frees him from the tangled wires of the lights. As he pulls Blackie out from the tree and puts him down, the cat is off running away out of the room.

As Daddy bends down by the tree stand to examine it, I remember how well he hammered the nails into the tree stand just last night and said that no amount of decorations, or anything else, could possibly tip the tree over.

"Goddamned cat!" Daddy mutters again.

"Patsy, watch your language; it's Christmas time," Mommy admonishes him.

Daddy frowns and complains further, "I can't believe it. How the hell can that crazy cat knock over a tree with a three-inch trunk nailed in the stand?"

Mommy says sarcastically, "Obviously, you did not nail the tree properly in the stand if a little cat could tip it over."

Biting his tongue, Daddy snaps back, "In a pig's tit! I nailed this tree in real good."

I think to myself that it really is virtually impossible for our cat to have pulled this gigantic tree down. Given the religious symbolism of the Christmas tree, I have no doubt but that the demon did it.

Buried underneath the rubble are our precious toys, some of which may have been damaged. We can only stand at the entrance to the room and watch. Soon, Mommy and Daddy have all the mess cleaned up. Daddy re-cuts the jagged end of the tree trunk so it fits back into the stand, then he nails it very securely in place... very securely!

Once the tree is back up, Mommy points out that the angel ornament at the top of the tree has lost its head! This is very disturbing and further confirms my suspicion that the demon in a rage attacked our tree and the angel figure in particular.

Mommy searches through the boxes of decorations to find another top for our tree. She finds an alternative, star-shaped ornament that has a small white light bulb in the center. Standing on the kitchen chair he brought in, Daddy carefully sets the star at the very top of the tree, then connects its electric plug into the set of plugs from the other light sets linked together in the back of the tree. The new top shines brightly at the top of the tree near the ceiling.

Pointing to the star ornament, Mommy says, "We don't have the angel ornament on top any longer, but now we have a beautiful bright star there that is like the bright star in the sky over Bethlehem. That star marked where the Infant Jesus was located in the stable with Mary and Joseph. Now we have our own star to remind us every year of the true meaning of Christmas... the birth of Jesus."

"And we will always remember how Blackie the cat helped us make that change," Larry says without meaning to be funny.

While everyone laughs, I realize that Larry's innocent observation **will,** in fact, help us remember this memorable event in our family's life... and the true meaning of Christmas.

Chapter 20

THE OLD LADY

January 1953

This Sunday morning, our Big Ben clock clangs loudly waking us up at eight o'clock signaling time to get up and get ready for our weekly 9 A.M. school Mass. Paddy, Kitty, and I dress in the chilly morning air while Mommy searches for three nickels to give us to put in the collection basket. Each of us receives a nickel. Then she gives Paddy a few dollars and tells him to buy the 'Sunday Daily News' newspaper and the 'Daily Mirror' newspaper, and then stop at the bakery shop on the way home to buy the usual dozen and a half rolls for breakfast.

I am envious of Larry who is allowed to stay in bed, warm and snug, sound asleep under the blankets. How lucky he is. He can stay in bed while we have to get up early in the morning and go out into the cold morning air for a long walk to St. Monica's Church. But then, we get to attend Mass. Now I feel sorry for him because Mommy and Daddy only take Larry and Geri to Mass twice a year on Easter and Christmas. They tell us that is their yearly duty as Catholics.

This is not correct. I remember one of the nuns telling my class that many older Catholics believe this, but they are wrong! Everyone is supposed to go to Mass every Sunday.

Paddy, Kitty, and I make our way to St. Monica's walking closely together through the brightly sunlit streets of Yorkville that are deserted except for kids like us on their way to the nine o'clock school Mass. The cold brisk air shocks my nostrils and lungs causing me to pull my jacket up in front of my mouth and nose. We rarely speak as we hurry on our early Sunday morning journey walking shoulder to shoulder alongside one another.

Immediately upon entering the church, Paddy reminds us that we have to meet right outside the church by the front steps after Mass. We split up now and head to where our respective classes are located in the church. There I check in with Sister Pascaline who marks in her little black book that I have come to the nine o'clock Mass. All the nuns do this for their respective classes.

If you miss this school Mass, when you go to school on Monday, the nun for your class calls your name out in the classroom and tells you to stand up and explain to the class why you were not at the nine o'clock school Mass with them. Then the nun asks to see a note that you had better have from your parents confirming why you were not at the Mass. Finally, the nun asks you to tell which other Mass you attended… and who the priest was that celebrated the Mass… and what the Gospel was about! Facing your teacher nun on Monday morning in school is really scary. It certainly is not worth it to me… no matter how sick I may be. I don't like to miss Mass.

At the nine o'clock school Mass, the nuns can always be found sitting in the last pew behind their class in their appointed area of the church. My pew is the one immediately in front of Sister Pascaline so when she checks my name off in her book, I genuflect in the direction of the Tabernacle where Jesus is located before I take a seat. The only time we genuflect together as a class in church is when we process in together, and sister uses a "clicker" which makes a distinctive sound we can all hear indicating we should genuflect together at that time.

Kneeling down in the customary manner, I bless myself by making the Sign of the Cross and as I do, I sense someone off to my left side in the center aisle. Looking over, there is an old lady limping toward me only a few feet away. I have seen her here in church once before. Her pale white face is soaked in more pain and sadness than last time. Judging by her shabby clothing, she appears to be very poor, may be even homeless.

Other schoolchildren notice her and begin to whisper and gesture in her direction. As she hobbles over, I can see her deformity more closely. It prevents her from standing erect. That sad, haunting expression on her face is heart breaking. Her arrival at my side causes a great commotion among my classmates and results in Sister Pascaline arriving to intervene.

"Excuse me, madam," Sister says politely, "I am sorry but these pews are reserved for the school children. You can't sit here; you can sit in the pews in the sides of the church."

The lady ignores what Sister says. Sister Pascaline repeats what she said, but with the same results. The old lady has her eyes set on me with a pleading expression. Sister Ramon, the seventh grade teacher, now comes to see if she can help but the lady ignores her as well.

"Please pray for me, sonny; I am so sick," she pleads as she reaches her thin, bony hands out to me.

Her haunting eyes reflect deep suffering within her spirit, not just her body. A great compassion for her wells up within me as I see and hear only her now. I reach out and gently hold her hands. Closing my eyes, I cry out to Jesus to have mercy on this poor, sad lady.

"Please heal her, Jesus. Please heal her mind, body, and spirit."

An exhilarating shower of graces descends upon me and travels onto the old lady causing her to flinch. God is hearing her faithful prayer. We are surrounded now by the nuns and some adult parishioners.

Sister Ramon, who is regarded throughout St. Monica's as quite

191

athletic, tells the lady she must leave and if she needs help, Sister says she will help her.

To everyone's surprise, the old lady abruptly stands straight up and cries out loudly, "I am cured! I am cured! God has healed me!"

Her words reverberate throughout the hallowed walls of St. Monica's Church stunning everyone. A miracle has taken place right in front of everyone's eyes! God, indeed, rewarded the faith of this poor old lady. He cured her right here, right now. She is standing up straight now as if nothing is wrong with her! I sense that God has also healed her broken spirit.

The nuns are especially taken back. They saw how badly crippled this lady was before I held her hands and prayed for her. Now she is standing perfectly straight and is loudly proclaiming her miraculous healing.

"Thank you, God, thank you!" she cries out loudly and buries her face in her hands.

Sister Ramon says, "Oh, my God... praise be to God. Please come to the back of the vestibule where you can thank God during the Mass."

She nods okay. The old lady may still be clothed in rags, but her whole countenance now exudes great joy and happiness as if she does not have a worry in the world.

Looking over to me, she says, "Thank you. You are an angel of God. Thank you."

As the ushers escort the old lady to the back, I turn to see that all my classmates and the nuns are looking at me apparently bewildered by what they just witnessed.

Sister Pascaline comes to my side and asks, "Are you all right, Robert?"

"Oh, yes, Sister, I feel wonderful; God healed her."

"Yes, I saw. That is amazing, Robert. You showed great courage and compassion for that poor lady, a wonderful example for all of us.

"Now Mass is about to begin so why don't you sit down and say a prayer of thanksgiving."

Turning to my classmates, she says, "All right, everyone return to your places now. Mass is about to begin."

During the Mass, I do thank God, and pray again for the old lady and all people who are suffering but have no one to pray for them.

After Mass, I meet Paddy and Kitty as planned outside the church in front of the center steps. They are anxious to hear the details about what happened with me and the old lady.

After telling them, Paddy scoffs, "You didn't heal that lady, Bobby. You can't heal anyone; you're just a kid."

Kitty protests, "That's not nice, Paddy; leave Bobby alone. He's a good boy. We've got to hurry otherwise Mommy will be mad if we don't get home on time."

"That's all right," I say. "Paddy is right, Kitty. I can't heal anyone; only God can heal people. I just ask God to heal people who are sad or suffering."

With Kitty's further urging, off we scoot to the newspaper stand near the corner of 79th Street and First Avenue where we buy the Sunday Daily News and the Daily Mirror newspapers. I clutch the bulky papers tightly to myself so I don't accidently drop them. Once before, I dropped them and had to chase the pages all over the street as the wind blew them. It seems there is always a strong wind blowing when I go in or out of church.

I hurry to keep up with Paddy and Kitty as we make our way to the German bakery on York Avenue between 80th and 81st Streets.

Paddy's comment reminds me how other people think the same way about me, but I cannot do anything about what other people think about me. It does bother me but have I no control over such things. It is God Who acts in ways and times that **He** believes are best for the good of people who cry out to Him. Sometimes God physically heals, sometimes He doesn't, but He **always** rewards the prayers of faith in ways that He knows are best.

I am just a bystander who is blessed to feel, and sometimes see, the healing graces of God descend upon those who cry out to Him. It is sad how so many people do not realize how God does, in fact, hear **all** prayers and answers every one of them... often in amazing ways.

Sadly, many people reject the reality that God can and does act in miraculous ways. I guess it is because they try to fit the limitless capacity of God into their limited human understanding. No one can do this. It is too bad that more people do not realize that there is nothing beyond God's ability as Jesus says in Matthew 19:26, "For mortals, it is impossible, but for God all things are possible."

News of what happened with the old lady in church spreads quickly throughout St. Monica's school and our Yorkville neighborhood. For the rest of the school year, I am teased by other children including some boys who bow in front of me and call me "Saint Robert," as they mock me and beg me to heal imaginary ills.

I know the devil is behind all this teasing, and enjoys every moment of my discomfort. It encourages others to hurt my feelings in the hope that this will discourage me from praying for people. How sad it is that given the choice, so many people choose to be mean and hurtful, rather than being kind and helpful. Even worse, how sad it is for people, young and old, to understand that demons exist and do everything they can to mislead and hurt us in any way they can.

Two weeks later, outside school on 80th Street during recess after lunch, Sister Cecil, the seventh grade teacher, comes over to where I am standing by myself.

"My, my... why are we being so anti-social today?" Sister says with a pleasant smile.

"You haven't budged one inch from that spot so far during recess! Your feet aren't glued to the ground now are they?"

I smile and tell her, "No, Sister."

Her humor and attention is appreciated.

"Well, seeing that your feet are not glued to the ground, why don't you join the rest of your classmates over there... while there is some recess time left."

I just don't want to tell her that other kids have been teasing me about healing the old lady in church.

"You will feel much better than standing around by yourself, you know... and your classmates will probably stop teasing you!"

Wow! She understands what I am going through.

"Try to understand, Robert, what you experienced is not what most people see in a lifetime! We Sisters are aware that God has blessed you in very special ways. Besides what we have witnessed ourselves, Father Kelly has shared much with us. So we know you are one of God's blessed children, and we can only imagine how confusing and difficult that must be for you."

This is such a comfort and relief to hear. I have great love and respect for the nuns. They are very special, holy women of God.

"You can come to me, or any of the other Sisters, anytime you need to talk. Okay?"

"Yes, Sister. Thank you."

"Now, about the children who tease you. They are not likely to tease you if you play with them, so why don't you give it a try?"

I am surprised and relieved to hear what Sister Cecil has said. Although Sister Cecil is sweet and gentle, I have heard that she also has a quick Irish temper that often results in a student getting a slap on the head.

I thank her again, give her my best smile, and quickly join the others. Playing relay races between the boys and girls doesn't help much, especially since my team of boys is easily beaten by the girls' team! I will probably be teased about this as well. It is not fair that we lost because we had some of the slowest boys in Yorkville on our team.

There is one redeeming aspect of this humbling experience, however. Judy was on the girls' team. I am always thrilled to be around her. She is so beautiful; her pretty face is framed by shiny jet-black hair; and, she is always smiling, happy, and kind to everyone.

194

One of the older boys bumps into me jostling me back to my surroundings. He and some of the other kids are laughing. He purposely ran into me to annoy me! I feel embarrassed and angry at him for doing this but there is nothing I can do because he is so much bigger than me. This is so unfair, I did not do anything to deserve this.

Ah, here comes Sister Cecil! She is walking very quickly toward the older boys with her hands clenched and a look on her face that shows she means business. She must have seen what that guy did to me, and now she is going to punish him. Coming up behind him, she slaps him in the head and yells at him for what he did!

"Nobody likes a bully! You understand what I am saying? Quit it and behave yourself or you and I are going to have a lot of trouble."

The shocked and embarrassed boy nods and slowly walks away as the boys and girls nearby laugh at him. I feel sorry for him but at the same time I am happy Sister Cecil taught him a lesson so now he knows what it feels like to be hit by someone bigger than you... and to be embarrassed in front of your peers. Hopefully, this will help him avoid a more painful experience in the future.

It's too bad Sister Cecil can't do the same with the spiritual bully, the demon that torments me.

Chapter 21

DEVILS IN DISGUISE

March 1953

"Hooray! Thank God that son-of-a-bitch devil in disguise, Joseph Stalin, is dead! May he rot in hell forever where he belongs!"

Daddy's hate-filled words rip through the air like venom from a snake as he rejoices in the death of this man who died on March 5th.

"The whole civilized world is rejoicing over his death," he adds.

"Why, Daddy? Who is Stalin? What did he do that was so bad?" I ask.

"Josef Stalin was the dictator of the Soviet Union who is responsible for the murder of millions of his own countrymen, and others," Daddy explains.

"He was the Premier of the Soviet Union from May 1941 to this month. He was one of the 'Bolsheviks' who brought about the 'October Revolution' in Russia in 1917. From 1922 until he just died, he was the General Secretary of the Communist Party of the Soviet Union's Central Committee.

"Like so many people in life, Stalin had the opportunity to achieve great things for the people entrusted to his leadership. Instead, he became one of the devils in disguise!

"Under his leadership from 1928 to 1930, there was the Ukrainian Holocaust where two million Ukrainian people were deported or jailed and another 400,000 were either hanged or shot. Women became 'communal property,' children were separated from their families and sent to China, and old people were burned so they would not consume any of the food supply!

"Then from 1932 to 1933, to squash what he considered 'Ukrainian nationalism,' Stalin starved the Ukrainian people by having all their wheat sent to Russia thereby creating an epic, unimaginable famine.

"People were forced to eat tree bark, leaves, milkweed, worms, rodents, cats, dogs, crows and anything they could find. There were reports that people died from hunger in the streets, in their homes, yards, fields, railway stations; dead bodies were everywhere. Bodies were collected and thrown into large mass graves and covered with lime. Millions of Ukrainians were starved to death according to reliable estimates!"

This is so horrendous, so terrible! How can anyone be capable of such mindless inhumanity? How can anyone be so cruel, so hateful to fellow human beings? Clearly, this is yet another work of the devil.

Daddy continues, "All told, it is estimated that through starvation, labor camps, and mass executions in Ukraine, Stalin was responsible for the death of over fourteen million of his fellow countrymen in Ukraine! That is more than all the people who died in all countries during the First World War!

"What he did in Russia was also demonic. In Russia during the 1930's, Stalin directed that Christian believers and their bibles be eliminated from society. This order was executed in an especially heinous way in the city of Stavropol. Thousands of bibles were taken away while huge masses of Christians were condemned as "enemies of the state," sent to prison, and ultimately died there.

"That is why I call Stalin 'a devil in disguise."

As Daddy was describing this horror, I pictured demons in and about the bad people who hurt innocent men, women, and children. Now every one of those evil people are likely spending all of eternity in the torments of hell for what they did.

"Another devil in disguise," Daddy continues, "is Adolph Hitler."

I immediately conjure up the image of a terrible demon in my mind.

"The evidence shows that he and the German people during World War Two tortured and killed over six million poor innocent Jewish men, women and children just because they were Jewish! He called them, 'useless eaters.'

"Hitler had the Nazis round up Jewish men, women and children from their homes and put them in what were like cattle-train cars and sent them a long distance to concentration camps. There they were all stripped naked, had gold teeth pulled out, were starved, and eventually were gassed to death in large gas chambers. The Nazis then burned their bodies in ovens!"

Daddy looks as sad as I feel as he adds, "That is not all. Hitler also had his Nazi doctors conduct experiments on these poor Jewish people. Some of the 'tests' the Nazi doctors performed included staking naked Jewish people to the ground outside in the winter time in below freezing temperatures and hosing them down with water to see how long they would survive. They also broke the bones of some of these people to see how long they could survive that way. Others they shot in an arm or a leg to see how long someone with gun-shot wounds could survive in the freezing cold!"

"Why did they do this, Daddy?" I ask.

"They conducted these 'experiments' as they called them so they could estimate how long a German soldier might survive in similar conditions during the war!

"Meanwhile, everywhere his 'SS' troops went they burned down whole villages and slaughtered tens of thousands of innocent people."

As Daddy was describing these crimes against God and man, I pictured demons once again in the background, and told Daddy that I am sure the devil must have reveled in all this.

"After the war ended," he adds, "most of the Nazis were brought to trial and many were executed for their crimes. Hitler was able to evade trial and punishment by killing himself and his girlfriend, Eva Braun, when he realized that the Nazis had lost the war.

"You know, Bobby, the German people followed Hitler even though they knew that he was committing crimes against humanity. In the end, that cost them all dearly."

"Just like all the angels who followed Lucifer," I observe.

"There are yet other devils in disguise who showed themselves during the Second World War," Daddy continues.

"The Japanese.

"First of all, look at what they did to us at Pearl Harbor pulling off a sneak attack killing thousands of our innocent young military men and women while they were asleep in their beds! In addition, do you know what they did in the prison camps? They went around gang raping the women and little girls in front of their families before killing them.

"They also played a game in which they put a water hose in a baby's mouth and ran the water until the baby's stomach was bloated. Then they threw the baby up in the air and used their bayonets to spear the baby in the air!"

Once again, I envision the presence of demons in all these unspeakable acts against God and fellow human beings.

Mommy protests, "Patsy, that is all a little too graphic for Bobby to hear. Please stop, no more."

"There is one last important thing I want Bobby to hear, then I will say no more," Daddy promises.

"For all those who committed such terrible crimes against humanity, and have eluded punishment here on earth, it does **not** mean that they will also get away with their crimes when they die and cross the lifeline. Without exception, every one of them will stand before God, and be held accountable for their crimes, and they **will** be punished accordingly.

"As Jesus says in Matthew 5:26, 'every penny must be repaid!'"

198

Chapter 22

BLIND CHARLIE

April 1953

Daddy has not been the same since his mother, Nana, died over a year ago. He still deeply grieves her loss. Uncharacteristically quiet and withdrawn, he hardly speaks or sings as he used to do. Mommy explains that because Daddy loved his mom so much and misses her so greatly, it is going to take him a long, long time to get over losing her.

How can you ever get over missing your mom, I wonder.

"Try to be quiet around your father, children," she suggests, "and Bobby, please don't talk about Nana like you did the other day."

Unfortunately, I was not thinking when I told Daddy about my memories of Nana. How loving and gentle she was with me, and how I miss her and our walks to visit her in her apartment on First Avenue. Tears rolled down Daddy's face even though he smiled and nodded his head approvingly.

Right now, he is asleep but he will soon be rising since it is nearly one in the afternoon. He has to leave at three o'clock in order to get to his job at the Railway Express Company.

Daddy often says how much he enjoys his job even though he works on the night shift until midnight. We do not like this because we rarely get to spend time with him during the week. Right now, Mommy is making a fresh pot of tea for him. Seeing that we are out of milk again, she gets irritated because she did not know we were running low. She always tells us to be thoughtful and tell her when we drink the last of the milk so we can buy more.

"Now I have no milk for your father's oatmeal and tea," she complains, "Why can't you kids ever remember to tell me when you drink the last of the milk?"

"Bobby and Larry, how would you like to earn two cents each by going to Carolina's store to get two quarts of milk?" Mommy entices us.

Hearing, "two cents each," is all the coaxing we need to come running. Of course, we would go to the store for Mommy for nothing as we have many times before.

"Make sure you ask if the milk is fresh before you pay for it," she reminds us.

Larry and I race each other down the stairs as usual, and run all the way to the grocery store. At the store, we enter and walk right over to the dairy case where we retrieve two quarts of milk and bring them to the front counter. Carolina and her husband, Ernie, are very pleasant people with a strong German accent. Sometimes when we go in their store, they speak German to us and giggle when they see the confused looks on our faces.

I tell them, "Our mother told us to ask if the milk is fresh before we pay for it."

"Oh, it is fresh, I assure you," the man smiles and assures us.

Taking our money and putting the milk containers in a small brown paper bag, he says, "Before you go, boys, how would you like to see something really interesting?"

Being on the other side of the counter from him, I feel safe in saying, "Sure."

He picks up an egg from a carton on the counter and says, "Now watch carefully, this is no trick."

Raising the egg slightly above the counter in his right hand, he taps it down lightly on the counter, cracks it, and in one fluid motion holds it up in the air above his open mouth. He opens the shell allowing the contents of the egg to flow down into his open mouth in one gulp!

"Mmmm, delicious!" he exclaims as he swallows it.

"Eeewww!" Larry and I protest, 'That is disgusting! Why did you do that?"

As they laugh at our reaction, he says, "Disgusting, eh? I will have you know that is one of the best foods you can eat! Raw eggs are filled with lots of protein to help you build big strong muscles and avoid all kinds of sicknesses. You should eat them just like I did."

"I could never eat a raw egg like that; it's too slimy," I tell him.

"How do you know if you have never tried it? Here take one and try it," Ernie says extending an egg toward me.

"No thanks, mister, not me!" I answer as Larry and I quickly exit the store to the sound of laughter behind us.

Rather than going right back home, I think it might be fun to go down the block first to spend our two cents on candy at Blind Charlie's candy store. As the name infers, Charlie, the sole owner and operator of this small candy store, is completely blind. I am intrigued by the black glasses he wears covering his eyes. Why does he wear them if he is totally blind? It seems silly to do so.

His store is a popular gathering place for kids. It is so dark and dingy inside, I do not think Charlie is missing much by not being able to see his store. Interestingly, all the candy he sells is enclosed behind a glass case that is only open on his side of the counter.

"Hi, Charlie," Larry greets him as we enter. "Why do you keep all your candy inside the case like that?"

Turning in the direction of Larry's voice, Charlie answers, "I do that because there are little bastards who come in here and steal the candy knowing I am blind and can't see them. That's why."

I am shocked to think that anyone would steal something from a poor blind man like Charlie.

"Do you see a small opening at the bottom of the front panel in front of you?" Charlie continues.

I nod that yes I see it, but then realize Charlie is blind and can't see that I am nodding yes.

Feeling embarrassed, I quickly say, "Yes, Charlie, we see it."

"Well, they come in here without saying anything and stick their fingers in through that opening to steal some candy before they run out. I yell at them, 'Thou shall not steal! I may be blind, but God is not!' One of these days, I'm going to catch their fingers sticking through that opening, and maybe I'll break them off!"

I do not think he would really break them off. Poor Charlie, he does not realize that he allows those boys to steal something far more valuable than the candy... his peace.

Larry and I decide to get a strip of colored candy dots on a long, narrow piece of white paper. They cost two cents each.

After we give Charlie our pennies, he hands over the two strips and tells us, "Enjoy them, boys."

He turns his back to put the pennies in a flat cigar box he keeps on a shelf directly behind him. As he does, the demon says it would be very funny if I grab a handful of candy through the small opening in the glass partition! My angel reminds me that the seventh Commandment of God is 'thou shalt not steal.'

Even though I know I should not do this, I decide it would be very funny to do it anyway after Charlie spoke about other kids stealing from him. A quick assessment of the situation convinces me that I can do it without getting caught by Charlie, so I quickly squeeze my right hand in and grab a few Bazooka bubble gum pieces.

Stuffing them in my pocket as I walk with Larry, I call out, "Thanks, Charlie."

"Come again, boys," he responds kindly.

Outside, Larry looks shocked, "Bobby, you just stole candy from Blind Charlie! That's terrible! How could you do that? That's so wrong!"

I immediately feel the shame of what I did.

"I know, Larry. The demon told me it would be funny to steal from Charlie after he told us how other boys do it."

Larry protests, "But that's wrong, Bobby. You're mean for stealing from poor Blind Charlie. Like Charlie said, God saw what you did, and will make you pay much more for the candy someday. Besides, if the police catch you, Mommy says they'll put you in jail where they beat you and you may never see us again."

Standing outside Charlie's store, I pull the bubble gum pieces out of my pocket and study them as I think about what I have done. I feel so badly that I stole something… especially from Blind Charlie.

"I'm going to give it back, Larry," I tell him.

I walk back into Blind Charlie's store followed by Larry.

"Back again," Charlie says.

Confused, I ask, "How do you know it's us?"

"I recognize the sound of your footsteps. You see, God has given me better hearing than most people to compensate for the fact that I can't see."

"Oh, I see," I reply, not trying to be funny.

"Very funny!" Charlie says good-naturedly.

"By the way, some kid stole some bubble gums from you so my little brother told him to bring them back. So, here they are."

I place the bubble gums on top of the glass case and wait for Charlie's reaction. He does not say anything; he just stands there motionless like a statue staring off into space.

Then slowly, a smile graces his face as he says, "You tell that boy for me that stealing is not what anyone should do. Remember what I said… God sees everything."

After a pause, he adds, "You know, a wise man named Wadsworth once said, 'None are so blind as those who do not see!' But on the other hand, honesty… like returning stolen property… is something that everyone sees and admires. You just did something very special by returning that gum to me. As a reward, I want you to take a piece for yourself… and one for your little brother too."

I reach up and take two pieces… and two pieces only… as I thank Charlie for the gum and the good advice.

A few days later, Daddy tells us he heard that Blind Charlie has died! I am shocked and greatly saddened with the loss of someone who I feel has been so much a part of my life. I am going to miss him dearly. Now I am so glad that I returned the gums I stole from him.

I am also happy that Charlie is no longer blind.

Chapter 23

FIRST HOLY COMMUNION

May 1953

I still miss Nana Walsh and often think about the happy times we spent with her. How I wish we could go for another walk up to First Avenue like we used to on our way to visit her in her top floor apartment. But now she is gone from this physical world. All I have now are the happy memories and the comfort in knowing that someday I will see her again in heaven.

As Mommy encourages us to do, I pray for Nana every day. If she is in purgatory as Mommy says might be the case, I hope my prayers help her to get out sooner. I also pray for Daddy who is in a kind of "purgatory of grief" here on earth because his heart aches missing his mother, Nana.

Mommy told me that God hears and answers our prayers that are said from the heart. I wish He would hurry up and comfort the people I pray for. Why does He take so long sometimes? Mommy says that everything must be in God's time, not ours, and that God's time is always the best time. I just wish that God would make His time the same as my time.

Often when I pray, I see the holy white lights surrounding me, and family members who have died before me. Mommy says that some of our relatives may be stuck in purgatory, and need our prayers to help them get out of purgatory sooner. She explained that God sometimes allows them to call out to us so we can know they need our prayers. When I pray for our relatives, I sense that they know I am praying for them, and they are grateful. Some of them need lots of prayers before they can get to heaven.

Good Friday each year is one of the most effective times to pray for the souls in purgatory. On that day, there are more souls freed from purgatory into the fullness of heaven than on other religious holidays because Good Friday is the day on which Jesus performed the greatest act of love and deliverance for us all. Jesus made restitution for all the sins committed by mankind over all the ages. While Good Friday is a day of enormous sorrow because of the suffering Jesus endured for us, it is ultimately a day of infinite hope and promise.

This past Good Friday I imagined how the demons must have celebrated when Jesus was abandoned by His closest friends, the apostles, the first bishops of our church, and that was after He was betrayed by one of them, Judas. Then later, when Jesus was being tried, Peter, the first pope, actually denied knowing Jesus three times! And no one came to rescue Jesus when the soldiers beat Him and forced Him to carry the heavy wooden cross a long distance to the place where they killed Him by nailing Him to the Cross.

How could the apostles abandon Jesus as they did? It greatly disturbs me that personally knowing Jesus was not enough for them. And yet, despite all this, Jesus still forgave them. That is why, I believe there is hope for sinners like me and for all of us.

I often think of all the stories I have been told of Jesus's life and teachings from Mommy, Daddy, Sister Pascaline, and the priests at St. Monica's. The demon often floods my mind telling me these stories are not true, that they are made up 'fairy tales' by people who are now long dead so we can't confirm anything the church tells us.

I ignore these blasphemous thoughts whenever I hear them. Instead, I think of Jesus in the midst of many people including small children. They must have enjoyed hearing the extraordinary quality of His voice that must have comforted all who heard Him. I am sure He enthralled young and old with entertaining stories on how to live in love, peace and happiness.

One of my favorite visions is of Jesus sitting on a hill with many men, women and children gathered around Him, listening to His counsel of love and salvation. The children especially must have enjoyed His stories, as I am sure He enjoyed telling them. He loved ministering to people's hearts, minds, and souls as evidenced by all the miracles of mercy He performed.

The bible tells us that news of His miracles and great love spread far and wide by word of mouth so everywhere He went large crowds of curious people gathered around Him to hear what He had to say and to witness his miraculous feats of healing.

What an indescribable joy it must have been for those who were so fortunate to be in His presence and gaze directly into His eyes and feel the reality of His infinite personage. His eyes must have conveyed the qualities of understanding, forgiveness, tranquility, and above all else... love.

A priest once told us in church that Jesus knows each one of us intimately well in all our humanness, all we have ever done, all we will ever do... and yet He still loves us!

By the time my thoughts return to my present surroundings, I recall that I will soon be receiving Holy Communion for the very first time. What an exciting moment in my life. However, the devil has been trying to discourage me from receiving by placing thoughts in my mind that I am not worthy, and that as a consequence, the host which is large and dry will get stuck in my throat and choke me to death! I dismiss such thoughts but they worry me any way.

The night before I am to receive my first Holy Communion, I find myself still struggling with the feeling that I am not worthy to receive Jesus, and therefore should not. My thoughts drift off to the Consecration of the

Mass when the priest places his ordained hands over the bread and wine at which point they are transformed by God into the Body and Blood of Christ!

The demon's sinister voice says, "That's just the point; no man can transform bread and wine into **His** Body and Blood!"

But I remember what the priest told us, "Priests only assist God during the Mass by offering the bread and wine up to God the Father Who transforms it into the Body and Blood of Jesus, and in so doing accepts our offering of Jesus as a sacrifice in reparation for our sins.

"Only in this way can offenses against God be relieved by the ultimate sacrifice from God's own Son. That's why Jesus died on the cross, and why we call the Mass, 'the Holy Sacrifice of the Mass.' We actually relive Jesus's death and resurrection during each Mass."

To this, I think about how Jesus walked on this earth as a man, He took on all the appearances and nature of a man. He, indeed, **was** a man. He looked, felt, spoke and lived as a man, but He is also the Son of God who chose to come live among us so that He could make restitution for our sins and show us how to live properly.

Some of the people who personally met Jesus must have had difficulty believing that He is the Son of God living within the human body they saw before them! How much more difficult is it for people to believe that Jesus is in the bread and wine we see consecrated during Mass! It requires faith and trust to believe in what our senses cannot prove or understand. The peace and certainty of sleep soon overtakes me.

It seems only moments later that Mommy wakes me up reminding me that today is one of the most important days of my life. Everyone else in the family is already busy getting dressed. The air of excitement in our home blends naturally with the glorious sunshine streaming in through the kitchen window. Mommy helps me get dressed in an outfit of brand new clothing including underwear, white shirt, white clip-on tie, navy-blue suit, blue socks, black shoes and finally, a large white satin bow that is tied around my upper left jacket sleeve.

"All these new clothes, Robert, are symbols of your new beginning today when you receive the Body of Christ for the first time," Mommy explains, "Other than the day you were baptized, this is the greatest day of your life."

"I don't feel good, Mommy; I feel sick and nervous," I tell her.

Mommy looks surprised, "Oh, I'm so sorry to hear that, honey, especially on such a special day for you. You probably feel sick because you have not had anything to eat since midnight. And being nervous is only normal, son. Don't worry about it. You'll feel much better once you get to church," she assures me.

"Mommy, why can't we eat anything after midnight?" I ask.

"Didn't Sister Pascaline explain that?" she answers with a question of her own.

I tell her I don't remember.

"Well, first of all, it is a personal sacrifice. Secondly, it's just to make sure that you don't have any food in your stomach when you swallow Holy Communion. It is done out of respect for the Body of Christ," she explains.

I wonder about this because at the very first Mass and Holy Communion at the Last Supper, Jesus and the Apostles received Communion right after eating dinner together! I reasoned that Jesus showed us that it is not necessary for us to fast before we receive Communion. In any event, what I am most concerned about right now is that I do not feel worthy to receive the sacred Body of Christ in Holy Communion. I feel so nervous and conflicted over this feeling.

As our family walks along York Avenue heading toward St. Monica's on 79th Street, we are bathed in the early morning Spring sunshine. On 80th Street, I see Judy and three of the girls in our class. They look so beautiful in their brilliant white dresses, white see-through veils, white pocketbooks, white gloves, white socks, and white shoes. Knowing they also went to their First Holy Confession, their souls must also be "white as snow."

How appropriate for first Holy Communion.

Mommy and Daddy leave me in front of St. Monica's School, give me a kiss, and wish me well. Daddy's kiss, of course, is a giant-sized, "schmushkypop" as he calls it. Paddy, Kitty, and Larry smile projecting the special bond of love and understanding shared by us. Geri is sound asleep, the early morning hour is too much for her so I lean into her carriage and give her a kiss on the cheek.

Inside our classroom, I huddle together with my classmates and listen to all the eager, nervous chattering going on. Suddenly, Sister Pascaline claps her hands loudly and puts her right forefinger across her lips signifying that we should now be quiet. Silence falls upon our group as we stand motionless staring at Sister, anxiously waiting for her next instruction.

She directs us to line up as we have practiced many times before - boys all together on the left in height order, girls on the right also in height order. I am happy that I am one of the tallest boys in our class because I get to stand near the back of the line that is closer to where Judy is located on the girls' line.

Sister reminds us of the holiness of today's celebration and says, "If you have committed a sin since you went to your First Holy Confession last Friday, please come see me before we process into church. For example, did you eat meat on Friday? Or perhaps you may have forgotten to confess a sin during your first confession."

Last Friday during school hours, all of us who are going to receive our First Holy Communion went to confession for the first time. Sister Pascaline spent a great deal of time in the weeks before explaining how confession is a sacrament in which God allows us to confess our sins to a priest, God's representative, and then receive forgiveness and then have to say some prayers for penance. Sister also taught us how to conduct a thorough examination of conscience before confession.

She explained that Jesus had created the ability for priests to represent Him in confession when told the apostles, "What you bind on earth is bound in heaven, and whose sins you forgive, they are forgiven."

No one responds to Sister's question about committing a sin.

Her eyes scan our class from one side to the other before she says, "Okay, children, I want all of you to close your eyes for a moment and think about what I just said. I want you to be sure that you have confessed all your sins and have been spiritually cleansed in preparation for your First Holy Communion. If there is something you are not sure about, just raise your hand and I will come speak with you privately."

After a long, painful pause she adds, "There are priests available right now to hear your confession if need be. Don't be ashamed or afraid to talk to Sister now, children."

I am the only one to raise a hand. Sister looks down the long line of boys until her eyes fall on my hand raised as high as I can to ensure Sister sees it. Sister looks very surprised to see anyone's hand go up, especially mine!

She quickly recovers and announces to my great embarrassment, "Okay, Robert, since you are the only one, why don't you and I stay here in the classroom so we can talk while the rest of the class goes to the sacristy with the other first grade class."

Everyone in my class turns around to look at me amidst a flurry of giggling. They are all probably thinking I have committed some sins that I need to confess! I am so embarrassed.

"Shhhhh, be quiet and turn around, children!" Sister scolds everyone, "Don't be so rude to Robert. What he and I must discuss is none or your business. Now be quiet!" she snaps.

"Thanks a lot, Sister," I think to myself. I will never hear the end of this now from my classmates. Everyone files quietly past in two orderly lines leaving Sister and me alone, standing perfectly still, staring at each other. Sister Pascaline gently puts her hands on my shoulders and asks what is wrong.

Looking away from her piercing eyes, I stare blankly across the empty room and summon up the courage to tell her that a voice keeps telling me that I should not receive my first Holy Communion because I am not worthy.

Sister smiles and says, "Robert! It is wonderful that you feel that way. That is how we all should feel; none of us is worthy! However, it is by the grace of God that He gives us this gift and He **wants** us to receive Holy Communion even though we are not worthy."

Placing her right hand firmly under my chin, she forces me to look up into her eyes and asks, "Do you understand, Robert?"

I try to pull my face away from her steady gaze but to no avail; she has an iron-tight grip on me. My heart melts under her maternal concern leaving me unable to hold back my tears as I tell her that I am also afraid that the dry host will get stuck in my throat and choke me.

"Oh, Robert," she laughs and shakes her head from side to side, "you can't possibly choke on the Eucharist! It is far too small and thin. The things you little people worry about never ceases to amaze me. Where did you get such an idea?"

"The evil voice keeps telling me that!" I confide in her.

"An evil voice! she repeats incredulously. "What evil voice?"

"The voice of a demon," I tell her.

Sister's smile quickly disappears and is replaced with a stunned look of serious concern.

"Robert, you must not pay attention to any 'evil voices' you hear telling you such things. They are **not** true. What **is** true is that Jesus loves you very much and wants you to receive Him in First Holy Communion. There is absolutely no danger that you will choke on the host. Do you understand?"

I know Sister would never mislead me; she is a nun and always tells the truth. I feel greatly relieved now so I tell her that I no longer worry about choking, but I still feel I am unworthy to receive Jesus in Holy Communion.

"Very well, Robert," she says apparently resolved that there is nothing more she can do to help me with my feelings of unworthiness.

"Father Kelly is available here to speak with anyone with concerns such as yours," she tells me, "why don't we go have a talk with him. Okay?"

This is good news for me because Father Kelly understands better than any of the priests at St. Monica's the extraordinary things happening in my life. Beginning with his first visit to my home three years ago, he has witnessed how the demon pursues and torments me. Through follow up visits, he has also seen evidence of the unique gifts of healing God has bestowed upon me. I know Father Kelly will be able to help me this morning.

Sister Pascaline escorts me quickly through the silent second floor hallway all the way to the sacristy where all my classmates are waiting in two long lines for Mass to begin. As we walk past them on our right, I can feel their eyes gawking at me, and I can hear an occasional whisper about me having to go to confession because I have sinned!

I walk directly behind Sister Pascaline as we briskly make our way into the sacristy first passing the area where the altar boys put on their vestments, then the area where the priests put on theirs before Mass. Sister's long flowing veil made of black solid material flows playfully behind her and partially blocks my forward vision as we hurry along faster and faster as if we must get somewhere before an imminent deadline.

The sacristy is located within the church building itself but is enclosed separately from the rest of the church. It is situated off to the front right side of St. Monica's Church and is cordoned off by two separate sets of double doors. One set is up by a landing three steps high where I see three priests and several altar boys waiting to enter the front of the church right now. The other set of doors is located at the foot of the three steps where they now stand wide open in front of the two lines of children who are nervously waiting to enter the church to begin Mass and receive their First Holy Communion.

The darkly colored stained glass inserts on the upper half of the four doors added sparkle and life to an otherwise somber-looking area created by the dark brown, wooden walls and closets lining the inside of the sacristy. Over to our left is a ten-foot long dressing table running along the long side of the rectangular-shaped room. There are many long, thin drawers located under the dressing table making it look like a gigantic, odd shaped dresser.

As we face this, directly behind us are four tall individual closets each separated by a bench with a dark stained-glass window overhead allowing light from the outside to illuminate the sacristy. I feel a great sense of reverence and comfort standing in this special room.

Sister Pascaline and I stand together without speaking. We are off to the left side just behind where Father Kelly is looking through the thin drawers of the dressing table. He seems preoccupied and nervous, as does the altar boy standing behind him to his left holding a large colorful garment across his arms. Altar boys help the priest by holding the liturgical garments the priest must put on.

Father Kelly is wearing his long, white surplus as he hastily grabs a long thin stole out of one of the top drawers. Quickly raising it to his lips, he kisses the figure of a cross-embroidered on the center of the stole, then whips it over the back of his neck allowing it to drape down in front of him.

He quickly swings around to the waiting altar boy who extends the neatly folded garment out toward him. Father snaps it up and shakes it out so that it makes a loud cracking noise. Within a second, he has it over his head and down over his body. The loose fitting half-sleeves give his arms plenty of freedom in moving about as he makes final adjustments to his ceremonial garments.

Noticing Sister Pascaline standing next to me, he looks surprised as he politely greets her with a smile and a nod. Looking at me, it is almost as if he expected to see me here having some difficulty on my First Holy Communion day.

Sister Pascaline apologizes for disturbing him and asks him to take a moment to speak with me. Stepping closer to him, she leans over and whispers something in his right ear while his eyes continue studying me.

Father nods his head acknowledging that he understands and tells her, "Everything will be fine; Robert and I are old friends. You can just leave Robert with me, Sister. Thank you."

Taking a step back, sister says softly, "Thank you, Father," then turns and walks briskly over to join the other nuns waiting by the line of First Holy Communicants.

"Father, will you be coming out with us?" one of the other priests calls out to Father Kelly, referring to the procession out to the center altar.

"No," he answers, "You go ahead, I'll be there soon."

All eyes turn to me in curiosity. I feel embarrassed and uncomfortable. The older priest nods to one of the altar boys who reaches up and rings the bell announcing to the waiting congregation that the priests are now coming out to begin the celebration of the Mass. As the altar boys lead the procession out to the center altar followed by the priests, the unique sounds of people rising from their squeaky pews fills the church proper outside the sacristy.

The church organ and choir adds beautiful, joyful music as the triumphant procession of boys and girls enter the church on their way to their first Holy Communion. Everyone, that is, except me.

I feel so out of place standing here next to Father Kelly as my classmates march in two by two past me. All are dressed the same, and have their hands folded reverently together in front of their chests. The girls look so pretty wearing their white dresses. As Judy passes, she smiles at me and for that moment all my embarrassment disappears.

Soon the last of them enters the church leaving only Father Kelly and me in the once crowded sacristy.

Father walks over to the first set of doors and closes them quietly, then he climbs up the three steps to close the other set of double doors. Standing there, he looks out into the church at people who can't see him in return. Father turns to me standing alone in the middle of the sacristy. No words are exchanged as we stand motionless facing each other. I wonder what he is thinking? He carefully steps down, walks over to my side, and crouches down to talk to me.

Speaking with his Irish accent, he says, "From what Sister tells me, you are upset about receiving you First Holy Communion."

I nod yes.

"Listen carefully, son; we don't have much time. There is only one thing you should be thinking about when it comes to your First Holy Communion, and it is this: at the Last Supper Jesus said, 'Do this in memory of Me.' What He means is that we should receive Holy Communion and do so often."

What Father says is important to me because it is what Jesus specifically said we should do.

"You see, it has nothing to do with any of us being worthy. None of us is worthy, not even the saints of our church. But we all receive Holy Communion because that is what Jesus tells us to do, and it is **His personal gift** to us, the greatest gift of all from God Himself!"

Gently resting his hand on my shoulder and looking deeply into my eyes, he says, "I understand what you are going through, Robert. We have spoken about this before. You know that God has blessed you in most extraordinary spiritual ways. You are what we call 'a blessed child of God.'

"You also know that the devil is aware of this, and so it does everything it can to dissuade you from focusing on God and the gifts He has given you. Knowing this, you should be able to recognize that the devil is trying to keep you from **the greatest gift** God wishes to give you… **Holy Communion**!

"The devil is the father of lies and will tell you anything and everything to keep you from receiving Holy Communion! So you must ignore everything it says, and remember only the words of Jesus Who personally invites you to receive your First Holy Communion today."

Father Kelly really understands.

I nod yes, of course, and for the first time today, I feel relieved so I can focus once again on this special once in a lifetime moment, my first Holy Communion. Father can tell that he has helped me to understand. Thank God for Father Kelly in my life.

"You know, Robert, there is no better time or place than right now to go march on out there and receive our Blessed Lord in Holy Communion, and I will be proud to walk out there with you!"

I nod yes and ask for a few moments to clear my mind of all things except that I am about to receive Our Lord in my First Holy Communion. I listen as an altar boy out at the center altar where Mass is being celebrated rings the hand-held bell three times signaling that the Consecration of the Mass is about to take place. Father Kelly kneels down on the floor in front of the bench and extends his right hand reverently in the direction of the main altar.

Staying right where I am, I also kneel down on the hard floor and am comforted by the warm sunlight streaming down on me through the stained-glass window behind me. I watch Father closely as I think about what is going on outside at the main altar. The bell is rung again, but only once this time. Although I can't see the priest, I know from the ringing of the bell one time that the priest is placing his hands over the host and chalice. I know that at this moment Jesus has arrived out at the main altar.

Now there is the sound of three bells signifying that the priest is raising the consecrated Host as an offering up to God the Father. "Ding-a-ling-a-ling, ding-a-ling-a-ling, ding-a-ling-a-ling," the bell echoes throughout our huge church reverberating throughout the church filling my ears with their magical sound and extraordinary message.

Jesus is here. Feeling His powerful, loving presence all around me, I call out to Him and ask Him to help me find the courage to go out into the church in front of the entire congregation to receive Him in my First Holy Communion.

Father Kelly is still kneeling in front of the bench. A feeling of panic rips through me as I realize that time may run out before I can receive. The distribution of Holy Communion will be over soon!

I jump up and shout, "Father, I would like to receive my First Holy Communion."

"That's wonderful, Robert!" he exclaims, "Let's go!"

Father jubilantly opens the double doors, grabs my right hand, and leads me out in front of the packed church. As we cross directly past the right side-altar speeding on our way toward the center-altar, we make a lightning fast genuflection then resume our fast pace toward the center altar.

As I gaze upon the sanctuary, a breath-taking vision greets me. The entire sanctuary including the main altar is awash in a brilliant, glorious, white light illuminating the whole area. This sacred area is completely filled with dazzling white spirits and angels all bowing in joyful reverence to the presence of Jesus in the Eucharist. A song of praise and adoration is being sung by these holy spirits.

In the midst of this, two lines of boys and girls extending up the entire middle aisle make their way up the altar steps where an older priest sits in a chair facing the congregation. He is giving Communion to each one who kneels down before him. Although there is a boy and girl at the very top step kneeling down before the priest, Father Kelly brings me up the altar steps to the top. My heart is pounding as Father tells me to kneel down to the side of the older priest. Emotions of great expectation swirl within me as my heart beats wildly.

The priest turns to Father Kelly and asks, "Why isn't this boy on line with the others?"

Father explains, "He hasn't been feeling well, Father, but he can receive now... right now!"

"I see," the priest says before reaching into the golden Ciborium filled with tiny, round, white consecrated Hosts. Taking one out, he holds It up directly in front of my eyes as he says something I can't hear. A brilliant white light flows outward from the Host as the priest extends It and places the Host in my mouth.

All else is suspended for me; I am not aware of anything else except the Holy Communion I have just received. A tingling sensation flows throughout my entire being as the Spirit of God fills me. Father Kelly's hands on my arms pull me straight up and away. I feel a little dizzy as I stumble down the altar steps.

As we make our way back to the sacristy, it does not seem right to rush away after having just received Holy Communion. I wish I could stay right there to revel in this wonderful, holy moment for a long time.

Father Kelly sits down on the bench next to me and says, "Congratulations, son. I am very happy for you. I know you will always remember this day... and receive Holy Communion as often and as you can."

Yes, Father," I think, "I will never forget."

We sit peacefully together as the Mass approaches its completion. For the first time, I notice the many beautiful flowers in the church today filling it with a wonderful, sweet fragrance. The sun pouring brightly in through the church's large stained glass windows creates a dazzling display of warm hues fitting, it seems, for the celebration of First Holy Communion this morning.

How wonderful it is to sit here with the One who loves me so completely... and with Father Kelly.

Chapter 24

CONEY ISLAND
AND STEEPLECHASE

June 1953

Mommy recently wrote to a writer at the New York Daily News who has a column entitled, **"A Friend in Need."** As the title indicates, this is an effort by the newspaper to bring attention to the needs of poor people in the greater New York area so charitable people who read the paper can help. Without mentioning our name, Mommy had described our large family, how poor we are, and what people can to help if they wish.

She never dreamed that her letter would actually get published in the newspaper, but here it is only ten days after she mailed it! I think she is more amazed than we are that her letter was actually published! Gathering closely around her, we listen as Mommy carefully reads the article.

Then she tells us, "I wrote that letter because Daddy often gets 'bumped off' at his job with Railway Express, and when he does, he earns less money so we can't pay our bills."

"What does it mean to get 'bumped off,' Mommy?" I ask.

"Well, they call it that, Bobby, because the men with the most "'seniority,' that means time working with the company, are the ones who get to work when there's only a limited number of jobs available. That's what happens when Daddy gets 'bumped off' his job by someone who has more seniority than he does."

"Why did you write to a newspaper about us?" Paddy asks.

"Because I thought some rich people who read the paper might feel sorry for us and send clothing and money to help. That's why I did it. Just watch, before you know it, someone is going to write asking how they can help us."

Mommy was right. A few weeks later, Mommy receives a letter that was sent to the newspaper for us. She is excited as she reads the letter and tells us it is from a lady who read the article about us in the Daily News Newspaper and now wants to help us. The lady says she is an older lady whose husband passed away, and she doesn't have children at home. She writes that she lives in Connecticut, and her name is "Mrs. Duden."

"Oh, wow! Listen to what she writes," Mommy exclaims. 'Please send me a list of all the clothes each of your children needs including their sizes. I can't promise that I will be able to get them all, but I will do my best. In the meantime, I have enclosed twenty dollars which I hope will help in some way."

Mommy holds up a crisp, new-looking twenty-dollar bill!

"Hooray!" we cheer.

"Does this mean we're rich?" Larry wants to know.

Mommy laughs, "No, it doesn't mean we are rich, Larry. But I tell you what, it'll certainly pay for a trip to Coney Island and Steeplechase Amusement Park!"

This sets off another frenzy of cheering. If there is one thing we are all dying to do, it is to go to Coney Island and go on the great rides at Steeplechase Amusement Park Mommy has told us so much about.

"When can we go, Mommy?" When can we go?" Paddy asks.

"I'll talk to your father and see if we can go this Saturday the 20th because it's Daddy's 37th birthday. I'm sure he'd love to go to Coney Island; it's one of his favorite places in the whole world."

More hugging and cheering follows now that we know we're finally going to go to Coney Island!

Saturday arrives, and since Daddy said we can go today, everyone gets up bright and early and quickly gulps down our favorite breakfast of Kellogg's corn flakes with bananas and milk. We already have our bathing trunks on under our clothes as Mommy instructed.

Daddy reminds Mommy to put sun lotion on us since we're not accustomed to being out in the sun all day.

"Without sun lotion," he said, "they'll get painful sun-blisters like I did years ago at Coney Island."

With a bag of bologna sandwiches packed for lunch, we eagerly start out on the most exciting journey we have ever taken. Daddy is carrying Geri as he leads us out the front door. Mommy is the last one out since she has the keys to lock our front door.

The sun is shining brightly, and it is already very hot out as we trek along the streets at a slow pace on our way to the IRT Lexington Avenue subway station at 86th Street and Lexington Avenue. Daddy reminds us to hold each other's hand so we can stay together and not get lost.

"Stay close together and watch where you're going," he warns us. "If you do get lost, don't panic. Just look for a policeman and tell him where you live. He'll see to it that you get home safely. Whatever you do, **don't go with any stranger**, no matter what he tells you, and no matter how scared you may be! Many strangers are bad people who might hurt you. If someone tries to take you away, scream as loud as you can, and keep screaming until they leave you alone."

We've heard Daddy tell us this many times before so we now understand how dangerous it can be to talk to a stranger, no less to go off somewhere with him. Mommy and Daddy have explained there are grown-ups who are mentally ill and enjoy hurting children like us.

For me, Daddy's comment about bad people includes the demon, and how it tries to take us away from God. Daddy's advice on how to react is also how we must react to the devil's attacks... scream in prayer for the spiritual policeman, God.

At the train station, Daddy carefully lowers the baby carriage one step at a time until he finally reaches the turnstiles on the level below the street. He tells us to duck under the turnstiles because we are younger than seven years old so we are allowed to ride for free. He puts a token in the turnstile for himself and then one for Mommy even though he wheels the carriage through the gate to the right of the turnstiles.

Riding the subway is part of today's treat because we've never been on the subway before. We wait for the train with our backs pressed hard against the cool ceramic tiled wall far back from the edge of the platform. Soon there is a rush of wind blowing from our left. Daddy says the wind is from the train coming from that direction.

He explains, "The wind is a sign that the train is coming because it pushes the air in front of it. Listen, and you can also hear the train coming."

Sure enough, within moments, I feel the platform rumbling as the train approaches. I am frightened by the ferocity of the sound and the rumbling caused by the train as it explodes into the station. It whizzes by, car after car, until it finally slows down and comes to a stop. The doors slide open, and Daddy and Mommy rush us onto the train telling us to step over the gap between the train and the platform. Terrified that I might slip down into that opening, I take extra-long steps over the gap.

Safely inside, we sit down just as the train jerks to a start and slowly rumbles on its way out of the lighted 86th Street station. Soon it bursts into the pitch black darkness of the subway tunnel where the roar of the train sounds much louder. This is scary.

I am intrigued by the golden-colored, straw-like seats. They're shiny to the touch and make funny squeaking noises as we bounce on them caused by the train racing along through the darkened tunnel. Their color blends nicely with the dark green walls and red tiled floor. The huge overhead fans offer a pleasant diversion as they gently spin around and around at a slow, methodical pace.

The train shakes violently creating deafening, screeching noises as it speeds wildly on its way at a breakneck speed. There is a refreshing breeze blowing in from the open windows of the subway car.

Although this ride is scary, Mommy and Daddy do not seem concerned by all the noise and the violent way the train is thrashing about.

They just sit there smiling and enjoying the subway ride. Daddy makes a funny face causing us to laugh... as well as some of the people sitting nearby. This helps pass the time and ease our anxiety as the train rushes in and out of one station after another. I wonder how long it will be before we reach Coney Island?

After changing trains twice, Daddy says we are finally on the D train that will bring us to Coney Island, the last stop.

"Keep looking out the window, kids, because the train will suddenly burst out of the tunnel into the daylight," Daddy tells us.

Other children on the train join us in eagerly looking out the windows.

"When you see a giant, round tank that is the size of a building, we'll almost be there," Daddy adds, "And when you see the sky-high parachute ride, then you **will** be there!"

All of a sudden, just like Daddy said, the train bursts out of the tunnel into bright sunshine.

"There's the big tank over there!," a little boy shouts excitedly.

The train car is filled with cheering children as the giant parachute ride comes into view off in the distance. I can actually see people sitting in swings underneath the large parachutes as it rises high up in the sky! When the parachutes reach the circular-shaped top, they quickly fall straight down to the ground, just like real parachutes do.

Kitty appears quite concerned.

"What's the matter, honey?" Mommy asks. "Why are you frowning?"

"I don't want to go on that thing, Mommy. It's too high and scary!" she cries.

Mommy laughs and assures her, "Of course it's too high for you to go on, Kitty; even your father is afraid to go on it! The rides you're going on are very nice, safe rides. You'll see."

Daddy obviously takes exception to what Mommy said about him, "Hey listen, it's **not** a matter of being afraid; it's a matter of being smart! You have to have rocks in your head to go on something that dangerous! Anything can happen at those heights. What if the cable holding the parachutes snaps? At that height, you wouldn't have a chance. You'd be dead before you hit the ground!"

"Yeah, yeah, we know," Mommy teases him.

Smiling, Daddy realizes she is kidding him.

At the last stop, we follow the crowd down a long wide ramp leading to the street. My sense of smell is pleasantly greeted with the scent of hot dogs, French-fried potatoes, cotton candy, and... ocean water. In addition, my

217

ears are filled with exciting carnival-like sounds from rides, children laughing, and people working at the game booths calling out to passersby to stop and play.

On our way to the boardwalk and the beach, Daddy points out a famous place. "Over there, kids, there's 'Nathan's' on Stillwell Avenue. That's where they serve foot-long hot dogs. Nathan's is known all over the world."

Mommy insists that we stop to buy one hot dog and one order of the crinkled French fried potatoes they serve in white, cone-shaped paper cups. Standing by Nathan's street-side counter, each of us takes a bite out of the hot dog, and a few of the crinkled fries. They taste even better than they smell!

"Hey, kids," Daddy says excitedly, "let's take a quick look at the 'Cyclone,' the scariest roller-coaster in the world!"

As we walk up the block, I watch the roller-coaster slowly, haltingly climb to the very top of the tracks making a loud "clicking" noise as it rises. Pausing for just a second at the top, it then goes over the top and races straight down on the other side! People on the ride are screaming at the top of their voices as the roller-coaster whips up and down and around the tracks making distinctive "clickity-clackity" sounds as it races at a tremendous speed.

"That's one rough ride!" Mommy notes, "You kids won't get to go on the Cyclone until you're grown up."

Kitty looks quite pleased to hear this as we resume our journey up the block toward a ramp leading to the wooden boardwalk. Along the way, I am fascinated by a small booth where two women dressed like gypsies are sitting at a table calling out to people to have their futures told.

Daddy shakes his head in disgust and says, "Going to a fortune-teller is stupid because only God knows the future, not the angels or the saints, and certainly not the devil! That's why going to a fortune-teller is against our religion; it's a sin."

At the top of the ramp, we cross over to the other side of the boardwalk where we stand for a while looking out over the crowded beach. I've never seen so many people in one place.

Daddy confirms this, "I've never seen so many people here before, Ellie. There must be a million people here today! Let's leave the carriage up here by the railing; we can keep an eye on it from where we stay on the beach."

Mommy agrees and tells us to sit down on the wooden boardwalk to take off our shoes, socks, and pants. After I take my shoes off, I discover to my utter dismay that the wooden boardwalk is boiling hot from the sun! Left with only my bathing trunks on, the rest of my body is now exposed to the red hot sun.

218

Leaving the baby carriage behind on the boardwalk, we make our way down to the beach where I have another unpleasant surprise. The sand is also red hot and is filled with hundreds of tiny, cracked sea-shells that sting the tender underside of my feet. Walking gingerly, and quickly picking up my feet, minimizes the pain. Fortunately, Mommy decides to settle down halfway to the water's edge.

Pulling out an old white bed sheet, she spreads it out on the sand, then tells us to sit down on it so the wind can't blow it off the sand. She doesn't have to tell us twice, we are all anxious to get off the painfully hot sand.

"Try not to get sand on the sheet, kids," she pleads.

Geri is thrilled running her hands through the sand where she sits on the edge of the sheet. Kitty is sitting next to her showing how to build a "sand castle." It looks more like a "sand hut" to me. Paddy, Larry, and I begin digging a huge hole in the sand. I am curious to see how deep down we can go. Much to my surprise, a little water appears at the very bottom.

After a while, Daddy invites Paddy, Larry, and me to go down to the water with him. Kitty and Geri are content to stay with Mommy. As we make our way to the water, Daddy reminds us to watch where we are walking so we don't step on any of the countless sunbathers lying on their sheets.

Down by the water, we hold hands as Daddy warns us not to go too far into the water. I am shocked to discover the water is absolutely freezing! Even though I am shivering, I inch farther into the ocean along with the others until we are in up to our waists with the water splashing wildly up into our faces. The ocean water tastes very salty. The white foam created by the ever-flowing incoming waves impresses me. Meanwhile, the sand under my feet is playing games with my balance as it constantly shifts under the movement of each surging and withdrawing wave. My feet are sinking straight down into the sand while the rest of me is being pushed and pulled by the powerful waves.

I am relieved when Daddy finally says we are going back to our blanket on the beach. It's a struggle to walk against the water as it pulls me backward toward the ocean as if it is resisting my departure. My legs feel much lighter when I finally break free from the ocean's powerful grasp. The sand now feels deliciously warm under my feet, but the rest of me shivers as the wind blows against my wet body. When I get back to the sheet, Mommy throws a warm towel over my shoulders and tells me and the others to sit down so we can have lunch.

As she unpacks and distributes a bologna sandwich to each of us, I notice a very sad-looking boy staring at me from where he sits on a sheet next to us. Behind him is his mother and some other kids. No one appears to be paying attention to him. I smile and offer him a bite of my sandwich but he shakes his head no and keeps staring. I think he just wants someone to talk with him.

So I tell, him, "My name is Bobby; what's your name?"

"Johnny," he quickly answers with a smile.

I go over with my bologna sandwich and sit next to my new friend, Johnny.

"We're going on the rides at Steeplechase after lunch," I tell him. "Are you going there too?"

Johnny looks down at his legs, and says in a barely audible voice, "I can't go on rides... I can't walk like other kids."

I notice now how very, very thin and frail his legs look.

"Why can't you walk like other kids?" I ask.

"I don't know. Mom and dad know, but they tell me I'm too young to understand."

"Bobby," Mommy calls over to me, "hurry up and finish your sandwich; we have to leave soon."

I tell her okay, and chomp away on my bologna sandwich. Then I ask Johnny to tell me what he can do and what he likes.

He says he likes reading, watching TV, listening to music on the radio, and... Christmas.

Why Christmas? I ask.

"Because every Christmas, I ask God for a present of being able to walk... and even run like other kids."

This is good news... he prays to God.

So I tell him, "You know, you can ask God for that gift at any time of the year, Johnny. You don't have to wait 'til Christmas."

"I can?"

"Sure. Why don't we both ask Him right now to give you that gift. Let's close our eyes, and ask Him right now!"

"Okay, let's do it... even though it's not Christmas!" Johnny says eagerly as he closes his eyes.

I close my eyes, and focus all my love and attention to God as I pray silently, "Dear God, please send your healing graces down upon Johnny so he can walk and run like other boys. Thank you, God."

The familiar tingling sensation surges over and through me indicating that God has heard and answered our prayer. I just don't know if that includes a physical healing. But that's okay, because God always knows and does what is best.

"Okay, guys, let's go," Mommy calls out, "it's time to head for Steeplechase Amusement Park!

I tell Johnny goodbye and promise to keep praying for him. He says he will do the same for me. How wonderful! After I pray for people, very few of them ever say that they will also pray for me.

Daddy leads the way over the hot sand to the boardwalk where we sit down to finish dressing. I brush the sand off my feet, then put on my pants, socks, and sneakers. All of a sudden, there is a big commotion with lots of yelling and crying coming from the area on the beach we just left.

Daddy says, "Oh, oh, it sounds like a wild fight with all that yelling going on. The heat probably got to some of the people!"

"I don't think so," Mommy clarifies, "Look, Patsy, do you see those people chasing that boy who's running like crazy all over the beach? That's the boy who Bobby was talking to on the sheet next to us."

Sure enough, I look out onto the beach, and see Johnny running so fast no one can catch him! I guess Johnny got his Christmas present a little early this year. Thank you, God.

"Come on, let's go," Daddy says, "time's a wasting."

Walking along the boardwalk, I see booths with various games of chance being played. In each one, there is someone calling out to the people passing by.

"Come and take a chance," they shout.

Daddy ignores them all.

Then sees a merry-go-round ride off to our right and says, "Look at the sign for that merry-go-round. Its name is misspelled, 'the B & B Carousell.' It has two 'L's' at the end but it's only supposed to have one L!"

Laughing, he says, "How'd you kids like to take a ride on the … Carousellllllll?"

We all shout "yes" at the same time and rush over with Daddy to a booth in front where he buys the needed tickets. There are so many colorful, life-size statues of horses on the merry-go-round. Some are supposed to go up and down like real horses. The other horses just stand still. Daddy and a worker make sure each of us is safely strapped on a horse. Slowly, the merry-go-round ride starts going around while beautiful music is played from somewhere in the middle. The wind is whipping through my hair while my horse goes up and down.

All of a sudden, I have an uneasy feeling of danger coming from behind. Turning around in the direction of the bad feeling, I see a man sitting in the bench area of the ride. Around his head, I see the unholy, black shadow I have seen on evil people! He looks like he is in a trance as he stares and sneers at me. Fortunately, Daddy also sees the man and how he is glaring at me.

As soon as the ride stops, Daddy goes over to the man and tells him,

"Get lost and don't come back if you know what's good for you!"

The man gets up and leaves.

Kitty asks Daddy to please let us go on again, so Daddy gets more tickets for another ride. Daddy stands between Kitty's horse and mine to make sure we don't slip off. Paddy is on a horse just ahead of us. After a few turns, Daddy tells us to watch him as he goes over to the edge of the merry-go-round and holds onto one of the silver poles there. Then he suddenly leans outward and grabs at a metal arm as we pass by it.

"I got it, I got it!" he shouts as he holds up a large metal ring. "For every ring you can grab as the horses go round, you get a free ride!"

When the merry-go-round ride stops, Daddy helps us off the horses and rushes over to tell Mommy how he got one of the rings. Mommy looks happy for him. Then he gives the metal ring to a father standing nearby with his little son. Daddy can be so kind and thoughtful.

Turning to us, he asks, "Hey, does anyone here want an ice cold custard?"

We all jump up and down shouting, **"yes!"**

"Well, come on then, let's go!" Daddy says. "There's a booth on the boardwalk nearby that sells swirled custard cones."

Sure enough a short distance away, there is the stand. Running up to the booth, I am the first to get there but I can't decide what to order. After much deliberation, I settle on a chocolate and vanilla mixed custard, swirled together. That way I can enjoy two flavors rather than just one. It tastes ice cold and delicious as we follow Daddy off the boardwalk and start walking up the street.

"I want all of you to see the big smiling face on the front of the Steeplechase building, kids. You're not going to believe it when you see it, kids," he promises.

Suddenly there are loud screeching noises, clicking and clattering, just above us. I look up to see people sitting on mechanical horses racing along steel tracks about ten feet above us. Frozen by the ferocity of the noise and action, I watch in amazement.

Daddy tells us, "I forgot to tell you about the Steeplechase itself, kids. Since a steeplechase is a long horse race, the park owners built a mechanical one right here for people to ride in a make-believe race."

"Will we get to race on the make-believe horses, Daddy?" Larry wants to know.

"Yeah, but you're going to have to sit with me on the horse, Larry, because they go pretty fast."

Daddy did not want to hurt Larry's feelings by telling him that he is also too young to ride on the horse ride by himself. Standing across from

Steeplechase Amusement Park, I am impressed to see the enormous sign of a man's smiling face high up on the top of the giant building housing the amusement park. I also notice stationed around the perimeter of the amusement park is a black wrought iron fence about six feet high.

We cross the street and enter by the corner ticket booth. Each of us is given a circular ride card that has eight small circles around the outside edge. These, Daddy explains, are punched out one at a time as we go on each ride. In the center of the card is a picture of the smiling man we just saw on the large sign on the outside of the building.

A string is supplied attached to each card, so Mommy places the string around our necks allowing the card to dangle safely in front of us. Off we go starting with a free ride, that is walking through a huge, revolving barrel located just past the ticket booth. It is so much fun trying to walk through the barrel without falling down. Only Paddy and Daddy are able to get through without falling down.

Next, we run over to a ride called the "Whip." As the name implies, it whips us around several times in little round cars along an oblong track. Coming off the ride, Larry's ticket somehow slips off his neck and falls straight down between two wooden planks of the walkway alongside the ride. We can see the card laying there with the smiling face looking up at us as if it is laughing at us. Despite how hard Daddy and the man in charge of the ride try to get it, they cannot reach it.

The man finally says, "Mister, if you tried a million times, I'll bet you could never fit that ticket in that little crack!"

Daddy looks so frustrated, and Larry looks heart-broken. I tell Larry he can share my ticket. Daddy goes over to the front booth where he is trying to get a replacement ticket from the man selling them there. But no matter how well Daddy explains what happened, the man says he cannot give Daddy another ticket unless Daddy pays for it.

When he comes back to tell us the bad news, Daddy points to a silver lining, "It's a good thing we didn't buy the more expensive ride cards with more circles on it. We would have lost even more money! I wish I could buy another ticket for you, Larry, but I just don't have the money."

Larry is crying so Mommy consoles him, "Paddy, Bobby, and Kitty will let you use one of the rides on their cards."

We are all greatly upset by this misfortune. I call out to God, and ask Him to please make it possible for Larry to get another card. As soon as I prayed this, a man and boy about Larry's age and size suddenly appear to our right and approach us. There is something quite unusual about them… in a good way, in a very good way. I sense extraordinary goodness radiating from them.

The man says, "We heard what happened and thought perhaps we could help. Since we can't use this ride card, why don't you take it and enjoy the rides left on it!"

"Gee, are you sure?" Daddy asks looking astounded at the kindness of a perfect stranger.

"Yes," the man and boy smile, "we are both sure we can't use the ticket."

The boy hands the card to a very, very happy Larry.

"Well, thank you, thank you so much," Daddy says.

The man and boy bow ever so slightly then turn to leave. Walking away, they both look back at me… and smile.

I will never forget their smiles and countenance.

Mommy says, "Patsy, you didn't even ask their names or where they're from. Please call after them so we can properly thank them."

Daddy turns to call out to them but there is no one anywhere in sight as far as we can see down the long, open lane!

"Where did they go?" Daddy wonders. "They were just here a second ago? How could they just disappear into thin air? There's no other place they could've gone!"

Daddy looks at the ride card they gave him.

Raising his eyebrows, he says, "Holy God, this is a brand new unused card with all eight rides still on it!"

Mommy and Daddy take another look up the long pathway. Then they turn to me.

I smile and say, "I asked God to please send Larry a new ride card."

Larry, being quite perceptive for his age, says, "Thank you, Bobby. God heard your prayer and sent that nice man and boy to give me a new card."

Mommy says, "I'm surprised they didn't have wings!"

Daddy says, "Ellie, I was just thinking the very same thing! They were angels!"

"Okay," Daddy says returning to business at hand, "Larry, now **please** be very careful with this card. It's as good as cash. If you lose it, that's the end of the rides."

Needless to say, all of us will be careful to hang on to our ride cards. Making our way inside the large building, I notice the air inside is much cooler because the sunlight is subdued.

Off to our right is a ride called "King of the Hill" which we decide to make our first stop. Once we are on it and the ride spins around, we scramble to get to the top of the slippery, highly-polished wooden top. However, the spinning of the "hill" throws everyone who gets close to the top back down to the bottom again. After the rides stops, we stand outside it and watch other

224

kids try as we did to get to the top. No one can stay on top, at least not for very long.

Our next ride is one with swings attached to a carousel that goes around and around in a circle at great speed up in the air. There is a girl about Kitty's age who is terrified by the ride. She is screaming for it to stop but the man controlling the ride will not stop it. He is ignoring everyone yelling for him to stop the ride!

All of a sudden, the girl starts throwing up chunks of pink and tan colored vomit. It sprays and splatters down over the people below... including the man who would not stop the ride! Covered with vomit, he now moves the lever that will stop the ride. As the swings gradually slow down, the man steps away so he won't get hit with any more vomit.

"Serves you right, Buddy!" Daddy admonishes him, "You got what you deserve for not stopping the ride when you heard the poor girl crying!"

The man, much smaller than Daddy, looks concerned that Daddy might come over and "slug" him as Daddy calls punching someone. Of course, Daddy doesn't hit the man.

"Get wise to yourself! Next time stop the ride!" Daddy shouts as we walk away from this unforgettable swing ride.

Far off to our left on the other side of the building, there is a slide that starts high up near the roof and comes down over a few waves in the slide. Kids and grownups are sliding down different lanes at incredible speeds.

"Patsy, you can't let the kids go on that thing. They'll get killed!" Mommy warns.

"I don't know about that, Ellie," he says with a mischievous smile. "What do you think, boys?"

Larry is the first to plead, "We can go on it, Daddy; it looks like fun. Please, Daddy, let us go on it, Daddy. Please!"

Paddy actually looks worried as he stares up the long flight of stairs leading to the top of the slide.

He says nothing but looks to me next, so I quickly let him know what I think, "I'm afraid, Daddy; I don't want to go on it."

Daddy chuckles and says, "Don't worry, boys, it's far too dangerous for you. I just wanted to see what you'd say. Let's go, there is something I know all of you will like."

We walk closely behind Mommy and Daddy as we head for the next adventure in this exciting place. On the other side of a three foot high wall, there is a theater with lots of seats facing a stage. There is a life-size statue of an elephant on the left side of the stage. It constantly moves slowly back and forth a distance of about two feet. Seated on top of the mechanical elephant is

225

a man dressed like an European Indian. The white turban on his head wobbles as the elephant jerks to and fro.

"Beware of the clown!" he shouts dramatically. "Beware of the clown!"

"What clown, Daddy?" I ask.

Daddy laughs, "Never mind, Bobby; you'll find out soon enough!"

As we walk along the winding wall, I can see many people sitting inside laughing and shouting things to a clown who is running around the stage.

Daddy tells us, "That clown is holding an electric prod that he uses to stick people giving them a nasty shock! That's what cattle ranchers use to control their cattle. The cattle feel that nasty sting and move real fast!"

Suddenly, the clown places his finger across his lips indicating that he wants everyone in the theater to be quiet. Now he runs off to hide on the right side of the stage. As we watch, a very large lady and a skinny man with her enter center stage through an open doorway there. Both of them look puzzled as they peer out at the giggling audience watching them!

Sneaking up behind them, the clown extends his electric prod toward the unsuspecting couple. With a burst of speed, the clown runs up behind the man and sticks him with the prod right on the backside!

The skinny little man jumps away and throws his arms up in the air as he yells, "Yow! Oh my God, sweetie, that clown stuck me with something. Run for your life, the clown is after us!"

The man looks terrified as he runs in the direction of the artificial elephant. In a flash, the little man runs past it and disappears off the stage but his wife is still standing in the same spot with her hands on her hips shaking her head.

"Henry, don't you dare leave me here with this maniac!" she shouts loudly. "Henry... do you hear me? You come right back here this minute!"

Her booming voice and words set off a riotous laughter in the theater.

"Are they acting?" Paddy wants to know.

"No, son," Daddy laughs, "this is for real."

The clown menacingly approaches the large lady who is clearly not amused by all this especially with the audience goading the clown on. The large lady keeps her eyes fixed on the clown as she slowly inches her way toward where her skinny husband had escaped.

"Sweetie," a voice calls out from some place behind the stage, "watch out for the man on the elephant, too!"

"Oh, great!" she complains, "Why don't you come out here and help me, Henry!"

There is no response from Henry wherever he is hiding off stage.

226

I can see how the lady is becoming more and more angry by the second as she looks back and forth between the clown and the man teasing her from on top of the elephant. When she is four feet from the elephant, she has to walk on rollers that are embedded in the stage floor. She wickedly swats at the clown as he creeps dangerously close to her as she steps gingerly across the rollers.

As she struggles to across the rollers, it looks certain that she is going to lose her balance and fall. The audience is in an uproar laughing at this poor lady desperately trying to evade the clown and get off the stage to end her public humiliation.

Finally reaching the other side of the rollers, she turns and glares at the clown. It is clear to me that she has gone as far as she is going to go in her attempt to evade the clown and his electric prod.

All of a sudden, a loud buzzing noise goes off as a powerful gust of air blows up from the stage directly underneath where the fat lady is standing. The powerful gust of air blows her dress straight up over her head exposing her completely bare bottom! She had no underwear on! With people in the audience screaming in laughter, the large lady turns her back to the audience and struggles unsuccessfully to get her dress down leaving her huge bare exposed buttocks quivering and shaking.

The man sitting on top of the elephant laughs so hard, he falls off the mechanical elephant and lands on the stage only a few feet from where the lady is flailing about fighting to hold her dress down in the upward blowing air.

"Do you see that, Ellie?" Daddy says excitedly. "she has no drawers on!"

Mommy smiles as she shakes her head from side to side.

"Serves her right for not wearing bloomers! Mommy adds.

Just then, the air stops blowing. The large lady is so furious she turns around with a look of hatred on her bright red blushing face. Without hesitating, she begins chasing the clown who had fallen down laughing. Seeing her charge like a raging bull, the clown jumps up and starts running for his life!

I think the clown is surprised to see how fast the large lady can run. In no time at all, she closes the distance between them. The audience is delirious seeing this enormous lady chase down and corner the clown. As she reaches to grab him, he escapes by ducking down and crawling frantically away on all fours.

Mommy say she does not want us to see what happens to the clown when the lady catches up to him so we are forced to move on while the fat lady is still in hot pursuit of the clown. Daddy consoles us by telling us that

227

our next ride will be on the Steeplechase horse race!

"Hold on tight, kids, whatever you do because those horses go pretty fast," Mommy warns as she starts toward the exit.

We follow Daddy through narrow corridors to an even more narrow staircase that leads to the ride. There are two lines of people waiting to get on, so I guess this must be the most popular ride in Steeplechase.

Up the dark brown squeaking wooden stairs we slowly climb one step at a time until we reach a platform where there are five mechanical horses waiting to be mounted. Daddy tells the man that we want to ride together. To do so, we let some people go ahead of us until at least four horses are available.

Daddy helps strap Paddy and Kitty onto the first and second horses while the man straps me tightly onto the third one. Daddy then places Larry on the next one and climbs up behind him. The man wraps the long belt all the way around them before buckling it in on the side.

After a boy climbs onto the last horse, the man steps back over to a long lever sticking up from the floor and says, "Hold on tight all the way. If the ride stops, do not, I repeat, **do not**, get off the horses!"

With that, he pushes the lever forward and the horses abruptly thrust forward on the tracks. My heart pounds wildly with excitement as the horses soon burst outside the building into bright sunlight and races straight ahead as people in the street below yell up to us. I am thrilled to be part of the attraction for people in the street where I stood earlier in amazement as I watched the mechanical horses race by.

My attention now turns to winning the race. The five metal tracks below the horses are a shiny silver color and they all go in exactly the same direction around the outside of the building. I am in third place ahead of Daddy and Larry. Kitty is in first place, and Paddy is in second.

Feeling the constant clicking sensation under me as my horse races along, I try to urge my horse to go faster to catch up to Kitty and Paddy. With the air blowing hard against my face, and my hair flying straight backward, I lean forward in my seat in the hope that this might help my horse go faster. I wish that my horse would turn on a burst of speed to take the lead.

As we round a wide turn, I can see the entrance that leads back into the building. I guess that is where the finish line must be. As our horses rush back into the building, I realize that my horse is **not** going to win the race. I have dropped back even farther before reaching the finish line. Paddy's horse passes Kitty's at the very last minute. Daddy and Larry came in third, the boy fourth, and I am dead last!

What a thrilling ride! After dismounting, we chatter about our perceptions of the Steeplechase race. Soon other people arrive from the race after us. This forces us to move on. Following Daddy, we make our way down another extremely narrow staircase. At the bottom, there is a choice to go either left or right.

"Which way should we go, Daddy?" Paddy asks.

"Go to the left," Daddy answers, "but let me go first. Just remember to follow me and stay close, kids."

Following directly behind Daddy, we enter a brightly lit area. I am partially blinded by bright lights shining toward us from an area fifteen feet ahead of us. To my horror, I see the evil-looking clown standing to our left with the electric prod in his hand. His diabolical smile sends chills up my spine because he reminds me of the demon.

I can't believe we are on the same stage where that poor large lady was teased and tormented earlier. The only reason I don't panic is because I know Daddy is in front of us and he will protect us from the wicked clown. Huddling close together behind Daddy, we slowly edge our way over to the right without taking our eyes off the clown.

"Don't scare the kids," Daddy warns the clown.

"And what about you?" the clown taunts.

"I am not afraid of you, buddy. If you want the audience to see you get your teeth knocked out, just come close to us!" Daddy snarls. "I'm no fat lady, mister, I'll knock you flat on your ass!"

Looking at Daddy's imposing size and demeanor, the clown takes Daddy's warning quite seriously. To the delight of the audience, the clown bows toward Daddy and cautiously steps backward a few paces letting us make our way safely off the stage to our right.

As we reach the floor area next to the huge mechanical elephant on our way out, the floor turns into rollers spinning under our feet. This is fun trying to walk forward as the floor rollers spin. I fall down twice before I get to the other side where I am blasted by a powerful burst of air blowing up through the slats in the floor directly below me.

With a final lunge forward, I am the first to get out the exit door and run over to where Mommy is standing with Geri. Soon we are surrounded by everyone else as we anxiously tell Mommy about our great adventure on the Steeplechase and the wicked clown.

"One at a time, one at a time, please," Mommy laughs. "Only God can hear you all at the same time!"

How true.

Chapter 25

THE LAZARUS EXPERIENCE

July 1953

I am so worried. Tomorrow Mommy and Daddy are sending Paddy and me off to a faraway place! We are being forced to go to the St. Vincent DePaul Summer Camp for poor children where we must stay for an entire week.

I can't think of anything worse than being sent to some strange faraway place far from home where the demon can attack me in an unfamiliar place. Also, I will be forced to live with people I don't know. Even though Paddy will be with me, I am still afraid. I've never been away from home before, but even worse, I sense a great danger awaiting me at camp. Paddy gives me the impression he's also not happy about being forced to leave home and go to summer camp.

Another part of my fear is that Mommy has often told us when we misbehave that she may send us to a "home" for disobedient children where we'll never see her or our family ever again! She also said that the adults there viciously beat the children with a "cat of nine tails," a whip that has nine belts attached to it. They also make the children kneel on uncooked rice in a corner. That's what happened to her when she was sent to a home as a child for playing "hooky" from grade school!

"You boys are going to love St. Vincent DePaul camp, it's one of the best camps in the country," Mommy tries to encourage Paddy and me.

"They have a big swimming pool, a baseball field, and they take you on hikes in the countryside. They also have camp fires at night where you sit around and toast marshmallows and sing songs."

I am afraid because of the stories Mommy told us about "homes for bad children." What if they accidentally take us to a 'home' instead of the camp?

"You guys are so fortunate," Mommy adds.

"There are a lot of kids out there who never get a chance to go to camp," Daddy chimes in, "I never got a chance to go to one. I hope you boys are grateful to your mother and me for making this possible."

"But I don't want to go to camp," I protest, "I am afraid of what might happen there, and we may never come back!"

"Oh, don't be silly, Bobby, of course you will come back, and they have all those great things at camp," Mommy says.

"I don't care about those things, Mommy. I don't want to go to camp, I want to stay home. Please don't make us go."

"You and Paddy are only going away for a week, and you'll have a great time. You'll see," she tries to assure me.

"No, I won't. The brothers down the block told me they went to camp last year and they were separated from each other because they were in different age groups. They are not going to allow Paddy and me to stay together."

Paddy tries to reassure me, "Don't worry, Bobby, I'll be there to look after you and make sure you're all right. At night, we'll just have to sleep in separate buildings. That's all. You'll be okay; I'll take care of you."

Paddy puts his arm around me for reassurance. Paddy is much bigger, stronger and braver than I am. He can do everything better than I can except in school where he has a difficult time learning and doing homework. Sometimes I feel safer around Paddy than I do with Mommy because he is tough and helps me when I need help. Mommy does not always understand like Paddy does.

I wish I could talk to Paddy about ghosts, but I cannot. When I have tried to tell him some of the things that have happened, he doesn't believe me, and teases me about it. Besides, after what happened to Larry's arm last year, I worry about something bad like that happening to Paddy also.

"Didn't you say the name of the camp is 'Spring Valley?" Paddy asks Mommy.

"Yes, it is," she answers. "Although it's a St. Vincent DePaul Camp, it's also called 'Spring Valley' because that's where it is located."

"How far is it from home?" I want to know.

"Oh, not far. It's about a two hour bus ride from St. Monica's," she explains. "That's something else I forgot to tell you boys. You're in for a real treat, a long, exciting bus ride into the country to where the camp is located. Now what do you think of that, eh?"

Mommy knows that I love bus rides so I suspect that is why she is telling us this. Since I greatly enjoy bus rides, the thought of going on a long bus ride almost makes the thought of going to camp acceptable. Almost, but not quite. The only bus rides I have been on were when Mommy had taken us to the health clinic to get our free immunization shots. Even that joy of going for a bus ride was tainted by the scary, painful needles we got at the clinic.

Thinking back, I can remember how we used to walk to the corner of York Avenue where we would wait for the bus at the bus stop near the corner. After a short time, a big green and white colored bus would rumble up the street and stop at the bus stop.

I was intimidated by the high steps I had to climb to get into the bus. Once inside, I was fascinated by the strange looking device next to the driver into which Mommy always put a coin. That paid for her fare while the rest of us rode free because we were all under seven years old. Mommy always got a "transfer ticket" from the driver. These are very thin, narrow pieces of green paper that allow us to go for free on a different bus going in another direction.

I remember walking back through the bus while it started moving. I always looked at the floor so I could avoid the eyes of the strangers on the bus. The hard, thin-ribbed flooring ran the entire length of the bus. I liked to sit in the very back of the bus. The dark green seats were well-cushioned. This helped when the bus bounced wildly and threw us up in the air. Some of the bumps in the road are so bad, they cause the bus to jostle us around like some of the rides at Coney Island's Steeplechase amusement park.

Soon we had to transfer to another bus going west on 79th Street. This bus was usually more crowded because many people took it who worked on the west side of Manhattan, like Daddy. Mommy reminded us that Daddy took this bus to work each day.

After four blocks, we would get off this cross-town bus to catch the Lexington Avenue bus going downtown to the sixties where the health clinic was located. I never enjoyed this part of the bus ride because it meant we were close to the clinic where we would get a painful needle from a doctor.

The needle always hurt badly, stinging and burning at the point of injection. What made it more frightening was the strong, painful grasp of the hands that were always there to hold me perfectly still. This only served to make me feel trapped and panicky at the thought of what was going to be done to me each time, and how much it was going to hurt.

My fear of going to the health clinic was heightened by the fact that none of the medical workers there ever told me what was going on, or what to expect. They just snuck up on me while I sat on a long, cold table in a crowded noisy room filled with other crying, frightened children. It was always a terrifying experience.

Much later, Mommy says, "Why don't you be smart and get off to bed early so you can get a good night's rest. Tomorrow is your big day!"

I reluctantly agree and give her a kiss good night. To my delight, Larry is still awake. I tell him I cannot sleep because I am so worried about going to camp tomorrow. Larry says, "You are lucky, I wish I was old enough to go with you."

"Yeah, I wish you could come with Paddy and me."

In the morning, I awake to find our apartment filled with bright sunshine and a sense of excitement. I dress for the day while Mommy prepares some pancakes and toast for breakfast. I am too nervous to eat, however. Our clothes for the upcoming week have been folded neatly and stacked in individual paper bags by the door. Paddy and I each have our own bag.

232

"Remember to take your clothes out of the bag as soon as you get there, boys, and save the bag so you can put your dirty laundry in it each night," Mommy advises us.

"Don't wander away from the group when you go for hikes and things," Daddy cautions, "and remember, if you see trouble coming, walk the other way. Don't go poking your noses into things that don't concern you."

When everyone is ready, we walk together to the front of St. Monica's Church where a big yellow school bus is waiting to take us to Spring Valley camp. I am so upset a painful lump has formed in my throat. I cannot speak as tears roll down my face. Mommy bends down to console me.

"Bobby, come on now, you don't want everyone here to think you're a big cry baby, do you?"

I don't care at this moment what anyone thinks about me being a big cry baby. I desperately want to go back to the comfort and safety of my home. Mommy has tears in her eyes, and surprisingly, so does Daddy.

"You be a big boy now, and go have a good time with your brother," she adds.

Turning to Paddy, she says, "Take good care of your little brother. Okay, Paddy?"

Paddy nods affirmatively but he also looks scared.

Mommy adds, "Bobby is afraid of being away from home, so you look after him, Paddy, and stay out of trouble yourself. Don't do anything you know is wrong. I'm proud of you, my big boy. Have fun, and I'll see you both back here in a week."

Mommy kisses each of us and then watches as we board the bus along with all the other children from St. Monica who are going to camp. The roar of the bus's engine fills the back of the bus where Paddy and I are sitting. Within moments, the view of St. Monica's Church and our family standing in front waving to us disappears as the bus speeds quickly past one street after another. The other children on the bus are jumping around and making lots of noise.

There are two young men sitting up front who came along as chaperons for our group. They are walking up and down the aisle trying to keep everyone calm.

"Sit down! Stop yelling out that window!" they shout.

We are gone only a few minutes and I already feel very upset, worse than ever. All the yelling and commotion makes me feel insecure as Paddy and I sit quietly in the back of the bus. In about an hour, we have gone over the George Washington Bridge high in the air over the Hudson River, and are driving on some major highway. Most of the kids have now calmed down except for an occasional outburst because of something they see outside.

The driver announces that we will soon be arriving at Spring Valley Camp so our chaperons tell us to gather up all our belongings. Paddy and I still have our bags of clothing tightly clutched on our laps. The bus soon turns off the highway and drives through a thickly wooded area with old, small houses off to the side here and there.

Finally, we pull into a wide open field as the chaperons announce that we have arrived at Spring Valley camp. Everyone starts cheering and hurries to get off the bus. Paddy and I sit quietly until we can get off the bus without being separated.

Outside, we are told to line up according to age. My worst fears are being realized! I complain to a camp worker but he just tells me it is all right. He says I must go over to my age group. Seven and eight year-olds to the right, nine and ten year-olds to the left. I look over into Paddy's eyes and I am surprised to see that he, too, is frightened. We have no choice but to obey the orders of the camp workers.

Paddy also tries to explain that we are supposed to be kept together, but the camp worker won't listen as he snaps, "Yeah, yeah, I know kid; we'll take care of that later. For now, just get in line over there in height order."

I keep my eyes on Paddy every moment to make sure I do not lose sight of him. Our lines are only ten feet apart, but it seems like a mile right now.

"All right, everyone stay in a straight line and follow me to our dormitory where we will be staying," the camp worker shouts to those on my line, "Move out, get the lead out of your pants, guys! Let's go!"

I look quickly over to Paddy who just shrugs his shoulders and calls out, "It is okay, Bobby. I'll meet you later when we all eat together."

That provides little consolation. I am heart-broken and terribly frightened at the thought of being alone in a strange place, so far from everyone and everything I have ever known, and now being separated from my big brother. I obediently follow the boys in front of me as we walk about one hundred feet across an open field to a large two story, stark white clapboard building.

Outside the building is a high staircase which we climb leading up into a damp darkened second floor. There are long, narrow cots neatly arranged filling all the available floor space from one side of the floor to the other. Off to the side is the large bathroom and a shower room. A strange, musty smell fills the air adding to my uncomfortable feelings.

"Okay, guys," the camp worker's voice booms out loudly throughout the hollow area, "grab a bed and put your things underneath it. That is where you are going to sleep while you're here at camp. Come on, don't just stand there looking at me, get going!"

There is an instant scramble for the beds as all the boys run for the beds they want. Running feet on the bare wood-planked floor makes loud thunderous "thumping" noises. I turn to the bed on my immediate left, place my bag under it then sit on it.

Once everyone is settled, the chaperon calls our attention to him so he can tell us about the camp's rules. First, he says we should call him "counselor." No one is to call him by his real name, John. Then he explains that we are expected to get up at seven o'clock in the morning, make our bed, eat breakfast in the main hall downstairs, come back to brush our teeth, go to the bathroom, follow him through each day's events, have lunch and dinner at the main hall, shower in our dorm, and be in bed before dark.

John the counselor raises his voice, "There'll be no cursing, fighting or stealing! And anyone who disobeys is going to be punished. Does everyone understand?" No one says anything.

"Are there any questions?"

Again, no one says anything, so he orders us to call out our name and tell everyone where we come from. When it is my turn, I yell out loud and clear that my name is Bobby Walsh and I come from Yorkville in Manhattan. I yelled loudly because the counselor criticized some boys for "sounding like mice."

Afterward, we hurry off to the main hall for lunch. Down the stairs and across the middle of the camp's center we walk in single file. I notice that there are two other buildings that look the same as mine, and I am surprised to see that my building is attached to the main hall. The building directly across from my building is where Paddy is located.

I see him come out of the building with all the other older boys! We greet each other with a big smile and wave before we quickly come together and enter the large, noisy main hall. Sitting at the first table near us, the smell of delicious food fills our nostrils.

"You've got to get on line over there to get your food," one of the older boys tells us.

Paddy and I follow everyone else over to the line by the left wall. We get hot dogs, French fries, and ice cold milk. What a treat this is! I am beginning to think I might like it here after all especially after I hear someone behind us say that we can eat all we want to, all we have to do is go up and get more of whatever we want!

"It is not so bad here, eh, Bobby?" Paddy says encouragingly. "You really like those hot dogs, don't you?"

Paddy is referring to the two hot dogs I just quickly gulped down in record time.

"Listen, Bobby, they're going to take us on a hike right after lunch so let's stay together if we can, okay?"

I happily nod in agreement.

Following lunch, our two groups are organized by our counselors directly outside the main hall. Paddy's counselor is taller and heavier than mine.

"Can I have everyone's attention, please?" he shouts to no avail as the boys keep talking and fooling around.

Looking very annoyed, he takes a whistle hanging on a chain around his neck and blows hard on it making a loud, screeching noise. That gets everyone's attention.

"We're going on a little hike into the countryside surrounding camp, but before we do, there are a few things we want you to know about so listen up! First of all, you should stay within an arm's length of each other, don't stray away from your group, and if you become separated from the rest of us, just stand still and keep calling out as loudly as you can until we get to you. We **will** find you so don't panic.

"One more thing, don't eat any of the berries you see on some of the bushes along the way. They may be poisonous. And don't pick up any rocks or wood. If it looks interesting, kick it over with your foot. You never know if there is a nasty snake or insect lurking underneath just waiting for someone like you to bite!"

This scares me. I've never been in any woods so I don't want to walk in woods with all kinds of snakes, bugs, and other creatures. Besides, I am worried that I may get separated from the group and get lost in the woods and never find my way out.

He adds, "If anyone has to go to the bathroom, please go now. It'll be more convenient than going in the woods!"

He looks around our group but no one steps forward so he says, "All right then, let's move out in two straight lines... and stay in line."

Looking over at us, the counselor asks as he points at me, "Hey, Paddy, is that your brother?"

"Yes, that's him!" Paddy answers looking at me.

"You can have him stay in line with you, okay? Keep an eye on your little brother."

Paddy shakes his head happily as we both smile.

We walk across the open field where we had arrived earlier, cross over a baseball field, and then enter the woods behind it. With the sound of twigs crunching under our feet, we trudge along as we make our way far into the woods. Looking around, all I can see now is Paddy in front of me surrounded by green and brown shrubbery that snaps back at me as we make our way forward. Paddy keeps looking down; I'm sure he is looking out for snakes and bugs.

"Stay close to me, Bobby!" he tells me.

No worry about that! I stay right behind him as we trudge along. Although I am nervous about being here, there are pleasant sounds and fragrances all around us that I have never experienced before. Occasionally, a bird flies about in the trees overhead and calls out to other birds.

Other sounds come from the boys on our line as they talk, and there is the constant sound of crunching caused by all our steps. After hiking briskly for about thirty minutes, we reach a small clearing that is right next to railroad tracks! The lead counselor tells us to gather around him in a circle so he can tell us something important.

"Sit down and take a break, fellas, while we take a head count to make sure we haven't lost anyone."

He, and the other counselor who is bringing up the rear of our line count off the number of us boys sitting on the ground.

"All present and accounted for, sir," the other counselor says.

"Very good," the lead counselor responds. "All right, we're going to do something interesting and adventuresome. We're going to walk right down the center of the railroad tracks for about a mile, and then we'll turn back."

I don't think he is serious because this sounds too dangerous to do but then I quickly discover he is dead serious!

He adds, "While you are on the tracks it is important to listen for the sound of the train whistle. You'll probably feel the ground rumble before you hear anything because the trains come behind us. Sounds are not heard as well when they come from the rear so if you feel a rumble on the ground, or you do hear the train coming, you must get off the tracks immediately and shout, 'Train, train!'

"Then I want all of you to go to the right side about ten feet away from the tracks and stay there until the entire train passes. And don't go back up on the tracks until I say it's okay! Did everyone hear me? Does everyone understand? Are there any questions?"

After a pause, the lead counselor says, "No questions? Okay, let's shove off, and remember... you **must** listen and watch for the train!"

Although I am a little nervous about walking on the tracks, I am also thrilled that Paddy and I are walking on the center of railroad tracks! What an adventure; we're actually walking on railroad tracks! This is so exciting. A short distance later, I feel the ground under my feet suddenly begin to rumble ever so gently... just like the counselor said it would if a train was coming!

Paddy turns to me and asks, "Bobby, do you feel that?"

I nod yes just as the counselor shouts, **"Train coming; train coming! Everyone get off the tracks and go to the right!"**

I turn to see there is a train all the way down the tracks from where we are standing! Everyone quickly scrambles off ten feet to the right side where we huddle closely together and watch as the train steadily approaches in our direction. The train whistle screeches out loudly warning to us that it is coming. Both counselors shout out to remind everyone not to go near the train as it passes.

Surprisingly, it takes several minutes before the train finally reaches us and thunders slowly by causing the ground to shake, one car after another in a seemingly endless line. As each train car roars by, I am impressed by the enormous size of the train's wheels and the powerful pounding sensations they cause. The counselor shouts that there are over fifty cars on this freight train and the reason each car is painted differently is because each car actually comes from a different part of the country!

It seems an eternity before the last of the train cars, the "caboose," finally passes. It continues on its way along the tracks following the other cars ahead of it. Soon the counselor calls out that it's now safe to go back up onto the tracks. We all scramble back up on the tracks as we chatter about the incredible experience it was to have this long powerful freight train go thundering right by us!

After we have walked another thirty minutes, the lead counselor tells us it is time to turn around and start back to camp. Watching the freight train go by apparently ate up a lot of our hiking time. The trip back along the tracks is uneventful, but not so for the woods. Now we are constantly plagued by gnats and mosquitoes flying around us and biting us as we push through the quickly darkening woods. This helps us move back over the trail to camp much faster than we came.

After washing up, Paddy and I meet outside my building then go into the main hall to eat dinner. We follow the line of boys and pick out a hamburger, potato salad and soda. As we gobble up this delicious dinner, we talk about the exciting trip into the woods and the train.

When we're finished, a counselor tells us that we must go to our own building for the night! This is the moment both of us have been dreading... we're going to be separated for the first time in our lives!

Fighting back tears, Paddy says, "I'll see you in the morning, Bobby. Don't worry. Everything is going to be all right."

I am so sad my throat aches. I can only nod my head okay as we walk our separate ways.

The counselors direct everyone to go by their individual groups out by the US flag pole in the open field. I cannot see where Paddy is located. I am very, very scared and sad. As we stand saluting the flag, someone blows 'taps' on a horn as two counselors take the flag down. One of the older counselors says something I cannot hear because he is speaking too lowly. I then follow my group to our dorm, climb the long outside staircase, then go directly to my bed where I nestle under the covers of my blanket.

Lying there in the darkened dorm, I listen for signs of the demon but all I hear are sounds of the night. Hundreds of crickets outside are calling to each other; what a nice sound. Inside, I can hear the sounds of muffled cries from some of the boys. They are homesick like me…but I am trying to be brave like Mommy and Daddy told me to be. They said "big boys don't cry!"

Lying here under the covers, I have a sense of peace. The crickets' sound like they are happy playing outside in the night air. They sound so happy.

I am more fortunate than the other boys because I have my big brother, Paddy, with me in camp to watch over and protect me. These thoughts combine with the physical rigors of the day to take me swirling into the welcome abyss of sleep.

The loud sound of reverie being played on a horn outside in the open field abruptly awakens me. Sitting bolt upright, I look over in the bright sunlight filling our dorm to see a puddle of yellow urine under the bed next to mine. The boy sitting on the bed has his face buried in his hands as he cries in shame.

Our counselor comes over and tells him he is **"a big baby!"**

That's so mean!

The counselor then threatens him, "If you don't stop wetting the bed, you're going to have to wear a diaper at night!"

I feel so sorry for the boy, I ask God to help the boy stop wetting the bed so he won't be embarrassed in front of all of us in the dorm. My prayer is interrupted by the counselor yelling at me to get up and get going! I hurry downstairs to the flag-pole where everyone stands silently saluting the US flag as it is raised. Afterward, we run to the main hall for breakfast.

As I run, I see Paddy standing off to my right waiting for me! I am so happy to see him. Together, we run to the main hall and enjoy a breakfast of cornflakes, milk and a buttered roll. As we eat, I tell Paddy about the bed-wetter and how mean the counselor was to him.

To my surprise Paddy says, "Don't worry about the boy wetting the bed, Bobby. You'd better worry about what they're going to force **you** to do today! Your group is the first to go down to the big swimming pool today where everyone must to go in the water!"

Instant panic! This is terrible because I have never been in a pool, and don't know how to swim! I might drown!

Seeing the fear on my face, Paddy advises me, "Your only hope, Bobby, is to tell your counselor you can't swim, and make sure they don't force you into the deep part of the pool. I'm not going to be there today, they're taking my group over to the gym so I won't see you until dinner time tonight. Please take care of yourself, and remember what I told you."

I feel sick to my stomach as I watch Paddy slowly walk away with his group. Before I have time to panic any further, my counselor announces that today is going to be our group's "pool day." As everyone cheers, he orders us to put our swim trunks on and bring a towel down to the pool. It is completely fenced in and is located between our dorm and the baseball field.

I reluctantly comply but complain to the counselor at the pool entrance that I am afraid because I do not know how to swim and have never been in a pool before... especially one with deep water. He listens to what I say then tells me not to worry about it, that everything will be all right. He brings me over to the pool's edge where he points to an area where he says the water is only a few feet deep so it will not be over my head.

Feeling safe enough about the level of the water, I slowly ease myself into the ice cold water at this end of the pool. The other boys from my group call this area of the pool the **"sissy's end."** While the boys swim around and enjoy the water, I am perfectly content to just relax in the water holding onto the side wall of the pool.

After playing for a while, all the boys leave the pool, one by one, to go play softball or basketball. Since I am the last boy in the pool, I decide to walk around a little in the waist high water. Feeling a little braver, I inch closer to the center of the pool where the water is up to my neck. There is a thick blue and white striped rope stretching across the entire width of the pool here in the middle. Wondering what this is for, I duck down under the water to see what is underneath.

Just then, someone violently shoves me from behind pushing me forward. As I try to put my feet on the bottom, I find that the floor of the pool here is incredibly slippery... and it is slanted downward! I frantically try to scurry backward away from what I realize must be the deep end of the pool! Both my feet keep sliding off the floor as if the floor is moving away from under me! With nothing to support me, I slip down under the water with my eyes and mouth wide open!

Hideous laughter from the demon fills my mind conveying a message of doom as I flail about! I now know who shoved me into the deep end of the pool. This means I am now in a life and death struggle.

I thrash about trying to grab the thick blue and white rope but it is nowhere near me! Torrents of water rush into my mouth and throat completely cutting off my air supply as I panic looking upward at the top of the water about two feet above me! Remembering that Mommy said if you go down three times, you will drown, I wildly thrash about in my attempt to

240

reach the surface. Nothing works!

All I can hear is the demon screaming in my mind that no one is here to save me so I am going to drown!

My lungs, throat and head feel like they are going to explode they hurt so badly. The harder I struggle, the louder the demon laughs! As I try desperately to scream out for help, even more water rushes into my mouth and throat further choking me! I feel myself sinking back down a second time. One more time and I'm dead!

The demon gleefully says, "Yes, you're going down for the last time… then you'll be ours!"

Hearing this threat, I struggle even more wildly to reach the surface and air but I can only keep my head above water for a second at a time. No matter how furiously I flail my arms on the surface and constantly kick my legs, I cannot get any air! My chest, throat, and head bursting for air feel like they are going to explode! I am crying inside, terrified that I cannot breathe or cry out for help, and there is no one to help me.

Suddenly, my arms feel like they weigh a ton as fatigue sets in so badly I cannot move my arms or legs any more. The surface looks like it is rising upward away from me as my body sinks down a third time into the profoundly silent world under the water.

My arms are positioned straight up toward the surface as if I am reaching out to God. Amazingly, all the events of my life to date flash by my mind's eye as I recall Mommy once saying that this is what happens when you are dying.

The demon screams one last time, "There's nothing you can do… even **He** can't save you"

Realizing that I am dying and have only a second or two of consciousness left, I instinctively cry out to God from the inner recesses of my soul to save me. I tell Him I am too young to die, and have not fulfilled the many things I am called to accomplish in helping others! Please, God, save me!

I am suffering excruciating pain as I pray these final conscious thoughts. My motionless body drifts downward, and my eyesight fades to utter darkness as my mind slips away into total unconsciousness like going into a deep sleep.

The mental, physical, and spiritual parts of my being blend together in one peaceful, harmonious union. This final second is devoid of all else.

My eyes open and are suddenly blinded by a glorious bright light! I cannot see anything else. I must have died and am now in heaven! But my nostrils, throat, and lungs are filled with wonderful, refreshing air! I must still be alive!

I am confused. What happened? A moment ago, the demon was taunting me as I was drowning, unable to breathe or move, in absolute agony. I remember drifting downward in the process of drowning to death. And now, I am relaxed breathing fresh air at the side of the pool!

Rubbing my eyes, my sight returns allowing me to see my arms are draped over the side of the pool. I don't feel any pain, and I don't have any trouble breathing. There is no one else in the pool but now I notice the dry legs of a tall young man standing right in front of me at the poolside.

Looking up at him, I complain, "Why didn't you help me sooner? I was drowning!"

The counselor crouches down and says, "From what I saw, you did just fine gliding under the water all the way over to here!"

I protest further, "I couldn't do that! I don't know how to swim! Why did you let me suffer like that before helping me. You're supposed to help me!"

"As soon as you called for help, I was sent to help you, and so I did!"

"But I couldn't yell; the water kept going in my mouth. How could you have heard me?"

"I was told."

Looking at his legs, I notice once again that they are completely dry.

"Hey, your legs are completely dry! You couldn't have been the one who saved me. If you were, your legs would be all wet!"

"We don't get wet," he says mysteriously as he smiles.

I look away from the brilliant sunlight shining off his face, and I look around the pool area to see who else could have saved me. There is no one else here except us.

Smiling as if he understands my confusion, the man asks, "Do you remember the story of the ten lepers?"

"Ten lepers? Yes, I do. Why?"

Nodding his head, he says, "Well... "

Rising, he turns and walks off toward the enclosed end of the pool area. As I watch, a brilliant flash of light momentarily blinds me. When my sight returns, he is gone! I look around the entire pool area, but he is nowhere to be seen! He vanished into thin air!

Recalling what he said about being "being sent," "being told," and that, "**they** don't get wet," I realize now that he was no counselor... he was an angel sent by God to save me in my dying moments. Remembering he asked about the ten lepers, I realize I should do the same thing the one leper did after he was healed. I must go back to Jesus and thank Him for helping me.

I thank Jesus, and have an idea now how Lazarus must have felt when Jesus saved him from physical death.

Chapter 26

THE LEAST OF OUR BRETHREN

October 1953

Daddy always says to look for the silver lining in the storms of life.
"Sometimes good things come from bad things," he says.

A good example he points out is the August 18th fire on the roof of St. Monica's Church. It caused so much damage to the church that it is still closed while repairs are being made. Daddy says the fire reminded everyone how important the church is in our lives, and in the life of our parish community.

"Very often, people don't appreciate what they have until they lose it," Daddy explains.

While the church is being repaired, Mass is celebrated in the auditorium beneath the church. Estimates are that it will take nine months to repair the damage. Unfortunately, the auditorium is not open to the parish as often as the upper church was even though Jesus is present in the tabernacle. Being locked out from our church at any time just doesn't seem right. I am sure Jesus would keep the doors of the church open to everyone at any time of the night or day.

Not having as much access to church leaves me with more time to spend at home and to play on our street with my brothers and friends who live on the block. This evening, Paddy and I just finished playing "hide and seek" with some of our friends. I am worried that at any moment Mommy is going to stick her head out our second floor window and call for us to come home. That is how most mothers call their kids home on our block. To get a few more minutes playing, we decide to go by the girls' high school building near York Avenue.

Our street is very dark at this time because it is cloudy tonight and there are only two street lights on either side of our street to illuminate the western half of our block. I am certain Mommy will not be able to see us so we can stay out and play a little longer before we have to go home.

As Paddy and I approach a group of older teenage boys by the school, I see the unholy, dark shadowy images of demons lurking behind these boys. Before I can warn Paddy about what I see, one of the biggest boys, Damian, extends his arms outward and orders everyone to be quiet as if there is danger nearby. Around his head, I see the ominous black shadowy outline I usually see around people who are very evil.

The villain he speaks of turns out to be none other than an adorable little stray kitten. It is crying and shivering in the cold night air. Maybe it is sick. Where is its mother?

Bending over and picking it up, Damian says with a mischievous tone in his voice, "Aw, look at what we have here, a poor, little pussy-cat, freezing out here... all by itself... alone in this terrible cold night."

Damian does not appear to be aware of the large, monstrous demon behind him. It is clearly fixed on him. Seeing this, I innately step back away and watch as Damian lifts the little kitten high in the air for everyone to see. It is a precious little gray and black striped kitten with rather large, round, adorable-looking eyes.

"Mew, mew, mew," it pleads as the four boys pass her around to one another.

Interestingly, the boys do not ask Paddy or me if we would like to hold the kitten. My attention is drawn to the shortest boy, "Bub," because there is another fierce-looking demon positioned right behind him. I feel we are surrounded on all sides by a powerful aura of evil permeating the area around us.

Bub is not the boy's real name; it's a nickname Damian gave him, "in honor of one of the greatest fallen angels, Beelzebul."

With a diabolical look, Damian turns to Bub and says in a sinister, singsong way, "I think we should do something to help this poor little kitty-cat keep warm, don't you agree, Bub?"

"Yeah, yeah," all three boys cry out and begin jumping around in wild, bizarre motions unaware of the demons behind them. This is terrifying. These boys are going to do something terrible to this poor little kitten. They are obviously not aware that the demons surrounding them may have similar diabolical plans for them.

Damian says again in a singsong way, "Oh, man, this is going to be soooo much fun. We're going to have a real **hot** time tonight!"

While the boys fight over who is going to do something to the kitten, I whisper to Paddy that we should leave because I can see demons around the boys. This indicates to me that the boys are going to do something very bad to the kitten. Paddy shakes his head no and says there's no reason to believe the boys would hurt such a cute little kitten.

Apparently hearing what Paddy said, Damian stares at us with a hateful, evil look and announces that it is his "honor" to offer a sacrifice to **'the devil'** by arranging some heat for **'this little lamb."**

Chuckling diabolically, Damian takes off his long, white sneaker laces while Bub holds the cat. Using the laces, Damian ties the kitten's tiny legs tightly together causing the poor thing to wiggle and cry even more desperately.

"Get some garbage, guys, from across the street in those trash cans," Damian orders.

The two other boys run over, get some bags of garbage, and bring them back to Damian.

"Pile them up inside the fence and get me some matches," he demands. "Bub, you crazy cat-lover, you'll have the honor of lighting it up!"

I see the demons heaving in hateful expectation of the ungodly thing the boys are about to do. With a twisted expression on his face, Bub takes a match out of his pocket, lights it, then drops it into the pile of garbage starting a fire. Quickly lighting more matches, he gleefully throws them in as well. Soon, the crackling fire becomes red hot.

Walking up to the fence with the kitten, Damian holds it up close to his face and speaks to it in a devilish tone of voice, "Well, senorita pussy-cat, this is where you and I part company because we have arranged something very special to keep you warm on this cold night. Adios, gatito!"

As Paddy and I look on in horror, Damian extends his arms outward so that the kitten is directly above the fire.

"Drop it, drop it," the three other boys scream out sounding like those who shouted, "Crucify Him, Crucify Him," before Pontius Pilate.

To my utter horror, Damian drops the tied-up, defenseless, little kitten down into the roaring flames! Instantly, its cries turn into nightmarish screeches of agony as the fire devours its fur. With its legs tied tightly together, there is nothing it can do to escape the merciless flames. As this poor little creature screams and spasmodically flips about, the boys diabolically laugh, cheer, and mimic the kitten jumping about… much to the satisfaction of the demons surrounding the boys.

My God, please have mercy on this poor little kitten, and forgive these sick, heartless boys. This revolting act of cruelty scorches me to the core so badly, I turn away and throw up on the sidewalk. Paddy pulls me away and forces me to walk quickly away from this horrendous scene. After a few steps, we run as fast as we can all the way to our building.

Climbing the stairs in the building where we live, Paddy stops to wipe away some tears, then tells me, "Bobby, let's not tell Mommy what happened. She'll be angry that we didn't do anything to stop those sick bastards, and then she won't let us play with **any** of our other friends on that block."

"It happened so quickly, Paddy, we couldn't do anything to save the kitten," I answer sadly.

"I know. There's no way we could have known they were going to do something so terrible. Before we knew it, they threw the poor little cat into the fire.

"Try not to look so sad, Bobby. You know how Mommy can tell whenever something is wrong. Let's go right into the living room when we go in. Try to avoid Mommy. Okay?"

I nod in agreement.

Mommy doesn't approach us when we go in... but I wish she did. Discussing the terrible, ungodly thing Paddy and I just witnessed might ease our feelings about not being able to help the poor kitten.

Visions of the kitten flipping about in agony flash through my mind followed by the image of the demons surrounding the terrible boys, and how they celebrated with the boys as the poor little kitten was mercilessly burned alive.

I pray that those boys do not someday face the same fate... the same merciless flames... they imposed on that poor little kitten.

Chapter 27

"NIGHT RAIDERS"

January 1954

Paddy asks Mommy if he, Larry, and I can go sled-riding by ourselves in Central Park while Daddy is sleeping. We don't bother asking if Kitty can also come because she doesn't like sled-riding since she got hurt the last time.

"Not with Larry," Mommy says. "He's too young, and the two of you couldn't watch him while you are sled-riding. You and Bobby can go but I want you home before it gets dark."

Larry looks hurt and unhappy but I understand Mommy's concern for his well-being.

Carrying our sleds, Paddy and I quickly make our way over to 79th Street then head west all the way into Central Park and Cherry Hill. After going down the hill a few times, one of the older boys there tells us that there is another great hill for sled-riding. It's called "Pilgrim Hill," and it's not far from where we are right now.

"Just follow this path; it will lead you right to Pilgrim Hill," he tells us.

We and some other kids head off south along the path, and after a short walk come to Pilgrim Hill. Looking up at the top, I discover why it is called this. There at the top is a large metal statue of a pilgrim. The hill itself doesn't look as long as Cherry Hill but it is steeper and has more bumps making for some elevated sled-riding when we hit them.

Pilgrim Hill is not too crowded so up and down we go on this fast hill for what seems hours. It is starting to get darker and colder so we decide it is time to head home. Paddy says he wants to go down the hill one last time before we leave. Standing at the bottom of the hill with my sled off to the side, I watch Paddy come flying down the hill. Near the bottom Paddy's sled hits a large bump and goes flying high in the air and crashes right into a solid wooden barricade resting at the bottom of the hill!

This makes a loud crashing noise. Paddy must be injured. I run over to him and discover my fears are realized as blood spurts out all over Paddy's face from a gash above his left eye. Some fathers seeing the accident come running over to help but no one knows what to do. Kneeling down next to Paddy as he sits on the ground, I put my hand on his shoulder and look into his stunned eyes.

"I got a pretty bad cut, heh, Bobby?" he says as if he wants me to disagree.

"It is just a nasty scratch," I tell him.

I am so worried for Paddy. The bleeding keeps coming, and we are in the middle of Central Park far from home, and it is quickly getting dark and colder by the minute.

My thoughts turn to terror as I remember what Mommy once told us, "You should never go into Central Park at night because the animals are released from the zoo at night so they can roam freely throughout the park until dawn! If the animals catch anyone, they tear them apart and eat them!"

That is why no one is allowed in Central Park at night. And now it is just about night-time, and everyone will be leaving the park for their own safety. What will Paddy and I do? I am terrified at the thought of some fearsome lions and tigers, polar bears and panthers coming after us! I remember seeing them in the zoo. They are strong and fierce with big sharp teeth and they can run faster than we can. We'll never be able to escape from them!

I am so scared I cry out to God and beg Him for help. I feel so scared, and I can tell Paddy is too.

Someone calls out, "Oh, thank God, here is a cop!"

A tall kind-looking cop suddenly appears and asks everyone to step back. Seeing Paddy's injury, he immediately pulls a white handkerchief out of his right pants pocket and places it directly over Paddy's cut as he explains that this will stop the bleeding.

"What happened?" he asks Paddy matter-of-factly.

Paddy explains how he lost control of his sled after going over a large bump on Pilgrim Hill then crashed into the barricade.

"It's not too smart for them to put a big barricade like that at the bottom of a hill where they know you kids go sled-riding," the officer says.

Paddy nods yes.

"Does anything else hurt?

Paddy says, "Yes, my head hurts a lot."

"Do you feel dizzy or nauseous?"

Paddy answers, "A little bit."

"That is not surprising. You got a pretty hard bump on the head. Are your parents here?"

Paddy tells the officer that Mommy and Daddy are home but his brother, Bobby, is here.

The cop looks over to me as Paddy points me out, then the cop asks Paddy, "What's your name and where do you live?"

"My name is Paddy Walsh, and I live on the eastside in Yorkville in Manhattan."

The police officer writes this down on his note pad, then he tells me,

"Here, hold this cloth on the cut over your brother's eye while I go call for a squad car to come give you guys a lift to the hospital."

Turning back to Paddy, he adds, "It looks like you may need a few stitches there to close that up, but it's no big deal."

Rising, he tells me, "Don't push too hard on that and don't move it around, that will make it bleed more."

I nod okay as I nervously hold the white handkerchief as still and gently as I can on Paddy's forehead.

Soon a black and white police car arrives to our left and stops right on the path near us. The cop in the car gets out and talks to the officer before coming over to us.

This other cop says, "Let's help get you over to my squad car. Get up nice and slowly, okay?"

The cops escort Paddy and me over to the police car and help us get into the back seat before putting our sleds in the trunk. Paddy and I thank the first cop for helping us.

"You are welcome, boys. That is what we are here for."

Before closing the door, the second cop leans in and jokes, "Now don't worry, guys, I am not taking you to jail!"

He laughs … but we don't.

I am still terribly worried about the animals coming out before we can get safely out of the park. As we drive away, the first cop smiles and waves goodbye to us.

"You guys are lucky that the officer came along when he did to help you," the officer driving tells us as he turns on his siren and drives slowly along the path leading out of the park on the west side.

I am relieved that Paddy is going to get medical aid, and we are safely getting out of Central Park before the animals are let out of their cages in the zoo!

The policeman drives us to Roosevelt Hospital that is located on 59th Street and Columbus Avenue on the west side of Manhattan. He leads us to the emergency room where he explains what happened to Paddy, and gives our names and address to a lady at the receptionist desk.

Soon, a nurse comes out and asks for our home telephone number so she can call our parents to get permission to treat him.

"I don't remember our phone number," Paddy explains.

"Oh that's great, and I suppose there are no other relatives who live around here who we can call either?"

Paddy tells her that we have lots of relatives but we don't know exactly where they live, or how she can contact any of them.

"Well, we can't let you bleed to death now can we?" the nurse says,

"Come with me and we will have a doctor take a look at that gash you have."

Bleed to death! Those words scare Paddy and me. Is his injury really that bad?

Turning to the police officer, she says, "You can leave now, officer, we can take it from here."

We thank the police officer as he wishes Paddy well and walks out. I wonder if we will ever see him again?

The nurse takes us past people lying on stretchers and brings us to an area that is set off by white curtains. She tells Paddy to sit on the stretcher, and tells me to stand off to the side where Paddy can still see me.

"I'm just going to take a close look at that cut and clean it up a bit before the doctor comes in, okay?"

Paddy hesitantly nods okay. I suspect he is very scared right now but is trying to be brave for my sake. And I guess having his brother with him must be comforting. Paddy winces and groans as the nurse gruffly rubs the wound with something she says will clean it up and kill any germs.

"This is important to do. If we don't kill the germs, an infection can set in and cause far worse damage than the injury itself. Some people can even die from such infections."

Die from such infections! Paddy's injury really must be very serious! It is not very wise for this nurse to be telling Paddy as he lies here suffering and scared in this unfamiliar place that people can die from an injury like his. I feel relieved as a doctor comes in and goes right over to Paddy and closely examines his wound that is now cleaned up although it is still bleeding a little.

Poking around at it causes Paddy to wince and complain, "That hurts!"

"Sorry. You're going to need a few stitches to close that up, but that's no big deal. I understand your parents and family can' be contacted. Is that true?" he asks the nurse.

"I'm afraid so."

Paddy explains why.

"What's your name?" the doctor asks Paddy.

"Paddy Walsh, I'm the oldest in my family. I'm named after my father." Paddy proudly announces.

"Oh, that's a wonderful, proud Irish name!" the doctor says.

"Well listen, Paddy, we can't let this injury go any longer without fixing it, so I must ask you under the circumstances if you want me to fix it for you?"

Paddy tells him yes, so the doctor tells the nurse to give Paddy an authorization form to sign. Once he does, the nurse then signs as a witness to

Paddy's agreement and authorization.

Paddy asks the doctor, "Can my brother, Bobby, stay here with us while you stitch me up? We're here by ourselves and I think he might get afraid if he has to sit outside in the waiting room all by himself."

As he closes the curtain to our cubicle, the doctor smiles and says, "Sure, your brother can stay right here... as long as he's willing to be my assistant!"

I eagerly nod yes.

"Okay, you have to stay right where you are until we are all finished. Can you do that?"

I nod yes again.

"Your job as my assistant is to tell me all about the sled-riding adventure you guys had in Central Park. Can you do that?"

I enthusiastically nod yes.

Leaning directly over Paddy's face, the doctor says to him, "I have to give you a little needle that will sting but it will quickly kill all the pain so I can stitch you up. Okay? You won't feel anything once I give you this needle but it might hurt a little as I inject it. Now try not to move."

The doctor injects a needle directly into Paddy's wound as Paddy winces and moans in pain.

"Remember, this is only going to sting a little but then it is going to numb the whole area so you won't feel any pain at all as I put a few stitches in. You still okay?"

Paddy nods okay but winces again as the doctor injects the area a few more times, twisting the needle around in different directions as he does.

"Okay, 'Doctor Bob,' it is time for you to assist me now by telling me all the details about today's sled-riding adventure," the doctor says as he puts some thread on a surgical needle and begins to sew up the nasty gash over Paddy's eye.

I know the doctor really wants me to talk about today as a distraction for Paddy and me as he operates, so he asks questions about sled-riding, the weather, Pilgrim Hill, and the cops.

"Is Pilgrim Hill better than Cherry Hill?" he asks.

"I like Cherry Hill better because it is bigger."

"How about you, Paddy?" he asks.

"I like Cherry Hill better too."

"Why?"

"Because I didn't get hurt on Cherry Hill; I got hurt on Pilgrim Hill," he explains.

The doctor and nurse giggle and say they don't blame him for not liking Pilgrim Hill.

251

"How're we doing?" the doctor asks Paddy.

"I'm okay."

"Feel any pain?"

"Nope."

"That's good because we're all done!" the doctor surprises us!

"You only needed a few stitches; you are as good as new now. You are a brave young man, Paddy... and your brother is an excellent assistant doctor!"

With the nurse's assistance, the doctor covers Paddy's wound with white bandaging over his entire forehead.

"There now, I am off to help the next patient. The nurse here will give you instructions on your follow-up care with some do's and don'ts's, okay?"

As he pulls the curtain to our cubicle open to leave, he smiles again and adds, "Oh... and let's stay away from hills that have barricades at the bottom, okay?"

Paddy and I laugh but you can be sure in the future, we will carefully examine the bottom of any hills before we do any sled-riding!

The nurse leads us out of the emergency room and stops at a desk and tells Paddy to sit down for a minute so she can give him some instructions. After explaining what follow up care is needed and that he should see the family doctor in five days, she gives Paddy a copy of the authorization form he signed and then asks if he feels all right.

"I just feel a little dizzy and my head hurts," Paddy says.

"Do you feel well enough to go home now?" she asks.

"Yes."

The nurse tells us we can leave but we must go directly home. She shows us the way out past the waiting room then leaves us. Standing there together, I realize that Paddy and I do not know where we are, and we don't know how to get home! I instantly become frightened. Paddy must be thinking the same thing I am.

"There's a cop over there." he says hopefully, "Let's ask him how we can get home."

Paddy and I walk over to the chubby, black cop sitting behind a desk by the door.

Paddy says, "Excuse me, officer, we are by ourselves and don't know where we are or how we can get home. Can you help us?"

"I am not a police officer, son; I am only a security guard but maybe I can help you. You are at Roosevelt Hospital on Columbus Avenue and 59th street in Manhattan. Where do you live?"

"We live on the eastside in Yorkville in Manhattan," Paddy says.

252

"Oh, that's all the way on the other side of town. Boy, you boys are a long way from home."

This scares me.

"Does your family know you are here?"

"No, we had an accident in the park while sled-riding," Paddy explains.

"Does your family have a telephone so I can call them?"

"We don't remember the number," Paddy explains.

"Oh, so I guess you boys don't have any carfare either to take a bus home."

"No, we don't have any money," Paddy answers.

Leaning over, he digs into his pocket and says, "Let me give you some change for the two of you to get home."

Handing Paddy some coins, he tells us, "Here's what you gotta do. When you go out this door to the street, go to the corner to your right, cross the street, walk one block toward the park, and wait there by the bus stop. When the bus comes, get on the uptown bus. Make sure you are on the uptown bus, ask the driver for a free transfer, and ask the driver to tell you know when you get to 79th Street because that's where you must get off to catch the bus that goes through the park to the east side. You take that bus all the way to the end of its route then get off. You should then be on 79th Street near East End Avenue, only few blocks from your home. Okay? Can you remember all that?"

Paddy says he can, and thanks him for helping us.

"Don't mention it, boys, I am happy to help."

Motioning toward me, he says to Paddy, "I hope you don't mind me saying this, but there's some powerful good energy coming from your brother here. Anybody ever say that?"

Paddy and I laugh and nod yes.

"I see. Do me a favor, will you. I have someone in my family who needs a lot of prayers, and I know that God's got a soft spot in His Heart for kids. He says in the good book, 'let the little children come to Me.' I'd sure appreciate it if both you boys would say a prayer for my loved one. Can you do that?"

"Yes," Paddy and I promise.

"God bless you," he says enthusiastically then adds, "Now you boys best be going along; your parents must be worried sick over where you are!"

We thank him once again and head toward the door feeling a little more confident that we can now find our way home. As we do, I ask God to bless the person this kind man has asked us to pray for.

Once outside, we are immediately hit with brutal, bone chilling cold

253

accompanied by a strong wind blowing so hard we have to push slightly against it. The thought of walking any distance in this terrible weather is disheartening, and I am afraid once again that we are lost and cannot find our way home. Dragging our sleds makes loud scraping sounds.

"Stay close, Bobby, keep your face down and walk as fast as you can so we can get to the bus stop as fast as possible," Paddy urges me.

We make it one long block to the next avenue, Central Park West; that is where the bus runs uptown. We stand back against the four-foot wall surrounding Central Park as we wait for the bus to come. It is so bitterly cold and dark. There are no people out on the street, just Paddy and me … and the howling wind and bitter cold of this night feels like it is getting worse by the second.

After what seems an eternity, Paddy says, "There are no buses in sight, Bobby. I don't know if they are running this late; they may have stopped for the night. If we stand here any longer, we may freeze to death."

"What do you think we should do?" I ask, trembling from the bitter cold... and the mounting worry that we are lost.

"I think we should start walking uptown along the park to 79th Street where the cross-town bus may be running. If it is not running, we will have to cut across the park to the east side where we live."

Alarmed, I tell him, "But Mommy said they let the animals from the zoo out at night into Central Park. Remember? She said they become **'Night Raiders'** roaming the park looking for people to eat!"

"I know, but we don't have any choice. Besides, maybe Mommy was just saying that to scare us so we won't go into the park at night. I don't think they really let the animals out at night, Bobby. Maybe they just let them out **inside** the zoo area.

"We don't have a choice. We have to get home or we are going to freeze to death out here on the streets. Let's start walking as quickly as we can uptown and keep looking to see if the bus comes along."

Block after block, we walk uptown freezing in the painful cold, arm in arm, terribly frightened. The park off to our right is cast in ominous darkness as it gives off frightening sounds from thousands of tree branches whipping about in the wind. There are many lights shining from the apartments in the tall buildings to our left on Central Park West. How I wish we could go inside one of those buildings to get warm. Meanwhile, the streets here are completely deserted... no cars... no people... no buses… nothing but the howling cold wind and... the loud scraping sounds of our sleds.

I encourage Paddy to stay away from the four-foot wall on our right enclosing Central Park as far as I can see uptown, "Some of those noises in the park may be from wild animals they let loose from the zoo, Paddy."

254

"That's just the wind blowing through the trees, Bobby; that's all," he reassures me.

A loud banging noise above us startles us and causes us both to run to the side away from the noise. Turning around, we see a loosened street sign waving back and forth in the wind. It reads Central Park West.

Just ahead there is an entrance to the park on our right. With the wind incessantly howling around us, Paddy shouts, "Bobby, I don't know if we can make it all the way up to 79th Street in this cold, and I don't think the buses are running anyway. I think we have to go into the park here and take our chances with the animals. We can walk quietly not to be heard, and we can use those big sticks over there to beat them off if they come after us."

"I'm afraid of the animals, Paddy. I don't think we should go in the park. They can be anywhere in there, hiding in the bushes waiting to pounce out on us."

"We don't have a choice, Bobby; we are going to freeze to death trying to walk all the way uptown to 79th Street. Cutting across the park here is a shorter way home. We have to do it. Don't be afraid, I'll beat off any animals that attack us. Stay close to me. Let's go!"

My big strong, confident brother's words are reassuring. Thank God he is with me, but I am still very worried as we enter the darkened park and follow the path which we hope will bring us to the east side... without encountering any animals along the way.

The few lampposts off in the distance along the pathway shed light on the area surrounding them. After walking against the brutal icy wind for quite a while, I see the faint outlines of buildings on the other side of the park, the east side! It looks like we have gone halfway across the park already.

The fearsome roar of a lion off in the distance cuts through the silence of the night! Although it sounds like it is far away, I know that lions are in the cat family, which means they can run very fast!

Paddy and I stop dead in our tracks and cling to each other in terror. Our worst fears are realized... a lion must be out loose somewhere in the park! Lions are man-eaters. If a lion is out, then other wild animals must be out in the park also! My God, please help us! Please protect us from the wild animals.

Paddy whispers so the lion cannot hear us, "Bobby, walk as softly and quietly as you can on the snow. If the lion comes, hit it as hard as you can on its nose! We'll have to carry our sleds now so they don't make scraping noises on the ground."

Walking gingerly on the snow-covered path, our steps still make crunching sounds. I am so afraid the lion or any of the other "night raiders" will find us before we get out of the park.

255

Paddy pleads, "Bobby, say a prayer... but not out loud! Say it to yourself so the lion doesn't hear you."

I cry out to God from the inner recesses of my heart, and beg Him to protect us from the lion and other wild animals... and to help us find our way home. I am so frightened. I thank God that Paddy is with me but I still feel so vulnerable and I am so cold, so terribly, terribly cold!

"Please, Jesus, please send someone to help us," I beg Him. "You were once hunted when King Herod sent his soldiers out to kill all the baby boys in his efforts to get You. Please send your angels to protect us from the wild animals, and get us home safely.

"What's that?" Paddy whispers as he stops and grabs my arm.

"What's what?" I ask.

Looking frantic, Paddy says, "It sounds like hooves coming up the path behind us, Bobby! Quick, run!"

We start running as fast as we can along the slippery path. Now I can hear the hooves behind us pounding on the ground. There is a lamp post up ahead on the right side of the path. It is going to cast light on us for the animal to see us! The ground is so slippery, it is hard to run any faster.

"My God, help us! Don't let the animal get us," I pray as I hear the beast behind us getting closer.

As we approach the lamp post, Paddy shouts, "Get your stick ready, Bobby, we're going to have to turn and fight for our lives! Stop by the lamp post so we can see what kind of animal it is."

My God, help us!

At the lamp post, I turn around ready to swing my stick as hard as I can at the beast. The ground shakes as the beast slows down in its approach to us. Coming into the light, I can see that it is a white horse with a police officer sitting on top of it!

A voice calls out, "For the love of God, it's good you called out for help in this terrible weather!"

I am so relieved to see the policeman and his beautiful white horse! Now he can help us get safely out of the park. Thank you, God, for hearing our prayers!

Paddy tells him, "I got hurt sled-riding and had to go to the hospital to get stitches, and now we are trying to get to our home on the eastside in Yorkville. We thought you were a wild animal from the zoo!"

The policeman laughs, "Well, we've been called a lot of things over the years, but never a wild animal from the zoo!"

I ask him if he has seen any wild animals from the zoo running out in the park now.

Chuckling, he assures us, "No, there are no wild animals from the zoo out in the park right now; they're kept locked up in their cages **at all times**. The only animals running loose in the park are the human type that feeds on innocent people. They're the worst kind of animal but you won't find any of them out here tonight; it's too cold."

Paddy and I are greatly relieved to hear there are no wild zoo animals out loose in the park... and that the "human-animals" are not out here either!

"You can follow me to the exit that will take you out of the park and leave you off on the east side on Fifth Avenue. From there, you walk to 79th street and walk east toward the East River until you get to St. Monica's Church. From Church, you can find your way home."

Smiling, he adds, "A wise man once said, 'Follow Me," so... follow me."

I am so happy hearing this; I would cry with joy if I wasn't too cold to even cry! We thank him and follow him and his beautiful white horse. The air about us is remarkably warmer as Paddy and I walk behind him and his horse. Oh, thank you, God!

Soon the policeman says, "You can go the rest of the way by following this path, boys. It will lead you to the exit out of the park."

We thank him again as he slowly rides off into the open field.

"Don't' forget to thank Him also... and always follow the signs!" he calls out mysteriously.

"What does he mean, 'thank Him also?' Thank who?" Paddy asks.

"I think he means that we should also thank God for sending him! I bet he's an angel who was sent by God to help us!"

We both turn to take another look at the policeman and his white horse but they have vanished!

Paddy says, "Hey, where'd he go?"

"Didn't you notice, Paddy, that there was no steam coming from his horse or from him breathing in the cold air? He was an angel!"

"Well... angel or no angel... we have to get going, Bobby. It's starting to feel deathly cold again."

Just ahead I can see that we are approaching the zoo.

"We can't go in there, Paddy!" I protest.

"Sure we can," he says. "The cop said all the animals are locked up in their cages. Besides, we have to go in that direction to get home. Let's go. Let's carry our sleds and walk quietly so we don't wake up the wild animals. You know they have great hearing."

We walk quietly and cautiously down a set of stairs leading into the zoo area. On our left are thick, black bars. These are the bars to the cage for the polar bears! This reminds me of the story Daddy told us about a man who had too much to drink and went past the restraining bar and went right up to the polar bear cage. When he stuck his arm inside to pet the polar bear, the bear grabbed the man's arm and ripped it right out of his socket! How horrible! That poor man! I remind Paddy about what happened to that man, and beg him to stay **far away** from the polar bears' cage.

Walking a little bit faster past this area, we reach a carved archway leading to four steps down to an open area. About fifteen feet ahead, we pause to look around and listen. Only an occasional grunting sound is heard.

Being here reminds me of the many happy times Mommy and Daddy took us here to see the animals in the zoo. Just thinking of those warm, sunny days helps me to feel a little less cold. Every time we came here in the past, there were so many people gathered to see the animals that it was difficult to get close to any of the animals' cages.

To our right about thirty feet ahead is the popular seal pond area. It is enclosed with three-feet high black metal fences that surround the entire pond area. Inside, there is a cylindrical concrete housing in the center; that is where the seals live.

Off to the right is a twelve-foot high cage. There is a similar cage on each of the other three corners surrounding the seal pond. Colorful birds live in each of these high corner cages. Situated neatly to our left is a long row of heavily restricted cages that house the gorillas, panthers, lions, bobcats, and monkeys.

I remember Daddy once telling us about one of the most popular animals in the zoo, a gorilla named "Carolyn." Daddy said Carolyn is the "Grand-dame" of zoo gorillas who has lived at the Central Park Zoo since 1943. Whenever I saw her, she always looked sweet and gentle, and was interesting to watch. I always wondered what Carolyn was thinking as she looked at us.

All the animals are in the inside area of their cages enclosed inside this red brick, one-story building. It is eerily quiet here in the zoo. I am very nervous and frightened that Paddy and I are here alone without Daddy and Mommy... and the angel on the white horse.

As we reach the last empty cage on the left side, I whisper, "Do you remember the time all of us were standing here in front of this cage watching that nasty little monkey, Jimmy, on his swing?"

This brings a smile to Paddy's face as he recalls, "You mean the time that wicked monkey peed on all of us and the other people standing in front of its cage!"

We both laugh remembering how this monkey peed on everyone that day.

Paddy adds, "Do you remember when it also threw its poop on the people standing in front?"

I nod yes but I don't laugh; that was so disgusting. The people were very angry but all they could do was yell at the monkey as it screeched, jumped around and laughed at them!

"Do you remember what Daddy did to get even with that crazy monkey?"

I laugh as Paddy retells how Daddy taught Jimmy the monkey a lesson.

"Daddy wanted to get even with the monkey for throwing its poop on the people and for peeing on us. So Daddy went over and bought a bag of peanuts from the man with the cart at the end of the cages. Then Daddy went over to the water fountain, filled his mouth with water, walked back over to the monkey's cage, and held out his hand. Gesturing toward the monkey, it appeared Daddy wanted to give the wicked monkey some peanuts.

"The monkey was suspicious of Daddy. It nervously climbed from one swing to another in his cage, hissing and spitting at Daddy all the while. But Daddy just stood there perfectly still and patiently waited for the monkey to come and take the peanuts out of his hand. Eventually, the monkey made its way near Daddy's hand. Then it hesitantly reached its arm toward Daddy's hand as its eyes darted from Daddy's hand to Daddy's eyes.

"When the monkey reached its arm out through the bars, Daddy spit the water out all over the monkey! The monkey was so shocked and wet, it screeched and jumped wildly all over the cage! Daddy and the crowd cheered and clapped. The monkey was so angry it spit toward Daddy and the crowd."

"That was so funny, Paddy! What a great memory."

At the end of these cages, off to our left we see the three open archways that span the northeast walkway leading out of the zoo area. Following that path, it takes us out of the park and onto Fifth Avenue.

I tell Paddy, "It looks like we've survived all the 'night raiders' from the zoo!"

Just then, the roar of a lion splits the silence of the night igniting our faster pace crossing Fifth Avenue. The cold night air doesn't feel quite as bitter and painful now that we are on the familiar, though deserted, streets of Yorkville.

At the corner of our street, I am so happy to see our block that I feel like running down the block to our building but I know Paddy must be weak from his injury and the stress of our long, cold, scary walk through Central Park. I put my free arm around Paddy's shoulders, and he puts his arm around my shoulders. Paddy and I are about the same size... but he will always be my big brother.

In the foyer of our building, Paddy rings our doorbell, the second one from the front on the right side. After a few seconds, the buzzer goes off allowing us to open the locked door to the hallway. At the top of the winding stairs, Mommy is standing there with her arms on her hips looking very stern and upset until she sees the large white bandage across Paddy's forehead.

"Oh, my God, Paddy, what happened to you?"

"Some fierce Indians attacked us as we were sledding on Pilgrim Hill in Central Park," Paddy jokes. "Then we had to fight off all the 'Night Raiders.' You know, all the wild animals from the zoo they let out into the park after dark! Well, Bobby and I took care of them all!"

Paddy then tells Mommy about the policeman who came on a white horse after I prayed to God to send someone to help us.

"He showed us the way out of the park; otherwise, we would have been lost all night, and would have frozen to death."

Mommy says, "Boys… there are no police on white horses at night in Central Park."

Exactly.

Chapter 28

ALL GOD'S CHILDREN

April 1954

"Do you think there is any truth to what Senator McCarthy says that America is infiltrated with Communists?" Daddy asks Mommy.

"I don't think so, Patsy," Mommy says, "President Eisenhower and Vice President Nixon wouldn't let Communist spies get into our country and spy on us," Mommy assures him.

"Some of the guys on the job say that Eisenhower and Nixon are far removed from our day-to-day lives so they depend on their staff to detect such things. The Commies know this, so they send spies in among us ordinary people. From there, they gradually work their way into positions to learn our country's military and technological secrets."

"Patsy, do they really think Communists would send their spies among ordinary people like you and me?"

Daddy explains, "Listen, don't you remember how the Germans did the same thing during the Second World War? They had their spies living in a regular apartment in a tenement right here in Yorkville on East 92nd Street! Spies try to 'hide in open sight.' That's why they mingle among us every-day people."

"Sure, but they did that during war-time, Patsy. This isn't war-time," Mommy points out.

"What makes you think so?" Daddy says. "There is a **'cold war'** going on as it is called between the Commies and us. McCarthy may be the only one in Washington who has it right. Time will tell.

"News reports indicate Communists are already making inroads in places like the Mid-east, Cambodia, Vietnam, parts of Africa, and even here in our own hemisphere. I wouldn't be surprised if we hear before the decade is out that there're Communists in Central and South America!"

Taking a drag on his Chesterfield cigarette, he blows the smoke up in front of his face and watches it slowly drift away, "Just like this smoke, they're right there in front of everyone's eyes but no one sees how harmful they are!"

Daddy does not realize how true his statement is… not just about the cigarette smoke either. In terms of smoking, I am convinced that someday people will discover how cigarette smoking does very serious damage to the lungs. In terms of the devil, I am not so confident that people will ever accept its reality or the harm it inflicts.

Daddy resumes, "Their plan to take over the world includes controlling religion often by nationalizing it, making clergy dependent upon the state by paying their salary, then declaring any talk against the state to be 'hate speech' so they can arrest and remove clergy from society. Once they remove religion from society, they create a 'God-less' population with little or no conscience or compassion for fellow human beings.

"Then they remove all the guns from private citizens. They do this by first requiring that all weapons be registered, then they declare that it is against the law for private citizens to own weapons thereby requiring that their weapons be turned in. Then, when only the state has guns, private citizens can't do anything as the state implements its full system of totalitarian government. That's actually what Hitler and Stalin did.

"Remember, the first thing they did was to remove God and religious worship from society!"

I can understand why they did that. If God is removed from society, the devil has far greater reign over the people.

Daddy adds, "Communists today spread their ideology across the world by causing political unrest and rebellion from within. The Soviets pay a fortune to traitors who help Russian spies overthrow governments by whipping up the local citizenry into a frenzy of revolt under some false pretense of injustices or a better way of life. Guns, ammunition and equipment are supplied by the Communists to rebels including how to strategically wage a war of rebellion."

As Daddy pauses, I say, "The Communists are so wrong in their thinking. They should be providing people with food, water, medicine, clothing, and **greater** access to religion."

"That's right, Bobby," both Daddy and Mommy say at the same time.

Daddy looks pleased as he adds, "You should've heard these two guys the other day arguing in Union Square Park near 14th Street where people gather to debate their views. I couldn't believe how prejudiced this one guy was, and the audacity he had to stand there in front of a large group of people and insult minorities!"

"What for example?" Mommy asks.

"Well, first of all, he was bad-mouthing colored people in our country, complaining how they're protesting for the same rights as white people. The other man argued that colored people are entitled to equal rights because they're American citizens **and** children of God!"

Mommy asks, "How did the crowd react to that?"

"Unfortunately, there was a lot of booing but the man stood his ground saying that colored people deserve to vote, go to decent schools, and use the same public facilities as any white person. Man, did that draw a lot of

262

bad words from the bigots in the crowd!

"The prejudiced guy then asked the other guy if he would mind if his daughter married a colored man and had little 'niglets' for children!

"This drew raucous jeering from the crowd. However, the good guy said, 'I love and respect my daughter, and if she wanted to marry a negro then that's perfectly all right with me! All men and women are children of God, no matter what the color of their skin may be. It's not the color of one's skin that determines a person's value, it's the goodness and love within!'

"Before the prejudiced man could counter, the good guy continued, 'Colored people deserve to be treated with dignity and respect the same as any white person. They fought in the wars defending our country and many of them died in the process. They pay their taxes, go to church, and they bleed red, white and blue just like we white people. And you know what? I'm sure Jesus loves His colored children just as much as He loves His white children!'

"This quieted the rowdy crowd until the prejudiced guy shocked everyone by saying, "Well then, I guess you feel the same way about **Jews, 'Wops,' 'Spics,'** and **'Mics!'**

"This drew an entirely different response from the crowd. They started loudly booing him until he stormed away!"

"Daddy," I ask, "what do those words stand for?"

"They're insulting, denigrating, racial slurs to describe different nationalities, Bobby.

"For example, **'Wop,'** refers to Italians because when many Italians came to America around 1908, they didn't have passports so they were said to be **'With Out Passports'** Hence, **'Wops.'**

"**Spic'** refers to Spanish people because many of them say they don't **'spic'** English.

"**Mic'** refers to Irish people like us because the last name of many Irish people begins with **'Mc.'** If an Irish last name begins with Mc, that stands for 'son of,' like McDonald would represent 'son of Donald."

"Bobby, God doesn't want us to use racial slurs, and He certainly doesn't want us to hate others just because they are different from us."

Mommy adds, "And that includes people who are mentally ill or handicapped. They're all God's children and should be treated with love and respect."

"That includes people like Vernon, doesn't it?" I ask.

Vernon is one of the saddest stories in our neighborhood, in all of Yorkville. He is a tall, thin, middle-aged homeless man who kids on our block call, "Vernon the Bum."

Mommy quickly replies, "Yes, of course, it also includes Vernon. He's homeless because he's an 'alcoholic', which is someone who drinks too much alcohol and accordingly can't live like most other people. It's sinful how the kids tease and torment him."

"Where does he live?" I ask.

"Vernon lives in the hallways of buildings… and sometimes in the street. During the day, he can be seen sitting on the steps of different stoops on the street watching people coming and going, and occasionally sipping alcohol from a bottle he keeps in his jacket pocket.

"He has family members who live somewhere down the block on that street. They help him as best they can but he never changes. His clothing is always dirty and wrinkled because he sleeps in them and doesn't wash them.

"On summer nights, Vernon can be seen sleeping on top of old clothes, rags, and cardboard on the sidewalk against one of the buildings. In the wintertime, he seeks shelter from the cold by going inside buildings on our block where he sleeps in an alcove behind the ground floor stairs… or in a basement near a warm furnace."

I tell Mommy and Daddy, "Instead of being kind to Vernon, some of the older boys say nasty things to him whenever he passes by. One time, in the middle of a hot day, I saw the figures of demons around the older boys. I watched as the demons followed the boys as they gathered up caterpillars from some trees nearby."

"Are you sure you saw demons… not shadows?" Daddy asks.

"Yes, I'm sure, Daddy; there's no mistaking them."

"Why in God's name would demons care about boys collecting caterpillars? That doesn't make any sense," Daddy reasons.

"They were tempting the boys into using the caterpillars to torment Vernon by throwing them on him while he was sleeping in an old armchair. After they did, they woke Vernon up by screaming like devils. When Vernon saw the caterpillars crawling all over him, he screamed and frantically jumped up as he brushed them off while the boys wickedly laughed at him.

"I helped Vernon brush them off, and told the boys what they did wasn't funny; it was cruel. They laughed at me and called me a 'holy-holy.' After I helped get the caterpillars off Vernon, he smiled and thanked me for being so kind to him. Despite what the boys had done to him, he looked happy as he walked away."

Mommy reassures me, "God tells us in the bible that He takes care of the birds in the field, so He certainly looks after poor people like Vernon. Jesus also says that when we help poor people, we are actually helping Him. God will reward us for being kind to people like Vernon… and anyone else who is less fortunate than we."

"There but for the grace of God, go I," Daddy says.

Chapter 29

PENNIES FROM HEAVEN

August 1954

Mommy looks surprised, "What are you doing home so early, Patsy?"

"I got bumped off today, Ellie, and I don't know when I'll be able to get back on. It may be a week or two," Daddy explains sounding so depressed.

Nervously puffing on a Chesterfield cigarette is a clear sign that he is greatly concerned.

"Oh, geez, Patsy, just when we need extra money with the kids going back to school. They need some clothes, shoes, and there are the book bills. It seems these layoffs always come at the worst time."

"I know, I know, Ellie. We'll have to skimp by and pray that I get back on the job soon."

Mommy reaches for a Chesterfield cigarette evidencing her concern. The two of them smoke way too many cigarettes! Daddy says he smokes two packs a day, and Mommy says she smokes "only one pack."

Only one? I think even **one cigarette** is too much. Smoking must do terrible things to the lungs. You can't inhale all that smoke directly into your lungs and not have it do terrible damage. The lungs are not made to deal with poisonous smoke. I wish Mommy and Daddy would stop smoking but every time I ask them, they tell me that if smoking was harmful, the government would not allow tobacco companies to sell cigarettes.

Even if the government says it is not harmful, I still think it is... very harmful.

"The last time you were out, you were out for nearly two weeks," Mommy reminds him, "We couldn't pay our monthly bills. It took us a **long** time to catch up. Remember?"

"Yes, of course I do."

Mommy worries more about paying the bills than Daddy does. This might be because Daddy usually gives his pay on payday directly to Mommy so she can pay the bills. She does so by going to the different bill-paying locations in Yorkville. Daddy keeps a little money in his pocket for carfare and lunch. Mommy says this arrangement is common among families in Yorkville.

"Well, there's no time like the present to 'stretch the dollar' as far as it will go, and to start cutting corners again," Mommy says.

"We need some milk, bread and eggs, so I guess I'll ask one of the kids to go to grocery store and get it on trust. Thank God the grocery has been so helpful to us and other families in the neighborhood. Every time someone gets hit with hard times, he has always been there to provide groceries on trust until they get back on their feet. I don't think he has ever turned anyone away. He is such a good man."

Daddy responds, "Yeah, but when people are on 'trust' with him, he doesn't let them get cigarettes or beer."

"That is because those are not 'essentials,' Patsy," Mommy explains. "When you have to cut corners, you cut out the beer and the cigarettes first before anything else. I am sure he does that to help people discipline themselves during hard times and avoid running up a big bill they may later regret. Otherwise, he gives people the food they need to tide them over."

"Yep, you are right, Ellie. That's why everybody sees to it that they pay him back every penny they owe him as soon as they can."

The process of "trusting" customers down on their luck is yet another common practice among the people of Yorkville where owners of small grocery stores help their regular customers when times get tough financially.

And so, I go to the grocery store to get the groceries we need now on trust. Mommy writes out a list of groceries for me to give to the grocer... assuming he will give us trust as usual. As I walk to the store, I think of how I will ask him to trust us for the groceries we need. I also wonder if anyone who knows me will be there in the store to hear me ask for trust.

Entering the store, a little bell goes off above the door. This tells the grocer no matter where he is in the store that someone has entered his store through the front door. Fortunately, there is only one other person in the store, an older lady, who is shopping. Standing off to my left, I don't know if she hears anything I say. Many older people cannot hear what you are saying no matter where they are standing.

I muster up the courage to say, "Hello, how are you today?"

Smiling, he answers, "I'm fine, thank you. What can I get for you?"

"Well, we need some groceries... but my father just got laid off today so my mother told me to ask you if you can trust us again for a while until Daddy gets back to work. We promise to pay you back everything."

He blinks then says, "Sure, son. What is it your Mom wants?"

I give him the list, which he uses to retrieve the items Mommy wrote down.

Carefully loading them into a cardboard box, the grocer then reaches under the counter, pulls out a notebook, and says, "I'm writing the amount your family owes in my book. I'll keep a running account until you can pay it back."

He looks happy he is able to help by 'trusting' us.

"You can tell your mother she can send any one of you kids and simply tell me to 'put it on the bill.' Okay?"

I nod okay and thank him.

I slide the box of groceries off the counter and turn around to leave. At the door, I realize that I cannot open the door because my hands are tied up carrying this heavy box. Before I can figure out what to do, the grocer suddenly appears and reaches around me to open the door.

"Have a good day, sonny," he tells me cheerfully.

Wow! He even opened the door for me! He may never become rich running his business like this, but his kindness and generosity certainly are earning him treasures in heaven.

As Jesus said, "What you do for the least of My brethren, you do for Me."

That means when he helps others, he is actually helping Jesus. Therefore, his reward will be much greater than any money people might give him.

When I tell Mommy and Daddy of the grocer's kindness and his promise to let us put groceries on the bill, they look greatly relieved.

"That's swell," Daddy says.

Mommy says, "Bobby, please say a prayer that God will help Daddy get back to work quickly!"

"Okay, Mommy, I will go pray right now."

I go into the room off the kitchen and lay down on the bed. With my eyes closed, I clear my mind of everything so I think only of God.

"Dear God, please help Daddy get back to work. Mommy and Daddy are so worried about all the bills they have. Can you please send them some money to help them? Thank you, God, for whatever You do to help. Thank you also for the gift of people like the grocer who help when things are difficult. Please bless him, Lord, and if **he** ever needs help from others, please send someone to help him. Amen."

As soon as I finish my prayer, a vision forms of my entire family going for a walk during which someone in our family finds a roll of money! I feel certain that this is God's answer to my prayer for help with money problems. He wants our entire family to go on a walk of faith to find the money we need.

I jump out of bed and run out into the kitchen and tell Mommy and Daddy, "God just showed me a vision of our whole family going for a walk and one of us finding a roll of money to pay our bills!"

Mommy and Daddy look at each other and smile. Having previously witnessed several miracles in my life, they don't hesitate to take our entire family for a walk, a walk of faith... right now!

Mommy calls out to everyone, "We're all going for a walk because Bobby says that God is going to let one of us find a roll of money!"

"Let's go, shake a leg!" Daddy urges everyone.

When everyone is gathered by the front door for our walk together, Mommy says, "Now remember, Bobby said God gave him a vision showing one of us finding a roll of money so everyone keep your eyes pinned to the ground to find that money!"

Daddy leads the way out of the apartment into the hallway followed by Paddy, Larry, Kitty holding Geri's hand, me, then Mommy. Everyone is looking down at the floor when all of a sudden, Paddy steps on something causing him to stop in his tracks and bend down toward the floor.

Holding up a thick roll of money in his hand, Paddy shouts, **"I found the money; I found the money!"**

Daddy rushes to Paddy's side as Paddy hands the roll of money to him. With his eyes wide with amazement, Daddy counts the money.

"My God, Ellie, there are over two hundred dollars here! That's more than enough to pay all our bills!"

A cheer goes up from everyone!

Mommy cries, "It's a miracle! Thank you, God. Thank you for hearing our prayers and helping us."

How wonderful and amazing it is that God answered my prayer this way. It required our entire family to go on a walk of faith trusting that God would help us in a most remarkable, implausible way.

I guess that puts us in the good company of someone else, St. Peter, who God also asked to take a walk of faith… only we were asked to walk on land.

Chapter 30

THE ALTAR BOY

September 1954

Monday morning finally arrives. Today, I am going to serve as an altar boy for the first time! I just became an altar boy along with other boys from my class. After attending several practice sessions to learn how to assist at Mass, my classmate, Johnny, and I are paired off as partners for our altar boy assignments.

For our first Mass, we have been assigned to the six o'clock morning Mass today, and every day this week. I get up at five o'clock and quickly dress for Mass. No sneakers or dungarees are allowed. Everyone in the family is still asleep as I head out the door.

No one is out on the streets of Yorkville at this hour as I walk to where Johnny lives in a building on 82nd Street just west of First Avenue on the south side of the street.

As I pass St. Stephen of Hungary Church, the demon's voice spoils the silence of the morning, "You're a fool to do this. No one cares. You are wasting your time... and you're committing a sin by not giving your body the sleep it needs!"

I ignore the demon's lies as I sit on Johnny's stoop and pray as I wait for him a short time before Johnny appears looking excited and happy. He is a little shorter and thinner than I am, but like me, he also comes from a large, Irish Catholic family.

"Are you nervous, Bobby?" he asks.

"Yes... very nervous!" I admit.

"Do you remember all the Latin words?" he asks.

"I think so. I stayed up late last night reading them over and over again from the Daily Missal," I tell him.

"I did too!" he confesses.

When we reach St. Monica's Church, we quickly make our way to the sacristy up front. Entering, we go to the room for altar boys and put on the long, black cassock that has to be buttoned all the way from under our necks down to our ankles. Then we put on a short-sleeved, white surplus that looks like a loose, puffy shirt that is far too big for us. Once we are fully dressed in our altar boy outfit, we go into the first room of the sacristy and stand by the dressing table where the priests put on their vestments for Mass.

Suddenly, the door to the far left that is connected to the Rectory where the priests live, flies open and in comes Father O'Connor who will celebrate this Mass.

Quickly descending the three steps in front of the door, Father says, "Good morning, boys. Ready to assist at Mass?"

"Yes, Father," Johnny and I answer together.

"Good! Is this your first Mass?" he asks.

Johnny and I again answer together, "Yes, Father."

"Don't worry, boys, the Holy Ghost will help you remember the Latin words and if you forget what you're supposed to say or do at a certain time, I'll just remind you. Don't worry about doing things right, rather, focus on the great joy of what is happening as Jesus joins us in Holy Communion!"

Johnny and I look at each other feeling less nervous hearing Father O'Connor's encouraging words. After quickly putting on his vestments, Father leads us over to the stairs on the right and tells us it is time for us to serve at our first Mass. Father O'Connor pulls the chain on his right ringing the bell alerting everyone in the church that he and his altar boys are about to enter. Our first Mass has begun!

Everyone stands up as we enter with our hands folded reverently in front of us. Father O'Connor follows us carrying the chalice covered by an ornate cloth. At the center altar, Johnny and I genuflect, make the Sign of the Cross, kneel down, and begin saying our Latin prayers that begin, "Ad Deum qui lae ti fi cat iu ven tutem me am."

The Mass quickly progresses as Johnny and I remember all the Latin words and all the actions expected of us. At the Consecration of the Mass, Johnny rings the bell as soon as he sees Father O'Connor extend his hands over the bread and wine as he faces the altar. An exhilarating, tingling sensation sweeps over me as Jesus miraculously becomes present.

Rising, I go directly up the steps of the altar and kneel on the top step immediately to the left of Father O'Connor. He is saying some prayers as he leans over the bread and wine. Rising, he then genuflects and as he does, I take the back bottom of his long vestment and hold it up so it does not touch the ground. Rising, he lifts the host high up in the air for everyone in the church to see.

As I look up at the uplifted Host, I see above and around us are countless angels and glorified souls in loving adoration of Jesus in the Eucharist. We are all immersed within an aura of indescribable love and joy. An exquisite fragrance fills the air while heavenly voices combine to sing words of love I never imagined possible.

The angels are in rapt adoration of the Eucharist in Father O'Connor's hands. When Johnny rings the bell again it brings me back to see Father lift the chalice containing the Precious Blood of Jesus high up into the air to the joy of all the angels and glorified souls present.

For the rest of the Mass, I am mesmerized by this incredible experience.

Soon Father O'Connor distributes Holy Communion as I accompany him and hold the Communion paten under the chin of those kneeling at the Communion rail to catch the Host if it accidentally falls.

To each person, Father says, "Corpus Christi," which is Latin for "Body of Christ."

Each person receiving says, "Amen!" which means "I believe" or "so be it" confirming that we believe the Communion Host is the Body of Christ. Soon Mass is over, and Johnny and I find ourselves standing in the sacristy waiting for Father O'Connor to speak to us.

"Thank you, boys, for assisting at Mass," Father says. "You both did an excellent job! Remember, it's a great privilege for you to serve Our Lord this way. Don't ever take serving at Mass for granted."

We thank him and go to the altar boys' area to take off our vestments. Walking back to 82nd Street, we congratulate each other and express how thrilled we are to have served. We are proud to be altar boys, and to be so close to Jesus during Mass.

As we part at the corner of 82nd Street and First Avenue, I hear the demon mock me for serving at my first Mass.

"You would have achieved more by staying home and sleeping. What a fool you are!"

A "fool for Christ," I think, and I say another prayer of thanks to God for allowing me to peek behind the curtain to see what actually happens at the Consecration of the Mass!

Every night this week, I go to sleep remembering the exhilarating experience I had at my first Mass as an altar boy. I cannot wait until morning so I can get up and serve again as an altar boy at the six o'clock morning Mass. To make sure I don't oversleep, Mommy lets me set the Big Ben alarm clock for five o'clock. The only thing she asks is that I keep the clock close to my bed so I can jump up as soon as it goes off and turn the alarm off so it doesn't wake everyone else up too early. I then have to reset the alarm for six in the morning for everyone else.

In its efforts to detain me from serving, the demon has been turning off the alarm clock. But my guardian angel wakes me up on time by gently rocking my shoulder back and forth. I thank my angel, and inspect the clock each day. Despite being set properly, the alarm clock simply will not ring when I set it to get up for Mass. The demon is not happy my angel wakes me up on time anyway.

Each day that I serve is like serving at my first Mass.

On Friday evening, I will be serving as an Acolyte for the first time at a Benediction service. Daddy and Larry have decided to come along to witness my first service as an Acolyte at a Benediction. My partner, Johnny, told me that he would meet me at St. Monica's. Looking out the window, I can see that it is starting to rain. I give Geri, Mommy, and Kitty a kiss, then I head for the front door. Pausing for a second, I grab an umbrella from the corner of the kitchen between the refrigerator and the wall then I go through our front door followed by Daddy and Larry.

Earlier, Daddy told me, "When you go to church you are **not** doing God a favor, He is doing you a favor! You get special graces **every time** you attend Mass.

"Remember what St. Brigid said, 'For every mass you attend reverently, God will allow one of your loved ones who died before you to greet you in heaven when you die!'

"And that is not all. Our church teaches that at Communion time, all the angels and all the saints who are with God, come surround the priest and the Eucharist at the altar!"

As Daddy, Larry and I climb down the steps outside our building, I look up to see Geri sitting on the window sill smiling and waving to us. She is so precious.

As we walk toward York Avenue, it begins to drizzle a little harder now so I lift the umbrella upward, snap it open, and raise it up. Immediately, I hear some strange sounds coming from the underside of the umbrella above me. Looking up, I am disgusted to see countless brown roaches crawling around inside the umbrella! I quickly pull the umbrella down and close it as I hold it by the handle outward away from my body. Larry, walking next to me, notices... but Daddy doesn't.

Larry tells me to dump the umbrella in a nearby garbage can but as I am about to do so, I think, why throw away an expensive umbrella? I will just shake it to get the roaches out. However, after shaking it a few times, only a few fall out. Rather than throwing it away, I will carefully carry it to church where I can leave it outside so the roaches will run away.

Once I see St. Monica's, I forget about the roaches as I go over in my mind what I am supposed to do during Benediction. Daddy, Larry and I quickly climb the stairs just in time as the rain really starts to come down. Inside the vestibule, there are many ladies gathered there visiting with one another as they wait for the beginning of Benediction. It is remarkable to hear so many words being spoken by them... even though they are speaking softly.

I have only a few moments to get to the sacristy to be on time to serve as an Acolyte for Benediction but I realize that I forgot to leave the umbrella outside the church. Figuring the roaches will stay inside the umbrella until I return, I place it on top of the long, warm radiator by the back wall next to the main doors.

As I walk away toward the right doors to head for the sacristy, I hear alarming cries from the women, "Oh my God, look at all the roaches!"

I turn around to see a rainbow of roaches running up the wall of the vestibule from the umbrella!

"Who's umbrella is that?" a woman cries out.

The demon whispers in my mind, "It would be so funny to tell them the umbrella belongs to your father so they will blame him!"

At this moment, the instinct to do something funny supersedes my aversion to the demon's suggestions.

Without thinking of the consequences, I point to Daddy and say loudly, "It's **his** umbrella!"

The ladies immediately begin shouting at Daddy to remove his umbrella... **and his roaches!**

His eyes are bulging and his mouth wide open as he realizes the ladies are blaming him for the invasion of the roaches in the church! Stepping quickly over to the umbrella, Daddy grabs it, and in one fluid motion opens the main door of the church and wickedly flings the umbrella out as far as he can. Returning to the heat radiator, he frantically swipes at the roaches on the wall and stomps on as many as he can.

Larry, realizing that Daddy is likely going to blame both of us for his humiliation, has already started moving over to the doors entering the church on the far left side. Taking a cue from him, I, too, quickly enter the church through the other side doors... just in time.

Walking up the right side of the church as fast as I can, I look over and see Daddy walking very quickly after Larry who is practically running ahead of him on the far left side of the church. When I reach the safety of the sacristy, I peer out through the glass panels of the doors and watch as Larry continuously circles around the church maintaining a safe distance between himself and Daddy who is still biting his tongue.

Realizing what I have done is wrong, I ask God to forgive me... and I also ask Him to chase all the roaches out of the church. Following Benediction, I fear the worst as I face Daddy in the back of church in the vestibule where the roaches escaped. I tell him how sorry I am for what I did. To my surprise and relief, he is forgiving!

He says, "That's all right, son, don't worry about it. It's not your fault that our apartment is overrun with roaches! Don't let this ruin things for you; just remember your first Benediction."

I thank him for being so understanding... and I realize that whenever I see roaches it will remind me of the first time I served as an Acolyte at Benediction.

Chapter 31

"ZIT-BANG!"

October 1954

We are all so happy… the New York Giants baseball team won the 1954 World Series in four games by beating the heavily-favored Cleveland Indians! During the first game at the Polo Grounds, the score was tied 2-2 in the top of the eighth inning with two runners on base for Cleveland when one of the stars, Vic Wertz, hit the ball over 450 feet into deep center field. If the ball was not caught, the Indians would have scored at least two runs to take the lead. The Giants young star centerfielder, Willie Mays, ran like a bullet with his back to the infield and made an incredible over-the-head catch of the ball out near the centerfield bleacher stands! That was to become one of the greatest catches ever made, and it saved that game for the Giants. The Giants also got great pinch-hitting from Dusty Rhodes who hit a few homeruns during the Series to help the Giants win the World Series.

"The 'Say Hey Kid' as he is called, in that one play became instantly famous **and** infamous at the same time," Daddy laughs. "He became an instant hero in New York, and a despised opponent in Cleveland!"

On the past few weekends, I have been playing softball with Paddy and his friends at John Jay Park, and playing tackle football at Carl Schurz Park with Larry and some of the kids from our block. The best field for tackle football is at Carl Schurz Park on the small field just before the bridge leading to the Mayor's residence at Gracie Mansion.

On weekend days, Paddy, Larry, and I have played card games like War, Casino, Go Fish, and 500 Card Rummy. I often win, but when I don't, Larry does. Paddy is clever but he has the worst luck playing cards. Another favorite pastime is watching television. Some of our favorite shows are on Sunday night: Lassie, the Ed Sullivan Show, Gun Smoke, and late at night, there is the Late Show, and Sherlock Holmes, a show about a famous, brilliant detective in Scotland Yard, London.

Unfortunately for Daddy, another one of our favorite pastimes has become teasing him! It all started from listening to his stories about the mischievous pranks he and his brothers pulled on people when they were younger. Now Paddy, Larry, and I think of ways to pull practical jokes on him.

Although Daddy loves to tell us his earlier escapades, he is **not** a good sport when it comes to being the target. In fact, he becomes greatly agitated when we do things to tease him. His reaction makes teasing him all the more fun and adventuresome.

One of the things I just started doing to tease him is drawing a picture of what I call a "devil Pig." My angel tells me not to do this, but I ignore his guidance because I don't consider it an especially bad thing to do. The image I draw looks like a pig's head except that I add horns, deeply wrinkled skin, and fangs. After I draw it, I leave it in places where I know Daddy will see it. He **hates** to see this drawing because he says it looks so evil.

Knowing that devil-pig drawings work well in getting Daddy all riled up, I decide to draw one right now. Rather than just leaving it in a place where he will see it, this time I will put it in an especially mischievous location. I am going to put it where he can see it but can't get to it right away... like on the far back-wall of our bathroom. When he sits down on the toilet bowl and looks toward the back of the room, he will see the devil-pig drawing hanging there looking at him, but he won't be able to remove it until he finishes going to the toilet!

After putting the finishing touches to the drawing, I go into the bathroom and walk past the tub to go to the far back wall of this long room. There, I use a tack to attach the drawing high on the wall where I know Daddy cannot help but see it. I quickly get out of the bathroom and position myself in the room outside the bathroom. Larry knows what I am doing and is as eager as I am to see if Daddy goes into the bathroom before Mommy does because she will tear it down before Daddy sees it.

Our hopes are realized as Daddy comes into the room carrying a newspaper and walks right over to the bathroom and enters. We get a little closer to the toilet door so we can hear what Daddy says when he finally sees the devil-pig drawing. We listen as he sits on the bowl and apparently opens the newspaper to read it.

After the sound of him turning the pages a few times, we hear him cry out, "Oh my God! Ellie, your goddamn son has drawn another devil-pig picture on the back wall of the bathroom!"

Hearing his cries, Mommy comes into the room where we are and sees us laughing hysterically at Daddy's expense.

"Bobby, what have you done? Have you drawn another one of those devil-pig pictures again? You shouldn't be teasing your father like this; you know how that spooks him. Now he's going to be mad as hell when he comes out. You two better go hide somewhere if you know what's good for you!"

Mommy slightly opens the door and apparently sees where I put the drawing on the back wall making it impossible for Daddy to remove it until he is done. Mommy giggles adding to Daddy's frustration.

"What's so goddamned funny?" he asks.

"Nothing," Mommy answers.

"See what your goddamn son has drawn again?"

"Yeah, I see," Mommy says as she goes to the back of the bathroom, removes the drawing, and crumples it.

"You have nobody to blame but yourself, Patsy," Mommy admonishes him. "I told you a thousand times you shouldn't be telling the boys about the practical jokes you and your brothers pulled on people when you were kids. Now you have the boys following in your own footsteps!"

"In a pig's tit, it's my fault!" he protests.

"No, in a devil-pig's head!" Mommy laughs.

"Very funny, Ellie, very funny," Daddy complains.

Larry and I make sure to disappear down to the safety of the street below before Daddy comes out of the bathroom. We will have to stay out of our apartment until he goes to work.

Later that evening, when he arrives home from work around one in the morning, we have planned a new practical joke to pull on him. Larry, notorious in the family for his smelly farts, has been purposely eating raw onions and garlic cloves all night. Our plan is to "bomb" Daddy with one of Larry's **SBD's,** "**S**ilent **B**ut **D**eadly" farts!

Knowing that Daddy has had several hours to cool off from seeing my devil-pig drawing earlier, I risk my personal safety staying in the kitchen as he walks in through the front door.

Immediately looking at me he says, "No more of those freaking goddamn devil-pig pictures, kid. That stuff is evil and has no place in our home. You especially should know better."

"Okay, Daddy," I promise him.

Daddy goes right over to the stove and heats up his dinner that Mommy left there for him as she usually does. Tonight's dinner is one of his favorites, spaghetti and meatballs. When the food is ready, Daddy positions himself at the head of the kitchen table facing the small television on the table at the opposite end from where he is sitting. Larry and I are strategically stationed on either side of the table with Daddy sitting in the middle at the end of the table.

As Daddy enjoys his dinner, Larry gives me the agreed signal that he is about to let loose with one of his dreadful SBD's. This gives me advance notice so I can prepare to make a run for survival from Daddy's anticipated rage.

Soon a drift of Larry's foul-smelling "SBD" comes wafting over to me after it passes right past Daddy's nostrils. It is so sickening I can't believe it! It smells like a thousand rotten eggs! Daddy freezes with a mouthful of spaghetti hanging down out of his mouth. His eyes are unmoving as he stares straight ahead. He is probably trying to figure out which of his mischievous kids farted.

In a flash, he whirls in the direction of the terrible odor and lunges at Larry who in that instant is out of the chair racing for the doorway out of the kitchen. In a crazed effort to catch Larry, Daddy dives like a Giants football player trying to tackle a runner! Daddy's flying tackle misses Larry near the doorway leading out of the kitchen, and winds up lodged in the corner between the refrigerator and the wall! He dove so hard that he is now stuck, tightly wedged, in that narrow space!

With his legs wiggling in the air, he screams at the top of his voice, "**Ellie**, come help get me out of the corner!"

Daddy's alarming scream wakes Mommy up from a sound sleep. Entering the kitchen, she cannot believe her eyes seeing Daddy wedged head first in the corner unable to free himself!

Laughing, Mommy says, "Oh, my God, Patsy, what in God's name are you doing in the corner like that?"

"Well, let's see," he says sarcastically, "perhaps I am wedged in here so I could eat my dinner in privacy!

"What the hell do you think I'm doing?" he shouts. "Your goddamn kid, Larry, was farting at the table while I was eating so I tried to catch that little bastard to teach him a lesson!"

"What does that have to do with your being stuck in the corner?"

"What the hell do you think it does?" he shouts. "I dove for the stinky little bastard but I missed and wound up stuck here in the corner! Okay? Now will you stop with the goddamn questions, and just help get me out of here so I can get that little fart-master!"

As Mommy helps by pulling Daddy's legs, I quickly make my own escape. I run through the rooms and go to the right window where I climb out onto the fire escape where I find Larry already stationed there. We know that Daddy never goes out onto the fire escape whenever he chases us. Mommy said it has something to do with his father falling out the window when Daddy was a little boy.

Soon enough, Daddy comes into the living room apparently knowing where to find us.

"Think it's funny, heh? Let's see how funny you think it is when you have to stay out on the fire escape all night! Let's see if you think it was worth it. You can fart all you want out there, Larry!"

He slams the window down and locks it so we can't get back in! We know that as long as Daddy is awake, we are not going to be able to get back into the apartment. It is so chilly out here, Larry and I huddle together as we sit propped up against the brick wall for support. The iron fire escape is ice cold against our legs. We know that Mommy will eventually come and unlock the window so we can go back in when Daddy goes to sleep but that is going to be quite a while.

We pass the time by talking about the New York Football Giants, and by playing games like guessing whether a car or taxi will be the next to come by, or whether someone will come walking on our side of the street or across from us. Thank God it is not too long before Mommy appears and unlocks the window allowing us to crawl back in. After whispering how crazy we are to tease Daddy like that, she tells us to get to bed.

The next day, Sunday, Paddy, Kitty, Larry, and I go to the 9 A.M. school Mass at St. Monica's. Afterward, we buy the Daily Mirror newspaper and the Sunday Daily News newspaper at the stand on the corner of 79th Street and First Avenue. On our way home, we stop at the German bakery on York Avenue to buy rolls for breakfast. When we get home, we put A & P black tea leaves in a pot of water and heat it on the stove until it boils. Knowing that when Daddy gets up, he will be looking to punish us for what we did last night. Accordingly, Larry and I eat very quickly.

While Daddy is still asleep, we head out to play tackle football at Carl Schurz Park with other boys from our area. When we arrive home before dark, Daddy has already left for work so Larry and I are safe from him... at least until he gets home after midnight.

I tell Larry I have another great way to have fun with Daddy. We can tease him when he rings the doorbell from the vestibule downstairs to get into the building. The only way he can get in is if someone upstairs rings him back making it possible for him to open the entrance door downstairs. The bell he has to ring is a distance from the entry door so it requires ringing the bell then quickly dashing over to the entry door before the return ring stops! This can be very frustrating for anyone who is slow moving.

Realizing this, I explain to Larry that if we only buzz him back for a split second, there is no way he can get to the door in time!

"We can call this joke, **'zit-bang!'** I suggest.

"What do you mean, zit-bang?"

"Zit-bang,' is the sound that results from our buzzing the bell for only a split second, **'zit'**, and **'bang'** is when Daddy slams on the door downstairs to get in!"

"I get it, 'zit-bang!" Larry laughs.

When the time finally arrives around one in the morning, Larry and I are in the kitchen by the round push button doorbell located to the right of the front door to our apartment. We hear the outside door open downstairs followed by the expected ring of our doorbell. As carefully, as quickly as I can, I push our doorbell only a little.

We hear "zit" downstairs followed by a distinct "bang" sound as Daddy pushes against the entry door down there. Utter silence follows for a moment before Daddy rings the doorbell again. Once more, I push our doorbell as quickly and briefly as possible creating another "zit" sound downstairs followed by another, louder, "Bang" noise. This time Daddy immediately rings the bell again, and I immediately repeat my return buzz creating yet another "zit-bang" noise - only much louder this time!

I hear the elderly ladies come out into the hallway from their ground floor apartment. They are yelling at Daddy through the glass paneled entry door telling him to stop all the banging noise because it woke them up! Daddy is trying to explain his dilemma to them but they do not sound like they are too interested in learning why he has awakened them again. Daddy asks if they will kindly open the door. To his surprise, they refuse and go back inside their apartment!

Larry and I are hysterically laughing at how a simple thing like getting buzzed into the building has become such an ordeal for Daddy. Hearing Daddy go out the front door of our building and onto the front stoop, Larry and I run into the living room to see what he is doing. Just as we arrive at the front windows, I hear Daddy jump onto the bottom rung of the fire escape ladder in front of our building. Rather than play zit-bang with us and fight with the elderly ladies, he is going to climb up to our apartment by way of the fire escape! This is not how I pictured our little prank working out.

All of a sudden, there is a blinding white light beaming up at Daddy on the fire escape ladder!

A voice booms out from the street below, "Freeze, buddy; hold it right there! We have you covered! Come down, nice and slowly, and keep your hands where we can see them!"

The police are getting out of their squad car that just happened to be coming down our street at the very moment Daddy was climbing up our fire escape! They have a powerful search light on the side of their car, which they are shining on Daddy, and they are using a loud speaker here in the middle of the night to shout out orders to him!

We hear Daddy say, "Don't shoot, officers, I live here!"

As we watch from the left window, Daddy carefully climbs back down and tells the cops that he lives in the first floor apartment. Neighbors in other buildings have come to their windows now to see what all the ruckus is in the street at this time in the night. Having neighbors see that he is the cause of the police action will undoubtedly frustrate Daddy even more.

One cop says, "If you live here, why don't you use your key?"

The other cop says, "In all my years, I have never seen anyone climb up a fire escape to get into their apartment!"

Daddy explains that he just keeps forgetting to bring his front door key when he goes to work, and he adds, "And my kids like to tease me by not ringing me in."

At Daddy's insistence, the cops agree to ring our bell so they can come up and speak to Mommy to confirm that Daddy really does live here. We hurriedly wake Mommy up and tell her what is happening. Saying that we are going to be the death of her yet, Mommy gets up and returns the doorbell ring letting the police and Daddy into the hallway downstairs.

When Mommy opens our front door, one of the two cops says, "I am sorry to disturb you so late at night, ma'am, but we found this man climbing up your fire escape. He claims that he lives here. Is that true?"

Larry and I peer over Mommy's shoulder and see Daddy glaring back at us… while he bites his tongue in anger! Mommy looks right at Daddy then tells the police, "Officer, I have never seen this man before in my life!"

Daddy is completely shocked by Mommy's answer… as I am! The two cops tighten their grip on Daddy's arms and begin to lead him back down the stairs.

Daddy shouts out, "Ellie, this is not funny; tell them I am your husband!"

When they are halfway down the winding stairs, Mommy walks out into the hallway and says, "I am just kidding, officers. I married that lunk-head years ago. He comes from a family of tree-climbers so every once in a while he has to climb up things. You know… like fire escapes! You can let him go."

"I told you so," Daddy complains to the officers as they release their grip on him.

One of the cops says, "Bring a key next time, Buddy … and talk to your kids!"

"Talk to your kids," I think. There is no way. It is going to be more like pound your kids! Not waiting to find out, Larry and I escape Daddy's wrath by scooting out onto the fire escape just as the police car leaves!

I tell Larry, "Thank God we have a place where Daddy will not go. Rather than calling this a fire escape, we should call it a **'Daddy Escape!'**

We both laugh but I think it is so strange that a big strong man like Daddy who will fearlessly climb up a fire escape from the street, will never go out onto the fire escape through a window from inside an apartment. I guess the horrific memory of seeing his father fall out the fifth story window to his death has seriously affected Daddy in more ways than he realizes.

It is interesting how a significant event… good or bad… can dramatically affect the rest of our life… like seeing demons and angels.

Chapter 32

GOD'S DELIVERY BOY

January 1955

"Happy birthday, Robert!" Father Kelly says, "Thank you for taking time on your special day to visit with me. How old are you now?"

"I am ten years old today," I tell him proudly.

"Ten, that is a wonderful age, Robert, if I remember correctly. But that was a long time ago for me."

"You have a good memory, Father!" I tease.

"Ah, you have developed a sense of humor, I see. Very good! You need to have a good sense of humor to make it through life these days."

'I'll bet Jesus had a good sense of humor," I surmise.

Father smiles, "Yes, I'm sure He did."

"The school Sisters have done a pretty good job in keeping me informed of your… 'doings.' Some of the things they tell me are pretty amazing. I don't know if you realize it, Robert, but we priests and nuns at St. Monica's are deeply moved by the remarkable things we see God doing in your life."

I am surprised to hear this because that is how I feel about the work of the nuns and priests. They do so much in serving so many.

"The nuns tell me you're relatively quiet and humble despite the extraordinary nature of what God does through you," Father discloses.

"That's because it's all so natural to me, Father. All the good things come from God; I'm only the **'delivery boy.''**

Father laughs, "That's a wonderful way to put it, Robert, God's delivery boy! It's good that you realize that on your own, you can't do anything. **All** healing comes from God."

"I sometimes forget that other people don't have the same experiences I do. That's why I get teased by kids who don't understand. I wish no one knew. People can be so mean."

"I know, and I'm sorry that happens, Robert. But you have to understand that for most people, not just kids, hearing about your experiences is really difficult to believe. There is a silver lining though. Having people doubt you, keeps you humble.

"Remember this, Robert… God knows every hair on your head and He knows what you're going through and will always give you what you need to use the gifts He's entrusted to you. Your challenge is to be faithful in using those gifts despite whatever hardships and sacrifices may come.

"In **this** life, no one knows better than your father what you're going through. While he's aware of the teasing by your peers, he told me his greatest concern is your exposure to the devil. And I couldn't agree more. Your father said the reality of the devil taunting you hit him like a 'ton of bricks' when he read what Jesus says in Mark 9:19-20.

"Let me read it to you. 'And they brought him to Jesus; and the spirit, when it saw Jesus, immediately threw the boy into convulsions, and he fell down on the ground, and rolled about foaming at the mouth. So Jesus asked his father, 'How long is it since this has come upon him?' And he said... **from his infancy!'**

"Understanding that such things can actually happen to little children, your father doesn't want to risk that happening to you. You're at greater risk than most children because God has blessed you with extraordinary spiritual gifts.

"While that's your father's greatest concern, he also wants to make sure you properly use the gift of healing. He tells me when you pray, God does miraculous things."

"Yes, Father, that's true."

"And so, your father has asked me to join him in doing whatever we can to be helpful to you. For starters, we put together a few suggestions we think may be helpful.

"First, we have asked the priests and nuns at St. Monica's to avoid treating you differently than your peers. We think part of the 'teasing problem' may have to do with how the nuns, in particular, treat you. You see, children are quite perceptive; they can pick up right away when the nuns treat someone in a special way."

"But I don't feel like I'm treated differently than anyone else, Father."

"I'm not surprised to hear you feel that way. But the reality is that the nuns acknowledge they relate to you much differently than any other student. However, they've promised to be more sensitive to the way they relate to you in front of others.

"Secondly, your father requested that you and I get together on a regular basis to discuss spiritual things. As such, I will be your 'spiritual advisor.' That's someone who understands what you're going through spiritually, and can assist and encourage you as needed.

"Does that sound like something you would like, Robert?"

"Yes, Father, I would like that."

"Very good. So why don't we meet every few weeks. Okay?"

"Yes, Father."

"During these visits, we can discuss anything you'd like including spiritual things that may have happened... good or bad... since the prior visit."

"That sounds very good, Father."

"Good. The last suggestion we came up with is aimed at fostering your spiritual development and understanding of the faith. We'd like you to complete a reading assignment from the bible, which you and I can discuss at the next meeting. Would you like to do that?"

"Yes, Father, I'd like that very much."

"Good! Now before we discuss some of those details, has anything unusual, that is, spiritually speaking, happened recently?"

"Yes, Father, there're a few things, but there's one thing in particular that stands out."

"Do you mind telling me about it?"

"Sure, Father. A really scary, evil-looking woman began appearing at the corner near my block."

"Why do you say, 'evil-looking?' What was there about her that appeared evil?"

"There was a dark black outline around her head. That's what I see around people who are bad. I also sensed the evil that was boiling inside her."

"I see. Please tell me what happened."

"Every time I passed her, she stopped me and asked me to go with her to her apartment. She told me that she and her friends knew about me and what she said were my... 'special powers.'

"I told her I don't have any special powers; I only pray to God and He is the One Who heals people. But she ignored what I said and insisted that I go with her. She said that she and her friends could show me how to do... real magic... through a greater power."

"I hope you didn't go with her," Father worries.

"No, of course not, Father. Each time she stopped me, I told her no thanks, I'm fine just praying to God. This always angered her especially when I added that I'd pray for her. Whenever I said this, she sneered and said she didn't want... or need... my prayers."

Raising his eyebrows, Father asks, "What did you say to that?"

"I told her I would pray for her anyway."

Father laughs and asks me to continue.

"The last time I saw her, she stood in my way and told me that I **must** go with her.

"When I told her I would **never** go with her, her face twisted in a very scary way as she shoved her right hand at my mouth and shrieked, **'Don't you just hate it when someone reaches in and rips the very soul out of your body!'**

"I was so frightened I backed away and begged God to protect me as the image of a demon appeared right behind her!"

Father looks deeply disturbed hearing this.

"But then, her face returned to normal, and she grabbed onto my shoulders and pleaded for me to help her!"

Father asks, "So what did you do?"

"I prayed out loud to Jesus and asked Him to send St. Michael the Archangel to drive the demon out of her."

"What did she do when you prayed for her?"

"She just stood there staring at me with a blank expression as if she was in a trance. When I told her to go to a priest, she sneered at me, then said some terrible curses, then slinked away all hunched over."

After a moment, Father says, "Robert, what you describe is very serious. Have you seen this woman again?

"No, Father, I have not seen her since."

"Thank God! You need to avoid her at all costs!"

"Yes, Father."

"Did you tell your parents about this?"

"Yes, Father. Daddy told me to stay away from the woman, and under no circumstances should I ever talk to her again. Daddy tried to find the woman but she no longer hangs out at the corner, and nobody knows who she is or where she lives."

"I see. There are times, Robert, when the devil does more than just taunt people as appears happened to you. Unfortunately, this can include far worse things the devil can do to influence, or even control, a person's actions.

"From what you describe, it sounds like this woman is such a victim. Do you understand what I'm saying?"

"Yes, I understand, Father. Mommy explained what the devil does and how it can hurt people. Daddy told me what to do if I ever come in contact with a person like that again."

"What did he tell you to do?" Father asks.

"He said I should walk away and keep saying, 'In the name of Jesus Christ, I command you to leave me alone and not return!"

Father nods in agreement, then says, "Only God fully understands how and why such things happen, Robert. Hearing that such disturbed people have approached you greatly concerns me. I am going to talk to your father about this.

"Robert, if ever again you find yourself confronted by people who appear to be disturbed by the devil, please refer them to me or to their parish priest… and keep your distance! This is an area of ministry that's as dangerous as it gets, and only specially-trained priests with the approval and

284

authority of their bishop may intercede. Do you understand?"

"Yes, Father, I understand."

"In the meantime," he says drawing a deep breath, "I have written down three Gospel readings which I'd like you to read and reflect on what you think Christ is telling us. These three are among my favorites, Luke 10:25, Mark 9:38, and, Matthew 15:21.

"It's interesting that I selected these readings before we had this discussion today. When you read them you'll understand. Please read them over, reflect on their meaning, take notes, and let's discuss your thoughts at our next visit.

"In the meantime, if you need to talk, you can call me at any time… day or night. I'll make time for you. Otherwise, I'll see you at our next meeting.

"Now bow your head for God's blessing, 'May God continue to bless and protect you, Robert, in the Name of the Father, and of the Son, and of the Holy Ghost. Amen."

"Oh, and by the way, tell your father I want to see him."

Chapter 33

THE JUNK STORE

February 1955

It has been nearly three years since Larry cut his arm swinging at the spirit-form of the demon. That is the injury he sustained when he put his arm through the glass panel in the left French door as he tried to punch the demon positioned in front of the door.

Sadly, the part of his arm that swung through the evil spirit is still terribly disfigured. It is an oval-shaped area that is about four-inches long and over one-inch wide covering the length of his left forearm. The skin covering the area now eerily looks like the transparent casing on a sausage. You can actually see the flesh and veins under the skin. Since that part of his arm came into contact with the demon, I don't know if it will ever properly heal.

The doctors say that a skin graft will not work so his arm is going to remain like this for the rest of his life. He'll never have normal skin cover that part of his arm ever again. It will serve as a life-long reminder of his encounter with the demon.

Perhaps worse than the physical scar, is the emotional one this horrific event left on him. Larry thought that he could scare the demon away from our home by punching it. He did not realize that his arm would go through the demon and crash though the glass panel behind it. I feel so guilty for my part in his terrible injury. If I did not tell him about the demon being there, he would not have tried to hit it.

Daddy is home from work today because it is one of his days off. Normally, he would be at work at this time of day.

"Hey, how would you kids like to go to the 'Junk Store' around the corner and get some comic books! Eh? What do you say?"

Paddy, Larry and I are thrilled to hear this; this is one of our favorite things to do. We jump up and immediately run for the front door!

"Whoa! Hold onto your horses! I'm not ready to run out the door this very second," Daddy laughs, "Give me a few minutes to get ready, will ya?"

The three of us wait eagerly for him by the front door as we watch his every movement. Daddy can be maddening when we are in a hurry to go somewhere because he always takes his "sweet time" as Mommy calls it.

"Hey, Ellie, do you need anything from the grocery store?" he calls out through the rooms.

"No, Patsy. Thanks anyway. You know, you'd better hurry. I don't know if the 'Junk Man' stays open late," Mommy cautions.

"Oh, sure he does. He lives in the back of the store, and always comes out when he sees me at the door... no matter how late it is," Daddy brags.

Soon we are out the door and quickly on our way to the little junk store located on York Avenue between 81st and 82nd Streets. As soon as we arrive in front of the store, Daddy walks up to the metal gate covering the top half of the locked door and begins to pound his chunky fist mightily against the gate causing a loud annoying ruckus. Besides creating such a terrible racket, I am afraid he is going to break the glass behind the gate, or injure his fist!

"Hey, come on, Pops, it's Pat Walsh!" he yells, "Open up! We want to buy some comic books."

When no stirring is seen or heard from inside, Daddy calls out again even louder, "Hey, come on, old man, we haven't got all night."

Daddy is kidding, of course. He has often said how much he and the old man like each other.

There is thick dust covering the glass panels behind the metal mesh. It is so thick, in fact, it looks like a smoke screen. In the darkness beyond the door inside the shop, I see a flutter of movement as a dark shadowy figure slowly approaches the door. My first reaction is one of fear; however, I sense that this is not an evil entity approaching us.

Soon the unshaven, pale, white face of the short old man presses against the glass and peers out at us.

"Oh, it's you!" he grumbles good-naturedly, "I should've known. Why do you always come so late at night when I'm closed and bang the dickens out of my door?"

"Well, if I come here at a civilized hour, would I be able to get the same bargains from you?" Daddy kids him.

"I swear, one of these days you're going to bang right through that glass," the old man says as he gradually loosens several locks and bolts on the door.

"You remember my sons, don't you?" Daddy says as he gestures in our direction, "They've come to pick out some more of your used comics. You're still selling them three for a nickel, aren't you?"

The old man smiles and nods his head yes as he appears to like seeing our eager faces. I sense a wonderful aura around this gentle old man. He must have lived a life of service for others. As our eyes meet, I feel a special connection with him... similar to the feelings I have with Grandpa Sheridan.

Looking around the store, I am impressed by the remarkable number of things the old man has piled up on the floor, on tables and wall shelves. There are pots, pans, old radios, tools, pictures, and much, much more. Most of the things can barely be seen under the dim, single light bulb that is swinging on a chain directly above us. It is still swinging from when the old man pulled the chain to turn it on. The farther back I look into the store, the darker and more mysterious it looks. I wonder what the back of his store is like where he lives?

The old man points in the direction where the comic books are neatly stacked about two feet high just to my left. Paddy, Larry and I each grab a group and begin to look through them to pick out the ones we want.

"Take it easy with them, boys!" the old man cautions, "I've got to sell the ones you don't want."

He reaches back into a darkened area and retrieves yet another pile of comic books, and says, "Here, look through these too; they just came in today. They are real good ones."

I carefully examine each one as I search for my favorite type … horror books. I especially like the ones about werewolves, but I also like scary stories about witches, warlocks, ghosts, and creatures from outer space. I eagerly sort these out and find six that I would like to bring home.

Larry and Paddy each have a similar number of comic books they would like to read including: Donald Duck, Archie and Jughead, Uncle Scrooge, Bugs Bunny, Superman, Batman and Robin, and some scary ones about werewolves, vampires, and zombies. We have so many, I am afraid we may have to put some back. Daddy never spends more than twenty-five cents at any time we come here.

"Okay," Daddy starts to say, but the old man interrupts him.

Smiling, he says, "You've got eighteen books there, so I'll give you a special deal since you come here so often. How does two bits sound for the whole bunch of them?"

Daddy looks surprised and happy, "Gee, that's swell of you, Pop. Here's the quarter. Thanks a million."

The old man looks a little embarrassed as he smiles and looks away.

As we turn to leave, the old man says, "Now take good care of the books, boys, and I'll let you trade them back, two for one, when you return."

Raising his eyebrows for dramatic effect, he looks at me and knowing that I like scary comics, he says, "Enjoy them, but remember… they are only make-believe!"

A chill shoots up my spine hearing this. After we all thank the old man, Daddy hurries us out the door. Back home, I nestle comfortably in my favorite place to read the comics - at the end of the thickly cushioned sofa in the living room with the light of the lamp on the end table shining its light and

288

warmth down upon me. My head is at the end by the window. I always position the lamp on the end table so that it casts its light fully down upon me and the comic books I hold up to read. Behind me, the steam heat in the radiator in the corner gives off a whistle every few minutes. Moments like these are among my most enjoyable.

I get drowsy whenever I read like this even though the comics are filled with lots of color pictures and interesting stories. Although I am a pretty good reader, there are still many words I do not understand so I must ask Mommy or Daddy to tell me what they mean. They do not seem to mind, and that is the only way I can learn to read all the words.

Soon I become too tired to read so I join Larry in bed in the next room off the living room. Larry tells me he cannot sleep either so he calls out to Mommy who is washing dishes in the kitchen where the sink is located to the left of our front door.

Larry calls out, "Mommy, we can't sleep. Can you sing us a song?"

She giggles, "Okay. Just give me a few minutes to finish doing the dishes and I'll be right in."

Meanwhile, Daddy, who is in the bed in the next room, calls out, "Hey, Larry."

"Yes, Daddy," Larry answers.

"Two lumps of sugar!" Daddy says and begins to laugh uproariously!

Puzzled, Larry asks, "What did you say, Daddy?"

Daddy shouts even louder, "I said... 'two lumps of sugar!'"

Daddy's laughter fills our home. What a wonderful sound.

"What does that mean, Daddy?" Larry wants to know.

"What do you think it means? It means that I want a cup of tea... with **two lumps of sugar** in it! You get it? **Two lumps of sugar!** Ha, ha, ha, ha, ha... "

I don't think I have ever heard Daddy laugh so hard and so long about anything. Larry and I join him in laughing as Mommy says, "I swear your father is losing all his marbles!"

When the laughter subsides, Larry calls out, "Hey, Daddy."

"Yeah," he answers.

"**Two lumps of sugar!**" Larry shouts at the top of his voice!

This brings a hearty laugh from all of us... except Daddy who obviously does not share our amusement. There is no response from Daddy in the next room, only dead silence. This is a sure sign he does not think Larry's clever maneuver of his joke is funny.

Hearing us laugh about pulling **his joke on him**, Daddy warns, "If the two of you don't be quiet and get to sleep right now, you're going to have **two lumps** on your heads!"

That is all the warning we need. We know when Daddy gets mad like this it is dangerous to proceed any further with whatever we are doing.

"Are you going to come sing to us, Mommy?" Larry reminds her.

"Yes, I'm almost finished, Larry. I'll be right in."

Wow, what a treat this is, Mommy is going to sing for us! She likes to sing, and we like to hear her sing with her soft, pleasing voice. At night, she often sits on the edge of the bed and sings to us, especially when we cannot sleep… or at least when we tell her we cannot.

"All right," Mommy says entering the room and sitting down at the foot of the bed, "You know the rules. You have to lie down and be perfectly still if you want me to sing to you. Now show me how well you can do it."

Larry and I quickly lie down and remain completely still as we eagerly wait for her to sing. Geri, meanwhile, is busy making all kinds of noises as she carries on her own little conversation. She must be talking to her dolls again. Mommy puts her finger to her lips encouraging us to be quiet while we wait for Geri to finish her baby talk.

When Geri finally stops, Mommy treats us to the wonderful song she sings to us at bed time, "An Irish Lullaby." As usual, she sings it several times in softer tones each time.

Finally, as she gets up to leave, Larry asks, "Mommy, are there really such things as vampires, werewolves, Frankenstein, and the other creatures I see in the comic books?"

Amused, she reassures him, "No, Larry, don't be silly. Monsters are make-believe; they don't really exist. Have you ever seen any monsters other than in comic books?"

I have… I've seen far worse.

Chapter 34

DELIVERANCE

April 1955

Father Kelly appears just as eager as I am to discuss the Gospel readings he assigned to me. After greeting me, however, he jumps right into what he obviously is more interested in addressing.

"Before we begin, Robert, please tell me... has anything **'extraordinary'** happened since our last visit?"

As usual, there were, in fact, a number of "extraordinary" things that have happened, but there is one in particular I would like to share with him.

"There was a mother who came from uptown asking if I would pray for her teenage son who she said was 'spinning out of control' drinking, fighting, cursing, and doing what she said were 'evil, lurid things.'

"She said she believed that a 'demon of self-destruction' had seized control of her son when he and some friends began fooling around with an Ouija Board, and dabbling in black magic!"

"Why did this woman come to you, Robert, and how did she know where to find you?"

"Some people in the neighborhood told her that I am a 'blessed child' who helps people with all kinds of spiritual problems. When she came to our door and explained what her problem was, Daddy told her to leave and take her son to a priest.

"But she persisted, saying that she had already taken him to several priests but none of them believed that her son's problem involved the devil. Each told her to take him to a physiatrist, which she did. When the doctors told her that her son wasn't mentally ill, she said she didn't know where else to turn. That's when someone told her about me."

Father interrupts, "So what did your father do?"

"He arranged for me to pray over the boy as I have done for others who were sick... like him."

"Others who were sick like him! Do you mean you prayed for other people who believed the devil was harassing them?"

"Yes, father. There were a few."

"Like who?"

"Well, like the eight-year boy from Brooklyn, the man living in John Jay Park, and... "

"What eight year-old boy? What man in the John Jay? Wait a second, **don't answer!**" Father holds up a hand, "Let's slow down here. Are

291

you telling me that your parents had you pray over people who believed the devil was tormenting them?"

"Yes, Father. My parents allowed me to pray over these people but Daddy was with me every time to protect me."

"This is terrible; I cannot believe your parents did this! Tell me about the teenage boy first, then I want to hear about the others."

Father leans forward on his chair as I begin.

"Daddy agreed to allow me to pray over the teenage son as long as specific circumstances were followed."

"And what were they?" Father asks.

"First of all, the mother was **not** to bring her son anywhere near where we live. Then, Daddy told her that unless her son truly wanted to be freed from the devil, and was willing to change his evil ways... no amount of prayer by anyone would work.

"So Daddy had her son go to confession because that sacrament itself is a powerful form of deliverance. Finally, Daddy said that no one from her family should attend the prayer if they were simply curious or thought a 'prayer of deliverance' was superstitious.

"The mother agreed to everything, so Daddy arranged for us to meet by the small baptismal room in the vestibule area in the back of our church. He explained that proximity to the baptismal room is powerful support for deliverance prayer because the Sacrament of Baptism itself is a powerful form of exorcism."

Father interrupts, "Your father conducts deliverance prayer?"

"No, father. I do. I pray for God to heal the person who is sick. If there is a devil involved, I pray that God chases the devil away. Daddy supervises everything and protects me in case anyone attacks me."

"I see... go on," Father says, appearing eager for me to continue.

"As arranged, the mother showed up with her troubled teenage son and two men from her family. They joined Daddy and me in the vestibule of the church by the baptismal room. The boy had a black shadowy outline around his head; that's what I see around people who have evil in them.

"While Daddy reminded everyone how we were going to pray, the son stood perfectly still and stared into the empty baptismal room as if he was watching something going on in there. But there was no one in there... at least... no one I could see.

"As soon as we made the Sign of the Cross, I prayed silently for the boy's healing... for whatever was needed."

Father interrupts, "Tell me what words you prayed."

"I prayed, 'Dear Jesus, please heal this boy, and send the Blessed Mother and St. Michael the Archangel to chase away any demons that may be tormenting him. Thank you, Jesus. Amen."

"Where did you get those words from?" Father wants to know.

"My father got them from the priest near his job."

Father says, "I want you to get that priest's name for me, but for now, tell me what happened when you prayed."

"As soon as we started praying, the son fell to the floor as if something knocked him off his feet. He remained there rigid as a board with his eyes staring straight up at the ceiling. He looked very scary. Daddy told everyone to leave the boy alone and continue praying.

"I kept praying that prayer over and over again while everyone else prayed the Our Father, the Hail Mary, and the Glory Be. As soon as we finished, the boy's body relaxed just as a strong wind whipped through the vestibule and exploded out through the double doors exiting the church!

"The boy sat up and smiled at his mother. Everybody started crying.

"Daddy and the men kept making the sign of the cross and thanking God. It appeared the boy was freed from the demon, or whatever it was that was troubling him. The faith and love of his mother is what Jesus rewarded... just like the mother in the bible who went to Jesus and begged him to drive the devil out of her daughter."

"Thanks be to God!" Father whispers, taken back by my report of what happened.

"Has your father heard from the mother since then? Is the son all right?"

"Yes. A few weeks later, she came to our door with a bunch of flowers for our family. She thanked us and said that the demons are gone. Her son has returned to church, and no longer does any of the 'bad' things."

Father stares in amazement, then says abruptly, "Now... tell me about the eight year-old boy from Brooklyn."

"Last year, a family contacted my father and asked if I could come to their home in Brooklyn to pray over an eight year-old boy who was acting very badly. They said they thought he was 'possessed."

"How? What was he doing?" Father asks.

"The parents said he'd wake them up in the middle of the night growling... **under their bed!** Other nights, they'd find him crawling around on all fours snarling like a wild animal. During the day, they'd find him crouched on top of the china cabinet, in the bottom of their closets, behind curtains, or in some other unusual place. When they asked him what he was doing, he'd say he was waiting. When asked what he was waiting for, his only response was to smile with his lips twisted in an evil way."

"It sounds like the boy has mental health issues, not demonic problems!" Father observes.

"There's more. Although his room was always cold, he preferred to

293

sit in it humming some strange tune, and mumbling words they couldn't recognize. Also, he was breaking religious statues and pictures in their home.

"The parents took him to doctors who said he was, in fact, mentally ill, but the parents were convinced there was also something spiritually wrong with their son. That's when they called in their parish priest who witnessed some of the unholy things going on."

"So what did the priest do?" Father Kelly asks

"Unknown to the boy, the priest put blessed water in the boy's glass of water without the boy knowing. The priest said that if a devil is involved, a person will spit out the holy water. The priest said this is one of the surest ways an Exorcist can determine whether or not the devil is involved.

"When the mother gave the boy the glass of blessed water, he spit it out and let out a piercing scream and quickly scampered around the room on all fours angrily cursing.

"The priest said that was a clear sign that something 'extraordinary' was involved, but he wasn't qualified to address such issues. He promised to discuss this with other priests and get back to the parents. He never did. That's when the family contacted Daddy and asked him to come with me to their apartment to pray over the boy."

"Did you?" Father asks.

"Yes, Father. Daddy took me to the family's apartment in Brooklyn. When we got there, we could hear the boy screaming throughout the building. Daddy greeted the parents and explained how we would pray. I sensed the terrible presence of a demon in the apartment as we approached the boy's room. Entering it, we found the boy cowering in the corner as if he was afraid of us! He had that evil, black shadow outlining his head.

"Daddy took out the bottle of holy water and splashed it all over the boy causing him to leap high in the air and run around the room screaming while Daddy continued to splash him with the holy water. At one point, it looked like he ran along the side of the wall above the bed. The parents were crying while I prayed and pleaded with God to heal the poor tormented boy.

"Then, all of a sudden, the boy fell down hard onto the floor. His body was limp... and no longer reacted to the holy water. A foul smelling wind swirled around the room and then disappeared. The boy woke up but he wasn't aware of what had happened. His parents wept with joy and relief to see their son was healing. Daddy told them they all have to attend the sacraments, especially confession.

"What happened then?" Father Kelly asks.

"Daddy and I went home."

"What I mean is... did the family later say if the boy was all right?"

"Oh, yes, he was, Father. In fact, Daddy was annoyed that the family didn't call to let him know; he had to call them to find out! They told him that everything was back to normal... there were no more problems."

Father nods approvingly but still looks very upset as he snaps, "I can't believe your father didn't think any of this was important enough for him to discuss with me! Why didn't he call me when these things were going on? This is really serious, dangerous stuff. And let me be clear, Robert, **you should not be involved in any of this.**"

The sudden appearance of red on his face confirms how upset Father Kelly is about what Daddy and I did without his knowledge or consent.

"Daddy was going to call you, Father, but a priest near his job told him that priests aren't allowed to do anything like this without a thorough investigation **and** their bishop's specific approval ahead of time. The priest said this is time-consuming and very difficult to achieve, so he said the Holy Ghost anoints certain lay people with the gift of healing to help such people."

Hearing this only appears to further anger Father Kelly, "Next time, **you** just call me! And tell your father I want to see him right away!"

"Yes, Father."

"I want to hear about these other people you mention, but we are running out of time. For now, let's move on and discuss your assigned readings. Which one do you want to start with?"

"I'd like to start with Luke 10:25, the parable about the 'Good Samaritan' where Jesus tells us about a man who was attacked by robbers who left him half-dead on the road."

"What impresses you most about this reading?"

"I am most impressed by the fact that the Good Samaritan was a perfect stranger who stopped to help the man who was injured. And he did so without looking for a reward; he just did it to help."

"Very good, Robert. That is, in fact, the central message Christ is telling us in that Gospel. We are all called to be 'Good Samaritans' in our lives. Was there anything else that impressed you about this Gospel?"

"Well, yes. I was shocked to hear Jesus tell us that a priest came down the same road but didn't stop to help the man. In fact, Jesus says the priest passed by on the other side!"

"What do you think Jesus is telling us?" Father asks.

"I think Jesus is telling us that even priests sometimes don't do what they are called to do. And when that happens, we shouldn't follow their bad example; we should do what we can to help... like the Good Samaritan did."

"That's very good, Robert! I couldn't agree more. We are all called by God... clergy and lay people alike... to be 'Good Samaritans' in all we do. Very good, very good.

"How about the next Gospel?"

"The next one I read was disturbing because Jesus sounds mean to a poor mother who comes to Him for help."

"Which reading is this?" Father asks.

"Matthew 15:21."

"Oh, yes. I figured you might have a problem with that one," Father admits. Tell me what bothers you about it."

"Well, there are actually two things that bother me. First of all, when the mother cried out to Jesus to drive a demon out of her daughter, the apostles told Jesus to send her away because she had been pleading with them first for help! That means the apostles had been acting just like the priest in the Good Samaritan story who crossed the road rather than help the victim. The apostles were doing the same thing by not helping the poor mother. In addition... they also told Jesus **not** to help the poor mother either!"

"Hmm, that's right," Father confirms, "good observation. Please continue."

"I was shocked to read how cruel Jesus was to the mother when He told her that it wasn't right to take food and 'throw it to the dogs' as He said, inferring that her daughter was as unworthy as dogs! I felt very sad for the mother, and was shocked that Jesus could be so mean to her.

"But then, the mother said that even dogs eat scraps that fall from the table. Jesus was so impressed by her faith in saying this that He then drove the demon out of her daughter just as the mother asked."

"What lesson do you think Jesus is giving us?" Father inquires.

"I think Jesus is giving us three pieces of advice in this Gospel. First, He is telling us that we should be persistent in appealing to God for help even if our priests, in the form of the apostles in this Gospel, don't do what Christ calls them to do. Second, we should not allow anything, including insults, to overcome our love for others when we cry out to God. And finally, I think Jesus is telling us **that it is faith that brings about His mercy.**"

Father looks impressed. "Very good again, Robert. I can tell you really did your homework on these readings. Now tell me about the final reading, Mark 9:38. I'm especially interested to hear what your thoughts are on this Gospel."

"I felt like Jesus was speaking personally to me in this Gospel, Father."

"Really? Why is that?"

"The apostles complain to Jesus that a man 'who is not with them' is driving out devils in God's name, so they ask Jesus to tell the man to stop. But Jesus tells them **not** to stop the man. Jesus explains why they shouldn't stop the man who was not with them. Jesus says, **'anyone who is not against us is for us!'**

"For that other man to be driving devils out of people tells us that the apostles were **not** doing what Christ called them to do... that is, drive devils out of people. Jesus also tells us that someone who is **not** a member of the clergy can **also** drive out devils using His Name! That is reassuring to me because I feel like the man in that Gospel because I feel that healing prayer is for all forms of suffering... including suffering caused by the devil."

"Your assessment and perspective on that reading is… quite extraordinary, Robert. Some of your observations, I had not focused on before.

"In terms of your feeling called to what some call 'lay deliverance ministry,' you are way too young to be involved in such things. So, I caution you, once again, to leave such matters in the hands of designated priests. This is **not** something you should be involved in… at least not until you are much older and have received the proper training. Do you understand me, Robert?"

"Yes, Father… but if priests don't help such people… just like Jesus tells us the apostles did… then don't I have an obligation to pray for their healing just like that lay person did in the Gospel?"

Rather than responding, Father says, "For your next reading assignment, please read Mark 10:46. Now bow your head for God's blessing, 'May God continue to bless and protect you, Robert, in the Name of the Father, and of the Son, and of the Holy Ghost. Amen."

Although Father tells me to leave deliverance ministry to properly designated priests, I leave today's visit convinced anyway that God calls me to include deliverance prayer as part of healing ministry.

As Christ tells us in Mark 9:38-40, "Teacher, we saw someone casting out demons in Your Name, and we tried to stop him, because he was not following us.' But Jesus said, 'Do not stop him; for no one who does a deed of power in My Name will be able soon afterward to speak evil of Me. Whoever is not against us is for us."

"Do not stop him!"

Chapter 35

FAMILY STORIES AND LEGENDS

June 1955

Mommy's younger sister, Aunt Anna, and her husband, Uncle Howie Gaugh, and their five children have arrived for another good old-fashioned family visit. We always have so much fun when we get together. My Gaugh family cousins are: Mary Ann who is 12, the same age as Paddy; Theresa, who is about the same age as me, 10; Mickey who is 8, about the same age as Larry; Helen who is about the same age as Geri, 4; and Katie, the baby of their family.

Every time we get together, Mommy and Daddy have fun visiting with Aunt Anna and Uncle Howie. They sit around the kitchen table while we have a great time playing games in the other rooms. Mary Ann and Theresa usually pal around with Kitty; Mickey hangs out with Larry and me and sometimes Paddy joins us; Helen and Katie play with Geri. There is never a dull moment when we cousins get together. We have more fun and happy times with them than with any of our other cousins.

While Paddy, Larry, and Mickey get reacquainted outside in the living room, I stand by the kitchen doorway and listen to the adults talking about the great times they had in what they call "the good old days."

Uncle Howie says, "No gathering of the clan would be complete without some proper libations so to lift everyone's spirits, I brought along some **'spirits'** of my own… two six packs of Rheingold beer!"

As Uncle Howie unloads the brown bottles of Rheingold beer, I think to myself that this is going to be another night of interesting family stories and legends. It does not take long for the stories to start.

After they have downed a bottle or two, Daddy kicks off their ritual telling of the tales.

"My brothers Eddie, Buddy and Donny and I used to go to the free outdoor concerts in Central Park during the summer. We would go there armed with lots of yellow lemons in a brown bag, and we would sit as close as we could to the first row facing the orchestra. When the musicians playing the horns started playing, we pulled out the lemons and began to bite them and suck on them right in front of the horn players. When they saw us sucking on the lemons, they could not continue playing because they could not blow into their horns with their mouths watering! We always got chased away but it was worth the laugh to watch them trying to blow into their horns!"

This story brings a round of laughter… with Daddy laughing the loudest.

When he calms down, he tells Uncle Howie, "Okay, now it is your turn now, Howie. Let's hear one of your tales."

Smiling devilishly, Uncle Howie says, "You want to hear one of my tales, heh? Okay, wait 'til you hear this one … a true story, mind you. Four of the Brooklyn Dodgers baseball team were in a car speeding to the Polo Grounds for a game against the New York Giants when they were stopped by a traffic cop.

Looking into the car, the officer recognized who they are so he says to the driver, 'Hey, aren't you the **'Duke,'** Duke Snyder, the centerfielder for the Brooklyn Dodgers?"

"The 'Duke' smiles and politely says, 'Yes, I am.'

"Then the cop says to the guy sitting next to the Duke, 'And you, you're Pee Wee Reese, the shortstop, aren't you?'

"Pee Wee smiles and says, 'Yes, I am.'

"Looking into the back seat, the officer then says, 'And you, you are Carl Furillo, the right fielder, and you are Roy Campanella, the catcher!

"They were all so pleased to be recognized. One of them then proudly said, 'Yes, officer, we are all members of the Brooklyn Dodgers baseball club, and we're on our way to play the New York Giants at the Polo Grounds in Manhattan.'

"The cop then smiles and says, 'Well, boys, I am a faithful New York Giants baseball fan and I am on my way… to giving you a speeding ticket!"

This brings another round of laughter from Aunt Anna and Daddy but Mommy and Uncle Howie just smile… they are die-hard Brooklyn Dodgers fans.

"Okay, Ellie, it's your turn," Uncle Howie says.

"What would you all like, a story, or a legend?"

"Whatever strikes your fancy," Uncle Howie says.

"Well, some people think what I'm about to tell you is a legend, but I'm telling you that this actually did happen. One day, Paulie, a family friend who worked as a mortician, was driving my father, Pops Sheridan, my sister Vera, and her daughters Margaret Mary and Flossy. They were going over the Brooklyn Bridge on their way back to Brooklyn after visiting old friends on 77th Street in Yorkville where they used to live.

"Halfway across the bridge, the car split in half right there in the middle of the bridge! Paulie said when they heard the metal breaking sound and felt the car come to a stop, he looked back and saw Vera and the girls sitting in the back half of the car a few feet away! Paulie and Pops were sitting in the front half of the car with nothing behind the front seat except air!

"Paulie said since the car was so old, he simply took the license plates off the car and they walked off the bridge leaving the car broken in half, leaking fluids right there on the bridge!"

Amidst the laughter, Uncle Howie wise cracks, "Considering all the weight in the car, I am surprised it didn't take the whole bridge down!"

When the laughter dies down, Mommy tells Aunt Anna that it is her turn now to share a story or a legend. Aunt Anna says she is not ready yet so she asks Mommy to tell another funny story.

Mommy says, "Sure, I have another 'humdinger' of a true story, **not** a legend.

"Anna, do you remember the story Pops told us about the time he was working nights at the cemetery?"

Mom is referring to her dad, my grandfather, Grandpa James Aloysius Sheridan.

"Oh yes," Aunt Anna giggles, "and I think I know exactly what you're going to say. Go ahead, Ellie, I don't think Howie and Pat have ever heard this one."

Mommy proceeds with the story, "Poppa and his co-worker decided it would be fun to pull a prank on a colored guy who worked with them. This fellow had a funny accent and was deathly afraid of dead bodies, ghosts, scary stories and all those kinds of things. Wait 'til you hear what they did. Pops went down into the basement of the building where they kept a few bodies waiting to be buried the next day in the cemetery's **'Potter's Field'** area for poor people."

"What is 'Potter's Field', Uncle Howie asks.

Mommy explains, "Potter's Field is a large area in the cemetery where they bury poor people in an unmarked gravesite. It's for people who don't have families to bury them, or are too poor to afford their own gravesite to bury their loved one."

"How sad," Uncle Howie says reflecting the great compassion he has for others who are less fortunate than the rest of us.

"Well, here's what Pops did. In the main building near the entrance to the cemetery, Pops put white powder all over his face and hair, black crayon on his teeth, and rubbed bright red lipstick on his lips. He then went into the dark, unlit basement and crawled into an empty wicker coffin in the far corner. His 'partner in crime' closed the wicker coffin and put a name plate on top of the coffin with the fictitious name, Mr. Rick A. Mortis, on it. Do you get it? Rick-a-mortis! That is what they call it when the body stiffens after death."

This draws a laugh from everyone, and encourages Daddy to add, "Yeah, that is why the cemeteries are filled with real stiffs!"

As usual, Daddy laughs harder at his jokes than everyone else.

"Yep, there are a bunch of dead heads there!" he follows with another quip and again laughs uproariously.

Aunt Anna laughs, but tells Daddy, "Okay, Pat, we get the picture. Your play on words is very amusing but now we would like to hear the rest of Ellie's story before we all wind up in the cemetery ourselves!"

"Okay, Anna... as long as you know that people are just dying to get into the cemeteries even though all the people there are rotten!" Daddy could not resist adding.

Another round of laughter from Daddy causes everyone else to laugh. I am not sure everyone is laughing because of his corny jokes or because of the way he laughs at his own humor.

"You want to hear this story or not?" Mommy complains to Daddy.

"All right, all right, go ahead, I will not interrupt again," Daddy promises.

Mommy quickly continues before Daddy can steal the floor again, "Pop's partner then went up to the office and called the colored worker into the manager's room where he told him he had to go down into the basement to get the name plate off the top of Mr. Mortis' coffin in the far corner. He told him that the name had been misspelled so he had to correct it.

"The colored guy complained bitterly that he did not want to go down there because he was afraid of the dark and was scared to go near all the dead bodies down there.

"Pop's partner, of course, ignored this and demanded that he stop being silly and go down there to get the name plate so it could be corrected.

"He gave a lighted candle to light his way and told him, 'None of the dead people down there are going to jump out and grab you. All those stories about Zombies coming alive in cemeteries are make-believe! Just go down and get that goddamn name plate!

"The colored guy slowly and reluctantly descended the creaking wooden stairs with his lighted candle as he complained aloud, 'Gid da name plate, gid da name plate! Wad's all da hurry 'bout giddin' a damn name plate outta a basement fulla dead people in da middle of da night? Dead people don't care wedda dare name's spelt rite or not. Gid da damn name plate, gid da damn name plate.'

"Pop's partner watched from the top of the stairs as the poor fellow was shaking like a leaf as he inched his way very slowly down into the darkened basement. All the while, the fellow kept encouraging himself aloud, 'Everyding's gonna be alrite, everyding's gonna be alrite; ain't no buddy down here but me an' dis liddle lite an' a coupla dead people. Why dey gotta gid a damn name plate outta da basement? Dead folks don't care how dare name is spelt. Jus' gid that damn name plate, da man sez, jus' gid dat damn name plate. Well, I'm gonna gid dat damn name plate an' gid maself outta here reel quick. No need to stay down here wid all dez dead folks. Yes siree, everyding's gonna be alrite, everyding's gonna be alrite. Jus' gid that damn old plate an' gid outta here.'

"When the colored fellow finally finds the coffin in the far corner with Mr. Mortis' name plate on top, he cautiously reaches out and snatches it as he says, 'Yes, siree, everyding's gonna be alrite, everyding's gonna be alrite. I god dat damn name plate!'

"That was Pop's signal to growl as he quickly pushed the squeaking coffin lid wide open and springing up into a sitting position he reached his arms out toward the colored guy!

"The poor fellow dropped the candle and screamed, 'Oh, ma God! Oh, ma God! Lord help me! Everyding's not gonna be alrite!'

"He was so terrified, he turned and with no light in the basement now, ran blindly right into another coffin. Scrambling through the dark, he ran into yet another coffin. He cried, 'Oh, ma God, gid me otta here! Everyding's not gonna be alrite, everyding's not gonna be alrite!'

"He practically crawled all the way over to the stairs and frantically climbed up on his hands and feet passing Pop's partner, on the way. At the top, he stood up and ran right out the front door of the building like a bat out of hell. They never saw him again; he never returned."

A subdued laughter follows the end of the story. I feel sorry for that poor fellow. What they did to that poor man was cruel; he must have been so terrified. Practical jokes like that hurt people, and should not be done just to get a laugh. I am surprised and disappointed to hear that Grandpa Sheridan could do such a cruel thing.

I think Daddy also senses that others feel the same way, so he grabs the floor and says, "You know, talking about running from danger reminds me of something **not** so funny. When I was about seventeen years old, I was standing on the corner with one of my friends when one of the trouble-makers in Yorkville, a real smart-alec, came by and asked me if I wanted to walk with him to the grocery store to get a pack of butts. Not trusting him as far as I could throw him, I told him no, I was just hanging out.

"My friend, however, does not take a cue from me, and goes with the smart-ass. Well, when they went into the grocery store, the trouble-maker pulled out a gun and told the grocer behind the counter that it was a stick-up! An off-duty detective who happened to be in the store at the time pulled out a gun and shot the robber dead! Then he turned the gun at my friend and says, 'Freeze or I will shoot you, too!'

"My friend tried to explain that he wasn't with the guy who was doing the robbery but the detective did not believe him. Even though he was completely innocent, nobody believed him! He was hand-cuffed, arrested, and later tried, convicted, and sentenced to a long prison term in 'Sing-Sing' Prison in upstate New York."

"Geez, **that**'s really scary!" Uncle Howie says, "Sometimes you have to have eyes in the back of your head and be Houdini the magician to avoid trouble. Holy God, that poor guy. I don't think there's anything worse than being sent to prison for something you didn't do!"

"Can you imagine if I had gone with that wise guy? I'd be the one sitting in prison right now rather than that other poor guy," Daddy says.

"Yeah," Mommy says, "that poor guy isn't the only one who's innocent in prison. Look at me, because you avoided prison I am in prison being married to you!"

This brings a really loud round of laughter... except Daddy who smirks, "Yeah, you are a 'prisoner of love,' you lucky lady!"

"Prisoner of love, ha!" Mommy replies, "Being married to you is more like what it was like when I was sent to reform school for playing hooky from school! I don't know if you remember, Anna, but Vera turned me in when I kept playing hooky!"

Aunt Anna looks serious as she replies, "I remember, Ellie. I missed you terribly and could not wait until you were allowed to come back home."

No longer looking happy, Mommy explains, "I was sent there for a few months that seemed like a few years. It was more like a prison than it was a reform school. I was put in with kids who had broken the law; kids who were really tough, and the guards there were so mean.

"We got punished for the slightest thing we did wrong. The way they punished you was to make you kneel in a corner on top of uncooked rice until your knees bled! If you tried to get up before they allowed you, they would hit you with a **'Cat of Nine Tails.'**

Uncle Howie asks, "What is a 'Cat of Nine Tails?'"

Mommy explains, a 'Cat of Nine Tails' is a whip with nine straps tied together. When they hit you with it, you would get nine welts wherever the belts hit your body! It was so cruel and painful. I couldn't wait to get out and go back home. I never did play hooky again! What a terrible experience it was, and it was so unfair to put me in there with all those vicious kids and guards just because I played hooky from school."

"I know what it's like to be in one of those so-called reform schools," Daddy surprises me.

Sounding somber, Daddy says, "I was put in a reformatory also along with my brothers, Buddy and Donny. We were put there when my mother was arrested for stealing a coat. She was put in prison for a while. Can you imagine a judge doing that knowing that my mom was a widow with so many kids to take care of! And the coat she was trying to steal was for a homeless lady living on the street where we lived. The judge just did not care; he sentenced her to prison like a common criminal, and had us kids sent to a reformatory where some of the city's worse kids are kept.

"Thank God my brother, Eddie, and my sister, Marion, were old enough to care for themselves so they avoided being sent to reform school. The judge let Aunt Marion off because she was sixteen at the time and he also allowed her to take care of my younger sister, Dotsy, who was just a baby at the time.

"In the reform school, they also made us kneel on rice, and used to beat the hell out of us with that 'Cat of Nine Tails.' The guards there were mean 'sons-a-bitches' who seemed to enjoy hurting and harassing us kids. I would not wish reform school on my worst enemy."

Mommy sees Daddy is emotional remembering this time of his life, so she adds, "You know, Patsy, your mother was lucky she was not caught and put in prison for what she did in all those apartments you guys lived in!"

Daddy's mood immediately changes as he chuckles, "After my Dad died so young, Mom did what she had to do to raise us kids and put a roof over our heads. Things were so tough then for us especially in the winter time. To create heat for us at night when the furnaces were turned off, Mom used to break the plaster off the walls so she could remove the wooden slats and burn them in the stove so we kids could have some heat in the apartment.

"When she ran out of wooden slats from the walls, she used to pull the wood moldings from around the doors and windows, and when that was used up, she would use some of the wood from the floors to burn them!"

Laughing, Uncle Howie asks, "What did she do when she ran out of wood in the apartment?"

Daddy chuckles, "Oh, she just moved us out in the middle of the night to another apartment she had arranged ahead of time!"

Mommy adds, "She was lucky that in those days the landlords didn't require a security deposit so your Mom was able to just keep moving from one place to another in the wintertime."

Chuckling, Uncle Howie nods approvingly, "Your Mom did the right thing, Pat. It's a good thing you didn't live in Brooklyn at the time because the landlords there were really tough. They would've tracked your mother down. Speaking of 'tracking down' reminds me of a legend that is based on fact.

"Two guys in Brooklyn were driving on their way to a dance when they saw a pretty girl all dressed up in a gown standing on the corner right outside a cemetery. They stopped and offered her a ride, which she accepted. When the driver invited her to join them for a night of dancing, she accepted.

After a night of dancing, he offered to drive her to her home. She gave him her full name and address but said she wanted to be dropped off at the same corner they picked her up… by the cemetery.

"The driver went around and opened the door for her. When he extended his hand to help her out, he was surprised to feel how cold her hand was. Being a gentleman, he insisted that she accept his jacket to keep her warm against the cold night air. He said that he could get the jacket back when he arranges to see her again.

"A day or two later, the driver goes to the girl's apartment building, rings the bell, goes up to the apartment, and introduces himself to the girl's parents. He tells them that he went dancing with their daughter the other night and now would like to ask her out on a date. The parents told him that he was mistaking their daughter for someone else because their daughter was dead! They said she had died a few years ago in an accident on her way to a prom!

"The man was thoroughly confused because the girl he danced with had given him her name, address, and told him about the apartment she lived in. Hearing this, the mother went over to the mantel piece, retrieved a picture of her daughter, and showed it to the man. It was the young girl he had taken to the dance the other night!

"Thinking he was the victim of some sick joke, the man said he wasn't going to leave until they tell him where their daughter is so he can talk to her.

"The father said, 'our daughter is buried in the cemetery!'

"The man became indignant thinking these people were persisting in this cruel, tasteless prank so he refused to leave. The parents called the police who came and when the guy insisted, they eventually went to a grave in the cemetery nearby where the parents said their daughter was buried. There, thrown across the tombstone with the girl's name on it was the man's jacket! Realizing what happened, the man became hysterical!"

"Ewww, that is very scary," Mommy says.

"It's a true story; I remember reading about it in the newspaper," Aunt Anna adds.

"Now, if you think that was a scary story," she continues, "wait 'til you hear this one.

"When Pops worked in the cemetery, we lived across the street in a ground floor apartment. One hot summer night, I was home alone and unable to sleep so I sat by the open window looking out at the cemetery across the street. That is when I saw a black, shadowy figure rise right up out of a grave!

"That scared the hell out of me but I thought it must be some wise-guy trying to scare little, gullible me sitting at the window across the street. But then, I could see that this figure was facing me. A terrible sensation of

305

danger swept over me as I realized this thing was fixed on me from the grave it was standing on!

"At that moment I knew I was dealing with something very bad, a ghost that had risen up from the grave! There was just enough moonlight to see that it had a black, full length hooded robe on… and a solid black mass for a face.

"I was so scared, I couldn't move until I noticed that it started moving in my direction. The closer it got, the worse I felt. I realized that it was coming after me. When I had turned away for a moment and looked back, it had already come halfway across the street! I slammed the window down closed, locked it, ran over to my bed and ducked under the covers, and started praying to God for help.

"I had the feeling that it had entered my room so I stayed under the blankets for what seemed an eternity. After a long time, nothing happened so I decided to peek outside the covers. When I lowered the covers, I found myself looking right up into the face of the ghost only two inches above my face!

"I was so terrified, I thought I was going to die! I couldn't breathe. Everything went black as I passed out.

"When I awoke, it was hours later. I was completely saturated in perspiration from the heat and the fear but I could tell that the ghost was gone. I couldn't stay there another second so I quickly got dressed, grabbed a few things, and ran out in the middle of the night to Vera and Emil's place where I stayed from then on. I never went back to that terrible place."

"Wow, that's scary!" Mommy says describing how I assume everyone felt who listened to this frightening story.

"Here's another scary story although it isn't as bad as that," Mommy continues. "You guys may also remember reading about this in the papers. Some robbers used to pour over the local obituaries to see if any rich people died so they could break into the funeral home at night to steal expensive jewelry left on the person who died. Some wealthy people actually bury their loved ones with their personal jewelry on.

"Well, these guys read about a rich lady who had just died and was being waked at a nearby funeral parlor so they broke into it in the middle of the night. When they found the lady's body in a coffin, they removed the jewelry except for an expensive looking ring, which they couldn't get off the lady's finger. So they cut her finger off in order to get the ring!

"To their shock, the lady's hand where they cut the finger off began to bleed! Even more shocking, the lady woke up and starting yelling at them! She was alive!

"It turns out, she had been in some kind of coma so when the robbers cut her finger off that brought her out of the coma! She was lucky she wasn't embalmed yet!"

Uncle Howie adds, "And she was lucky the robbers cut her finger off to get that ring!"

"What about the robbers?" Daddy asks. "Were they caught?"

Mommy explains, "The report said that they were so scared they dropped everything and ran out as fast as they could! The lady held her hand to stop the bleeding, climbed out of the coffin, and used a phone in the funeral home to call the police for help. She gave the police a good description of the robbers so they were later found and sent off to prison."

Uncle Howie says, "I guess you could say they were **'fingered'** by a dead woman!"

This play on words brings a lot of laughter.

Daddy now takes the floor, "Okay, talk about missing chances. I missed my chance years ago to hit it big when I went to see the Mills Brothers performing at a club in Manhattan. After the show, I went backstage and told them I have always been a big fan of theirs. They were very nice and polite and thanked me for my kind words.

"I told them I compose my own songs and asked if they would be kind enough to listen to one. After I sang a few lines, they clapped and said they liked it, and would like to sing it when they perform! I was so happy. I showed them the sheet music. After looking it over, they began to sing it. It sounded so good!

"When they asked me to leave my sheet music with them, I told them no, that it was not wise to leave your sheet music with anyone these days. As soon as I said that, and seeing the insulted look on their faces, I realized what a big mistake I made. I blew it; it was too late. Being colored, they probably figured I was prejudiced and did not trust them because of their color. This, of course, was not true... but the harm was done. There was no taking back the words; the moment was lost.

"They wished me luck and walked away. Boy, how I wish I could take that moment back. One unfortunate comment, a few words without forethought, and your life can change forever."

"But that can go the other way too, Pat," Aunt Anna says. "A kind word, a word of encouragement, words of forgiveness, can have the same good and lasting effect on someone's life."

"Yeah, I guess so," Daddy agrees.

Mommy interjects, "You know, you also have to be careful about what you tell people. Tell them about what happened to your father, Patsy."

Nodding his head, Daddy explains, "My father claimed that he thought of the concept of a cement truck before anyone else. Figuring he was going to become rich with the idea, he went drinking with his friend and over a few beers in the gin mill, my Dad told him about his invention of a cement truck. He even made a drawing of it on a napkin so his friend could understand what he was talking about.

"Well, his friend took that drawing and had the idea patented under his name! He went on to become very wealthy but never gave my father any credit for the idea he stole from him."

Mommy says, "Your brother, Eddie, also had some pretty bad luck. Why don't you tell them what happened to him."

"Poor Eddie. He was a great middleweight prize fighter who was undefeated and needed only one more win to get a shot at fighting for the world championship. So in that last fight, Eddie was winning every round until the last round. He was winning so easily, he got careless and let his guard down. The other fighter saw the chance and punched him so hard that Eddie was knocked out for the first and only time in his life!"

"The last round, that is terrible. What tough luck," Uncle Howie says.

"He was counted out," Daddy adds, "and that ended any chance he had to get a shot at fighting for the championship. Those who control the fight game knew that Eddie had a good chance of beating the champion were it not for that one lucky punch so they never gave him a shot."

"That's too bad," Uncle Howie says, "He will never know whether or not he would have won."

After a pause, Uncle Howie continues, "I can tell you about a guy who did win, and win big! There was this guy who got rich by advertising that for only one dollar you could buy a 'guaranteed way to kill roaches.' He said it could be used again and again if used as directed! This guy got thousands of orders which he filled by sending people a block of wood with instructions to, 'place wood on top of roach and press down until roach is dead!"

This story brings a round of laughter.

Uncle Howie adds, "Some people tried to have him arrested but they couldn't because what he advertised worked exactly as he said it would! The guy made a fortune!"

"How clever," Aunt Anna says, "now why didn't you think of something great like that, Howie?"

Smiling, Uncle Howie says, "I thought of something even better... I married you!"

Mommy says that Uncle Howie should have been a politician.

Daddy says, "Hey, how about the guy who saw two ads in the newspaper on the same day. One ad said that they needed steel; and the other

308

ad said that they had steel for sale!

"So the guy called from a phone booth on the corner and asked the company selling the steel how much they had and what price were they looking for. He got them to agree that if he could get a higher price, he could keep the difference for his efforts. They agreed, so the man then called the company that was looking for steel. He asked them how much steel they wanted and then quoted a higher price than the selling company was looking to get. The buyer agreed so the man had the selling company deliver the steel requested at the agreed price.

"When the deal was done, the selling company gave the man the difference in price... and then they hired him as a salesman!"

Mommy says, "Smart, very smart. Well, let me tell you something **very** interesting, and Anna can confirm this. The Sheridan family is related to the Vanderbilt family, the millionaires! Really. Every summer, a limousine would come to where we lived in a Brooklyn tenement and drive us out to the Vanderbilt estate on Long Island. There we would play with our Vanderbilt cousins.

"I remember the big black wrought iron gates at the entrance to their estate. We would stay there a few days playing games, playing the piano, singing songs, and running all over the grounds of their estate chasing one another. Our favorite game was 'Hide and Seek' because there were so many places to hide. At the end of our visit, the limousine would drive us back home.

"At Christmas time, our Uncle Robert would come in a limousine to our building in Brooklyn and give each of us expensive Christmas gifts. I named Bobby after him because Uncle Robert is such a kind and wonderful man.

"Uncle Robert said if I named a boy after him, he would leave some of his fortune to that boy. Well, Uncle Robert knows that I named Bobby after him, and he's heard through the family that Bobby is a 'blessed child.' Since Uncle Robert is deeply-religious and has not married, there's a good chance that when he dies, he will include Bobby in his last will."

Uncle Howie says, "If that happens, Bobby will be sooo rich!"

He doesn't realize... I am already very rich.

Chapter 36

BARTIMAEUS

August 1955

"Do you realize, Robert, that Hurricane Connie last Saturday, the 13th, will go down in history as one of the worst hurricanes we have ever had in New York City!"

Father Kelly is greatly impressed with the enormous power of this storm and the damaging effect it had on New York City in only one day.

"It was by far the heaviest rain seen in over fifty years dropping a ton of water on New York City in twenty hours! Huge sections of the city were flooded including thousands of houses and subways, and over 100,000 people had no electricity!"

"That's terrible, Father," I agree.

"Well, enough about Hurricane Connie. How are you, Robert, and how have you been enjoying this summer?"

"It's been very interesting, Father, very interesting," I tell him.

"Hmmm, so what was **the most interesting** thing that's happened since our last visit?"

There were several "interesting experiences" so I select the one I feel is most important to share.

"An older man came to my apartment and asked my parents if they would let me pray for his nephew who lives out of state. He was just diagnosed with malignant cancer, and the doctors said it spread so there was nothing they could do to help him."

"How sad," Father says. Tell me, how is it that the man knew about you and where you live?"

"He said some people in the parish told him I'm a 'blessed child' through whom God works miracles. They gave him my name and address."

"I see," Father says. "Since his nephew was out of state, I assume you could not go pray over him. So what did you do?"

"I couldn't physically pray over him, but I could pray for him from a distance… like the Centurion's faith that Jesus could heal the Centurion's servant from afar. The Centurion's words were 'I am not worthy you should come under my roof; say only the word and my servant shall be healed.' So Jesus healed the servant from afar simply due to the Centurion's faith."

Father nods approvingly, and asks, "So is that what **you** did?"

"Yes. My father arranged for the man to meet us in St. Monica's after all the Masses one Sunday. We stood at the center Communion rail where Daddy told the man how he could be like the Centurion as we pray before Jesus in the tabernacle at the main altar.

"As I prayed, I pictured a thin young man, and asked God to take away the cancer… and anything else that may need healing. The familiar tingling sensation poured over me. That happens when God answers my prayer."

"Does that mean God healed the person?" Father asks.

"No, Father. It's just a comforting sign for me that God heard my prayer, and will do whatever is best for the person who is ill. I never know if God is going to grant a physical miracle like most people want, but I do know that God hears **every** prayer and **always** does what is best."

"Yes" Father interjects, "God gives us what we need, but not always what we want.

"What happened to the man's nephew?"

"God healed him. Days after we prayed, the man came to our home and told us that his nephew had been miraculously cured. The doctors said the tumors just disappeared."

"Thanks be to God!" Father says looking quite impressed.

"Do I know this man?" Father asks.

"I don't think so, Father. He said that he has been away from the church for quite a while but after seeing God miraculously heal his nephew, he's going to go to Mass again at St. Monica's."

"When you see him, please tell him I'd like to speak with him."

"Sure, Father."

"Okay, now it's time to tell me about the assigned reading, Mark 10:46. What do you think of it?"

"This story of Bartimaeus, the blind man sitting by the Jericho Road, is one of the best I've heard! In it, Jesus provides several important lessons."

"Why don't you read that scripture for me, Robert," Father asks as he hands me the bible opened to that passage.

Sitting up straight, I read, "They came to Jericho. As He and His disciples and a large crowd were leaving Jericho, Bartimaeus, son of Timaeus, a blind beggar, was sitting by the roadside. When he heard that it was Jesus of Nazareth, he began to shout out and say, 'Jesus, Son of David, have mercy on me!' Many sternly ordered him to be quiet, but he cried out even more loudly, 'Jesus, Son of David, have mercy on me!' Jesus stood still and said, 'Call him here.' And they called the blind man saying to him, 'Take heart, get up, He is calling you.' So throwing off his cloak, he sprang up and came to Jesus.

"Then Jesus said to him, **'What do you want Me to do for you?'** The blind man said to Him, 'My Teacher, let me see again.' Jesus said to him, **'Go, your faith has made you well.'** Immediately, he regained his sight and followed Him on the way."

"Well read, Robert. Please tell me what lessons you think Jesus is conveying to us in this Gospel?"

"The first thing I notice is that Jesus tells us that there are holy men and women walking with Him including the very first pope, bishops, priests, and deacons. And yet, they are the very ones who tell Bartimaeus to shut up! I find that very disturbing. Walking with Christ, they are supposed to hear the cry of the poor, **not tell Bartimaeus to shut up!"**

"Let me stop you right there, Robert," Father says, "What do you think Christ is telling us right there? Why do you think God made sure that part of the Gospel was included?"

"I believe that God is telling us that no one, not even the holy men and women of God, the clergy, should keep us from crying out to Him. That is why He made sure that we hear about what Bartimaeus did when the people walking with Jesus told him to shut up. He cried out even louder!"

"Very good," Father says, "that's right. Continue, please."

"I also notice that Jesus stopped as always when people cry out to Him. This time He responded to Bartimaeus' cries for mercy by telling the apostles to tell Bartimaeus to come to Him. To me, this means that each of us must find our own way to God despite whatever obstacles we have in life... like Bartimaeus had to find his way to Jesus despite his blindness."

"That's true, Robert. What else do you think Jesus is telling us in this Gospel?"

"Jesus is telling us the critical role played by faith. He tells us that Bartimaeus threw off his cloak. That was significant because that cloak was Bartimaeus's protection against the elements. Being blind, Bartimaeus knew that throwing off his cloak he might never find it again. But He had such faith in Jesus that he believed he wasn't going to need that cloak any more. Jesus is telling us to have that same type of faith when **we** go to Him."

"Good observation, Robert. Is there more?"

"Yes, Father. I think the most impressive part of this Gospel is when Bartimaeus, a blind man, stands before Jesus, the Son of God, and Jesus asks, 'what is it you want Me to do for you?' I note that Jesus did **not** ask Bartimaeus if he wanted to see; He asked him what it was that Bartimaeus wanted Jesus to do for him!"

"Very good, Robert, very good," Father exclaims, "I confess I've never focused on that before.

"So what do you think Jesus is telling us there?"

"I think Jesus is telling us that we should, first of all, be specific in our prayer requests, and that sometimes what we think is most important... perhaps is not. Also, what we ask of God perhaps shouldn't be only for ourselves, but for the needs of others as well."

"That's true, that's true," Father says.

"Jesus then tells us the importance of faith, when He says to Bartimaeus, 'Go, your faith has made you well.' The sight that Bartimaeus once had and lost, was restored by Jesus right there, right then, in front of all

312

the holy men and women. I can just imagine what it must have been like for Bartimaeus to open his eyes and the first thing he sees is the face of Jesus! No wonder he then followed Jesus… much like what happened to my patron saint, St. Paul the Apostle."

"Excellent, Robert. I am very impressed. You see important things God tells us in scripture that are often overlooked. Very good, you've done quite well!"

"Thank you, Father."

Handing me a bible, Father tells me, "I found a reading in the Old Testament that struck me as applying to you. I'd like you to read it; please open the bible by the bookmark, and read **Isaiah 61:1-3**.

So I read, "The Spirit of the Lord is upon me, because the Lord has anointed me to preach good tidings to the brokenhearted… to console those who mourn in Zion, to give them beauty for ashes, the oil of joy for mourning, the garment of praise for the spirit of heaviness."

"I think this applies to you, Robert. I'd like you to read that every day, and as you do, remember Christ's words, 'To those whom much is given, much is expected.' You have a serious responsibility to use the gifts God has blessed you with.

"I want you to pick out a New Testament reading every week, pray over it, focus on what you think Christ is telling us, and take notes so we can go over your thoughts at our next meeting.

"For now, my time unfortunately is short which seems to be the story of **my life** these days. Allow me to extend a blessing for you. May God continue to bless you, and protect you, Robert, in the Name of the Father, and of the Son, and of the Holy Ghost. Amen."

"Give my regards to your parents, and thank you for sharing your thoughts with me about the Bartimaeus reading. Your comments **opened my eyes** in a number of ways."

Chapter 37

PASSAGEWAY TO HELL

September 1955

After my last visit with Father Kelly, I find it difficult to sleep each night as thoughts of God, angels, miracles… and devils fill my mind. As usual, the voice of the demon tries to cast doubt upon my thoughts of God, His teachings and how they all apply to me. I resist listening to the demon's statements and questions.

Here it is two in the morning and I still cannot sleep with all these thoughts flooding my mind. One of the reasons I cannot sleep is because I am so uncomfortable lying here on the sofa in the darkened living room. In the next room, there is a small lamp shedding light throughout that room. It sits on the right side of a large corner bureau that has a large attached mirror facing me.

Seeing the light in the next room and the utter darkness of the room I am in provides a reflection of my life wherein so much good is intermingled with the evil torments of the devil. Thinking back over past experiences, a voice I do not recognize suggests that the events involving demons perhaps never really happened, and to prove it, I should challenge a demon to come right now if it really exists.

"That would settle the matter for once and for all," the voice states.

Without reflecting on the enormity of the dangers involved, I foolishly give in to this suggestion and challenge the demon if it really exists to come and show itself to me. I instantly realize that I have made a horrendous, catastrophic mistake, one that may well end my life as I know it. Without appropriate forethought about what I was doing, I have called the devil to come and show itself.

Instant fear, panic, and terror grip me as I realize that the devil is wasting no time in accepting my indirect invitation... it is coming and I feel there is nothing I can do to stop it.

As I stare into the next room at the mirror on the corner bureau facing me at a diagonal angle, the black shrouded figure of the demon enters that room and moves in front of the corner bureau. Composed of consummate evil, it is four feet tall. Its right shoulder is pointed in my direction. Slowly it glides in front of the bureau and moves toward the right end of the bureau.

To my horror, I can see that the demon has no reflection in the mirror! As it passes in front of the lamp, it doesn't block the lamp's light! Reaching the end of the bureau, the demon stops moving and stands perfectly still. Then this demonic creature slowly turns to face me, and in a flash, it rushes upon me and envelops me within itself casting me into total darkness, evil, despair, and hopelessness.

In the next instance, I feel myself, the essence of my being, my soul, being carried away by not one, but several demons. At a herculean speed, I am being carried away in a tunnel of complete darkness. There is no light anywhere, only pitch black nothingness as I am being carried away in this black endless abyss. I am not dreaming, this is really happening to me.

I am terrified and powerless to save myself, and I realize there is no one here who can help me. But then... I remember that God exists and that wherever He is, He must know what is being done to me. So I cry out to Him from the inner recesses of my being and beg Him to please forgive me for my foolish mistake.

"Please save me, God, from these demons that are carrying me off into the abyss of eternal horror where they want to torture me forever, and keep me from ever seeing You or my loved ones again."

Nothing happens as the demons continue to carry me away into the utter darkness.

"Please, God," I cry even louder, "Please, God, have mercy on me! Please spare me, please save me from the demons. I am so sorry for what I did. Please have mercy on me. I am too young to die; I have too much yet to do in leading others to You. Please give me another chance, God. Please don't abandon me to these demons!"

My soul, my spirit, suddenly pops out of the path rushing to desolation. I am moved off to the right suspended perfectly still in the middle of nothingness.

There is only stillness, no light, no sound, no scents, absolutely nothing other than the demons hovering in the utter darkness around me. They surround me and direct indescribable hatred at me. It appears that they are being commanded by God, the superior being, to stand off, but they remain, seething, apparently waiting for permission to seize me once again and carry me off with them into the hellish abyss.

As I hang suspended in nothingness, I wonder if this is where and how I will spend all eternity for my foolish mistake inviting the demon to show itself to me. Maybe they were forced to stop by God because I called out to Him. With no hope other than God, I continue to cry out and beg Him for mercy.

"Forgive me, God," I cry, "spare me, protect me from the demons. Give me another chance at physical life where I can complete my spiritual mission."

I feel the demons loosen their hold on my being as they slowly withdraw backwards and angrily fade off into the darkness. My spirit is slowly turned so that I am now facing downward, perpendicular to whatever is below. I feel myself slowly drift downward. I can now see my body frozen

315

still as it lays on the couch in the darkened living room. My eyes and mouth are open and I am completely motionless. It looks like I am physically dead.

Gradually, my spirit floats down to inches above my body, parallel to my body to a point where my spirit faces my body.

Then I feel the remarkable sensation of my spirit pouring into my physical body as if my spirit is made of liquid. Once my spirit has fully re-entered my body, I again can feel temperature, hear silence, and I can breathe. God heard my cries for mercy and rescued me out of the clutches of the demons in the darkness of the abyss!

Now I have an idea of how Bartimaeus must have felt when Christ heard his cries… and rescued him out of the darkness.

Chapter 38

THE CAPTAIN'S CHAIR

October 1955

Since it nearly succeeded in carrying me off into the abyss last month, the demon has become even more fierce and audacious in its efforts to consume my spirit, my soul.

I am afraid to sleep at night now because I have been awakened several times from a sound sleep to discover the demon lurking in the shadows of my room seething, leering at me, casting its intense hatred and disdain upon me. It appears to be waiting for my weakest moment to seize me and carry me off again into the darkness. As soon as I remember to pray in the name of Jesus, though, it leaves.

Several times during daytime, I see things fall over or be violently thrown about in whatever room I happen to be in. Wherever I go, I sense its presence nearby… except when I am in St. Monica's Church or in our school.

Right now, it is late at night as Larry and I lay down opposite each other in what has become our shared bed… the two thickly-cushioned chairs pushed together in the living room. There are no lights on. The rest of the family is just now trying to sleep in beds located in the other rooms of our apartment home.

Suddenly, at the same time, Larry and I both sense the approach of the demon. It is heading toward the living room where we now sit bolt upright facing each other.

Larry quickly moves next to me, and whispers, "Bobby, I sense the devil is coming toward us! Do you sense it too?"

As I acknowledge his words, the closed French doors slowly swing open as the demon enters our room and positions itself to the left of the left French door facing us. It is the same frightening demon but it presents itself now in enormous size. Even in the darkness of our room, its jet-black figure can clearly be seen. The top of its featureless head nearly touches the ceiling. Strangely, slight puffs of dark charcoal-colored smoke slowly come out of the middle of its shrouded figure.

Larry screams out loudly, "Mommy, please come help us! There is a devil in the room with us!"

Mommy doesn't respond so Larry cries out even louder, "Mommy, **PLEASE** come help us! There is a devil in the living room by the French door! **PLEASE help us!**"

With the monstrous demon glaring down on us, the left French door now slowly moves away from the wall and closes… squeaking eerily all the way! As Larry cries out again for help, the French door starts moving again as it opens and rests against the wall… squeaking once again as it does.

The French door remains still for the moment as I finally hear that Mommy is awake! Thank God! She wakes up Daddy, and tells him that there is a devil is in the living room where Larry and I are trapped.

"You've got to go help them, Patsy," Mommy cries.

"Oh, for God's sake," Daddy complains, "what now? Can't a man get a decent night's sleep around here? For God's sake!"

"Stop complaining, and go help them!" Mommy shouts at him.

While Daddy goes out to put on the kitchen light, Mommy comes boldly right into the living room. Being eight months pregnant, she moves slowly and cautiously.

Without realizing it, she walks in front of the demon then says, "Oh, my God, it is so cold in here!"

Mommy apparently does not see the demon as Larry and I can.

As soon as Mommy turns on the lamps to the right and left of the sofa, I can no longer see the demon… but I can sense it is still stationed there to the left of the French door.

Stepping over to the open French door, Mommy watches as the door begins to move away from the wall toward her. Protecting the baby in her tummy, Mommy quickly backs away. When the French door is halfway closed, she abruptly raises her right hand in front of the door. Surprisingly, the door flashes back away from Mommy's hand so fast that it suddenly is back against the wall! It all happened so fast that I almost did not see it happen!

Daddy now arrives and immediately says, "Holy God, this room is freezing!"

The mention of God obviously angers the demon. The left French door slowly moves away from the wall and begins closing again all by itself as it continues that eerie squeaking sound. Seeing this, Mommy steps away but Daddy steps over to the door and rips off the heavy curtain hanging on it. As he does, the door slowly opens once again right in front of him!

Seeing this, Mommy, Larry, and I quickly go into the next room, and watch as Daddy steps over to the door and firmly grasps the doorknob with both hands and leans all his weight against the door holding it securely against the wall. I can sense that this only further infuriates the demon.

Shockingly, the French door slowly begins to open despite Daddy's mighty efforts to prevent it from moving!

"God damn it!" Daddy cries as he finally has to let go of the doorknob and step back out of the way of the squeaking door. As the French door slowly closes, Mommy begins to pray out loud. Daddy stomps out toward the kitchen saying that he knows exactly how to "stop all this nonsense."

He returns dragging along the very, very heavy wooden "captain's chair" from the kitchen.

"Be careful, Patsy," Mommy cautions him, "there is an evil creature in there doing that to the door!"

Without hesitating, Daddy goes right over to the French door, and wickedly jams the heavy captain's chair at a forty-five degree angle under the doorknob of the door virtually locking the door into place against the wall.

Stepping away, Daddy says, "There, that should keep the God-damn door in place! Now let's see something move it!"

Daddy steps back over to stand between Larry and me in the next room. Mommy, afraid of what might now happen, stands directly behind Daddy to protect her and the baby she is carrying. We stand together in silence and watch to see what, if anything, will now happen. I sense the intense anger of the demon; it is absolutely furious to be so challenged by Daddy... especially with me and the others standing by Daddy looking on.

A powerful atmosphere of evil envelopes us as the captain's chair shockingly begins to slowly scrape a few inches against the living room floor while the French door slowly moves away from the wall! It stops moving as if to make sure we are watching.

Mommy prays even louder; Daddy begins to shake.

In the flash of a moment, the captain's chair is violently turned to the left even though it is still jammed up against and under the doorknob of the French door! After a few seconds, the heavy captain's chair violently flies high up into the air to our left and lodges itself in the area between the ceiling and the adjoining wall. The French door remains perfectly still.

The captain's chair just hangs up there in the air lodged against the wall and ceiling. Then in a flash, the captain's chair is slammed down at lightning speed onto the floor where it is broken up into countless little pieces! Now, the French door slowly closes and casts off that terrible, eerie squeaking sound.

Larry and I hold onto each other as Daddy collapses, falling hard to his knees, onto the floor next to Larry and me. He is sobbing and repeatedly making the Sign of the Cross. Mommy stumbles backward and nearly falls as she also makes the Sign of the Cross and prays for God's help. Seeing this, I am filled with righteous anger that the demon has so frightened and bullied my family this way.

Making the Sign of the Cross, I shout at the demon, **"In the name of Jesus Christ, you must stop and leave... NOW!"**

A stillness fills the air. Other than Daddy's sobs, and Mommy's prayers, there is no other sound. Thanks be to God, the demon's attack has ended, and it has left... for the moment.

It is time to call Father Kelly to come again.

Chapter 39

SPECIAL THANKSGIVING GIFT

November 1955

This Thanksgiving I have special reason to be thankful. My third sister, Dorothy Elizabeth Walsh, was born on November 23, 1955 at Lenox Hill Hospital on Lexington Avenue and 77th Street in Manhattan. Daddy says Mommy is doing just fine and the baby, of course, is the most beautiful girl in the whole nursery.

"What a gorgeous baby!" Daddy boasts, "She's got that beautiful look that all the Walsh babies have. You can tell a mile away that she is one of us!"

They will be home in a few days. Meanwhile, Paddy, Kitty, Larry, and I are on our way to attend the Thanksgiving Mass that will be celebrated by our new pastor at St. Monica's, Bishop James H. Griffiths. He came to our parish in September along with some other new priests: Father Gilhooley, Father Moore, Father O'Neill, and Father Cannon who is in charge of the altar boys and St. Monica's co-ed choir.

Sadly, the bishop has already alienated some of the school children and adults in the parish due to what Daddy calls his "pompous, arrogant manner." Mommy adds that his homilies are way too long and not very interesting.

"Perhaps the reason he shouts during his sermons," Mommy jokes, "is to wake people up who have fallen asleep in the pews listening to him!"

I and several of my school friends are afraid of him because it seems he is always yelling at someone for something. This morning, I try to ignore these feelings about the bishop, and focus on the miracle of the Eucharist during the Masses I attend.

Paddy warns me, "You'd better hope that none of those old ladies go into the sacristy looking for you before Mass, Bobby. If that happens, you know the bishop will get very angry and blame you for people invading his sacristy and disturbing him!"

Paddy is right. From what I've seen, it seems the bishop is self-centered, and is always bossing everyone around him. I am sure that is **not** how Jesus wants him to behave. In terms of old ladies coming into the sacristy to ask me to pray for someone, there is nothing I can do about that. Why should that be a problem? Praying for one another is what we are all supposed to do, and what better place is there than in church?

I know all the priests, except Father Kelly, get annoyed when people

320

come into the sacristy to see me before Mass to ask me to pray for someone while I serve as an altar boy. The priests tolerate these intrusions because they have heard the many stories of healings involving me.

After Mass this morning, two ladies stop me at the back door of the church and ask me to pray for members of their families.

The younger looking lady with tears in her eyes speaks first, "Please pray that my son will be able to walk again. He was in a terrible car accident in which his legs were badly injured. As soon as the doctors told me they don't know if he'll ever walk again, I thought of you and how you healed that crippled man."

I tell her, "I'll pray that God heals your son. But you should know that it is God, and God alone, who heals… not me. On my own, I can do nothing."

"That's the same thing you told my friend when her father was in a coma and wasn't expected to live," she says. "But when you prayed for him, he came out of the coma and is doing fine."

"I remember," I tell her.

"We all know that you can't do any healing on your own; that's not what we ask of you. All we ask is that you pray on our behalf to God because when **you** pray to God, miracles happen! God listens to your prayers!"

"I promise I will pray from the bottom of my heart for your son."

The older lady says, "Please pray that my two sisters forgive each other and reconcile. They had a terrible disagreement years ago and haven't spoken since. It's kept our families apart."

"I will ask God to send the graces of forgiveness upon them and their families. Please remind them that Jesus tells us to forgive everyone, everything, including forgiving ourselves… sometimes that's the most difficult thing to do.

"God also tells us **how** to forgive. Three times in the bible, He tells us when He forgives, **He also forgets** what we did wrong! And, in the "Our Father," Jesus tells us we will be forgiven as we forgive others!

"One last thing, did you know there was one person who got Jesus to change His mind? Do you know who that was?"

They both admit they don't know.

"It was a mother! And that mother's name was Mary, the Blessed Mother. At the marriage feast at Cana, when Mary indicated she wanted Jesus to perform a miracle with the wine, Jesus said it wasn't time to begin His public ministry. And yet, out of love for His mother, Jesus changed His mind and transformed water into wine!

"That is why I encourage you when you pray to God, to do so as a mother, and ask the Blessed Mother to intercede on your behalf to her Son as she did at the marriage feast."

I see my brother, Paddy, patiently waiting for me at the foot of the steps in front of church so I tell the ladies that I must be going.

On our way home, Paddy says, "More ladies asking you to pray for something, heh? Anything interesting?"

"Every request is interesting and important," I answer.

"You know, you have to be careful, Bobby. The more people who hear about the miracles, the more people are going to be coming after you to pray for things! Pretty soon, you won't be able to get into or out of church," he laughs.

Paddy immediately shifts the conversation to our baby sister as he reminds me that Daddy wants us to call our new sister, "Dotsy." When we arrive home, Aunt Marion is in the kitchen fussing with the Thanksgiving dinner she cooked and brought over for us. I am grateful to her but I miss not having our traditional Thanksgiving routine this year. Mommy usually prepares the turkey the night before by putting it in the oven overnight to cook until morning. All during the night, the delicious aroma of turkey being cooked fills our home.

Thanksgiving Day follows our traditional routine. We attend the nine o'clock school Mass, come home, watch the TV movie, "March of the Wooden Soldiers," watch Daddy cut the turkey, then sit down to eat the best meal we have all year. Along with the turkey and stuffing, Mommy usually cooks potatoes and all kinds of vegetables.

At the dinner table, Mommy usually leads us in saying grace, "Bless us, oh Lord, and these Thy gifts which we are about to receive from Thy bounty through Christ our Lord. Amen."

Daddy, always more anxious than any of us kids to eat, usually waits to say grace but then quickly says, "Okay, everybody, dig in!"

This year, Aunt Marion has us help set the table then she gathers us around the table to say grace. As soon as we finish, Larry beats Daddy to saying, "Okay, everybody, dig in!"

Aunt Marion joins us all in laughing, then says, "I've got to leave in a minute to get back to my own tribe, but before I go, how would you kids like to hear your Daddy and I battle over who knows more witty sayings?"

We all, of course, encourage Daddy to compete.

Being a good sport... and also being quite smart... Daddy agrees but says, "Okay, but ladies first."

Aunt Marion says, "Oh, no, **you** have to go first, wise guy! You say one, then I will say one after you. The one who can't think of a witty saying within ten seconds loses! Okay, let's go!"

Daddy says, "Haste makes waste."

Aunt Marion counters, "Sticks and stones may break my bones, but names will never hurt me."

Daddy says, "Early to bed, early to rise, makes a man healthy, wealthy and wise."

Aunt Marion counters, "Don't cross your bridges 'til you come to them."

Daddy says, "The early bird catches the worm."

Aunt Marion counters, "Don't cry over spilled milk."

Daddy says, "He who hesitates is lost."

Aunt Marion counters, "Don't count your chickens before they are hatched."

Daddy says, "You're pretty good at this, Marion! Okay, how about this ... 'Don't judge a man 'til you walk a mile in his shoes."

Aunt Marion counters, "If you lay down with dogs you will get up with fleas."

Daddy says, "A stitch in time saves nine."

Aunt Marion counters, "A rolling stone gathers no moss."

Daddy says, "Every dog has its day."

Aunt Marion counters, "Don't burn bridges behind you!"

Daddy says, "A miss is as good as a mile."

Aunt Marion counters, "Two shakes of a lamb's tail."

Daddy says, "Don't look a gift horse in the mouth!"

Aunt Marion counters, "Time flies when you are having fun!"

Daddy says, "Birds of a feather, flock together."

Aunt Marion says, "Let sleeping dogs lie."

Daddy pauses and laughs, "And good brothers let their sisters win so they can get home to their own families!"

Aunt Marion laughs victoriously then gives Daddy and each of us a big kiss and wishes us a happy Thanksgiving. In a flash, she is out the door. As she leaves, Daddy announces that we are now going to add another family tradition to the Thanksgiving meal. That is each of us thinks of all the things we are especially thankful for.

Daddy starts it off, "I am thankful for many things but I am most thankful that God has blessed me with your beautiful mother and each of you, my precious children."

Paddy being the oldest sibling goes next, "I am thankful for our family, and Aunt Marion... even though she still calls me 'Paddy Boo."

This draws a laugh as Kitty quickly says, "I am thankful that I now have **two** sisters!"

This brings another laugh as Daddy turns to me to share.

"I am most thankful for all of you, our Catholic faith, and our wonderful country."

Next in line, Larry, says, "I am thankful for my friend, Kenny up the block… even though he's not allowed to come up to our home anymore."

Daddy asks, "What do you mean he is not allowed to come to our home anymore? Why?"

Larry explains, "After Kenny was here a few days ago, I went to his home to meet his mother. Kenny told her we have 'thousands' of little brown creatures with thin hairy legs that run all over our home, on the floor, the walls, the ceiling, and the furniture!

"So Kenny's mother said he can't visit our home anymore because some of those little creatures might get into Kenny's clothes and come back home with him. She told me it was best that I don't come back to their home either because some creatures may be hiding in **my** clothes and escape into their home."

Daddy looks indignant, "Listen, the next time you see Kenny's mother you tell her that your father said that **you are** not allowed to go up to her apartment either so **we** don't get any of **her** roaches!"

If everyone in Yorkville felt that way, no one would ever visit anyone else's apartment.

Chapter 40

MIDNIGHT MASS

December 1955

I am looking forward to singing with the boys and girls combined choir in St. Monica's tonight at the Midnight Mass. I have a strong sense that something quite eventful is going to happen during Mass that will make this evening one of the most memorable of my life.

Here I am in the top middle section of the choir loft located in the back of the church high above the congregation. The boys' choir is located on the right side facing out toward the front of the church; the girls' choir is on the left side. From where I am standing, I can see the front half of the congregation and the entire sanctuary including the main altar and side altars.

Our combined choir sounds very good. Before Mass, starting at 11 P.M., we sang all the popular Christmas carols. A loud speaker piped our singing to the outside of the church so people throughout Yorkville can hear us. Thus far in tonight's Mass, we sang Gregorian Chant and liturgical music without any mess-ups by anyone.

Now it is time for the main celebrant, Bishop Griffiths, to give his sermon. He was recently appointed to be the new pastor of our parish, and unfortunately, we have already learned that his homilies are very, very long.

Our chubby bishop lumbers on his way over to the pulpit on the left then slowly, laboriously climbs the winding stairs up to the top. Since what he is saying is so boring to me, my thoughts wind back to how I first joined the boys' choir here at St. Monica's. Father Canon, the choir director, auditioned all of us. Most of us were selected but there were some who sounded so bad they were told to try out again next year. Once he selected all the singers he wanted, Father Canon combined the boys and girls choirs into one large choir.

The first song he taught us was, "The Animal's Fair," which he had us sing over and over again. The lyrics are,

"We went to the animal's fair,
the birds and the beasts were there,
the big baboon by the light of the moon,
was combing his auburn hair.
The monkey he got drunk,
climbed up the elephant's trunk,
the elephant sneezed,
went down on his knees,

and that was the end of the monk,
the monk, the monk."

He had us sing that song repeatedly as he went around and listened up close to each of our voices. Occasionally, he corrected how someone was singing. During Christmas time, he taught us how to sing popular Christmas carols. We were so good that Father Canon was able to get us to sing Christmas carols at several wonderful places. These included Grand Central Station; the Mayor's Gracie Mansion residence in Carl Schurz Park; the giant tree in Carl Schurz Park playground; and, on the Ted Steele Hour on Channel 9 television!

The bus ride to and from the television station was at night. Boarding the school buses right in front of St. Monica's school, were several nuns who came along to chaperon our large group. We joyfully sang one Christmas carol after another as the bus rumbled through the streets of Yorkville in the pitch-black evening and freezing cold weather outside. I remember watching Sister Placide enthusiastically singing along with us from her seat in the very last row of the bus.

In the television studio, I was surprised to see the many large bright lights high overhead above the stage. They gave off a tremendous amount of heat. Father Canon told us to keep our eyes on him at all times while we were singing, look as happy as we could, and to smile whenever we were not singing.

"Sing as we have practiced all along, and do not look at the camera!" he ordered.

Singing on television was fun to do, but I will long remember the bus ride to and from the television station with greater pleasure. When I got home, everyone said the television camera stopped right on me as I was singing!

Mommy said, "That must be because the film crew could see how handsome you are.

These pleasant memories are now disrupted by the sound of Bishop Griffiths delivering his sermon. I know I should try to listen, but I just cannot get interested in the things he speaks about. I wonder if any of the adults attending Mass have the same reaction. Many of the boys and girls in the choir have said how they also do not particularly care for the bishop's sermons; they are too deep and intellectual.

All of a sudden, I see a big, dirty, mangy-looking dog slowly strolling straight up the center aisle heading toward the front of the church! The bishop also must see the dog approaching because he has suspended his homily!

Murmuring sounds and audible giggling rises up from the

congregation. At the very front of the middle aisle of the church, the dog turns left toward the area just below the pulpit, stops right at the foot of the pulpit, sits down, and looks right up at the bishop as if it has come to listen to his sermon!

This is hilarious! Rolling laughter cascades through the church as Bishop Griffiths leans over the pulpit and scowls down at the dog as if it has some nerve to interrupt his homily! I am surprised that the dog is so relaxed and cooperative with so many strangers about him and with the commotion going on.

The bishop thrusts his right arm straight outward and shouts to the ushers, "Get that dog out of here!"

As the congregation laughs openly now, the ushers come rushing up to retrieve the dog but it sees them coming and begins running away from them. This is so funny. What a welcome, implausible treat this is to see a mangy old dog running around the church being chased by a group of ushers in pursuit!

"Now what was I saying?" the Bishop says, "I lost my place!"

Hearing this, the congregation erupts into loud cheers and wild clapping! I cannot believe the deeply respectful adults of our parish are laughing and cheering because the bishop forgot what he was saying!

The bishop is so insulted; he storms down the winding stairs of the pulpit and stomps angrily over to the main altar to resume saying the rest of Midnight Mass! Wow! What a great treat this is! I wonder if God allowed all of this to happen to teach the bishop a lesson in humility… and give everyone attending tonight's midnight Mass a special Christmas gift… an abrupt end to the bishop's long sermon.

After Mass, Mommy, Daddy and I enjoy a good laugh over the newest legend, Bishop Griffiths and the dog! Walking home with my beloved parents on either side of me, I take in this precious moment with them. Listening to the unique sounds of the snow crunching under our feet, I revel in the extraordinary peace and sounds of this holy night.

As we make our way along York Avenue heading toward home, there is no one else in sight. We are the only ones walking along York Avenue. As we do, I look up and admire the many colorful Christmas decorations in the apartment windows. Adding to this magical moment are the faint sounds of Christmas carols playing in people's homes.

Mommy and Daddy also appear to appreciate this special, holy moment we are sharing. I feel so much love for my parents and family, the nuns and priests, my classmates and friends. Thank you, God, for blessing me with all these special people in my life. And a very special thanks also goes to God for the gift of that mangy old dog tonight at Midnight Mass!

Chapter 41

THE BISHOP

January 1956

Bishop Griffiths has become a legend in Yorkville, both good, and not so good. Stories abound in Yorkville about what a brilliant priest he is as second in command to Cardinal Spellman in the Archdiocese of New York. He also represents the Holy See at the United Nations. Unfortunately, there are also stories that he is overly proud, and mean-spirited. This past September, he was appointed to serve as our pastor at St. Monica's.

I am nervous this morning because I am scheduled to serve today as a "Communion Altar Boy" at the nine o'clock school Mass with Bishop Griffiths! My job is to hold the paten under the bishop's large, chunky hand as he distributes Holy Communion. The purpose of this is to catch the sacred Host if it should inadvertently fall.

In the sacristy before Mass, I reluctantly go over at the last possible minute to ask the bishop if I can help him get his vestments on. The bishop stops what he is doing, whips around, and glares at me! His face is so red it looks like it is going to explode at any moment!

His big red cheeks jiggle as he yells at me, "It is too late! The bus has already left the station!"

I am so embarrassed and afraid of him; I look down and immediately begin to back away. He is so mean and scary. What does he mean, "The bus has already left the station?" There is no bus here in the sacristy. What does he mean? I must ask Mommy what this means when I get home later… if I survive serving Mass with the bishop.

He is still glaring at me as we process out of the sacristy. I am so afraid he is going to yell at me during the Mass, I can't pay attention to the sacredness of the Mass as it progresses. As the Mass proceeds, I notice how nervous the two main altar boys are as they go about serving.

Finally, when it comes time for Holy Communion to be distributed, I pray to God to help me avoid making any mistakes to anger the bishop.

As I try to lead the way as I am supposed to do, the bishop bumps into me as he storms past me on his way to the far right side of the sanctuary. Once there, he immediately starts distributing Holy Communion before I can get there! To my horror, all the little second-graders are kneeling at the Communion rail with their chins resting right on top of the rail! There is no room for me to get the paten under the bishop's chunky hand as he extends Holy Communion to each one of the little children!

I hear him huffing angrily as I put the paten so close to his hand a few times that he bumps it and pushes it away! It almost seems as if he is purposely bumping his hand into the paten to knock it away.

At the center of the Communion rail at the center of the church, the bishop steps back from the Communion rail, faces me, and shouts at the top of his voice, "I cannot distribute Communion, now can I, **if you keep putting the paten in my way! Keep it out of my way!"**

I am so embarrassed. My worst fears have been realized in front of the whole church filled with all the nuns and all the students from St. Monica's School. Everyone is looking at me as if I am doing something so terribly wrong that the bishop has to stop the nine o'clock Mass to scream at me like I am an idiot! Carefully, I draw the paten back and keep it away from the angry bishop for the rest of Communion time. I feel so badly doing this, but the bishop will not let me use the paten to protect the Communion Host should it fall.

The rest of the Mass is a blur. As it ends, I find myself kneeling down in the sacristy alongside my altar boy partner, Johnny. After Mass, we are supposed to kneel here by the priests' dressing table in the sacristy until the bishop chooses to address us.

I watch in fear as Bishop Griffiths yanks off his vestments then rushes over to where I am kneeling. I know we altar boys are expected to kiss the bishop's ring after Mass, but I don't feel right kissing his ring. I don't feel it is appropriate to show such homage to anyone other than Jesus... especially if the person is someone like Bishop Griffiths.

The bishop holds out his ring for me to kiss which I do only because I feel obligated to do as a sign of respect. Then a sharp thunderous pain flashes across the left side of my face! The bishop has wickedly slapped me! My eyesight is temporarily blinded and I am nearly knocked off my knees to the floor he has hit me so hard! I can't believe he hit me, and so hard!

"Next time keep the paten out of my way when I am distributing Communion," he thunders so loudly the people in the church must have heard him!

I can't believe he had the nerve to hit me! And for what? Jesus would not hit me, and I am certain that He would not want the Bishop to hit me either. I am so offended. Who does he think he is that he can wickedly slap me? If my father was here, he would punch the bishop so hard he would send him flying… or at least rolling! I get up and storm away as I fight back the tears.

The bishop shouts after me, "Where do you think you are going? I didn't dismiss you! Get back here this moment!"

I ignore his bellowing and proceed to the dressing area for altar boys where I quickly take off my altar boy vestments. I am so offended and hurt, both physically and emotionally. Furthermore, the three priests there in the sacristy who saw the bishop slap me didn't say or do anything! They just stood there silently as the bishop outrageously carried out his tantrum! How sad.

They are cowards to stand there and not say one word when they saw the bishop slap me! They behaved just like the apostles when Jesus was being beaten and abused. What a bunch of cowards. I am so disgusted! Shame on them and shame on the bishop.

As I storm into the priests' area of the sacristy, I look over and purposely sneer at the bishop... **and** at the cowardly priests. They all appear to be surprised to see me blatantly sneer at them. Standing there motionless, they watch me walk over to the door leading out of the sacristy... sneering all the while.

The bishop angrily protests, **"How dare you sneer at your bishop! Get over here!"**

How dare I sneer at him? How dare **he** treat me in such an un-Christ like way while distributing Holy Communion, and then slap me in the face!

Opening the door, I give the bishop the most disrespectful, insulting sneer I can muster up as I walk out the door of the sacristy. I can hear him loudly complaining to the priests about me. Sadly, I don't hear any of the priests saying anything in my defense.

Now I am not so sure I want to be a priest when I grow up.

Chapter 42

BERTHA

February 1956

"If you don't teach 'miss goody-two shoes' a lesson... we will! Besides, teasing her is no big deal."

The demon's threat is aimed at Bertha, the tall, chubby German woman who works at the bakery shop on York Avenue not far from where we live. I understand right away why the demon has directed its venom at Bertha... she is one of the nicest, kindest people in all of Yorkville. She treats everyone who shops at her bakery like they are her best friend.

The "the father of lies" wants to hurt Bertha because she is so kind and loving to others. But some innocent teasing doesn't strike me as such a terrible thing.

My angel says, "There is no such thing as an unimportant sin. Every time you hurt someone, you are also hurting Our Lord. As He said, 'What you do to the least of my brethren, you do to Me."

After mulling everything over, I still don't think subjecting Bertha to a little teasing is so bad. Besides, since Bertha is so kind and understanding, I am sure she won't be unduly offended by an innocent practical joke.

When I tell Larry what I have decided, he says he isn't sure who Bertha is so I tell him that she is the big, chubby German lady with red hair who works at the German bakery on York Avenue.

"Oh, that lady," Larry recognizes who I am talking about, "You're right, Bobby, she'll be a great one to tease. Let's go there."

I get some money from Mommy to go to the German bakery to buy buns or rolls for breakfast as we usually do on weekends. We rush down the stairs and quickly make our way to the bakery on the west side of York Avenue.

Along the way, I suggest, "You do the ordering, Larry, because Bertha especially likes you. She's always happy to see you, and says how cute you are. You can order some buns, and then keep changing the number and type of buns after Bertha gets the ones you requested. You can tell her you made a mistake and were supposed to get different buns or a different number of them. After she does that, you can change that too! With such a large selection of buns to choose from, we'll have Bertha running crazy from one side of the bakery to the other!"

The stage is set as we enter the bakery. A bell over the entrance doorway makes a delightful jingling sound as it does every time someone enters or leaves. A delicious fragrance greets us from the wide variety of baked goods here. The air is warm and moist from the continuous use of the large baking ovens in the back.

The bell over the entrance doorway jingles again as a man enters the bakery and stands on line behind us along the glass case of cakes and cookies on our right. Behind the counter are slanted shelves across the entire length of the bakery. Each shelf contains rows of delicious looking buns of every variety.

There is Bertha walking back and forth as she fills a brown bag of delicacies for the customer ahead of us, a short, elderly man we often see around the streets of Yorkville. Bertha is so large, she can barely fit in the narrow area between the glass cases in the front and the pastry shelves behind her.

Her auburn hair is neatly arranged in a big bun on the top of her head. Her eyes dart over to Larry and me and she smiles. She is so sweet and gentle, I feel safe in proceeding with our plan to tease her.

As Bertha completes the order, the old man pays her and says, "Have a good day." The bell over the entrance doorway jingles as he leaves. Now it is our turn!

"Good morning, Bertha," Larry greets her cheerfully, "I hope you're having a good day."

"Good morning to you, little boy. What good manners you have!" Bertha says in her slight German accent. "What can I get for you?"

Larry starts right in, "This morning we're going to get some buns."

"How many?" She asks.

"Three dozen!" Larry tells her.

"Oh, that's a lot! Are you sure you want that many?"

"Yes. You see, we have many kids in our family. There are sixteen of us!" Larry exaggerates with a straight face.

Bertha looks aghast and says, "Oh, my God, that's a lot of kids. God bless your mother and father!"

Larry seizes an unplanned opportunity to begin teasing Bertha, "Mommy's name is Ellen Marie Sheridan Walsh, Daddy's name is Patrick Victor Walsh, my older brother's name is Paddy Walsh, my older sister's name is Kitty Walsh, my older brother standing here is Bobby Walsh, my name is Larry Walsh which is a nick name for Lawrence Anthony Walsh, and... "

Bertha abruptly cuts off Larry's long recitation of family names, "Very nice, very nice names. So do you want me to put them in a big bag, or do you want them in a box?"

"One big bag will be fine, about this size," Larry says gesturing the size desired. Still gesturing, he says, "What do you think, Bobby? Perhaps it should be this big… or… maybe this big… "

Larry and I exchange mischievous glances as Bertha reaches down under the counter and comes up with a large brown bag to put the buns in.

Before I can answer, Bertha shakes her head causing her huge jowls to shake like Jell-O, "So that's your brother, how nice! Now listen, we have only one size large bag, so this is it! Now what buns do you want?"

"Yes, he's my older brother, Bobby. He is eleven years old. He's not too talkative, but he's very smart… he thinks of funny things to do all the time."

"Oh, that's wonderful. You must have a good sense of humor in life today if you want to be happy. Okay, which ones do you want to start with?" she asks appearing to grow impatient.

Larry has a real goofy-looking smile on his face as he just stares at Bertha, as she looks back at him anxiously waiting for him to order. The jingling of the bell over the entrance doorway announces the arrival of two new customers.

Larry continues to just stand there staring at Bertha with that silly smile on his face trying to look as if he is adoring her! Bertha glances over at the other customers waiting on line then she looks back to Larry who continues to stand there and smile at her.

Looking nervous, Bertha says, "Come, come, little boy, the day is awasting. We ain't got all day you know. What buns do you want?"

Rather than answering her, Larry tilts his head and tells her that he's sorry, and begins to look back and forth at all the buns on **all** the racks behind Bertha… but he still doesn't say what he wants! Now he walks over to the far left and stares up at the shelves of buns there. Bertha also walks over in that direction expecting him to order some buns on that side.

"Sorry, Bertha, that I'm taking so long," Larry says slowly as he continues to look as thoughtful and innocent as he can. The bell over the entrance doorway jingles again as yet another customer comes into the bakery, and joins the growing line of customers standing on line.

Bertha makes an attempt at a smile that is clearly forced, as she grows frantic waiting for Larry to begin ordering.

"Never mind with the 'sorries,' little boy, what buns do you want? Let's go, let's go!"

Larry says in quick succession, "We'll have four crumb buns, three cinnamon buns, two cheese buns, four black and whites, six jelly donuts, three crème-filled, one apple turnover…"

"Wait a minute, wait a minute! Are you crazy?" Bertha says incredulously, "I can't follow that; you must go much slower! Now tell me one bun at a time, little boy!"

This brings some laughter from the customers waiting on line.

That is all Larry needs to hear as he slowly, very slowly, "Oh… I am… so… sorry… Bertha."

"That's too slow, little boy, go a little faster than that," Bertha instructs him as she shakes her head with each word for emphasis. She is now glaring at Larry.

"Okay, let's have three crumb buns over there," Larry says as he points to the rack of crumb buns all the way over on the left side of the bakery on an upper rack.

"I thought before you said you wanted four crumb buns," Bertha reminds Larry.

"When before?" Larry asks.

"When? When you said that before; that's when! When do you think?"

The bell over the entrance doorway jingles again as another customer enters. Now there are five people on line behind us! Seeing all the customers waiting, Bertha looks nervous… and it looks like she has run out of patience with Larry.

"Come on, is it three or four, little boy? Time is awasting!" She snaps.

"Three, I think," Larry teases as he rubs his chin with his right hand as if struggling with a terribly important decision.

"You think? You think? Well, what is it, three or four?" Bertha shouts at him.

"Three," Larry answers as if he just solved a difficult riddle," It is three!"

Bertha rumbles mightily over to the rack of crumb buns all the way over on the left side of the bakery on an upper rack as she grumbles, "Three crumb buns coming up!"

At the rack, she sounds quite annoyed as she counts, "One, two, three," while quickly retrieving the crumb buns. Putting them in the bag, she turns back to Larry for his next order.

Breathing heavily now, she glares menacingly as Larry as he holds up four fingers but clearly says that he wants **three** cinnamon buns from the rack all the way over on the other side of the bakery… on a lower rack.

Bertha looks confused, "Wait a second, you're holding up four fingers but you're saying three. Which is it? Do you want three, or four?"

Larry looks at his four fingers and thoroughly examines them before answering, "Oh, I'm sorry; Bertha, I have an extra finger up, don't I! How silly of me."

334

"Never mind, what is it, three or four?" Bertha shouts at him.

"I meant three," Larry answers, as he feigns embarrassment.

The customers on line are amused at Larry's apparent "little boy mistake."

Meanwhile, Bertha puts a wax paper in the bag on top of the crumb buns, then wobbles quickly all the way over to her right where she quickly counts off "one, two, three" as she retrieves the cinnamon buns. Looking exasperated, she turns and looks to Larry for his next request but he is gazing slowly from left to right apparently pondering his next selection as if it is a critical decision.

Looking nervously at all the customers waiting on line right up to the front door, Bertha says, "Come on, little boy, what do you want now? We have a lot of people waiting on line!"

"What's next, what's next?" she hurries him.

"Let's see… I'll take… five… no… six… yeah, I'll take six jelly donuts, please," Larry points to the rack of chocolate donuts all the way over on the far right side of the bakery.

"Those are **not** jelly donuts!" Bertha snaps, "They're chocolate!"

"Oh," Larry says, then he just stares at Bertha without saying anything.

"Well, what is it… jelly donuts or chocolate?" she shouts.

Turning slowly to me, Larry asks, "What do you think, Bobby?"

"Hmmm. I think it's jelly... yeah, it's jelly," I tell him.

"Come on, boys, come on, we haven't got all day you know," the old man on line behind us complains.

This makes Bertha all the more frantic.

"Jelly it is!" Larry says joyfully as if he just won a contest!

Bertha is greatly irritated. With a look of total frustration, she thunders all the way over to the rack of jelly donuts, and shoves them into the bag. Without turning around, she asks what is next.

With her back to Larry, he knows that Bertha is not be able to see what he points to so he points to the tray of 'black and white' pastries on the far left side of the bakery and purposely says in a tone of voice too low to be heard, "I'll take four of those, please."

"I can't hear you; speak up!" Bertha shouts.

"Bertha," Larry says trying to sound like his feelings are hurt.

"Never mind with the **Bertha**, little boy! Tell me what buns you want!" Bertha shouts.

"I want four of those," he says as he continues to point knowing that Bertha cannot see where he is pointing.

"Four of which buns?" Bertha shouts with her back still turned away from Larry. It appears she cannot stand to look at Larry now.

"Four of those!" Larry resists saying the name of the buns as he continues to point in the direction of the black and whites knowing that she cannot see where he is pointing.

"Maybe if you turn around, you'll see what he wants," the old man chastises Bertha.

Bertha turns around to face Larry. Her face is bright red with anger. Frowning and breathing heavily, Bertha means business now. Being such a big person, she looks scary like this. My idea of teasing her has worked much better than I thought... now I am worried about how long it will take Larry and me to get safely out the front door before she can run around the counter to pummel us!

Bertha glares at Larry as he stands looking right back at her with an obnoxiously angelic smile plastered across his face.

Glaring at him, she growls, "Four of what?"

"Four of the black and whites, of course," Larry answers as if Bertha should have known as he points at a glass case facing us toward the back of the bakery.

"There are no black and whites in that case! They're on the shelf over there," she complains and nods toward the rack of black and whites on the rack to the left behind her.

"I know that, Bertha, I was just trying to help you because you look sooo tired this morning," Larry tells her trying to sound like a sweet, considerate little boy.

That draws a fearsome glare from Bertha as she hustles over to the tray of black and whites and mumbles something in German. She grabs the black and whites and throws them in the bag. It's clear she is **not** enjoying this experience with Larry.

"Do you want any other buns from **this** side of the bakery?" She asks as she finally realizes this is wise to do with this "little boy."

Recognizing that Bertha is at her breaking point, Larry carefully maintains his look of innocence as he points and tells her, "Yes, Bertha, I'd like three plain cahrollums, please."

"They are called, crullers!" Bertha corrects him.

"Yes, cahrollums," Larry says clearly.

"No! It's crullers!" Bertha shouts again saying the word more slowly and distinctly for Larry's benefit.

"Cahrollums," Larry says as he nods his head.

"No! It's crullers!" Bertha says again in total frustration.

This is too much for the old man, "For the love of God, will you **please** just give him the crullers so we can all get out of here!"

"Crullers," Larry finally says clearly and easily.

"Yes. My God! I can't believe it!" she complains as she grabs three plain crullers and gruffly shoves them into the bag then turns around to face Larry.

I nod to Larry indicating that it is time for us to stop while we still can get out of here alive and in one piece. Getting my meaning, Larry turns to me and shouts, "Oh, my God!"

Bertha freezes and with her eyes bulging, she yells, "What, what? What is, 'Oh, my God' for?"

With a phony look of surprise, Larry looks back to Bertha with his eyes bulging and his mouth wide open.

"**What? What is it?**" Bertha shouts again.

"I just remembered," Larry says nodding his head up and down as if what he has to say is no big deal.

"You just remembered what?" she shouts.

"Mommy wants us to get **rolls** this morning... **not buns!**"

The man next to us on line complains, "For the love of God, kid, make up your mind! Let's get this show on the road!"

Bertha's face transforms into one of rage. Her eyes have a look of madness as her hands squeeze the bag of buns into a much smaller bag! She looks like she is going to climb right over the counter and pound us! If she could get us, I think she might kill us with her bare hands!

In a delayed reaction, she shouts angrily, "What are you saying? After all this, you don't want all these buns?"

Acting like he is hurt and insulted, Larry admonishes Bertha, "I'm surprised at you, Bertha. You shouldn't yell at us like that; we're just little kids. Now we are **not** going to buy any buns **or** rolls here! Come on, Bobby... let's go to the **good** bakery on First Avenue where people aren't mean to us!"

As we make a quick exit, Bertha is so frustrated, she can't speak as she struggles to get some words out.

As we reach the door, she is able to say, "You are dumb little boys! Don't come back here asking for buns or rolls unless you know what it is your mother wants you to buy!"

Outside the bakery, Larry and I laugh uproariously and congratulate each another for our highly-successful venture. I tell Larry we had better hurry now and get to the bakery on First Avenue to buy the rolls for breakfast.

To this, Larry asks, "To get buns or rolls?"

On our way to the bakery on First Avenue, the demon's voice sounding victorious, violates my inner peace, "Good job... blessed child!"

Instantly, I realize what a terrible mistake I made not listening to my guardian angel. I realize now that I did something cruel and sinful. In my defense, I tell Larry that I didn't think Bertha would let it go as long as she did. I thought for sure she would catch on after a while. We really upset her and the people waiting on line.

"You're right, Bobby," Larry replies. "We're lucky we got out of there alive after what we did."

"What we did was sinful," I add.

My angel says, "Both of you should tell God you are sorry right now, and go to confession as soon as you can."

I share my angel's advice with Larry, "My angel tells me we should tell God we are sorry right now, and we should go to confession as soon as possible."

Larry replies, "We also should go back to the bakery someday and tell Bertha we're sorry for teasing her. But let's go to confession first, Bobby. I don't think it would be such a good idea to visit Bertha for a while."

I know God will forgive us... I hope Bertha will also.

Chapter 43

DRINK FROM THE CUP

March 1956

Mommy and Daddy are still fighting over Senator Eugene McCarthy and his statements about the influence of Communism in America. Their disagreement at times has broken down into heated words. For two people who love each other so much, this is so upsetting to witness. It has created a tense, uneasy atmosphere in our home.

Last week on Geri's fifth birthday, March 10th, something happened to set off a screaming match at the kitchen table. They exchanged heated words with one another while the rest of us sat there with a chocolate birthday cake perched directly in front of us.

At my angel's suggestion, I lit the five candles on the cake and started singing, "Happy birthday to you, happy birthday to you, happy birthday, dear Geri, happy birthday to you!"

Paddy, Kitty, and Larry had joined me in singing... much to Geri's delight.

Mommy and Daddy stopped fighting for the moment and joined us in time to watch Geri make a silent wish and blow out the candles. I wondered if her wish was that Mommy and Daddy stop fighting. I know it was mine.

I suspect that the devil is behind all the discord and unhappiness between Mommy and Daddy. If the devil can tempt Jesus in the desert, then it can certainly tempt my parents.

Whenever I feel tempted to do something wrong, I say the same words Jesus used to chase the devil away, "Get behind me, Satan!"

How I wish Daddy and Mommy would say those same words. Here it is now a week later and they still find things to quarrel over. I keep praying for peace between them but things don't seem to improve. I am disappointed that Daddy, in particular, cannot rise above the pettiness that mysteriously consumes him these days.

He quarrels with Mommy over the slightest things. In my view, Daddy has instigated most of their disagreements. At times when Daddy gets mad, he declares that he is the "King of the Castle," and, therefore, what he says goes! This sounds so proud and disrespectful of Mommy. Once again, I suspect the devil is involved tempting Daddy through the sin of pride. I don't think Daddy realizes how proud and self-centered he sounds. If he did, I am sure he would stop.

It is obvious that he is blind to the possibility that the devil is manipulating him. This is ironic because Daddy has always said we are called by God to be humble in all we do. Hearing them arguing in the kitchen, I decide to go see if I can say something that may help bring peace.

As soon as Daddy takes a breath from arguing, I tell him, "You know, Daddy, Jesus said that 'He came to serve, not to be served!' And He also said 'He who is first will be last in the kingdom of God!'"

"Get inside, and mind your place!" he yells at me.

"You hear what Bobby says, Patsy?" Mommy says, "It' time you stopped and listened! What's gotten into you lately?"

"What's gotten into me? I will tell you what's gotten into me. I have finally wised up! No more being 'mister nice-guy' letting everyone disrespect me."

"God forgive you, Patsy!" Mommy says as she escorts me out of the room with her.

Lying down on the bed in the second room, I fear that Daddy's recent arbitrary nature is a result of the devil's false whisperings. The devil, the ultimate spiritual predator, apparently has Daddy as its target.

Living in fear of Daddy's volatile temper, we all try to stay out of his way… just what the devil hopes to achieve in bringing discord and unhappiness into our family circle. What is happening reminds me of what a priest said in Mass one time. He said that Jesus tells us in the Gospel of Matthew that , "A house divided against itself cannot stand."

The priest added something else that is in Matthew's Gospel. He said, "How can one enter into a strong man's house and spoil his goods, except that he first bind the strong man and then spoil his house!"

Wow, that sure sounds like what is happening in our family! I must continue praying to God for peace in our family… and protection from the wiles and wickedness of the devil.

The next day passes quickly and peacefully without Mommy and Daddy fighting even though Daddy has been home all day on his day off from work. Lying in bed in the room before the living room, I listen to Daddy and the rest of the family watching television. I am still praying for Daddy and for peace in our home when the demon's sinister voice invades my mind.

"There are things you can do to punish your father and teach him a lesson."

I recognize I should not listen but I am curious what it is that I might consider doing to teach Daddy as lesson.

"Spike his tea with salt!" the demon suggests.

Spiking his tea with salt sounds like a harmless thing to do but it comes with the danger of getting caught and beaten. It is also sinful to do something that hurts someone, and wastes food.

My angel cautions me, "Don't do it! You are called to be kind and loving, not mean and hurtful."

Despite this, I view spiking Daddy's tea as a small thing so I decide to do it.

Since he enjoys having a cup of tea while watching television, I will spike his tea by adding lots of salt to the large pot of tea! When I am certain everyone is thoroughly engrossed in the television show they are watching, I quietly slip out of bed and tiptoe out to the kitchen. There sitting atop the stove is the delightful vision of the large silver pot of tea with a bed of loose tea leaves floating across the top. The pleasant aroma of freshly brewed tea fills the kitchen air, a familiar scent in our home.

I look through the rooms to make sure no one is coming to the kitchen... especially Daddy. Certain that I am not seen by anyone, I grab the round box of Diamond salt from the closet and go over to the pot of tea. I pull out the little metal pouring spout on the top of the box and holding it open over the pot of tea I pour a generous amount of salt into the pot!

After quickly returning the box of salt to the closet, I thoroughly stir the tea, then quietly go back to bed unnoticed by anyone. Scurrying under the blankets with my back to the room, I make believe I am sleeping.

It appears no one saw me get out of bed and go into the kitchen to do my evil deed with the salt. I lie perfectly still and patiently listen for the sounds of a commercial break on TV knowing that Daddy will immediately head right out to the kitchen to get his cup of tea. The tea has now been brewing with the salt for some time.

Sure enough, when the commercial starts, Daddy rises up and begins his predictable journey out to the kitchen to retrieve his cup of tea. As he passes, I continue to lie perfectly still making believe that I am sound asleep. I hope this works; if it doesn't, I am in for a beating!

I listen to the sounds of Daddy moving about in the kitchen. First, he strikes a match in order to light the gas jet on the stove under the pot of black tea. Then he walks over to the kitchen sink on the other side of the room where he rinses out one of the plain white cups. Now he gets the sugar container and the quart of milk from the refrigerator, both of which are stored there to protect them from the roaches.

While waiting for the tea to boil, I think about this sinful thing I have done. I now realize too late that I am doing what the devil wants... causing harm and discord in my family. I feel so badly but it is too late for me to do anything now without getting a ferocious beating from Daddy! I have made a terrible mistake; the devil must be happy it succeeded in tempting me but I can't bring myself to stop what I have done.

A minute passes; then I hear Daddy dip his cup into the full pot of black tea before he adds sugar and milk to it. In his typical manner, Daddy takes a big slurp out of the cup of tea and swallows. Instantly, I hear the sound of gagging and spitting as the overpowering taste of salt undoubtedly fills Daddy's mouth! He must be leaning over the kitchen sink now because I hear him wretching and spitting as he apparently struggles to rid himself of the horrible taste of salt.

I hope he is all right.

An ominous silence follows. I strain to hear what Daddy is doing, and I pray to God that no one will get hurt as a result of my foolish, cruel prank. From what I hear, it sounds like Daddy is examining the pot of tea to determine what is wrong. It does not take him long to deduct that someone purposely spiked his pot of tea with a ton of salt… with him as the intended victim!

I expect the worst now. Daddy is probably furious that someone would dare to strike out at him like this. He is surprisingly quiet and calm as he goes about his business in the kitchen. I wonder what he is doing.

The familiar sound of a cup being dipped into the pot of tea on the stove is followed by the sound of sugar and milk being put into the cup. What is he doing?

Now he is walking slowly back through the rooms heading for the living room. I can barely breathe I am so nervous. I have to lie perfectly still when he comes into the room to convince him that I am sleeping. Otherwise, he may figure out that I was the one who spiked his tea.

Sure enough, Daddy pauses next to my bed and hovers over me as he calls out in a singsong way, "Bobby, oh, Bobby… are you asleep?"

With my back to him, I resolve not to move no matter what he says or does.

"Bobby," he calls out a little louder.

I refuse to answer or move; I can't afford to get caught.

Thank God, he is moving on! I tricked him into thinking I am asleep.

Daddy walks into the living room, walks directly over to Paddy and says, "Here Paddy, have a cup of delicious tea, why don't you! I am sure you will enjoy it."

I can imagine the look of confusion on Paddy's face wondering what in God's name Daddy is doing. He knows that Daddy never, ever gets a cup of tea for anyone except himself. Daddy is usually the one who asks everyone else to get him a cup of tea!

"Why are you offering me that? I don't want a cup of tea!" Paddy protests.

"What's the matter, don't you like freshly-brewed tea?" Daddy asks sarcastically.

"I don't know what you're talking about," Paddy tells him.

Daddy now turns to Larry, "How about you, LaLa? Why don't you take a sip of tea?"

"No way, I'm not drinking whatever is in that cup!" Larry answers.

"Why not? Is there perhaps something **wrong** with this tea per chance, Sir Lawrence?"

"I don't know what you are talking about but the way you are acting, there must be something wrong with the tea. I am not going to drink it," Larry says emphatically.

"Well, one of you is going to drink it because someone made a scrumptious pot of tea for me, and I just **have to share it** with whoever made it for me. Now, come on, one of you take a sip," Daddy demands of Paddy and Larry.

"Patsy, what the hell are you doing? What are you babbling about? Have you lost all your marbles? We can't hear the TV," Mommy complains.

"The hell with the TV," Daddy raises his voice, "One of these little bastards poured a ton of salt in my pot of tea. I almost choked on it! What do you think of that, heh?"

"What?" Mommy asks.

"Yeah. You want to take a sip and taste for yourself!"

"No thanks, I'll take your word for it. Whoever did it I am sure just wanted to kid around with you. Why don't you just forget about it and sit down and enjoy TV with us."

"In a pig's tit, I will. This is serious! Someone purposely spiked my tea!"

"Oh, stop making a federal case out of it, will you!" Mommy complains.

"I can see you don't give a damn that one of the kids just tried to poison me, do you?

"What am I supposed to do, Patsy; I don't know who did it either."

"Maybe Bobby did it," Larry suggests, "He likes dong funny things like that."

Daddy snaps, "There is nothing funny about this, and Bobby is sound asleep in the next room."

"Maybe he's acting!" Paddy suggests, "He's a good actor."

"Stop trying to blame your brother; he could not have done it," Daddy says.

"Well, since you are not going to chastise your children, woman, I will!"

The next thing I hear is the sound of Daddy throwing some of the

343

spiked tea on Paddy and Larry as they run out of the room. Mommy unfortunately is in their path so she also got some of the tea thrown on her.

"For God's sake, Patsy," Mommy complains as she gets up out of the chair.

"Why did you do that? You got it all over me and the floor!"

"It serves you right for not correcting your children… **mother**. If you did your job right, these kids would not be trying to poison their father!"

Larry and Paddy pause by my bed and wonder if I did it.

"Did you do it, Larry?" Paddy asks.

"No, I swear I didn't," Larry answers.

"Did you?"

"No. That means the only one who could have done it is Bobby! He must have done it before he went to bed."

Mommy exits the living room and goes into the kitchen followed by Paddy and Larry. I can hear her examining the pot of tea by dipping her finger into it.

"Ewww," she complains, "Someone **did** spike the tea with salt. Who did this? Larry? Paddy? I want to know who did this!"

Both of them protest their innocence.

"Come on, boys, I wasn't born yesterday, someone had to do this. Tea does not come out of the package tasting like the Great Salt Lake! If one of you did not do it, then who did? Not Kitty, not Geri. The ghost? Come on, someone did it."

"We did not do it, Mommy," Paddy insists, "It had to be Bobby before he went to sleep!"

Daddy enters the kitchen and snaps, "Get to bed the two of you before I beat the living daylights out of you!"

Without hesitation, Paddy and Larry quickly head off to bed grateful to escape Daddy's wrath. I continue my charade making believe that I am asleep. I feel so guilty and cowardly but I can't subject myself to the consequences of what I have done including a likely beating.

I am so sorry I did this and caused so much unhappiness. The evening is ruined for everyone; Daddy is deeply offended that someone did this to him; Paddy and Larry were nearly punished for something they didn't do; and, Mommy is upset. Had I thought more about the consequences of my actions and the harm it might cause, I would never have fallen prey to the demon's temptation. What I did was sinful.

I end this day feeling ashamed and sorry for what I did, and resolve not to do something like this ever again. Forgive me, Lord, and please send the graces I need to resist the temptations of the devil.

Meanwhile, I won't be making a pot of tea anytime soon.

Chapter 44

WHITE AS SNOW

April 1956

"Mommy, what's for dinner?" I ask.

"Bobby, you know it's Friday so we must refrain from eating meat today. We're having our usual Friday night dinner of macaroni with mayonnaise and salmon, sardines with onions, and fish cakes."

"Why can't we eat meat on Fridays?" I ask.

"I'm not sure;" Mommy replies, "I think it's a tradition we Catholics maintain out of reverence for Christ who died for us on a Friday. Ask one of the nuns or priests, Bobby. I'm sure they know."

"Speaking of traditions," she continues, "today being Friday means you should be getting to church to go to confession. Please get Paddy and Kitty and tell them I said to get going!"

We usually go to confession on Friday nights even though the nuns are not there to take attendance like they do for the Sunday nine o'clock school Mass. So, off we go to St. Monica's for our weekly confession.

The two confession booths in St. Monica's Church are located on the left side against the wall up near the very front. The booths are recessed about four feet within three alcoves. Each confessional booth has a door in the middle where the priest goes in, and there is an entrance on either side of the priest's door where sinners enter. Each sinner's entrance is covered by a dark, maroon-colored drape.

The nuns tell us we go into confession as sinners, and come out "white as snow." The whole area around the confessional booths is dark compared to the lighted area in the church proper. For me, this further symbolizes what confession is all about. We go into the confessional with our souls cast in darkness from sins, but we come out with the light of Christ upon us after we are forgiven.

It is customary in St. Monica's that those waiting to go to confession, sit in the pew outside one of the confessional booths. Each person goes in according to the order they arrived in the pew. After the person on the end goes in, everyone left in that pew slides over closer to the end.

Not knowing which priest will be on duty to hear confessions, makes me very nervous because it may be Father Gilhooley who often yells at people in the confessional... and everyone in the church can hear. Not hearing any shouting coming out of the confessional booth right now, I hope and pray that Father Gilhooley is not the priest in there.

Paddy, Kitty, and I genuflect outside the pew and go sit next to a girl who is already waiting there. Three more kids come into the pew to our right and sit next to us. I am relieved that all I can hear coming from the confessional are faint murmuring sounds.

After thinking of the sins I must confess, I sit and wait for my turn. I recall how some kids in my class told me they go to St. Stephen's Church on 82nd Street between York and First Avenues. They go there for confession just to avoid Father Gilhooley. Some say they even skip going to confession for that reason! That is risky. What if they die unexpectedly before they go to confession?

I don't understand why anyone would take a chance on possibly dying with sins on their souls when all they have to do is go to confession to be forgiven... regardless of who the priest is hearing the confession. The nuns also taught us that until we can get to confession, we should talk to God and ask Him for forgiveness.

Once I asked Daddy a series of questions regarding confession: "Why do we go to a priest to confess our sins? Where does a priest get authority to forgive our sins? Doesn't forgiving sins belong strictly to God alone?"

Daddy explained, "It's very simple. You see, Jesus created the Sacrament of Confession. In John 20:23, He told the Apostles, 'Whose sins you forgive, they are forgiven; whose sins you retain, they are retained.' That means priests who are direct descendants of the Apostles have been given the power and the authority by Jesus Christ Himself to forgive our sins... or **not** forgive them if we are not sincerely contrite!

"You know, Bobby, Protestants have a problem with our belief about confession. They say it's enough to pray to God directly, that we don't have to go to another person, a priest, to confess our sins. They don't understand that Christ Himself created confession. This authority to forgive sins is also written in the bible in Luke's Chapter 10, Verse 16 where Jesus says, 'Whoever hears you, hears Me, and whoever rejects you, rejects Me.'"

Daddy adds, "I always quote the Bible when talking to my Protestant friends because their religious beliefs are heavily dependent upon what is written in the bible. I also tell them, if confession is not needed, then why did Jesus create it? That usually stumps them. It's something they can't explain off. Since Jesus created confession, it has special value and benefit in the form of special graces that strengthen us to live better. I know I always feel spiritually clean and refreshed when I come out of confession."

My thoughts are interrupted by the sound of loud words coming from the confessional booth. Oh boy, Father Gilhooley is in the confessional booth! I can't believe our luck. Father Gilhooley is on duty so we will have to go to confession through him. I feel sorry for Paddy, Kitty, and myself, but I feel even more sorry for the person in the confessional right now. He must be worried about everyone outside hearing what Father Gilhooley is saying. When the boy comes out, he will have to walk past all of us waiting here. There is no way to avoid being seen when he comes out.

The beautiful voice of my angel tells me, "That is **not** the way God wants His priests to treat those who come to confession. God wants them to be like the father of the prodigal son... welcoming, kind, and forgiving."

That is what I think, too. I try not to listen to words I hear being said in the confessional... but it is difficult not to hear. I wonder if Father Gilhooley knows how loudly he speaks when he hears confessions? Whether or not he knows, I don't think he should raise his voice as he does. I ask God to please help Father Gilhooley to speak softly.

"I'm not going to confess anything really bad!" the boy to my right says out loud. "I don't want to take a chance he'll yell at me!"

"You have to," I tell him. "If you don't confess a sin, it won't be forgiven, and if you die with that sin on your soul, you may go to purgatory or even hell!"

The boy stares at me, then looks down. I hope he is going to confess everything. My own words give me courage to face Father Gilhooley myself in order to be forgiven and avoid the possibility of going to hell.

I hear the confessional screen inside the booth slide closed on one side and the screen on the other side open. The boy in the confessional on the right comes out looking embarrassed with his eyes cast down as he quickly walks to the Communion rail up front to say his penance prayers.

The girl at the beginning of our pew gets up and goes into the confessional. She looks very concerned. Only murmuring sounds come out from the confessional as I pray again that God will keep Father Gilhooley from screaming at whoever goes to confession through him. My prayers are answered as a boy soon comes out of the left side of the confessional looking quite relieved on his way to say his penance prayers.

Now it is Paddy's turn so he gets up and goes into the left side pushing aside the heavy cloth drape. Kitty and I look at each other and wonder if Father Gilhooley is going to yell at Paddy. I pray once again that God will keep Father from talking too loudly.

Kitty looks scared so I lean over and whisper, "Don't worry, Kitty, just remember what sins to confess and think of Jesus. I promise I will not listen if Father Gilhooley yells."

No yelling comes from Father Gilhooley as he hears the girl's confession on the right side of the confessional. All I hear are murmuring sounds. Soon the confessional screen is heard closing as the girl comes out smiling and walks up to the Communion rail to say her penance prayers. Kitty gives me one last worried look as she rises and enters the right side of the confessional.

Now it is Paddy's turn to have his confession heard by Father Gilhooley. I ask God to keep Father from yelling at Paddy. Only faint words are heard coming from the confessional, and then the sound of the sliding screen indicates Paddy is finished. He looks relieved as he smiles in my direction before making his way up to say his penance prayers. I now ask God to please keep Father Gilhooley from yelling at Kitty as I go over and enter the confessional.

Pushing aside the maroon-colored drape, I enter the dark, unlighted confessional booth. I kneel down on a padded kneeler and hear Father Gilhooley saying something to Kitty on the other side. He's actually speaking softly to her! Soon I hear the screen slide close on Kitty's side and my screen opens. It is now my turn!

I lean my face toward the screen and say the usual beginning for making a confession, "Bless me, Father, for I have sinned, my last confession was a week ago."

"Speak louder, I can't hear you!" Father yells!

I don't want anyone outside to hear my confession but at this moment I care more about receiving absolution for my sins. So I will speak very loudly for the rest of my confession… and hope Father Gilhooley doesn't yell at me.

"I was angry a number of times; I cursed a few times; I didn't do what I was told a few times; and I let the devil tempt me into spiking my father's tea with salt. I'm sorry for these sins and the sins of my whole life."

I fully expect Father Gilhooley to start yelling at me, but instead, he surprises me by speaking in a relatively low voice, "What do you mean… you let the devil tempt you?"

"The devil tells me to do bad things all the time, Father. It doesn't force me; it only encourages me to do things I know I shouldn't do."

"You think the devil talks to you?" Father says incredulously.

"Yes, Father, it talks to me all the time in my mind."

After a pause, Father asks, "Are you… Robert… from the school?"

"There are a few boys in the school who are also named Robert, Father."

"You know what I mean!" he yells. "Are you **'the Robert,'** the one the nuns call a 'blessed child?"

"Yes, Father. I am."

"Ooookay," Father says more calmly but strangely. "Now, I understand."

"Tell me, Robert, what makes you so sure it's the devil that talks to you, and not your own imagination?"

"Who else would tell me to do bad things, Father? It **IS** the devil."

"I imagine your parents know all about this?"

"Yes, Father."

"And what do they say?"

"They tell me not to listen to it, to listen to God instead."

"That's good advice; you should always talk to God... not just when bad thoughts come into your mind."

"I do, Father, but the bad thoughts come into my head anyway."

"Let me ask again. What makes you think they're not your own bad thoughts?"

"Because sometimes when I am thinking of something else, especially something good, the devil interrupts and talks over my thoughts."

Silence fills the confessional booth. It is as if Father Gilhooley has gone to sleep.

Finally, he speaks in a lower tone of voice, "Tell me some of the things this voice tells you to do."

I have to think for a while before remembering, "Well, things like spiking my father's tea; not doing what I am told to do; lying to avoid punishment; wishing bad things happen to people who annoy me. Things like that, Father."

"I see. Does this voice ever say anything about God?"

"Sometimes."

"What does it say?"

"It says that **He** doesn't care; that **He** lets bad things happen to good people; that praying is a waste of time because **He** doesn't care; that going to Mass is a waste of time because **He's** not really there. Things like that, Father."

"I see," Father says.

After another pause, he asks, "How long has this been going on?"

"For as long as I can remember... from when I was little."

"From when you were little, heh."

"Yes, Father."

"You can remember things from when you were little?"

"Yes, Father. I remember most things that ever happened in my life."

"How old are you?"

"I'm eleven, Father."

Silence sets in again.

"You know it is a sin to make up things like this, don't you?" Father surprises me.

"Yes, Father, but I am telling you the truth."

More silence.

"I understand that you are also supposed to hear a **good** voice telling you to do **good** things. Is that true?"

"Yes, Father."

"And who do you think this 'good voice' is?"

"I am pretty sure he is my guardian angel."

"Your guardian angel, heh," Father says.

"What are some of the things your 'guardian angel' tells you."

"He tells me **not** to listen to the devil; **not** to do bad things even if no one can see what I'm doing; pray to God more often; be kind to others; and always do what Jesus would do. Things like that, Father."

"Interesting. When was the last time your guardian angel said something to you?"

"Just before, Father, while I was waiting to come into the confessional."

"Oh really! And what did he tell you?"

I hesitate to tell Father what my guardian angel said but my angel encourages me to tell him anyway because God wants Father Gilhooley to hear this!

So I tell him, "My angel said it's not Christ-like to yell at people like you do when they come seeking mercy and forgiveness."

There is dramatic silence on Father Gilhooley's side of the confessional so I add, "My angel also said you should go to confession yourself!"

Silence continues.

"Thank you for telling me that, Robert. I really should not yell at people who come for forgiveness, should I? It's not a good thing to do. Thank you for telling me this."

Almost as an afterthought, he adds, "And yes, I **will** go to confession myself to another priest.

"From what I've heard about you from Father Kelly and the nuns, I understand you have some pretty amazing things happen in your life… and some very difficult things too. But they also tell me that you have an understanding of spiritual matters far beyond your years. Just remember, you must stay close to Our Lord in all you do, and resist temptations that come your way. Otherwise… "

This advice is quite familiar, but the way he says it is scary.

"The devil tries to pull us all away from God's graces a little at a time," he continues. "It begins with what may appear to be 'little sins.' But sin is like a sharp-pointed triangle inside your soul. The first time you do something wrong, the triangle turns a little inside your soul and hurts badly. Each time you sin thereafter, the triangle turns creating a groove in your soul so that the pain is a little less each time. And if you sin often enough, the triangle no longer hurts when it turns. In other words, you get so used to committing that sin, you don't even notice all the damage it does to your soul.

"Do you understand what I am saying?"

"Yes, Father, I understand."

"Good. I'd like you and your parents to make an appointment to come speak with me. I want to help in any way I can. Now, for your penance, I want you to say one Our Father, one Hail Mary, and one Glory Be. Now say a good 'Act of Contrition."

As Father says some prayers, I pray aloud the Act of Contrition, "Oh, my God, I am heartily sorry for having offended thee, and I detest all my sins because of thy just punishment and the pains of hell, but most of all, because they offend thee, my God, Who art all good and deserving of all my love. I firmly resolve with the help of thy grace, to sin no more and to avoid the near occasion of sin. Amen."

While I make the Sign of the Cross, Father also makes the Sign of the Cross with his right hand as he says, "I absolve you of all your sins in the name of the Father, and of the Son, and of the Holy Ghost. Amen. Now go in peace... and say a prayer for me."

"Yes, Father, I will. Thank you."

As I step out of the confessional, I feel so clean, so new, so wonderful! I am "white as snow' as Jesus says!" Thank you, God, for the gift of the Sacrament of Confession.

While walking up to the Communion rail to say my penance prayers, Father Gilhooley's voice booms out from inside the confessional booth, **"And don't spike your father's tea anymore!"**

Oh, my God, I am so embarrassed he said that! Now Paddy and Kitty… and everyone else in church… know that **I am** the one who spiked Daddy's tea! I guess Father Gilhooley has a short memory; he has already forgotten he said he wouldn't yell any more. And what about God's words to forgive **and forget?**

Well, if I didn't do such a cruel, misguided thing, I wouldn't be suffering the consequences. For now, I will fervently say my penance prayers, and thank God that **He** forgives and forgets.

For my penance, I begin with praying the "Our Father," "Our Father Who are in heaven, hallowed be thy name, thy kingdom come, thy will be done on earth as it is in heaven. Give us this day our daily bread, and forgive us our trespasses as we forgive those who trespass against us, and lead us not into temptation, but deliver us from evil. Amen."

Next I say a "Hail Mary," "Hail Mary, full of grace, the Lord is with thee. Blessed art thou among women and blessed is the fruit of thy womb, Jesus. Holy Mary, mother of God, pray for us sinners now and at the hour of our death. Amen."

Finally, I pray the "Glory Be," "Glory be to the Father, and to the Son, and to the Holy Ghost, as it was in the beginning, is now and ever shall be, world without end. Amen."

I thank God for the gift of forgiveness, make the Sign of the Cross, rise, and make my way out of church. When I join Paddy and Kitty outside on the church's steps in front, I am relieved to learn that they did **not** hear Father Gilhooley shout that I should not spike Daddy's tea anymore! They were already outside the church. Thank God!

At home, I tell Daddy about how I told Father Gilhooley what my guardian angel said about shouting at people in the confessional. I don't, however, tell him about how Father yelled out that I should not spike my father's tea anymore.

Daddy responds, "Actually, I am very glad that he yells at people! That's what people need these days, some good old-fashioned fire and brimstone! Maybe being afraid of getting yelled at in the confessional will encourage people to avoid sin. Did you ever think of that? What's worse, getting yelled at in the confessional... or burning in hell forever? Catch wise, kid? Listen to your old man; I've been around long enough to know what's needed."

Building up a head of steam on the subject, Daddy continues, "What Father Gilhooley is doing is right! I think priests today are too easy-going. Too many of them are more worried about offending parishioners and becoming unpopular than they are about what they're going to tell God when He asks why they didn't do their job as they're called to do."

"But I think that being **too** stern and yelling at people may also keep some people from ever going back to confession," I tell him.

"Let me tell you something, it would be a good idea to give repeat sinners today a 'Quadragesima' for their penance. Maybe that would help them to reform their evil ways and help to save their souls!"

"What's a 'Quadragesima?' I ask.

"Quadragesima is a Latin word meaning **forty**. There was a time in our church's history from the fourth to the ninth century when the church extended the period of fasting during Lent to forty days. Before that, from the first to the third century, fasting originally lasted between one to two weeks. Only one meal a day toward evening was allowed, and meat, fish, eggs, and dairy products were **all** strictly forbidden during the Lenten season."

"What does that have to do with confessions today, Daddy?"

"Don't you get it, Bobby? Priests today are too soft in terms of the penances they dole out, so there's little incentive for sinners to stop what they're doing wrong. They know they can go out and commit sins, go back to confession again, be forgiven, get an easy penance, and go out and sin again!"

"I see what you're saying, Daddy, but do people really do that?"

Daddy explains, "If sinners are given a really tough penance like having to do a 'Quadragesima' you can bet they'll think twice about committing the same sins again knowing they'll have to deprive themselves and suffer badly. That's what a 'Quadragesima' has to do with confession!"

"But Daddy that might also turn a lot of people away from going to confession," I tell him.

Daddy explains further, "People go to a priest to confess their sins so they can be reconciled with God. The priests accordingly have a sacred obligation representing God to properly administer this sacrament. Priests should not give sinners the wrong impression that certain sins are no big deal because the priests are too soft and lenient. Priests must encourage genuine contrition and absolute resolution not to commit those sins again. If a sinner is not truly contrite and resolute, his confession is not valid. In so doing, he may risk eternal damnation in hell!

"Giving out Quadragesimas, or at least tougher penances, would go far in helping sinners truly mend their ways. That's what I think, kid, and I am sure that God agrees with me! You remember this for when you are a priest yourself when you grow up."

Perhaps priests could provide tougher moral leadership when it comes to advising and encouraging sinners to be truly contrite and resolute about avoiding sin. I am not so sure, however, that giving out Quadragesimas as penance is the right answer. I am afraid that giving out wicked penances would likely result in fewer people going to confession.

I tell Daddy how Sister Bernadino, my third grade teacher, once explained to our class that Penance is **not** a form of punishment. It is a tool to help convert us from sinful ways to a Christian life style. Also, Father Kelly spoke to our class about confession and the vital importance of forgiveness.

He told us about the story of the Prodigal Son in Luke 15:11 in which Jesus tells us how a son goes off and dishonors his father by living poorly and wasting his entire inheritance. When the son is sorry and returns home, the father runs out in the field to forgive his son and welcome him back home! The father in this story is like God Who is always ready to forgive us, and to welcome us back home.

When Father asked what we thought about this reading, I was the only one who raised a hand. I told Father Kelly that for the Prodigal Son to be forgiven, he had to first acknowledge the things he did wrong, be truly sorry, and be serious about changing his sinful ways. But to do all this, the prodigal son had to first forgive himself.

"Father Kelly said he was very impressed with my answer. He said that is something many people have great difficulty doing… that is, forgiving themselves. They can forgive others more easily than they can forgive themselves.

"Father said that Jesus tells us in Mark 11:25 if we do not forgive others, God will not forgive us! He also told us was how Jesus forgave the people who crucified Him, even though they didn't ask for forgiveness. Jesus prayed, 'Father, forgive them, for they know not what they do!"

I told Father Kelly that if sinners understood how wrong their actions were, or what the consequences were for their actions, perhaps they would not do sinful things.

"Father agreed and added, 'Jesus tells us to forgive **everyone** including those who hurt us, and those who don't ask for forgiveness.' One of the boys in my class said that his relatives say they can forgive, but they **can't** forget. Father said that is not true forgiveness.

"He explained, 'What good does it do if they forgive someone but will not forget what they did wrong? And who do they think they are hurting by not forgetting? Do they **really** think the person who offended them goes around feeling badly about it? I doubt it! By carrying around the memory of who and what offended them, all they do is hurt themselves. It's like carrying around a huge, heavy boulder everywhere they go!"

"In support of what he was saying, Father said, 'There are three times in the bible, where God tells us that when He forgives, He also forgets what we did wrong! Twice in the Old Testament in **Isaiah 43:25** and in **Jeremiah 31:34**, and once in the New Testament in **Hebrews 10:17**.' Hearing that God forgives and forgets, I realize that we should do the same."

"Those are pretty powerful words of God," Daddy says.

"I don't recall ever hearing them before. What healing that could bring to so many people. One of the big reasons marriages wind up on the rocks today is because the husband or wife can't forget some hurtful thing their spouse did."

God forgets… the devil doesn't.

Chapter 45

PENTECOST

May 1956

Larry's ninth birthday on Thursday, May 14th is joyful as most birthday celebrations are in our family. There is the traditional lighting of the birthday cake candles, one for each year of life, and one in the center for good luck. That candle is not lit. Mommy leads us singing in the birthday song,

"Happy birthday to you,
Happy birthday to you,
Happy birthday, dear Larry,
Happy birthday to you!"

In keeping with our family custom, Larry makes a silent wish as he stares wide-eyed at the brightly lit candles. Afraid that the candles are going to melt down onto the cake, Daddy urges Larry, "Larry, blow the candles out before they burn down the house!"

Larry ignores Daddy as he does so often to tease him. He knows Daddy does not like to be ignored. Larry continues to stare at the cake with a silly expression. This further infuriates Daddy who realizes that Larry is purposely taunting him.

Daddy snaps, "I know what you're doing, kid. If you know what is good for you, you had better blow out those candles before I knock your lights out! Don't be such a wise guy!"

Heeding Daddy's warning, Larry slowly blows the candles out … one at a time. Mommy removes the candles and lets Larry lick the chocolate frosting off each one.

Kitty asks Larry, "What did you wish for?"

"Ballet lessons," Larry answers knowing that this will annoy Daddy who has often said he thinks men who are ballet dancers are "queers" as he refers to such people.

Larry does not have to wait long for a reaction from Daddy.

Angrily biting his tongue, Daddy snarls, "Why do you want ballet lessons, kid? Ballet is not for real men!"

"Oh yeah," Mommy chimes in, "I'd like to see you jump high in the air like the men do in ballet, and dance so gracefully. We would see who the 'real men' are! Then again, I don't think anyone would like to see you, Patsy, jumping around a stage in tights!"

Everyone giggles… except Daddy.

Biting his tongue, he snaps back, "Keep it up, Ellie, and **you'll** be

355

high in the air… without jumping either! Like Jackie Gleason says, 'Bang, zoom, to the moon, Alice!"

"Yeah, yeah, yeah," Mommy laughs.

The rest of Larry's birthday evening passes quietly and peacefully so my thoughts turn to the great joy coming in two days for me... the day I receive the Sacrament of Confirmation. On Saturday, I will confirm my Christian beliefs through this sacrament at St. Monica's Church. I have looked forward to this day for a long time.

When Saturday arrives, I wake up early and feel the excitement in the air as I go about preparing for this special event in my life. Unlike when I received my first Holy Communion, I not only feel worthy, I can't wait to receive this important sacrament.

Mommy and Daddy bought a brand new navy blue suit for me to wear today. It is our family's custom that whenever someone is to participate in a sacramental celebration, he or she gets a new outfit of clothing to wear for the special occasion. This is a fitting gesture symbolizing the importance and special nature of such milestones in our physical and spiritual lives.

I have looked forward to receiving the Sacrament of Confirmation because it is an exhilarating encounter with God, a specific point in time when I know the Spirit of God Himself will come and personally descend upon me and fill me with one or more spiritual gifts: Fear of the Lord, Fortitude, Knowledge, Piety, Understanding, Wisdom, and Counsel. These aid us in our journey through physical life. Like any gift though, unless it is used properly, it cannot bring the intended joy. The gifts of the Holy Ghost, in particular, should be acknowledged, appreciated, and used.

I can only imagine how pleased God is when He sees us using the gifts He gives us, and how disappointed He must be when we don't use them. In this regard, I often think of Jesus' words that "to those whom much is given, much is expected!"

While I get dressed, my thoughts now shift over to our big mean bully of a pastor, Bishop Griffiths. Since he is the bishop, he is the one who is going to slap me on the cheek during the Confirmation ceremony today. Knowing how dramatic and insensitive he is, I can assume he is going to wickedly slap me rather than just giving me a symbolic tap on the cheek.

I sense that all this worry about the bishop may be the devil trying to disturb my sense of eagerness and joy. I understand the meaning of this slap in Confirmation. It is to remind us young adults that there may be times in our lives when we will suffer because of our Christian faith. There may even be times when we are called to personally to stand up and be counted in defense of our faith knowing that doing so may subject us to pain, suffering, rejection and recrimination. Confirmation gives us the special graces to face such difficult times and to deal with them courageously.

This special sacrament also helps us deal with a spiritual danger that is not so obvious… doubt. It can lead to a loss of faith, hope, and trust in God leaving us to depend solely upon ourselves. It is then that the devil can more easily lead us away from God and ultimately ravage our souls.

Confirmation also helps us maintain an awareness and respect for God and all He has created. When we cease to see God in fellow human beings, and do not respect all He has created, we leave ourselves open to the wiles and wickedness of the devil. So many people allow this to happen when they lust after money, material things, and/or personal gratification to the exclusion of God and all He has taught us. In so doing, the devil can subtly turn us away from God by causing us to place such other things at the center of our lives rather than being God-centered.

Daddy told me the devil is the same evil, hateful monster that tempts and torments people everywhere today as it first did with Adam and Eve.

Looking at the clock, Daddy says, "Oh wow, it's time to go. Hurry up or we'll be late for church, Bobby."

All of us quickly gather around Daddy and Mommy then follow them out the front door. Downstairs in the street we are greeted with golden sunshine and a gentle breeze. The peace, tranquility, and solitude of this early morning in Yorkville is so appropriate for my Confirmation day.

At St. Monica's, I join my classmates in the auditorium of the church while my family goes directly into the church to wait for the liturgical celebration to start. The nuns line us up in our predetermined places around the perimeter of the auditorium with the boys on the left side, the girls on the right. There are about one hundred of us who will be confirmed today.

There is a lot of chattering going on. Occasionally, one of the nuns comes by to tell us to speak softly. Suddenly, a hush comes over our large group as the greatly feared Bishop Griffiths enters the auditorium with some of our priests following behind him. Whenever I see the bishop, I am afraid he is going to come over and hit me again. He always looks so angry and annoyed. For his good, not just for mine, I ask God to bless him today with peace… and a joyful spirit.

Bishop Griffiths and the priests take their positions at the head of the line in the rear of the auditorium to lead us out through the back stairs up to the street and into church. As I walk along, I try not to think about the bishop. I instead focus on the fact that the Holy Ghost is coming soon to descend upon me and fill me with His gifts.

As we go up the front steps of St. Monica's and proceed into my beloved church, I think about the very first Confirmation when the Holy Ghost descended upon the Apostles in the upper room where I believe the first

Mass was previously celebrated by Jesus. How fortunate they were.

The massive organ is playing loudly inside the church as we process in two straight lines. Everyone in church is standing and looking at us as we proceed to our assigned pews. Occasional flashes go off here and there as people take pictures. I have a sense of importance as I stand in my place knowing that the Holy Ghost will soon be personally coming.

As the ceremony progresses, I reflect upon my life and beliefs pausing at times to thank God for the many good things He has blessed me with. I thank Him for the gift of life, my family, my friends, the nuns, the priests, our great country, the spiritual gifts God has given me, and the greatest gift of all... how Jesus made it possible for me and all others to avoid the horrors of hell.

I also realize how fortunate I am to know first-hand that God really and truly does exist, that there really is spiritual life after physical death, that angels and heaven really do exist, as does that terrible, terrible place called hell where the devil and its army of demons reside.

We are now getting closer to the moment of Confirmation, the descent of the Holy Ghost. The bishop says today's reading from the Acts of the Apostles tells us of the very first 'Pentecost,' the very first Confirmation when the Holy Ghost descended upon the Apostles.

"As such, this also marks the 'birthday' of the Catholic Church," he adds.

"In the same way, the Holy Ghost is about to come right here in St. Monica's to descend upon and bless the young adults gathered here to confirm their faith!"

Wow, that is the most interesting, impressive thing I have ever heard the bishop say in any of his sermons!

The time soon comes for me to go up the center aisle of the church to where Bishop Griffiths sits on a chair at the top of the steps of the main altar. As I watch those ahead of me kneel down in front of him to be confirmed, I think of the name I have chosen for Confirmation, Patrick.

I selected Patrick as my Confirmation name because it is the first name of my father and my brother, and it is also the name of the patron saint of Ireland. I so greatly admire the good traits of each of these; I select their name to forever remind me to emulate all that is good about them. And so, forevermore, my name will be Robert Thomas Patrick Walsh.

My thoughts suddenly turn to Grandpa Sheridan who also felt so strongly about the Sacrament of Confirmation. I feel his presence by my right side as I step up next in line to be confirmed. This feeling is so strong that I look to my right side to see if I can see him there. He may not be physically visible, but I sense his personal presence here along with other family members.

A sea of thoughts and emotions race through my mind as I step forward and call out to God in my mind telling Him how greatly I wish to confirm all that I have been taught. My legs feel wobbly as I kneel down. The bishop's big-rosy red cheeks jiggle as he says the prayers of Confirmation. I close my eyes and sense a golden light surrounding me, immersing me. The bishop's heavy hand thuds on top of my head as he continues praying.

The sounds about me fade as I feel the graces of the Holy Ghost cascade over my entire being flooding my soul. I luxuriate in this holy moment, and thank God for all the graces and gifts He has blessed me with.

The bishop wickedly slaps me across the left side of my face snapping me back to the harsh realities of physical life. Stunned for a second, I recover and focus my eyes on the bishop as he stares down at me. He appears to be waiting for a reaction from me. I remain kneeling for the moment and wonder if the bishop can also sense the presence of the Holy Ghost as I do. I don't think so; however, the bishop will for all time be the one who served as the intermediary between God and me as I was confirmed. He will forever be an important part of my life's story.

And so, I smile and say, "Thank you, your Excellency."

To my great surprise, he smiles back!

As I rise, I feel a distinct new inner strength, a joy, and confidence I did not have when I knelt down a moment ago. The Holy Ghost came and knighted me as a Soldier of Christ. I am now better equipped to walk in the shadow of Christ.

Sitting back in my pew, I feel surrounded by my family members who are with God, along with the angels and saints. They are undoubtedly here in church with me.

I thank God for the gift of my faith, my family, the nuns, the priests, my classmates, my good fortune to be confirmed here today by Bishop Griffiths at my beloved church, St. Monica's.

But now, my thoughts are disrupted with a flashback to some of the terrible encounters with demons. I quickly realize, however, that I am better equipped now through the Sacrament of Confirmation to face such challenges.

As soon as we arrive back home, the phone rings. Daddy hurries over to pick it up and answer in his usual formal manner, "Walsh residence, may I help you?"

Daddy listens then says, "Oh... I am so sorry to hear that."

His face suddenly looks quite sad as he rocks back and forth.

"When did it happen? Was anyone with him? Do you know what the arrangements are yet?"

Daddy calls out for a pen and piece of paper to write something. Speaking somberly, he writes down some information the person on the phone is telling him. Whatever is wrong, it sounds like it is something pretty bad. After thanking the person for calling, Daddy hangs up the phone, and walks slowly over to Mommy who looks very nervous and sad.

With tears filling his eyes, Daddy places his hands gently on Mommy's shoulders, and says, "That was Vera on the phone, Ellie. It's Pop. I am so sorry."

Mommy shakes her head and begins to cry, "No, not my father!"

I am shocked and heart-broken! My Grandpa Sheridan has died.

Mommy asks, "When did he die?"

"Vera said it was late this morning… just before Bobby's Confirmation."

"Was anyone was with him?"

"Yes, Vera and her girls were with him. She said Pop had a smile on his face."

Daddy hugs Mommy as they cry together.

I am so sad. I lie down on the bed and bury my face under the pillow and cry. Images of time spent with Grandpa Sheridan flash by. Now I will not be able to visit him here on earth. Just like Nana Walsh, I must wait until I am in heaven to see him.

The day of the funeral wake for Grandpa comes all too soon. The funeral parlor is in Brooklyn close to where he lived at the time he died. Entering with Mommy, Daddy, and Paddy, I smell the powerful fragrance of flowers. There are so many people here, and most of them are dressed in black. Walking past some of the rooms, I see a coffin in the front of each room containing the body of the person who died. The person's family members and friends are gathered there to "pay their respects" as Daddy says.

When we come to Grandpa Sheridan's room, I immediately see Grandpa lying in an open coffin in the front of the room. His hands are folded across his chest. He is dressed in a full-length brown Franciscan robe in honor of the fact that he was a third-degree lay member of the Franciscan order. His full head of thick white hair rests prominently on top of his deeply wrinkled face. Grandpa looks much older than his 71 years. Perhaps this is a reflection of the long, difficult life he lived.

Before coming here, Daddy told Paddy and me to be quiet and respectful, and to do whatever we see him and Mommy do. Right now, they kneel down on a padded kneeler facing the side of the coffin. They make the Sign of the Cross and say a silent prayer. Mommy looks so sad as she stares at Grandpa. She appears to be lost in a lifetime of memories. Poor Mommy.

Finally, they make the Sign of the Cross again, then rise so Paddy and I can do the same as they did. As I look at Grandpa, I sense his spirit nearby... quite alive and well. In fact, more alive and well than ever.

After we finish saying a prayer for Grandpa, we rise and go over to stand behind Mommy and Daddy. They introduce us to our relatives on Mommy's side of the family; there are so many we have never met before. After politely greeting all our distant relatives, Daddy tells Paddy and me to go sit in two nearby chairs.

As we do, Daddy tells us, "Be quiet and respectful to everyone. Remember, everything you say and do reflects on our family."

I watch as more and more people arrive to pay their "last respects" to Grandpa and his family. A well-dressed woman comes over to Mommy, and introduces herself as one of Grandpa's good friends from St. Jean the Baptiste in New York City. She says that she knew Grandpa quite well.

Speaking in low reverential tones, she says quite dramatically, "You know, your father prayed over hundreds of people at St. Anne's Shrine in St. Jean's Catholic Church on Lexington Avenue and 76th Street in Manhattan. I personally witnessed some of the miracles that happened there. People who were crippled, dying from cancer, and other terrible things were cured after your father prayed over them.

"But the greatest thing he did was to bring **so many** people into the Catholic faith."

"I know." Mommy acknowledges. "Thank you for sharing that with me."

The woman adds, "Your father truly lived up to his vows as a third-order lay Franciscan. We are all going to miss him. What a good and holy man your father was!"

"He still is," I clarify. "Now that Grandpa is in heaven with God and all the people he helped to get there, he can do even more to help us and other people.

"Just because Grandpa died, doesn't mean he is dead. He is more alive now than ever!"

The woman looks surprised and pleased to hear this so I continue, "When you die physically, you don't cease to be who you were on earth. In heaven, you continue to be whoever you were, a mommy, a daddy, a grandparent, a son, a daughter, a friend. It is **then** that you can do so much more to help the people you love."

Appearing quite impressed, the woman smiles and says, "Why that's beautiful! I don't think I've ever heard that before."

Turning back to Mommy, she says, "That sounds like something your father would say."

Looking back now at me, she adds, "Hmmm. He often spoke of a

361

'blessed child' in his family, someone he said was spiritually gifted as he was. Oh my… you must be that child."

Looking proudly, Mommy nods, "Yes, he is. The last time my father visited, he confirmed what we've known for some time; Bobby is one of God's blessed children."

Hearing these words, I imagine Grandpa smiling from where he is in heaven. A wave of understanding floods my mind including a foretelling of the kind of life that lies ahead for me. It will be a remarkable journey filled with miracles, healings… and the ongoing assaults of the devil.

With greater faith in God than I have fear of the devil, I look to the future with confidence, unafraid of whatever the devil may do to interfere with God's plan for my life. After all… I am Jimmy's Boy.

"We'll see," the devil hisses, "we'll see."

INDEX

364